THE SEARCH FOR A CIVIC VOICE

THE SEARCH FOR A CIVIC VOICE

CALIFORNIA LATINO POLITICS

KENNETH C. BURT

Ken Burt

11-17-08

Regina Books
Claremont, California

THE SEARCH FOR A CIVIC VOICE
CALIFORNIA LATINO POLITICS

Book design: Mary Stoddard
Cover design: Mindy Pines

ISBN 1-930053-50-9 / 978-1-930053-50-2

Library of Congress Control Number: 2007923807

Regina Books
Post Office Box 280
Claremont, California 91711
Tel 909.624.8466
Fax 909.626.1345

Manufactured in the United States of America

This book is dedicated to Sonia Sotelo Burt,
our children Stephen and Katherine,
and to George R. Sotelo, my late father-in-law,
who returned from World War II committed to increasing the
role of Mexican Americans in civic life.

Contents

FOREWORD

For years, Latinos operated on the margins of civic life. Today that has changed. More than one thousand Latinos currently hold appointed or elected office in cities and counties across the state, and represent an influential force within the State Legislature, where three of the last five Speakers of the Assembly have been Spanish-surnamed.

A lot has changed since the 1950s and 1960s of my youth in East Los Angeles when it often seemed that Edward Roybal was the sole representative for millions of Spanish-speaking people. As the lone Latino at City Hall and then as the only California Latino in Congress he spoke for the disenfranchised and the powerless.

Roybal was the role model that younger women and men such as myself sought to emulate. But he was much more that a pioneering elected official, as impressive as that was. Roybal played a pivotal role in the first large-scale voter registration drive in the Latino community, and through groups like Viva Kennedy helped Latinos emerge as a force in state and national politics. Equally important, Roybal pioneered the model of multi-ethnic and multi-racial coalition politics effectively utilized by Mayor Tom Bradley, and that served as the blueprint for several other campaigns, including my own.

Kenneth Burt makes several invaluable contributions with this book. First, he helps the Latino community understand its own history, beginning in the 1930s with the efforts to elect Latinos to public office and to insert the community into the larger New Deal Democratic majority coalition. Second, by examining the formation and operation of the Roybal coalition he illuminates a side of Latino politics that is important for activists and elected officials in this multicultural city and state.

The Search for a Civic Voice: California Latino Politics is both an academic book and one that will be enjoyed by readers interested in history and current events. For those who have recently awakened to the large and growing role of Latinos in civic life, Burt answers the question: How did it all begin? For young people seeking to become active citizens, this book provides inspiration and insight into better understanding both the past seventy years and ongoing political developments. Finally, this is a powerful tribute to the sacrifices, struggles, and successes of women and men who were often unsung heroes.

Antonio Villaraigosa
Mayor
Los Angeles, California

ACKNOWLEDGMENTS

The Search for a Civic Voice, some two decades in the making, owes a tremendous debt to a countless number of activists and elected officials, some but not all of who became part of the story, as well as to archivists and librarians, and the larger community of scholars.

Carlos Muñoz, Jr. provided the initial inspiration for the project that was shaped by Martin Ridge who, unfortunately, passed on prior to publication. A number of scholars provided invaluable insights during seminar and conference presentations before the Center for Recent United States History at the University of Iowa, the Los Angeles History Group at The Huntington Library, the Pacific Coast Branch-American Historical Association, the Southwest Labor Studies Association, and the Western History Association. These presentations led to publications in *Labor's Heritage, Legal History,* and the *Southern California Quarterly,* and the opportunity to work with Stuart B. Kaufman, Bradley B. Williams, and Doyce B. Nunis, Jr.

Special thanks to Robert W. Cherny, William Issel, and Shelton Stromquist who, prior to publishing a pair of my essays in their respective anthologies on organized labor and the Cold War, asked the critical questions that deepened my understanding of the 1939-1955 period and helped me place Latino Los Angeles in a national context. Thanks also to Martin Schiesl who commissioned an essay on "The Promise of Politics" for his collection on multicultural Los Angeles, *City of Promise*, that resulted in my drawing parallels between the 1940s and 1990s.

That piece also led to a fortuitous meeting with Richard D. Burns, my erstwhile editor, whose subtle yet powerful hand is present in this book, and to whom I remain eternally grateful. I am likewise grateful to Celeste Brown, my executive assistant, who provided invaluable editorial assistance, and to Gloria Martínez, who read the manuscript and also offered editorial comments.

A number of scholars also gave generously of their time. Francisco E. Balderrama, Jaime A. Regalado, Martin Schiesl, and Michael Nye read the manuscript. Others read specific chapters and/ or provided resource documents. These included Luis Leobardo Arroyo, Kay Biegel, Martin J. Bennett, Albert Camarillo, William Deverall, Michael E. Engh, William Issel, George J. Sánchez, and Raphael J. Sonenshein. George Sánchez also provided stimulating insights on Boyle Heights, a neighborhood that is central to understanding Latino Los Angeles and coalition politics. Leo Chávez and Vicki L. Ruiz generously invited me to a conference on Latinos and Jews that provided feedback to my paper on garment workers as coalition builders.

So, too, have a number of librarians and archivists provided invaluable assistance. The following in-state institutions were particularly helpful: Bancroft Library at the University of California at Berkeley, Special Collections Department at Stanford University, ILWU Library and Archives (Eugene Vrana), Labor Archives & Research Center at San Francisco State, California State Archives, California History Section of the California State Library, the Huntington Library, Los Angeles City Archives, Special Collections at the California State University, Los Angeles (David Siegler), Southern California Library for Research and Social Studies (Sarah Cooper), the Special Collections Department at UCLA (Octavio Olvera), the Urban Archives Center at California State University, Northridge (Robert Marshall), and the San Diego Historical Society. The Texas A&M University-Corpus Christi (Grace Charles), the University of Iowa at Iowa City (Earl Rogers), the Archives of Labor and Urban Affairs at Wayne State University, the Minnesota Historical Society, the Historical Collections & Labor Archives at Pennsylvania State University, the Wagner Labor Archives at New York University (Gail Malmgreen), the Catholic University of America, the George Meany Center for Labor Studies, and the National Archives helped complete the historical mosaic, as did the presidential libraries of Franklin D. Roosevelt, Harry S. Truman, Dwight D. Eisenhower, John F. Kennedy, Lyndon B. Johnson, and Richard M. Nixon. The FBI provided thousands of pages of documents due, in part, to the intervention of U.S. Representatives Howard Berman and Hilda Solis. The *Sacramento Bee*, the *Fresno Bee*, and *Los Angeles Times* provided access to their clipping files; and the Hispanic Link News Service, former CSO president Tony Ríos, the Mexican-American Political Association, Atara Mont, and the Los Angeles Anti-Defamation League provided access to their private historical files.

This book became a reality in significant measure due to Bruce E. Cain and Gerald Lubenow at the Institute for Governmental Studies (IGS) at the University of California at Berkeley. IGS named me as its Carey McWilliams Fellow and provided a supportive research and writing environment, particularly during my sabbatical, generously granted by Mary Bergan and the California Federation of Teachers. The Institute for Labor and Economics at UC Berkeley provided additional research support, as did the United Labor Bank, led by its president, Malcolm Hotchkiss, and board member Michael Nye. The Minnesota Historical Society provided a grant to use Hubert H. Humphrey's papers. The Southern California Historical Society and the Haines Foundation provided a stipend to complete the essay, "The Power of a Mobilized Citizenry and Coalition Politics: The 1949 Election of Edward R. Roybal to the Los Angeles City Council," that won the society's Doyce B. Nunis, Jr. Award in 2004.

Finally, I am indebted to Los Angeles Mayor Antonio Villaraigosa for writing the foreword to this book. He is a civic giant who continues to make history.

Kenneth C. Burt
Sacramento, California
April 2007

Introduction

Antonio Villaraigosa's election as Mayor of Los Angeles in 2005 caught the attention of the national and international media. In its cover story, entitled "Latino Power," *Newsweek* emphasized that Villaraigosa's dramatic defeat of an incumbent mayor in the nation's second largest city was emblematic of the rise of Latinos within the political arena.[1] The following year, half a million people took to the streets of Los Angeles, with tens of thousands more gathering in San Francisco, Sacramento, and San Diego to protest efforts in Congress to criminalize undocumented residents. Mayor Villaraigosa, California Assembly Speaker Fabian Núñez, and the California State Senate, led by Senator Gloria Romero, a professor-turned-politician, supported the demonstrators. Additional backing came from Los Angeles Cardinal Roger Mahony and other religious and labor leaders, including María Elena Durazo, head of the Los Angeles County Federation of Labor. U.S. Senator Edward M. Kennedy (D-Massachusetts), co-author with Senator John McCain (R-Arizona) of a comprehensive immigration measure, headlined the star-studded rally at the Washington Monument. Senator Kennedy invoked memories of his brother, President John F. Kennedy, who penned A Nation of Immigrants and who won Latino voter affection in California and other states some fifty years earlier.

The ever-changing state of Latino politics in California continues to draw attention from academics, journalists, and political leaders. With the dramatic expansion of potential Latino voters in the 1990s—not only from Mexico, but other nations in Central and South America—the number who register and turn out at the polls has become a major issue. However, an increase in the Latino population has not automatically translated into additional Latino voters.[2] Academics are currently engaged in the national dialogue over the impact of recent immigration relative to the political status of Latinos, their ability to achieve the American Dream, and the nature of American society.[3] Those examining Latino politics have focused on issues of identity, leadership, and immigration, as well as gender, class, and ideology. Generational characteristics are also used to define larger trends, with academics focusing on the Mexican American generation (generally described as those coming of age in the 1930s, 1940s, and 1950s) and the Chicano movement of the late 1960s and early 1970s.[4]

The Search for a Civic Voice: California Latino Politics advances the thesis that Latino involvement in electoral politics occurred much earlier than is commonly understood and was achieved by mobilizing voters and developing coalitions.[5] It reflects an understanding that in California, as in other states like Texas, Latinos, in the words of Mario T. García, "viewed the attainment of effective political representation as the first step in equalizing their status with Anglos."[6] To fill important gaps in the state's historical record, the book addresses three essential questions: 1) How did modern Latino electoral politics begin and who and what groups played major roles? 2) What are the lessons learned from the early ventures and what is the legacy of these political pioneers? 3) What is the state of politics in California today and how was it shaped by these earlier forces?

The answers to these questions emerge in a narrative technique, combined with analysis, to capture the historical record. This account is based on two hundred oral histories, extensive archival research, and academic literature drawn from the fields of Chicano Studies, History, Political Science, Labor Studies, and Religious Studies. The unique lens used to survey the cultural-political landscape reflects this author's career in politics as a participant-observer in the tradition of Ernesto Galarza and Carey McWilliams.

The term Latino is used as the primary expression of group identity because of its widespread use in political circles and in the media. It was also prompted by the realization that since the 1930s a small but significant number of activists in California did not identify themselves as Mexican American. They were known as Californios (from pre-statehood families), Spanish-Americans or Hispanos (from pre-statehood New Mexico), or by their family's country of origin in Cuba, Guatemala, Nicaragua, Puerto Rico, and Spain. The early political groups used terms such as Spanish-speaking to incorporate such diversity.[7]

In seeking out the roots of today's political activists and elected officials, this study becomes a story of "firsts." It identifies the first appointees to state, local, and federal boards; the first judges; the first city council members; the first state legislators; the first members of Congress; the first gubernatorial chief of staff; the first to create a national organization behind a presidential candidate; and the first to represent a president of the United States as a mediator between the Latino community and the presidential administration.[8] Some of these names will be familiar. Others will be new.

These political achievements have occurred in a state with weak political institutions, where candidates assemble their own coalition by courting interest groups and wooing voters often with low levels of partisan loyalty.[9] Moreover, politics in California are in constant flux due to population changes. The state has grown steadily in terms of absolute numbers, and so has the percentage of Latinos relative to the nation as a whole. The dramatic population gains can be seen in the apportionment of congressional seats. In 1910, at the start of the Mexican Revolution, which first brought large numbers of Latinos to California, the state had only eight of the 435 members in the U.S. House of Representatives. The California delegation was the same size as that of Kansas and Mississippi, and smaller than that of Minnesota. By the 1930s, when this story starts, California claimed twenty seats, the sixth largest total. In 1960, California surpassed New York to become the most populated state and was awarded thirty-eight seats. Today the state's fifty-two-member delegation is by far the largest. Observed another way, the seven Latinos serving in Congress today represent more constituents than lived in the entire state one hundred years ago.[10]

This study also suggests a reevaluation of the dominant narrative concerning the impact of the Cold War.[11] In *Labor Rights Are Civil Rights: Mexican Workers in Twentieth Century America*, Zaragosa Vargas states that anti-communism "undid the civil rights-trade union alliance" and "set back the fight for full citizenship."[12] *The Search for a Civic Voice* suggests a more nuanced understanding of Latino politics by expanding on the observations of Ralph C. Guzmán, a participant-observer in post-World War II Latino politics, who described the coalescing of former servicemen, "labor unionists, civic leaders, and religious leaders in new alliances."[13] This new liberal alignment was successful in getting the California State Legislature to enact fair employment and fair housing laws, as well as to outlaw school segregation and to strengthen Latino voting rights. In *The CIO: 1935-1955*, labor scholar Robert H. Zieger concurs that "in state capitols CIO (and later AFL-CIO) legislative representatives played significant roles in the enactment of civil rights laws whose provisions are now commonplace but that were in the 1950s and 1960s great victories for human rights."[14]

This new approach to understanding the state's post-World War II civil rights politics also explains other seeming inconsistencies in the literature. How could a militant group such as the Community Service Organization (CSO)—which fought racial discrimination and police beatings, and operated successful voter registration drives and get-out-the-vote campaigns—thrive in a hostile environment? The answer to the apparent paradox lies in a fuller understanding of CSO's leadership, including its founding president, Edward R. Roybal, and its affiliation with the Industrial Area Foundation and its labor and religious ties and with the liberal-left in Los Angeles. Progressive elements within the local Catholic Church and the Jewish community embraced CSO, and these groups enjoyed their own interlocking relationships with the two pillars of CSO's labor support. Jewish socialists led the International Ladies Garment Workers Union and the Catholic "labor priests" heavily influenced the United Steel Workers of America, two progressive but anti-communist unions with large Latino memberships in Los Angeles in the 1940s and 1950s.[15]

An examination of how CSO expanded the number of Latino voters and established important political allies illuminates a specific time and place. It also sheds light on a larger dynamic. When César Chávez and Dolores Huerta left CSO to found the United Farm Workers, they adopted the model of organizing workers and the community, and stressed the centrality of civic participation. Not coincidentally, some of the periods of greatest frustration for Latino political activists are tied to either a low-level of self-organization and/or limited allies within the political arena. Too often scholars have avoided the dynamics of specific situations in favor of a larger theory of disenfranchisement. Based on archival documents and interviews with participants, this study will correct the historical record in a number of instances.

Coalition politics remains vital because, even with the dramatic increase in the number of Latino voters, candidates must still assemble an electoral majority to achieve victory. This is true in largely Latino legislative districts where candidates often divide ideologically or have ties to rival elected officials or competing interest groups. In ethnically diverse districts, a Latino candidate must reach out to Latino voters while appealing to the larger electorate, which in many urban districts is a mix of Anglo, African American, Asian Pacific Islander, Gay and Lesbian, and Jewish voters. Candidates must also court labor and business interests in their efforts to raise funds and support—unionized voters are a significant block in many Democratic primaries.

Coalitions are likewise important at the municipal level, where Latinos have been elected mayors in Los Angeles, San Jose, and Sacramento—cities where the majority of voters are non-Latino. This is particularly true in Los Angeles. Antonio Villaraigosa won the mayoral election because he simultaneously animated Latino voters and formed alliances with non-Latino groups. The press focused on Villaraigosa's efforts to reach out to union voters and African Americans. Less recognized has been the critical role of Jewish voters. The Latino-Jewish relationship rooted in the Boyle Heights neighborhood of the 1940s goes a long way to help explain why Villaraigosa won in Los Angeles while another Latino, Fernando Ferrer, twice lost his mayoral bid in New York.[16]

Though *The Search for a Civic Voice* begins as a story of firsts, these events do not emerge in a vacuum. The study of the coalitions built by Latino political pioneers and their descendents among labor, business, religious, and other groups sheds light on the organic process of an immigrant community finding its civic voice. Illuminating these well-organized networks and their patterns of struggle and success makes each political victory seem much less an isolated event in a sea of adversity and much more an integral block in the bridge to overcome it.

CHAPTER 1

THE BIRTH
OF
CALIFORNIA LATINO POLITICS

On a Friday evening, April 28, 1939, Eduardo Quevedo looked out over the packed second floor ballroom of the New Mexico-Arizona Club at 230 1/2 South Spring Street in the older section of the Los Angeles downtown commercial district. The area, replete with offices, storefronts, and neon signs for movie houses that once showed silent films, was physically tied to the spread out city by a network of streetcar tracks that shared the roads with a limited number of automobiles. From the stage, where he sat with California's Lieutenant Governor Ellis Patterson and other political, minority, and labor dignitaries, Quevedo knew the political influence of America's forgotten Latino minority was on an upward trajectory. The First National Congress of the Mexican and Spanish-American Peoples of the United States, known as El Congreso, was underway, and enthusiastic delegates packed the ballroom behind banners designating their home states. Most of the representatives were from the five states of the American Southwest—Arizona, California, Colorado, New Mexico, and Texas. Others, however, had traveled from as far away as Butte, Montana and New York City. Along with the delegates, a myriad of honorary guests, fraternal representatives, and political activists from throughout Southern California were in attendance. They were drawn by the promise of Latino empowerment, the opportunity to expand the progressive coalition, and by entertainment provided by Mexican musicians and Hollywood film stars.

The diversity of El Congreso delegates was remarkable—refugees from the violence of the Mexican Revolution, their American-born children, immigrants from Central and South America, and descendants of seventeenth-century Spanish settlers. Roughly one thousand women and men had arrived by train, streetcar, and automobile. Colorful banners captured the objectives of El Congreso: "Let Us Form a Committee for the Congress in Each Town," "In

Youth is the Future," "We ask for Justice for the Latin Race," "Citizens or Non-Citizens Unite our Strengths," "In Defense of Our Homes, Let Us Fight Against Deportations," and "Let's Unite for Progress."[1]

With the overflow crowd spilling into the street below, Los Angeles community leader Eduardo Quevedo banged the gavel to bring El Congreso to order. The self-taught Quevedo, thirty-five, had left school at age fourteen to work in a New Mexico mine with his father. He left the mine and the state after being told that the only way become a manager was to change his name so as to appear to be an Anglo. Upon his arrival in Los Angeles, he threw himself into community activities and progressive politics, campaigning for Franklin D. Roosevelt in his first presidential election in 1932. Two years later, he served as a spokesperson for muckraking author-turned-Democratic gubernatorial candidate Upton Sinclair. From 1934 to 1937, Quevedo worked for the federal Works Project Administration and spoke out against forced repatriation, discrimination, and poverty and advocated greater cohesiveness among Latinos. He participated in a wide range of groups, including the New Mexico-Arizona Club, the Mexican Chamber of Commerce, and the Catholic Church. The previous year, 1938, Quevedo took a leadership role in Culbert Olson's campaign for governor of California. Olson expressed his "grateful appreciation and thanks for the effective work [Quevedo] did in the campaign for [his] election" and invited the Latino leader to attend his inauguration at the State Capitol in Sacramento.[2]

In his opening remarks to El Congreso, Quevedo emphasized the importance of unity within the Latino community. "We must be thoroughly convinced of the fact that with unification we have strength," he stated. Quevedo stressed that "in the Hispanic-American Congress movement there is room for organizations and for individuals who wish to cooperate with those of us who work in the Congress." The overflow crowd's support for El Congreso reflected the urgent need for an organization to address discrimination. According to Quevedo, "The unification of our people is due to the fact that they are no longer willing to suffer inequalities." Unity within the Latino community could be further strengthened by alliances with forces in the larger society. Then he outlined El Congreso's plan to create a movement in alliance with other progressive organizations that would address Latino concerns, fight for working people, and oppose the rising threat of fascism abroad. The latter was an increased concern to Latinos because General Francisco Franco, an ally of Germany's Adolf Hitler, now led Spain, the mother nation to most of Latin America. The "forces represented here," Quevedo stated, "will crystallize in reality. It is time the world knows we will be unified in our objectives."[3] Governor Olson reinforced Quevedo's message in a congratulatory letter urging El Congreso delegates to work "in union with other progressive elements and proceed to work for a solution to the economic problems that beset the community." California's new chief executive emphasized that "[t]he problems of one are the problems of all."[4]

California Lieutenant Governor Ellis Patterson represented the New Deal Democratic coalition at the opening session. He pledged that "President Roosevelt and the present administration in California is sincerely fighting to bring real democracy into being."[5] A descendant of William Patterson, a signer of the U.S. Constitution, this educator-turned-state legislator ran on a platform supporting the "Militant Protection of Racial, Religious, Economic and Political Minorities in their Civil Rights."[6] Before El Congreso, he emphasized the shared agendas between the president and governor, and between Roosevelt and President Lázaro Cárdenas of Mexico. The United States and Mexico must stand "courageously against the aggression of nations that will stoop to the breaking of international law and the use of force in breaking democratic rule." He added, "We must struggle for the ideals of Presidents Cárdenas and Roosevelt . . . The lamps of democracy will not go out here or in the rest of the world."[7]

Carey McWilliams, chief of California's Division of Immigration and Housing, followed Patterson to the podium. Attorney, author and activist, McWilliams was the scion of a once-privileged Colorado ranching family. He had developed an affinity for the poor and powerless when his family's economic misfortunes resulted in his widowed mother running a boarding house in Los Angeles. In his address, McWilliams warned of numerous "anti-alien bills pending in the U.S. Congress." He said his office would work with those present "to solve the many problems of the Congress relating to repatriation, immigration and the migratory workers."[8]

On Saturday, the second day of El Congreso, the official delegates divided into issue groups to develop El Congreso's program and vision. John F. Fernández, a state legislator in New Mexico, chaired the morning session. Group leaders included Latino, Jewish, Black, and Anglo coalition partners.[9] Reid Robinson, president of the International Union of Mine, Mill and Smelter Workers, headed the labor committee. Assisting was Donald Henderson, president of United Cannery, Agriculture, Packing and Allied Workers of America (UCAPAWA). They were part of a larger progressive social movement in California that began in 1934 when Harry Bridges led longshoremen on a coast-wide strike. The same year, tens of thousands of farm workers under the leadership of the Communist Party struck throughout the state. The following year, 1935, John L. Lewis formed the Congress of Industrial Organizations (CIO) as a subdivision of the American Federation of Labor (AFL) before becoming a rival organization. The CIO, of which the longshoremen, Mine-Mill, and UCAPAWA represented the militant left wing, perceived itself to be a social movement and organized workers by industry, not by craft, as was the tradition within the AFL. These actions led to the formation of the "popular front," a network of labor and community groups with an activist bent that captured the imagination of those seeking to address poverty, inequality, and the general state of the working class.[10] Secret communists or those close to the party played a major leadership role in many of these groups. The inchoate CIO, led in California by Bridges, the president of the new International Longshoremen and Warehousemen's Union (ILWU), played a pivotal role in President Roosevelt's 1936 reelection in the state and in Olson's 1938 election. The CIO membership consisted largely of racial or ethnic minorities who worked in lower status jobs on farms or in mines and factories. Jerome Davis, the Yale University theology professor at the helm of the American Federation of Teachers, was the lone AFL union president to send fraternal greetings to El Congreso.[11]

The Great Depression led to unemployment or underemployment for half the population and this dramatically changed the contours of state and national politics, as if a raging stream had carved a new riverbed out of the parched earth. Gone were the days of un-regulated capitalism. The rise of large factories that replaced shops with specialized laborers had made a few fabulously wealthy but dehumanized the work for the masses that did not share in the profits generated from increased productivity. To address these issues, the federal government taxed millionaires and enacted a series of new programs to stabilize industry, labor, and agriculture. This included new laws to protect workers, such as a minimum wage, and restrictions on child labor. Also enacted were a series of new programs, such as hiring the unemployed to build roads, schools, and libraries; Unemployment Insurance for those laid off from their jobs; and Social Security so that seniors could retire with dignity and would not become dependent on their children for economic survival. Roosevelt also sponsored the National Labor Relations Act that encouraged workers to join unions and to collectively bargain with employers regarding wages and working conditions.

In this environment, the ideological spectrum was wide. Many of those on the right wanted to return to the days before the federal government started to regulate business activity. This included rolling back the right of workers to form unions and to pressure employers through strikes and boycotts. Some on the right were fascinated by the rise of fascism in Europe, particularly Nazi Germany. Industrialist Henry Ford's anti-Semitic tracks influenced a young Adolph Hitler and, in 1938, Germany presented the seventy-five-year-old automaker with the Grand Cross of the Golden Eagle.[12] Media mogul William Randolph Hearst paid Hitler to write for his newspaper chain, and the publisher flew to Berlin to meet with the German dictator.[13] Those on the liberal-left sought even greater government intervention in the economy, including the prohibition of racial discrimination in employment. The American Communist Party, with its link to the Soviet Union, dominated the left although numerous groups competed for adherents and advocated different party lines. President Roosevelt led a liberal government with support from the center-left, including organized labor, intellectuals, immigrants and their children, Irish-led political machines in the East and Midwest, the Southern States, and western progressives.[14]

In the 1938 election in California, the Republicans sought to discredit Olson by linking him to Harry Bridges, the CIO, and the

Communist Party. In seeking to portray the Democratic candidate as outside the mainstream, the Republicans replayed the strategy that had proved devastatingly effective against Upton Sinclair in 1934. They utilized the major newspapers that served, in a weak party state, as a key vehicle for communication, while their conservative owners served as pillars of the business community and the Republican Party. The *Los Angeles Times*, *San Francisco Chronicle*, and *Oakland Tribune* played a central role; two smaller papers, the Hearst-owned *Los Angeles Examiner* and *San Francisco Examiner*, likewise expressed a virulent anti-Roosevelt and anti-New Deal viewpoint. The strategy of attacking the Democratic candidate as a dangerous leftist proved less effective the second time around. A major reason for this is that Olson was a well-known liberal with a track record as a state legislator, unlike Sinclair who had served as a Socialist Party leader and as a prolific author whose material could be quoted, often out of context. The Republican strategy also failed in 1938 due to demographic changes in the state, the most important being the arrival of large number of Dust Bowl refugees from Oklahoma, Texas and Arkansas, who helped expand the Democratic party registration advantage. Finally, voters were eager to bring the New Deal to California.[15]

El Congreso positioned itself squarely within the Roosevelt coalition. The organization's progressive values reflected its activist orientation and commitment to using government and unions to improve the lot of workers and minorities while remaining internationalist in its worldview. Within El Congreso, leadership, ideological and organizational distinctions broke down along a liberal vs. left lines. President Quevedo demonstrated his progressive credentials by working for Roosevelt and Upton Sinclair. While he remained comfortable working with liberals and the left, Quevedo remained at his core a New Deal Roosevelt Democrat. El Congreso founder Luisa Moreno and staff person Josephina de Bright likewise operated as progressives promoting a reformist agenda; however, like Harry Bridges, they maintained a radical outlook and organizational ties to the Communist Party left. This kind of liberal-left coalition within the Latino community was possible because the communists abandoned their revolutionary vanguard activities to work with others to promote reforms within the two-party political system.[16] The

A youthful Luisa Moreno, a decade prior to her organizing of El Congreso.
The extraordinary Guatemalan-born woman gave up a life of privilege to
empower Latinos in California and other states through union organizing
and civic engagement.   *(Courtesy of Vicki L. Ruiz)*

liberal and left distinctions within El Congreso's leadership were generally unrecognized by activists who focused on the group's goals and objectives.

On the third day, Sunday, March 30, 1939, the delegates listened to Richard Olson, Governor Olson's son and top aide, heard from Los Angeles County Supervisor John Anson Ford and received greetings from representatives of Arizona Governor Robert T. Jones and New Mexico Governor John Miles. Former New Deal Congressman and soon-to-be San Antonio Mayor, Maury Maverick, served as El Congreso's most prominent Texas supporter. Such support from Anglo politicians was as impressive as it was unprecedented. Yet the organization did not start with the support of the nation's most prominent Latino elected official: U.S. Senator Dennis Chávez of New Mexico. Chávez had won his seat with the assistance of President Roosevelt. This furthered the realignment of longtime Hispano voters in the state from "Abe Lincoln Republicans" to "Roosevelt Democrats." However, El Congreso's leftist ties had led to an imbroglio necessitating the moving of the group's founding convention from Albuquerque to Los Angeles.

Louisa Moreno, at age thirty-two, the nation's best-known Spanish-speaking labor organizer, traveled the country to organize the first truly national and pan-Latino organization. Then based in San Antonio, Texas, where she organized Mexican American cotton and pecan pickers into UCAPAWA, Moreno was born into privilege in Guatemala. As a teenager she attended the College of Holy Names, a Catholic women's school in Oakland, California, before rejecting Catholicism and religion generally. She went on to assist Puerto Rican garment workers in New York's Spanish Harlem, Cuban and Spanish cigar makers in Tampa, Florida, and Mexican tuna cannery workers in San Diego. While in New York, Moreno came to identify with the struggles of the dispossessed and briefly joined the Communist Party. These experiences gave her a unique understanding of working class Latinos' concerns around the country and resulted in an expansive network of labor and leftist political activists.[17]

California welcomed Moreno and El Congreso, in part, because the state government was bucking the national trend—the state had moved left in November 1938 as the nation moved right. This is because the New Deal had come late to California. By the time Democrats captured top offices in California, voters in other states had started to tire of the reform agenda.[18]

The delegates spent the third day of the conference debating proposed resolutions and addressing a variety of pressing social ills. They manifested an interest in extending the New Deal to working class Latinos through a combination of generally pro-worker policies and actions to address the specific concerns of the Latino community. They called for the construction of public housing without racial barriers and bilingual education through the eighth grade. The delegates also sought to eliminate "prejudice . . . caused by false theories of race supremacy" through the inclusion of Latino history in the public schools. Ahead of their time, the delegates proposed the "formation of departments in colleges and universities that will deal exclusively with the study of the social, economic, educational and political development of the Spanish-speaking people."[19]

The delegates also recognized the importance of Latinos becoming more involved in electoral politics. El Congreso urged "all Mexican and Spanish-Americans who are citizens to register [to vote], to participate in all democratic-progressive organizations, and to actively engage in the lawmaking of this country." Given the relatively small number of Latino voters (Congreso founder Luisa Moreno put the number of immigrants who had become citizens at "five or six percent"[20]), coalitions promised an effective way to extend the group's influence within the political arena. El Congreso went "on record urging the Mexican and Spanish-American people of the United States not to follow the policy of endorsing and supporting candidates simply because they are Mexican or Spanish-American." Instead, Latinos should judge candidates on what they "have done and are doing in the fight of the Spanish-American people against economic discrimination and for educational and cultural equality."[21]

The emphasis placed on voting expressed at El Congreso expanded on the political gains made six months earlier, when Latinos had helped elect Governor Olson and other progressives. Dr. Rafael Vernaza led the Hispanic-American Division within the Olson campaign and the California Democratic Party organized a Spanish-

American Division. The Latino community likewise formed its first political action committee: the Federation of Spanish-American Voters of California, and endorsed Olson. A fourth group, Amigos de Culbert Olson, sponsored a large pre-election reception and dance for Olson. The dance also honored two Latino political figures: Los Angeles County Sheriff Eugene Biscailuz and state assembly candidate Pedro Despart. Sheriff Biscailuz, a Californio, or descendant of early Spanish settlers, was the lone Spanish-speaking elected official of note in California. Despart was a garment worker active in youth activities. He won nearly ten percent of the vote in Assembly District 44 that incorporated the Mexican colony around Olvera Street, the founding site of Los Angeles. Despart also symbolized the conflict between labor and Latino voters; while hailed by groups like Amigos de Olson, he was not supported by the unions. His successful opponent, John Pelletier, sent greetings to El Congreso's delegates.[22]

The dilemma over when the Latino community should rally behind a one of their own, and when the effort would be better spent backing a supportive Anglo, was complicated by the small number of Spanish-surnamed voters and the political and governance structure of the state. California had none of the traditions that had helped integrate immigrants into the political structure in the cities of the Northeast and industrial Midwest: California's political parties were by design weak and municipalities were nonpartisan with strong city managers and an absence of patronage jobs. Moreover, the political affiliation of state legislative candidates was not listed on the ballot. The result was a political dynamic that rewarded candidates who could put together ad hoc coalitions and raise money to promote themselves. Voters in California could also go over the head of the politicians and adopt laws through voter initiatives.[23]

External interests and ideology could also magnify the importance of Latino community events or concerns. For example, the presence of so many Olson administration officials at El Congreso undoubtedly reflected an appreciation for Latino participation in the 1938 campaign; yet the limited number of Latino voters hardly justified the administration's strong interest. Their engagement was due to a confluence of two other factors. The first was the Olson administration's progressive inclusiveness and anti-racist orientation.

The second was desire by the CIO, arguably Olson's single most important supporter, to use El Congreso to expand its reach into the Latino community for the purpose of organizing unions among low-wage, minority workers. The CIO's political importance was based in part on the reflected glory that came from being central to Roosevelt's reelection in 1936. Within the state the CIO's influence also resulted from supporting Olson and Patterson against more traditional Democrats who enjoyed AFL support in the 1938 primary. Labor's perceived importance was also elevated by the ability of the CIO, AFL, and community allies to defeat Proposition 1 that would have severely limited picketing and outlawed the sit-down strike and the use of boycotts to pressure employers.[24] The success of El Congreso's founding conference showed its ability to bring together elected officials with established Latino community and labor leaders who had worked together in the Olson campaign. It also revealed the ability of its leftist organizers to submerge their ideological ambitions. YMCA-organized college students observed that "Congreso is a non-profit, non-political organization. There is no room for 'isms' although no one is barred."[25]

Pragmatism and idealism contributed to the Los Angeles CIO Council's strong support for El Congreso, which was organized out of its downtown office. The CIO was driven by the desire to organize new members. The interest in Latino workers reflected their numbers in the local manufacturing sector and the ideologically driven interests of key leaders, such as council head Philip Connelly, a secret communist. It was likewise shaped by the CIO's competition with the larger AFL in Los Angeles. The AFL Central Labor Council, unlike the CIO body, did not have a targeted outreach program to bring Latinos into the union movement. It did, however, utilize its weekly newspaper, *Los Angeles Citizen*, to restate national AFL anti-discrimination policy.[26] For their part, the Latino CIO leaders were often leftists who saw themselves as part of a powerful social movement and who enjoyed access to a range of resources such as staff, political funds, newspapers, and attorneys.

El Congreso leaders had utilized every opportunity to expand the organization in Los Angeles in the months preceding the first-ever national gathering. They organized geographically-based clubs, reached out to potential members, and attacked anti-immigrant public officials to help brand the organization as a militant fighter for social justice. Such was the case in El Congreso's conflict with the Los Angeles County Board of Supervisors. The five-member board represented 2.8 million people, almost double that of the City of Los Angeles, and forty percent of California's nearly 7 million residents. Their regular Friday morning meeting on March 21, 1939 began well enough as Supervisor John Anson Ford sought to place county policy within the context of Los Angeles' Hispanic heritage, which was represented on the chamber walls in a series of murals. Ford made the successful motion to embrace Pan American Day. At the time, Roosevelt and the presidents of the twenty Latin American nations were planning to celebrate the 1939 Pan American Day at the San Francisco International Exposition. However, the goodwill dissipated when Supervisor William Smith argued that the county could save money by refusing relief to non-citizens. "We want them to go somewhere else," stressed Smith, himself a Scottish-born immigrant.[27]

Supervisor Ford deftly deflected the controversy by getting the supervisors to pass a motion directing the County Superintendent of Charities to discuss the issue with the state chief of Immigration and Housing. Ford was well informed of the liberal views held by Carey McWilliams and knew Smith would not be successful with his call to end aid to non-citizens.[28]

Despite Ford's parliamentary victory on behalf of the Latino community, Congreso President Eduardo Quevedo publicly attacked Supervisor Smith in the press. "No doubt Supervisor Smith has been reading literature written by the Fascist leaders, and so engrossed has he probably become that he forgets he is now residing in a country that enforces democracy," Quevedo was quoted as saying in the Communists daily newspaper on the west coast, the *People's World*. Quevedo went on to say that dropping 1,800 relief recipients from the rolls and deporting them was inhumane. "The Mexican people or other Latins are not Jews in Germany," stated Quevedo, "and will not tolerate to be treated as such, since the best years of their lives have been spent in toiling in helping to make California what it is today."[29] *La Opinión*, the Los Angeles Spanish-language daily, predicted El Congreso would be "the first lit torch for the sake of our social redemption."[30]

In the months after the founding of El Congreso as a national body, the organization in California looked repeatedly to Governor Olson for help in promoting a progressive, pro-Latino agenda and in blocking conservative anti-immigrant policies. The challenge for the Los Angeles-based Congreso was that most of the state's legislative and administrative functions occurred in Sacramento, four hundred miles north. The only way to get there from Southern California was to drive on Highway 99, a dusty two-lane road that traversed a number of small agricultural towns in the Central Valley. Not that Sacramento lacked Latinos. Mexican Americans labored there in low-paying jobs in agriculture, canning, and maintaining the railroads.

Most of the work lobbying legislators and administration officials fell to two people: Congreso President Eduardo Quevedo and General Secretary Josephina Fierro de Bright, as founder Luisa Moreno moved to Colorado to organize beet workers and then to the UCAPAWA headquarters in Washington, D.C. Quevedo and Fierro de Bright worked out of the Congreso office in the Music Arts Building at 233 S. Broadway in Los Angeles. Only eighteen years old, Josephina Fierro de Bright was three years shy of voting and was known as a "housewife" who lived in Beverly Hills and volunteered her services to the organization. According to Frank López, the vice president of the Los Angeles CIO Council, she was "the driving spirit, and the individual that worked behind the scenes to put things together."[31] Born in Mexicali, a small town on the Mexican-Californian border, she had inherited her radical politics from her parents. Fierro entered the University of California Los Angeles (UCLA) with plans to become a medical doctor, but left college to marry a young Anglo screenwriter, John Bright, who was a secret member of the Communist Party. He had been Orson Welles' roommate at Harvard University, and was a founder of the Screen Writers Guild.[32]

The challenge of lobbying posed by geographic distance was compounded by the larger political environment. Stanley Mosk, the governor's appointment secretary, later recalled the "general legislative indifference" to minority concerns in Sacramento.[33] Before the election he had served as an attorney for the American Civil Liberties Union (ACLU) and for organized labor, which accounted for his interest in civil rights. Of the 120 state legislators, there were only two "minority" legislators—one African American, Augustus Hawkins, from Central Los Angeles, and one Jewish, Benjamin Rosenthal from Boyle Heights, a neighborhood on the Eastside of Los Angeles. Jews and Blacks—like Latinos—benefited from alliances with organized labor and other groups within the Democratic Party majority coalition because of their limited number of voters and elected officials. El Congreso also benefited from having the governor's ear, the support of progressive Democrats, and the moral blessing of the official party platform. For his part, Olson stayed true to his campaign pledge to "affirm that all citizens everywhere, of whatever group, are entitled to equal social, political, and economic opportunities."[34]

In the polarized environment within the State Capitol, a number of progressive legislators introduced legislation to end discrimination in employment and housing and to outlaw hate crimes in 1939. Most bills died in committee, including one by Assemblyman Hawkins that sought to reduce the ability of employers to screen out minority applicants by "prohibiting the inclusion of questions relative to race or religion in application blanks or forms."[35] Another Hawkins measure was enacted in June 1939. The 45-word bill outlawed discrimination on public works because of "race, color or religion." It was based on the theory that state government could stipulate hiring practices on jobs for which it was the ultimate funding source. This was a significant first step in reducing job discrimination and in setting a precedent for future legislative action. For his part, Hawkins believed in coalition politics and had sent fraternal greetings to El Congreso's founding convention.[36]

El Congreso did not rely solely on political relationships to protect its interests. It brought Latinos in large numbers to the State Capitol to underscore the importance of defeating the anti-Latino bills. The most threatening measure was Senate Bill 470, authored by Ralph E. Swing, a Republican from San Bernardino. The measure would have prohibited "relief or aid from any monies" appropriated by state or local government for people who could not document their legal status as well as for those who had entered legally but who had failed to pursue naturalization. This would negatively impact the Latino community because many of the families who came to the state from Mexico did so when the border was open and there was little formal immigration procedures. In the context of the depression when state politicians were looking to cut costs, it was easy to target non-voters without a political voice. The measure breezed through the Senate on a lopsided 28 to 2 vote; in the Assembly it narrowly achieved the needed majority, passing 43 to 28. Progressive Democrats joined Latinos in opposing the measure. Opposition culminated in a rally at the State Capitol in July 1939. Governor Olson vetoed the measure in the presence of Congreso leaders. He then addressed the assembled activists. The crowd erupted with the news of Olson's veto. "It was the biggest hurrah you ever heard in your life," Fierro de Bright recalled.[37]

Other times, the state legislators defeated measures before they got to the governor's desk. One bill would have denied non-citizens the right to serve as elected union officers. The measure was aimed at Australian-born Harry Bridges; the greatest impact, however, would have been on Latinos, many of whom, like Congreso founder Luisa Moreno had not completed the process to become a naturalized citizen.[38] Another ultimately unsuccessful bill would have made it illegal for poor people to enter the state. Such a law would have hurt Latinos even though it was directed at stopping poor whites from the Dust Bowl from coming to California.[39]

Governor Olson also used the power of public pronouncements to tear down racial stereotypes. Having already proclaimed Pan American Day, he now utilized the backdrop of the Golden Gate International Exposition to declare Race Relations Day. "I declare that anyone who generates racial misunderstanding and hatred is a demagogue of the most subversive type," emphasized Olson. "He becomes an enemy of society just as truly as a tax evader, an embezzler, or a murderer. In fact, he does infinitely more harm."[40]

These overlapping economic, social, and political interests came together in 1939 in El Centro, a small, geographically and politically isolated agricultural town in Imperial County, adjacent to the Mexican border. The independent Fresh Fruit and Vegetable Workers Local 78, through Labor's Non-Partisan League, had applied to use the County Fairgrounds for a Memorial Day mass meeting. The union enlisted Lieutenant Governor Patterson and Dr. Towne Nylander, regional director of the National Labor Relations

Board, as the primary speakers. The Fair Board denied the request at the behest of the Brawley Chamber of Commerce and the Associated Farmers. Patterson immediately labeled the fair board's actions as "unAmerican" and publicly appealed for Olson to intervene. The governor pressured the board to reverse itself. Then, to the local sheriff's consternation, Olson ordered state law enforcement officers to ensure the safety of the attendees and sent his son to represent him on the podium. Richard Olson explained to the 1,500 workers his father's philosophy that "reform always comes from the bottom up, never from the top down." The press also reported that the unnamed representative of Mexico's labor movement encouraged Mexican Americans to back Roosevelt and Olson.[41]

This was probably the first time that a California governor had allied himself with largely Latino farm workers and forced the growers to accept the free speech rights of a progressive pro-labor organization. The next request to aid struggling farm workers would not go so well. Predominantly Mexican American cotton pickers in Madera and other towns throughout the Central Valley went out on strike in the summer of 1939 when the growers refused to follow the state orders by Carey McWilliams to raise wages. Olson was unable or unwilling to force the growers to comply with state orders or to physically protect the strikers. In the unsuccessful contest, the workers received aid from El Congreso, which had chapters in Shafter, Tulare, and Bakersfield. Quevedo and Fierro de Bright organized food and clothing drives. Celebrity support came from actor Will Geer and singer Woody Guthrie.[42]

El Congreso next turned its attention to an urban dilemma. On August 11, 1939, thirteen-year-old Benjamin "Benny" Moreno was found hanged in his cell at the Whittier State School for troubled boys. Acting in the name of the Mexican American community, El Congreso called upon Olson to investigate and began to mobilize the community. More than one thousand attended a Congreso-inspired mass meeting in Belvedere. This unincorporated section of East Los Angeles was "the largest Spanish-speaking neighborhood in the country," according to one CIO publication. El Congreso also reached out for support to its other Los Angeles area committees as well as those in Ventura, Orange and San Diego counties, and in the Central Valley.[43]

The governor ordered Aaron Rosanoff, M.D., state director of Institutions, to look into the matter. Rosanoff investigated and ten days later confirmed that Moreno's death was due to suicide. Unconvinced, El Congreso demanded a further investigation, as did groups such as the ACLU. Olson responded by appointing a six-person fact finding committee chosen by El Congreso and the Moreno family. The committee included Quevedo and Fierro de Bright. It also included two of the left's more able advocates: attorney Leo Gallagher and International Labor Defense organizer La Rue McCormick. The two brought specific skills to El Congreso and further illuminated its placement in the constellation of the popular front. Governor Olson's decision to appoint controversial figures to the fact-finding committee, as requested by El Congreso, is also a testament to his deep respect for the left and the Mexican American community.[44]

The investigation received wide coverage in Los Angeles' English and Spanish language press throughout the fall of 1939. The committee interviewed family members, various experts, and witnesses. They also went to the "Lost Privilege Cottage" where Moreno died, and even performed an autopsy on Moreno's exhumed body. "The autopsy climaxed an inquiry that began more than a month ago when the committee was appointed to run down rumors that the boy had been beaten before his death," reported the *Los Angeles Times*.[45] The investigators found evidence of brutality but not of murder.[46]

Olson's naming of Quevedo and Fierro de Bright to investigate the death of Benny Moreno made them his first Latino gubernatorial appointees. Soon thereafter the governor, committed to diversity, made his first appointment of a Los Angeles Latino to a permanent board or commission. In mid-October 1939, he tapped Anthony P. "Tony" Entenza to serve on the board of directors of the Veterans Home at Yountville. A labor attorney and the Past National Commander-in-Chief of the United Spanish War Veterans, Entenza was an elder statesman in the Mexican American community.[47]

Despite such a close relationship between Olson and the Latino activists, there were points of disagreement, particularly over the populist retirement program promoted by Dr. Francis Townsend. Popularly known as "Ham & Eggs," the proposal called for the state to pay seniors $30 a month. This program was a response to the dire conditions facing older persons who received no financial support from either their former employers or the government. The newly created Social Security program covered only a few retirees and specifically excluded government, farm, and homecare workers. "Mrs. Josephine De Bright and Edward Quevedo, of Los Angeles, spokesman for the half million California population of Spanish-American origin, predict an overwhelming Ham and Eggs vote from their people," noted one paper covering the issue. The two made a tour of the state drumming up support for the measure among Latinos.[48] Despite sympathies with its stated objective, Governor Olson opposed the initiative as fiscally irresponsible, as did President Roosevelt, and it was soundly defeated at the polls.[49]

For its part, El Congreso—which in the second half of 1939 changed its name to the Spanish Speaking People's Congress— was preparing to hold its second national meeting in San Antonio, Texas, as part of its long-held dream of becoming a truly national organization.[50] The meeting never took place, however, due to international events that shattered the organization.

The divisions within El Congreso followed the decision by Nazi Germany and Communist Russia to sign a Non-Aggression Pact and then militarily divide Poland between themselves. As World War II began, the communists and their allies, including the California CIO, undertook a three-pronged attack on President Roosevelt and Governor Olson that forced the Democratic Party's progressives to choose between leftist and liberal factions. First, it labeled Roosevelt a "warmonger" because of his commitment to continued military preparedness. Second, it pressed popular front organizations like El Congreso to drop their opposition to fascism. Third, the Communist Party helped organize a so-called "grassroots" delegation against the Olson-led, pro-Roosevelt slate to the 1940 Democratic National Convention. These efforts had a dramatic impact on El Congreso, in part, because of the essential role the liberal-left and the CIO played in its formation and founding conference in Los Angeles.

The fractured relationships in El Congreso were also illuminated by changes in leadership, the size and compositions of its members, and the group's position relative to fascism. While there are no contemporary statements by either Quevedo or Fierro de Bright describing the breakup, the change in membership from the Los Angeles-based national Congreso in April 1939 and the state Congreso in the same city just eight months later, in December 1939, was dramatic. The changes started at the top. El Congreso President Eduardo Quevedo disassociated himself from the organization as did the New Mexico-Arizona Club. Not only were ethnic oriented community groups absent from the second convention, so too were most of the liberal reform groups that once operated within the popular front. These included the Hollywood Anti-Nazi League, the John Steinbeck Committee Aid to Agricultural Workers, and the Spanish-American Division of the California Democratic Party. Those choosing to remain in El Congreso generally fell into one of three categories: CIO unions, Workers' Alliance chapters, and local El Congreso clubs.[51]

The changes in the composition of El Congreso resulted from a changing perspective toward fascism after the Hitler-Stalin pact. The first conclave in April 1939 had endorsed the Lima Conference "for its efforts to block Nazi and Italian fascist domination of the economies of Central and South America" and praised Warner Brothers for producing an anti-Nazi movie, "Confessions of a Nazi Spy." By contrast, the second convention in December 1939 declared that the "European War has as its aim the redivision of the colonial countries and the conquest and reconquest of the markets and the resources of the world." It further declared that "the peoples of the United States, Mexico and all Latin America desire peace and complete neutrality."[52]

Lieutenant Governor Patterson headed the so-called "grassroots" delegation opposing the Olson-led, pro-Roosevelt slate to the 1940 Democratic National Convention. Having previously heralded Roosevelt and Olson at the founding of El Congreso and at the rally in El Centro, Patterson now characterized the president's preparedness efforts as a "Blueprint for Fascism." Further, the slate's campaign brochure stated that "[b]oth Olson and Roosevelt think they are bosses and dictators instead of servants of the people."[53] Joining Patterson was Los Angeles CIO Council head Philip Connelly and Immigrant and Housing chief Carey McWilliams (who offered to

resign his post in the Olson administration). In addition to their effort to deny Roosevelt reelection, the leftists sought unity with their
opponents on the right to recall Olson.[54]

The internecine struggle severed relationships and divided former allies. The increasingly isolated labor-left soon discovered their
limited ballot box appeal. Despite its prominent supporters, the leftist "grassroots" slate competing to go to the Democratic National
Convention received fewer than 50,000 votes, less than ten percent of the 700,000 for the Olson-Roosevelt slate. It even came
in behind a conservative slate pledged to Vice President John N.
Garner. The Roosevelt slate included Lucretia del Valle Grady. The
Berkeley-based Latina was a member of the Democratic National
Committee. She was a Californio, with roots into the California's
Spanish and Mexican period, and joined other Latino delegates to
the 1940 convention from New York, Florida, and New Mexico.[55]

Before the ruptures caused by the Hitler-Stalin pact, the left-
oriented Latino activists were able to guide organizations in which
they were a numeric minority by placing one of their own in
key staff positions and by adopting popular and reformist goals.
Progressives outside the communist orbit, such as Quevedo, served
as articulate spokesmen for El Congreso goals. Fierro de Bright
stated: "We were able to control [Congreso President] Quevedo
pretty good." [56] By contrast, leftist Bert Corona was less critical
in his account. "While Quevedo may have had some differences with both Moreno and Fierro, by and large he seemed politically and ideologically compatible with them, despite his strong
Catholicism." Corona added that Quevedo's role in El Congreso
was an important one: "He bridged the gap between the Mexican
activists of the 1920s and early 1930s and the new activists of the
late 1930s."[57]

Two other Latino activists within the popular front explained
why the divisions in late 1939 and 1940 were so painful and long
lasting. "In a very comprehensive way the [Hitler-Stalin] pact was
a stunner and a splitter," recalled leftist Jaime González, a CIO
steelworker union leader close to the Los Angeles CIO Council's
leadership, and a Workers' Alliance activist. "The general run of us
union workers were of New Deal loyalty. The Mexican American
community went further—as idolaters of FDR. It would have been

hard to deviate from that."[58] For Henry Santiestevan, an American Student Union activist at Occidental College in Los Angeles, the divisions on the liberal-left destroyed relationships and profoundly reshaped his personal outlook. The discovery that "communists are not liberals" and that "anytime the USSR changed its policy, the Communist Party here changed its policy," Santiestevan declared, was painful because friends within the communist orbit had great organizational skills.[59]

The rise and fall of El Congreso revealed much about the value of votes, coalitions, and leadership. Leadership was especially important. Without Luisa Moreno, there would have been no El Congreso because the organization grew out of her vision and pan-Latino experiences in New York, Florida, and the Southwest. El Congreso illuminated the dynamic nature of coalition politics, both in terms of bringing together the Latino community and in working with non-Latinos. The organization achieved rapid recognition and several successes because of its support from important segments of the Latino, labor, and political worlds, as well as legal organizations such as the ACLU. Even though the number of Spanish-speaking voters was small, El Congreso was viewed as the representative of an emerging constituency with powerful friends. The growing importance of Latino voters was reflected in the formation of Amigos de Olson and the Federation of Spanish-American Voters, as well as a Latino division within the Olson gubernatorial campaign and the California Democratic Party. In the final analysis, the Olson administration's participation in the April 1939 Congreso, its defense of the right to assemble in El Centro, its investigation into the death of Benny Moreno, and the governor's veto of anti-alien legislation was due to a confluence of leadership, voters, and coalition work—and an ideological belief in fighting for minorities and against discrimination.

The Congreso experience also illuminated how policy differences between coalition partners shaped long-term relationships. Governor Olson did not support every Congreso initiative. While he aided farm workers in El Centro, neither he nor Carey McWilliams were able or willing to assist cotton strikers in the Central Valley. El Congreso and its allies disagreed with Governor Olson over the Ham & Eggs initiative to expand funding for senior citizens. These differences resulted in disappointment and anger, but did not shatter the basic relationship. By contrast, the reaction of the left to the Hitler-Stalin pact that led to the demise of El Congreso as a broad-based group and to intense enmity between leftists and Governor Olson would have enormous consequences at the end of the next decade with the beginning of the Cold War.

Despite its short life span as a broad coalition, El Congreso represented an historic milestone as it brought together Latinos, unionists, and liberal-left activists under the rubric of the New Deal. El Congreso was the first organization in California to appeal to diverse groups within the Latino community and to unite them with Anglos, Jews, and African Americans from a variety of labor and political organizations. It thus provided a model for progressive, multiracial political coalitions. El Congreso also demonstrated the convergence of electoral and issue advocacy as the Roosevelt and Olson administrations sought to advance a New Deal agenda to uplift workers and the foreign-born. Moreover, it was the first group founded on the principle of a national pan-Latino coalition and thus the group's importance was far greater than its history indicates.

Finally, El Congreso attracted talented young leaders and provided them opportunities to develop organizational skills and to expand individual political networks. A number of El Congreso leaders—on both sides of the liberal-left organizational divide—would subsequently play important roles in the community's political development in California. In the aftermath of El Congreso's collapse as a broad-based organization, neither faction withdrew from the political process. The two major factions chose instead to focus their attention on different goals. Those close to the left-led Los Angeles CIO Council sought to empower workers through unionization, and engaged in a number of community issues with a racial overlay. In the political area, the labor-left often backed CIO-endorsed Anglo candidates over liberal Latino candidates, despite the second Congreso's stated commitment to "fight for political recognition" in "Federal, State, County, and Civic Life."[60] Eduardo Quevedo and the community-oriented liberals, often small businessmen, assumed the primary role as ethnic advocates. They also undertook responsibility to recruit, finance, and otherwise support a number of Latino candidates for public office.

CHAPTER 2

EDUARDO QUEVEDO
AND
THE SEARCH FOR A WARTIME VOICE

The collapse of El Congreso as a broad-based organization in late 1939 led Eduardo Quevedo and other California Latino community leaders to utilize the Federation of Spanish-American Voters of California as their organizational vehicle. They adopted a more traditional strategy for ethnic political empowerment through the election and appointment of Latinos to public office. Almost all of their successes were "firsts," positions that no Spanish-speaking person had held in the modern era. For a people largely new to the United States and to its political system, even minor positions held enormous group importance. Latino activists also sought to use the political process to advance group goals. This included efforts to ensure the fair treatment of Latino youth, and advocacy of state legislation to establish a fair employment law and another to end school segregation. To obtain these goals, Latino political activists pledged themselves to work within the context of President Roosevelt's New Deal Democratic coalition. The New Deal represented an ideological framework, an administrative staff, and a set of public policies aimed at helping workers and the poor, a large number of who were foreign-born or their children. Equally important, at the start of 1940, the liberals who controlled the White House and the governor's office in California were in a position to advance Latino concerns.

Little is known of the origins of the Federation of Spanish-American Voters, but its founders appear to have been motivated by the desire to inject Latinos into the political area within the context of liberal pluralism and the New Deal. Under Quevedo, the group became much more dynamic, recruiting six Latino candidates for the August 1940 primary election. One ran for Congress, two focused on the State Legislature, and three set their sights on the Los Angeles County Democratic Central Committee. "This is the first time in history that we have the privilege of electing six of our own people into jobs that will enable them to draw the attention and services of officials to our immediate problems for immediate action," journalist A. de Hoyos wrote. His column, titled "The Dawn of Prosperity," ran in a small English language newspaper serving Mexican Americans. He emphasized that participation in politics will "uplift our standards of living to the highest possible degree!" De Hoyos specifically appealed to those focused on events in Mexico. "Some of us would like to go back to Mexico to live and are not interested in the outcome of events that affect our colony here. Even if we do go back to the old country, would it be too much to help our neighbor here with your vote?" he asked. "Never place insignificant value on your vote for it may mean the turning point in an election of close rivals."[1]

The most prominent candidate was Eduardo Quevedo. As president of the Federation of Spanish-American Voters, he agreed to run for the "east of the river" 52nd State Assembly District that was less than ten percent Latino. Oversized numerically and geographically, the district started in the older, working class communities of Boyle Heights and Belvedere, moved further east to pick up Anglo-dominated Huntington Park, and then south into the newer industrial cities of Vernon, Bell, Bell Gardens, and Maywood, replete with steel, auto, and rubber factories.

Eduardo Quevedo lived in Boyle Heights, the entry point for many immigrants in Los Angeles and a cauldron of working class, radical politics. The largest ethnic bloc was unassimilated Yiddish-speaking Jewish immigrants from Russia and Poland. The heart of the Jewish community and civic life was Brooklyn Avenue, with its retail shops, union halls, and houses of worship. Boyle Heights was both "Jewish" and "integrated," according to one resident.[2] Members of a dozen other groups called the area home, including Mexican Americans, Japanese Americans, and Russian Molokans who still spoke their native tongue. The district was also home to African Americans, Irish Americans, and other white ethnic groups. Politics was a centralizing force and always the topic for daily conversation, where labor folklorist Archie Green recalled that everyone saw themselves as minorities: "Americans were WASPS [White Anglo Saxon Protestants]."[3] All shades of New Deal Democrats were active in Boyle Heights, as well as the organized left—communists, socialists, Trotskyists—and those too independent to follow any party line.[4]

Quevedo's New Deal platform championed progressive labor legislation, funding for relief and public workers, old age pensions, and legislation addressing the concerns of California's youth. He also endorsed President Roosevelt's approach to the crises in Europe, arguing for "national and state defense for our own protection." He likewise stressed that Mexican Americans "have problems that are not only peculiar but very acute." Quevedo charged Latinos had "been the victims in too many instances of unfair discrimination [by] unscrupulous employers" and by the legislature that sought "to deny relief to aliens."[5]

Two weeks prior to the California primary election on August 27, 1940, the Federation of Spanish-American Voters sponsored a "Big Political Rally" at the Mi Club Auditorium, on the second floor of a Brooklyn Avenue establishment in Boyle Heights. The hall also served as Quevedo's campaign headquarters. The campaign invited voters to "Come meet Eduardo Quevedo, candidate for the Assembly," and other Latino and Latino-friendly candidates. Attorney Ernesto R. Orfila chaired the rally along with fellow attorney and candidate A.P. "Tony" Entenza.[6]

Quevedo came in fifth among seven contestants by garnering 2,028 votes, or 10 percent. A look at the candidates' campaigns provides insight into the low-budget, interest group-driven electoral process. Quevedo spent $120, all of which came from the Federation of Spanish-American Voters and he obtained free publicity from several small Latino weekly papers. The victor, William Pool, spent twice as much, or $240, and was backed by the CIO, which had its newsweekly, the *Labor Herald,* and a political apparatus that included labor and community partners. The second place finisher spent roughly the same as the winner and was backed by the rival AFL, which communicated to its members through its own weekly paper. The third place candidate was Jack Y. Berman, a liberal Boyle Heights theater owner who won in heavily Jewish precincts, and was supported by outgoing Assemblyman Benjamin Rosenthal and the weekly *Eastside Journal.*[7]

Entenza likewise made a big impression in his unsuccessful campaign. The governor's first Mexican American board appointee, to the state Veterans Home Board, the Spanish-American War veteran ran unsuccessfully for the Belvedere-based congressional district.[8] The election was not without Latino victories; Joseph Acosta and José Armand won their respective races for the Los Angeles Democratic County Central Committee.[9] The Latino community thus gained a voice in the lightly organized party structure. The collective candidacies advanced the community's interests by providing a reason for Mexican Americans to go to the polls, by increasing the group's perceived political importance, and by inserting Latino community concerns into the larger political dialogue.

The 1940 elections stood out for yet additional reasons: U.S.-Latin American relations assumed a central role in the unfolding presidential contest, and President Roosevelt selected the Spanish-speaking Secretary of Agriculture, Henry A. Wallace, as his vice presidential runningmate. In this race, liberal Latinos eclipsed leftists, due in large measure to the neutrality of the national CIO and its state and municipal bodies following the internal divisions that arose with the signing of the Hitler-Stalin pact. Tony Entenza—the Olson appointee, Quevedo ally, and primary election candidate— was the lone Latino listed as a sponsor of the labor-oriented mass meeting featuring Henry Wallace at the Hollywood Bowl. In the election Latinos joined workers and other ethnic and racial minorities in California and other states to reelect Roosevelt to an unprecedented third term. The post-election analysis on nationality groups by the Democratic National Committee included Mexican Americans in California. Even before being sworn-in as vice president, Wallace attended the inauguration of Mexican President Manuel Avila Camacho in Mexico City. He stayed for several weeks thereafter to work with Mexican farmers to increase their yield on corn, a principal crop.[10]

During the fall election campaign, the death by hanging of a second Mexican American boy at the Whittier State School triggered new demands for a wider investigation into the reform school's operation, and to the reopening of the Benny Moreno case. The investigation in 1939 where Governor Olson involved El Congreso leadership now continued with Quevedo and the Federation of Spanish-American Voters representing the Latino community. Unfazed by the earlier state investigation, the reform school apparently had continued their past practices. This time Olson named Superior Court Judge Ben Lindsey to head a three-person investigating committee. As a result, a number of state employees were fired for mistreating the young people in their charge, a first in the history of California, and reforms were undertaken.[11]

No sooner were the November 1940 elections for state and federal offices over than municipal contests began in the spring of 1941. This time the Federation of Spanish-American Voters and other Los Angeles Latinos chose not to endorse either the intractable incumbent, Parley P. Christensen, or to run one of their own. Instead they decided to ally themselves with the Jewish community in backing Al Waxman. The Federation of Spanish-American Voters sponsored a "monster rally and dance in the auditorium above Everybody's Super Market" on Brooklyn Avenue where Quevedo introduced the candidate. The Latino-Jewish alliance, while politically significant, did not produce an electoral majority. Consequently, Christensen used the power of incumbency and the backing of organized labor and the Communist-led left to effectively cut into the two ethnic voting blocks and once again win reelection.[12]

Quevedo and the other Latino leaders worked with Governor Olson to obtain additional state appointments. Olson named attorney Ernest Orfila to the Veterans Welfare Board. It was a fitting slot given that he was a veteran of the First World War who was active in the American Legion.[13] Ethnic leaders failed in their efforts, however, to have Orfila appointed to the Los Angeles Municipal Court. Olson used the judicial opening—one of only thirteen he would get statewide in his four-year term—to appoint the first African American, Edwin Jefferson, who was a brother-in-law of Assemblyman Hawkins.[14] But Governor Olson did use one of his limited judicial appointments to name Ataulfo "A.P." Molina to the San Diego Municipal Court, making him the first Latino judge in modern times. Molina was a Mexican-born, forty-eight-year-old graduate of the University of California, Berkeley Law School.[15]

Governor Olson's appointment of the first Latino and African American judges, and his opposition to discrimination, stood out in an era when discrimination in employment, housing, and throughout society was pervasive and widely accepted as a fact of life. The

Judge A.P. Molina, appointed to the bench by Governor Olson.
(San Diego Union-Tribune Collection, San Diego Historical Society)

Los Angeles CIO Council, led by Philip Connelly, played a significant role in forcing newly organized employers start changing their behavior. "Phil was a [secret] Communist and a progressive guy," James Daugherty, an Irish American comrade and the organizer for the Utility Workers, declared. "He would call us guys who were heading up various unions—rubber and steel, and the whole bunch—and he would get us together. We mapped out a program," Daugherty related, "to increase our members among Black people and among Mexican people." For his part, Daugherty helped open the "all white" utility industry, which had refused to hire Mexicans to dig pole holes for transmission lines. He negotiated a non-discrimination clause in the first union contract and then pressured management to diversify the workforce. "The end result was that we got great support [for the union's program] from the Mexican workers," according to Daugherty.[16]

Even when they agreed on fighting discrimination, liberal and leftist Latinos of this era had a different set of motivations and alliances. The dominant liberal faction worked through the Federation of Spanish-Speaking Voters, promoted the election and appointment of Latinos to public office. By contrast, the leftists promoted El Congreso and the CIO, backed CIO-endorsed Anglo candidates. While the liberals had the broadest support within the community, the leftists had access to greater political resources because of ties to the CIO. By the fall of 1941 the most pressing differences over foreign policy—accentuated by the Hitler-Stalin pact—had been resolved. The German invasion of the Soviet Union once again made communists anti-fascists; it also aligned the interest of the Soviet Union with that of the United States in opposing Hitler's continued aggression.[17]

For Latinos and other racially marginalized communities, President Roosevelt's executive order in 1941 prohibiting discrimination on the basis of "race, creed, color or national origin" in government agencies and in defense industries represented a promising opportunity. The number of jobs covered by the executive order increased dramatically after Japan bombed Pearl Harbor on December 7, 1941 and the nation boosted the level of economic production to exceed even the pre-depression years. A number of the "home front" jobs went to young Latinos, some of whom became supervisors. For example, John Gutiérrez oversaw 28 others on the Center Fuselage Assembly line at the Douglas Aircraft's plant in El Segundo.[18] The home front also provided new opportunities for Latinas like Hope Mendoza and Margarita Salazar, who found work as a "Rosie the Riveter" at Lockheed Aircraft in downtown Los Angeles.[19] Ultimately, some 17,000 Latinos found work in Los Angeles shipyards, after Pearl Harbor.[20] Roosevelt's order, issued to deflate the threat by A. Philip Randolph, the head of the Brotherhood of Sleeping Car Porters, to sponsor an African American March on Washington, did not fully eliminate discrimination in the war-related jobs. The spring 1942 issue of *Mexican Voice*, published by Los Angeles area college students associated with the Mexican American Movement (MAM), printed an article, "Discrimination—And Us." The article urged readers to report instances of discrimination to Guy Nunn, head of the Pacific Coast Committee of the Minority Group Branch of the War Production Board. "Working hand in hand with Mr. Nunn, in his work, are a group of OUR most able leaders." It listed more than a dozen Spanish-surnamed leaders serving on "various committees," including YMCA executive Tom García, student leader and *Mexican Voice* editor Frank Gutiérrez, middle class activists in Quevedo's circle, a number of CIO labor leaders, and a priest, Father González. Collectively, they represented the largest number of California Latinos ever appointed to federal advisory posts—and the first effort to involve Latinos themselves in combating job discrimination.[21]

Latinos were also among the first to sign up for military service which, according to Raúl Morín of Los Angeles, "made us feel like *genuine* Americans, eligible and available to defend our country." In fact, Latinos were part of the war from the very beginning. Rudolph M. Martínez, from San Diego, was among those killed in the Japanese attack at Pearl Harbor. Pedro Despart, the Los Angeles-based Assembly candidate in 1938 and 1940, was among the first group of draftees on October 29, 1941. Soon a trip through heavily Mexican American neighborhoods in Los Angeles, and throughout the state, revealed streets lined with homes displaying government issued blue star banners, with one star for each son in the military. Governor Olson used the prestige of his office to recognize the community. This included appearing with Quevedo at a Latino-oriented war bond rally. The federal government sold war bonds to pay for the salaries of soldiers and to manufacture tanks and planes.[22]

Despite the efforts going into winning the war, liberal Latinos adopted the same "Double Victory" strategy as their liberal African American counterparts to overcome fascism abroad and discrimination at home. In April 1942 Governor Olson issued an executive order outlawing racial discrimination. In its coverage of the order, *La Opinión* also reported on resolutions against employment discrimination issued by the Federation of Spanish-American Voters and El Congreso.[23] Congreso founder Luisa Moreno, once again living in California, focused her energies on organizing cannery workers in Southern California and the Central Valley.[24] For their

Eduardo Quevedo with Governor Culbert Olson at a rally to promote war bonds. Note the women's sashes represent the different nations of Latin America.

(Courtesy of Department of Special Collections and University Archives, Stanford University Archives)

part, Quevedo and the Federation of Spanish-American Voters placed a premium on electoral politics. "American citizens of Mexican descent should participate and be prominent in every election," reported the *Aristo News* in 1942, adding: "it is time that the Spanish Speaking peoples in California should have representation in the government legislative bodies."[25] The Federation of Spanish-American Voters decided to run two of their own candidates for the Assembly in 1942. Quevedo would run in the newly redistricted Boyle Heights-based 40th Assembly District and *Aristo News* publisher Fred Rubio would campaign in the new 51st Assembly District that included the Latino enclaves in Belvedere. Quevedo and Rubio promoted themselves as "Roosevelt Democrats" who were "qualified to serve their respective districts."[26]

Quevedo expanded his Latino-based political coalition to include the two most prominent African Americans in Los Angeles: Assemblyman Hawkins and Fay E. Allen, a leader of the AFL Black Musicians union and a member of the Los Angeles School Board from 1939 to 1943.[27] Absent from this multiracial coalition supporting Quevedo were El Congreso leader Josephina Fierro de Bright and the Latino CIO activists. Not supporting Quevedo was "a toughie," reflected Bert Corona, then the twenty-four-year-old president of ILWU Warehouse Local 26. "We had to swallow our pride. We had to follow the CIO line because we needed labor."[28]

In addition to running their own candidates for the legislature, the Federation of Spanish-American Voters endorsed Latino and supportive Anglo candidates for state and local office in 1942. The group supported Los Angeles Sheriff Eugene Biscailuz and many statewide Democratic candidates. "I want to express my appreciation to you for signing a petition and being one of the sponsors of my candidacy for reelection as Governor of the State of California," Olson wrote Quevedo prior to the primary election. In another letter Olson wrote: "I am extremely grateful for this expression of continued support of our progressive democratic administration by the Spanish American citizens of our state." Lieutenant Governor Patterson asked Quevedo to "Kindly convey to the Federation my grateful appreciation for this endorsement."[29]

On the eve of the 1942 primary election Governor Culbert Olson purchased radio time and appealed directly to Latino voters for support. "During the whole period of my administration as Governor, I have felt within me the assurance that you were standing by my side, giving me your wholehearted support in my efforts to give our great State of California a people's government." California's chief executive reminded Mexican Americans of his political appointments, the firing of the Whittier State School staff who had abused Mexican American youth, and his efforts to combat racial discrimination. He also praised their commitment to the war effort and restated his own commitment to fighting bigotry. Governor Olson, who had done more for Latinos than any previous chief executive, asked the community for their help at the ballot box.[30]

A month later Governor Olson made an even more dramatic appeal to Latino voters. He arranged for President Franklin D.

Roosevelt, a hero to Latinos throughout the Americas, to send Vice President Henry A. Wallace to keynote the September 16th Mexican Independence Day festivities in Los Angeles. Wallace spoke in Spanish to a crowd of 7,500 who gathered at the Shrine Auditorium for the El Grito festivities that kicked off the celebration. He conveyed the personal greetings of President Roosevelt. Mexico's Secretary of the Interior Miguel Alemán, acting as the personal representative of Mexico's President Manuel Avila Camacho, praised the cooperation between the two neighbors and delivered an impassioned speech in support of the Allied cause in World War II. Governor Olson and Los Angeles Mayor Fletcher Bowron joined them on stage, along with Latino community leaders, led by Eduardo Quevedo.

The presence of Wallace and Alemán in Los Angeles was front-page news in the *Los Angeles Times* and other papers.[31] The *Times* editorialized that the usual "spirit of fiesta" had been replaced by "a solemnity in keeping with the hour that is so critical in Mexican and United States annals."[32] The mood of the paper reflected the uncertain direction of the war at a time when the Axis countries were conquering new territory. Nazi Germany controlled most of Europe and had moved deep into Russia, while Imperial Japan had seized much of Asia, including a large part of China.

In this environment, thousands turned out the next morning for the Mexican Independence Day parade, which included much more than the usual collection of colorful floats, marching bands, and youth groups. Wallace, Alemán, Olson, and Bowron filled the reviewing stands along with top military leaders from both sides of the border. They joined more than five thousand people, who watched as American Army units marched ten abreast, the sound of boots rhythmically pounding the pavement. Jeeps and armor vehicles followed, as did anti-tank and anti-aircraft batteries, portable radio stations, troop carriers, and assault boats. Before it was over, two thousand infantry men, including many Spanish-speaking soldiers, marched south on Spring Street, before turning west on First Street and proceeding past the reviewing stand set up in front of the State Building.[33]

In the program that followed, John J. Cantwell, the Irish-born Archbishop of Los Angeles, and a leader within the Bishops'

Committee on Catholic Action Among Spanish Speaking People in the United States, delivered the invocation.[34] Vice President Wallace followed, addressing the crowd in Spanish. He praised the mixing of Latinos and Anglos in the state, calling California "a fusion ground for two cultures."[35] Mexico's Secretary of Interior Alemán then praised Mexico's partnership with the U.S. and the "spirit of justice for which the democracies" fought and complimented California's efforts to provide relief and other benefits to Mexican immigrants. The civic leaders proceeded to the Biltmore Hotel where Wallace, Alemán, and Olson addressed the people of Mexico and Latin America over a continent-wide radio network.[36]

The decision by the United States and Mexico to use Los Angeles as the backdrop for an important statement of multinational unity against the Axis powers reflected the region's growing military importance and its large vibrant Latino community. The White House's decision to send Vice President Wallace emphasized two important points: a desire to help Governor Olson politically without formally endorsing his lagging candidacy and to boost Latino morale.[37] In yet another linkage between Latinos and Wallace, national CIO leaders sent Ernesto Galarza, a Californian living in Washington, D.C., to discuss the best way to direct labor money in the 1942 campaign. Galarza informed Wallace that communists in the CIO continued to attack his friend, CIO Secretary James Carey, despite efforts to unite against Nazi Germany.[38]

Governor Olson was not the only California gubernatorial candidate courting the Latino vote in 1942. Republican Attorney General Earl Warren sought out Quevedo in a vain attempt to gain the support of the Federation of Spanish-American Voters of California.[39] Warren differed from earlier Republican nominees in his search for the political center, in courting minority voters, and in his nonpartisan approach to problem solving that attracted to public service "men and women of all faiths, all creeds and races and colors, without partiality or preferment."[40]

Warren personified the emerging Anglo middle class. His father had been blacklisted for joining a socialist-led railroad union, necessitating relocation to Bakersfield, an oil drilling and farming town where the young Warren went to school with Mexican Americans. For the 1942 election, Warren appointed actor Leo

Carrillo to chair his "Loyal Democrats" committee. The great grandson of California's first Provisional Governor, Carrillo had maintained his Catholic and Democratic memberships while becoming a favorite of the Republican business and political elite. Warren easily defeated Olson to win the November 1942 race.[41]

The mistreatment of Latino youth burst into the public spotlight with the Sleepy Lagoon case. Some two-dozen members of the 38th Street gang were arrested, tried, and convicted for the Eastside murder of José Díaz—without a shred of evidence. The supporters of Quevedo and Manuel Ruiz, the chair of the Coordinating Council for Latin American Youth, the primary advocate for young Latinos, were unable to pay for legal services for these or the hundreds of others detained in the city's mass arrest of Latino youth, according to Jaime González. The labor leader who would soon become a YMCA councilor had a unique vantage point. He was a member of the liberal Coordinating Committee for Latin American Youth and the chair of the leftist Los Angeles CIO Council's civil rights committee.[42]

The arrests and travesty of the Sleepy Lagoon episode provided a political opening for the leftists who had lost much of their influence within the Latino community after the split within El Congreso. La Rue McCormick, the head of the International Labor Defense, formed the Citizen's Committee for the Defense of Mexican-American Youth, along with Bert Corona, Jaime González, and others. McCormick had been part of El Congreso's investigation of the Benny Moreno prison death but was also controversial because she was the Communist Party's candidate for State Senate in Los Angeles.[43] This produced some private consternation in the Latino left. "She was using the Sleepy Lagoon case— and those kids' lives—to get votes, and it would have deterred from this investigation, from our defense," recalled Congreso staff person Fierro de Bright. "That's why she wanted to be president of the defense committee."[44]

The defense group had access to resources not available in the Latino community, including attorneys. They arranged for George Shibley, an attorney for Longshoremen's Local 13, ILWU-CIO, to take over the case. After the case was lost, the committee retained Ben Margolis, another CIO attorney and leader in the National

Lawyers Guild, to handle the appeal. Los Angeles CIO Council head Philip Connelly arranged for national labor attorney Abraham Isserman to "supervise the preparation of the brief."[45] UCAPAWA Vice President Luisa Moreno raised money from organized labor and Carey McWilliams took over the renamed Sleepy Lagoon Defense Committee during the appeal process.[46]

The committee's work in the Mexican colony was often difficult, according to Alice Greenfield, the young Jewish activist (and open communist) that McWilliams hired to staff the defense. She was frequently asked, "But are they good boys?" She then would seek to reframe the question to, "Were they treated justly?" For their part, Quevedo and most of the other Mexican American leaders declined to allow the use of their names by the defense committee. They appeared distrustful of the motives of the communists and their allies, having been burned politically when El Congreso aligned itself with the policies of the communists at the time of the Hitler-Stalin pact. Liberal actor Anthony Quinn, an original committee member, left the group although he used his celebrity status to help raise money for the cause.[47]

Then, for ten days in June 1943, U.S. servicemen beat up Mexican Americans on the streets of Los Angeles, negating much of the good will painstakingly built up by Roosevelt and Wallace. The papers sensationalized the situation and incited more violence by portraying the clean-cut, uniformed servicemen as honorable men teaching a lesson to the Zoot-Suit dressed, drug-crazed, violent youth. As the beatings continued day after day, it became evident that the violence was not targeting gang members, but Latinos generally.[48] "It was discrimination. They didn't give a hoot how you were dressed," stated George P. Sotelo, then in the ROTC at Pasadena City College. He noted "Mexican American youth got a bum rap" because "there were a lot of Mexican Americans in the Army."[49]

Eduardo Quevedo and other community leaders sought to end the conflict by appealing to governmental leaders. As the chair of the Coordinating Council for Latin American Youth, he sent a "night letter" to Elmer Davis, Office of War Information, with copies to Foreign Language Division chief Alan Cranston and President Roosevelt.[50] Los Angeles Supervisor John Anson Ford sought federal assistance to end the rioting by U.S. servicemen by contacting Nelson Rockefeller, head of the Office of Coordinator of Inter-American Affairs.[51]

The strongest White House statement came from First Lady Eleanor Roosevelt. She linked the causes of the riots to long practiced discrimination. "For a long time I've worried about the attitude toward Mexicans in California and the States along the border," stated Mrs. Roosevelt.[52] The California State Chamber of Commerce promptly denounced Mrs. Roosevelt. The *Los Angeles Times* backed them up, editorializing that Mrs. Roosevelt's comment "shows an amazing similarity to the Communist party line propaganda devoted to making a racial issue of the juvenile gang trouble here."[53]

The violence ended when the military restricted the servicemen's movement. "Everybody claims that [they themselves] put a stop to the Zoot Suit Riot," stated Jaime González, head of the Los Angeles CIO Council's civil rights committee. "I made a declaration, which Phil Connelly put in my mouth. We demanded the military be declared off limits, that they all be punished to the full extent of the law. You know what stopped it? Franklin Roosevelt sent the Office of Public Information out here."[54]

Alan Cranston served as the representative for the Office of Public Information (OPI). The youthful head of the OPI's Foreign Language Division oversaw relationships with thirty-nine language groups within the United States. According to Cranston, having "Anglos and Latinos fighting each other in the streets of Los Angeles [was] harm[ing] the war effort."[55] He met with newspaper editors in Los Angeles and was able to persuade them to run less sensational headlines, as well as to report positive stories about Latinos. He also met with a bevy of elected officials, religious and ethnic leaders, and Mexican American youth. He relayed one bittersweet case that illustrated the challenge of restoring ethnic harmony, and the extent to which wartime Washington was forced to exert its influence to overcome ingrained prejudices.

> I came out to see what I could do about [the situation]. I met with some of the leaders in the Hispanic community, Eddy Quevedo was one. And then I met with some of the young people. Then I met with some of the girls who had a plan. There were all sorts of wild rumors that they were members of gangs and you had to sleep with the male leader in order to be allowed to be in the gang, and they were

very upset about this. They wanted to organize a march on city hall where they would demand an examination to prove that they were all virgins. I didn't think that was too helpful to resolve the matter. So I thought about it a while, and I talked to Monsignor O'Dwyer and other people, and eventually I suggested to them that instead of that they organize a blood bank to show their patriotism. Not to organize a blood bank, but to go to the blood bank to donate blood. The Red Cross was running blood banks for the Army. To my horror, the Red Cross didn't want to accept Mexican blood. They thought Anglos might not want it. So then I had to go to Washington to the Red Cross and raise hell back there to get them to change their policy.[56]

The Red Cross changed its policy and the blood drive "got a lot of publicity," according to Cranston, demonstrating that the young Latinos "were supporting the war effort."[57]

Cranston also joined a delegation led by the Rt. Rev. Monsignor Thomas O'Dwyer that visited Mayor Fletcher Bowron and the Board of Supervisors. The politically connected O'Dwyer was a logical choice because he was the former president of the National Catholic Welfare Council, to which the Roosevelt administration looked to help represent Latinos on social justice issues, as well as the representative on such issues locally for Archbishop Cantwell. Together, they "outlined a program," according to one newspaper account, "designed to stop strife by gangs of youths which has been seized upon by Axis propagandists." Manuel Ruiz represented the Mexican American community at the meeting. Two days later, the Board of Supervisors appointed O'Dwyer to head a fifteen-person committee to investigate the situation that included a number of Latinos, including Quevedo, attorney Ernest Orfila, Dr. Reynaldo Carreón, labor leader Bert Corona, *La Opinión* manager Luis Flores Díaz, and Sheriff Eugene Biscailuz.[58]

A number of other public agencies and private organizations also rushed to investigate the causes of the disturbance.[59] Over breakfast, Carey McWilliams gave Attorney General Robert Kenny, the only statewide Democratic elected official, a list of politically "acceptable" members for a state committee that he thought should be established. The Attorney General then pitched the idea to Governor Warren, with whom he had long enjoyed a bipartisan friendship. Warren accepted this list and established the Governor's Special Committee on the Los Angeles Emergency, chaired by Joseph T.

McGucken, Auxiliary Bishop of Los Angeles. Warren added actor and former campaigner Leo Carrillo as his representative on the committee.[60]

Eduardo Quevedo traveled to northern California to help address problems facing young Latinos there. About 700 attended the San Jose Coordinating Council for Latin-American Youth sponsored event at Roosevelt High School. In addition to Quevedo, president of the Los Angeles Coordinating Council for Latin-American Youth, a number of local leaders spoke. These included José Villareal, president of the San José Comision Honorifica and representative of Mexican Consul Rodolfo Elías Calles, Jr.; José García, of the Pan American Society of San Francisco; and Maurice Hazan, field representative of the Coordinator of Inter-American affairs, from Washington, D.C.[61]

The trip to San Jose and the partnership with a variety of federal officials demonstrate the degree to which Eduardo Quevedo's reach had grown. His sphere of influence was to expand even further over the next two years due to an alliance with another son of New Mexico, U.S. Senator Dennis Chávez. The two political pioneers would work closely to promote fair employment, to maintain good relations with Mexico and the nations of Latin America, to reelect President Roosevelt and to promote Quevedo's candidacy for city council. Senator Chávez, one of the princes of American politics, used his considerable influence to promote the interest of Quevedo and California Latinos. (The importance of Chávez cannot be overstated; neither African Americans nor Jewish voters had one of their own in the United States Senate.)

Three weeks before the November 1944 election, Senator Dennis Chávez arrived in Los Angeles to keynote a Roosevelt "Good Neighbor" Rally at the Shrine Auditorium. Formally, it was an opportunity to laud the president for his relations with Mexico and to rally support for Chávez's bill, S.B. 2048, to create a "permanent" Fair Employment Practices Committee (FEPC). Extension of this law by Congress was necessary because the wartime FEPC, which had opened jobs to Latinos and other historically discriminated-against groups, would expire with the cessation of fighting. The rally served to advance two other political objectives: first, to encourage Latino voters to go to the polls, and second, to further elevate Quevedo's standing within Latino Los Angeles and the political community generally.

Quevedo welcomed Senator Chávez at Los Angeles' Union Train Station as did California's junior U.S. Senator, Sheridan Downey, and Los Angeles County Supervisor John Anson Ford. Chávez's press conference set the tone for his visit. "Many of our people in the Southwest have been discriminated against economically," he stated. "War manpower shortage has helped to cure this situation temporarily. We want to see it cured permanently."[62] A reporter for the communist *People's World* asked Chávez to comment on the Sleepy Lagoon case and the "communistic agitation" on behalf of the defendants. "Americans of Mexican parentage don't seek preferential treatment, but they do want fair play," asserted Chávez, "and they want to obtain it as their right as American citizens and not as a gratuity thrust upon them by political agitators."[63]

That night Senator Chávez dined privately with Quevedo

Eduardo Quevedo (on the right) meets with U.S. Senator Dennis Chávez at the Biltmore Hotel prior to the 1944 Roosevelt "Good Neighbor" rally in Los Angeles.

(Courtesy of Department of Special Collections and University Archives, Stanford University Archives)

and thirty prominent Mexican Americans.[64] The following evening, Senator Chávez shared the platform at the Roosevelt "Good Neighbor" Rally at the Shrine Auditorium with Senator Downey, who had labored to ensure the participation of Mexican Americans in "defense training schools."[65] The master of ceremonies, Manuel Ruiz, had promoted the rally through a radio broadcast sponsored by the Democrats' Foreign Language Division.[66] Entertainers from Mexico and Hollywood shared the stage, including Latino movie stars Rita Hayworth and Anthony Quinn.[67]

A brilliant orator, Quevedo warmed up the crowd by introducing Senator Chávez. After urging those in attendance to support the reelection of President Roosevelt and Senator Downey, Chávez attacked intolerance. He labeled prejudice "unfair and indecent but as American as a hot dog" and declared that "The FEPC has helped greatly to provide equity of job opportunity for all, regardless of race or color." The senator emphasized that "the activities of the committee have furthered our Good Neighbor policy by indicating to our Latin American allies that our government is determined to bring about an arrangement whereby equality of economic opportunity will be the right of every citizen of North America."[68]

Following the rally, Quevedo turned his attention to ensuring a strong Latino turnout on Election Day via a radio address to Los Angeles Latinos. "The reason why Spanish-speaking people should re-elect President Roosevelt can be answered very simply," Quevedo began. Roosevelt "has fought against racial, national and religious discrimination within these United States and he has extended a hand of friendship and international goodwill across the continents."[69] As a result, Latinos were making great strides in their social integration in the U.S., a process that was being advanced through military service with other Americans in World War II. He added that soon it would not matter "whether you say VIVA ROOSEVELT or THREE CHEERS FOR THE PRESIDENT."[70]

As 1944 turned into 1945, Manuel Ruiz and Eduardo Quevedo, acting as leaders of the Los Angeles Coordinating Council for Latin American Unity, continued to work with Senator Chávez in support of his national fair employment legislation. They also rallied to support state legislation being carried by the Assemblyman Hawkins, working through the Southern California Committee for

State FEPC, headed by Judge Isaac Pacht. They placed discrimination in the context of World War II. "Enemy bombs and bullets don't discriminate between one American fighting man and another . . . the blood of Catholic, Protestant, and Jew, of Negro, Mexican, and a dozen other 'minority' groups has been spilled in the fight for democracy and freedom," stated one flyer. "It isn't going to make much sense to them if they are told, when they come home: 'You were good enough to FIGHT for us, but you can't WORK for us because you are a Mexican (or a Jew, or a Catholic, or a Negro, or . . .)'."[71] Both the state and national measures failed passage.

Latinos not only joined representatives of other groups to lobby for fair employment legislation, they headed up an effort to outlaw school segregation. Assemblyman William Rosenthal from Boyle Heights authored the measure, AB 1257, which the Quevedo and Ruiz-led Coordinating Council of Latin American Youth sponsored. The issue had arisen when districts in "Orange County, Carpenteria, Oxnard, Montebello, El Monte and other Southern California areas" justified segregation of students, according to Ruiz, "on the grounds that they may have some Indian blood." State law allowed for separate schools for Asians and Indians. Quevedo lined up support from Los Angles Mayor Bowron, Los Angeles County Supervisor Ford, and Dr. Rufus B. von KleinSmid, president of the University of Southern California.

Mexican Americans in Los Angeles opened a campaign, "financially supported by more than a dozen Latin American groups," to lobby state legislators on behalf of the anti-segregation bill in the State Senate. Attorney Manuel Ruiz proudly noted that the lobbying effort "represents the first occasion on which Latin organizations have employed the methods followed so effectively in the past by other American interests in support of legislation which affects them directly." The bill passed the assembly but died in the senate in 1945.[72]

Assemblyman Glenn Anderson authored a similar measure passed two years later. That bill, AB 1375, was co-authored by Augustus Hawkins, William Rosenthal, and Elwyn Bennett, and sponsored by the California Teachers Association. It received the backing from the PTA, Monsignor O'Dwyer and the California Catholic Bishops, the Los Angles Democratic Party, the Los Angeles

Daily News, and a number of school administrators. Governor Earl Warren signed the bill shortly after Judge Paul McCormick of the U.S. Circuit Court ruled in *Mendez v. Board of Education*, in a case brought by the League of United Latin American Councils (LULAC), that the segregation of Mexican Americans in Orange County was illegal.[73]

In addition to fighting for fair employment and anti-school segregation legislation during the spring of 1945, the Los Angeles Latinos were engaged in a campaign to elect Quevedo to the Los Angeles City Council. According to supporter Dionicio Morales, he "knocked himself out going from event to event."[74] Quevedo emphasized his "abundance of practical experience." This included serving as president of the Federation of Spanish-American Voters and the president of the Coordinating Council for Latin-American Youth. He had also represented the Latino community on a variety of local and national government bodies, including the Los Angeles City Housing Authority's Citizens Advisory Committee, the federal government's Los Angeles area FEPC, and the U.S. Treasury Department's Latin-American Financial Committee.[75] But what made the campaign especially noteworthy was the support it received from Senator Chávez.

Senator Chávez arranged for Quevedo to be the lone Californian to testify before Congress on behalf of his FEPC bill. He used the opportunity to speak about the power of the federal government to improve the lives of ordinary Latinos while enhancing international relations. Quevedo shared conversations with former Mexican President Adolfo de la Huerta and Inter-American Affairs Coordinator Nelson Rockefeller about his insights and experiences in California. Quevedo also related a number of specific examples where employers worked well with the Latino community as well as instances of discrimination. He highlighted the case of Mary Delgado, who had obtained a job at Consolidated Aircraft in San Diego only through the intervention of Senator Chávez. "We do not want any special privileges whatsoever. We do not even want a job, or feel that we are entitled to a job just because we happen to be of a certain racial extraction," stated Quevedo. "But inasmuch as we accept our duties and responsibilities as Americans, even to the extent of losing our lives as Americans, we do not want to be

★ ★ ★ ★ ★

QUEVEDO'S Platform

★ ★ ★ ★ ★

QUEVEDO will submit an ordinance for a Fair Employment Practices Commission (F.E.P.C.) for the City of Los Angeles similar to the federal and state legislation. (Quevedo appeared at a U. S. Senate hearing in Washington, D. C., March 12-13-14, 1945.)

QUEVEDO will support legislation for the appropriation of city funds for the prevention of juvenile delinquency in Los Angeles.

QUEVEDO will demand that a Junior College be built in the 9th District.

QUEVEDO is in favor of modernizing the City Charter.

QUEVEDO will fight for more adequate and modern transportation.

QUEVEDO will work for the elimination of sub-standard housing areas and the improvement of streets in the district.

★

HEADQUARTERS
206 South Spring Street, Suite 100
Phone MUtual 8558

EDUARDO QUEVEDO Notary Public	X

A panel from Eduardo Quevedo's campaign brochure. The issues he raised in the 1945 city council campaign—beginning with the need for a fair employment ordinance—helped establish the agenda for Latino Los Angeles in the post-World War II era.   (Courtesy of Annemarie Quevedo)

deprived of a job on account of our ancestry or national origin or race."[76] Despite the strong campaign, Quevedo and all of the other would-be council candidates lost to the aging but entrenched incumbent, Parley P. Christensen.

The two most enduring images from this period—the Sleepy Lagoon case and the Zoot Suit Riots—served as graphic reminders of the extent of racism within society and the institutions of government. Yet a fuller exploration of the war years also illuminates multiple examples of progress and cause for optimism. For California Latinos, particularly those in Los Angeles, the early to mid-1940s was a time of significant firsts. The Federation of Spanish-American Voters of California served as the first explicitly political organization with deep roots in the community and ties to local and state elected officials, including Governor Olson. It supported Mexican Americans running for the city council, the state assembly, and Congress in the Los Angeles area. Latinos obtained political appointments to boards and commissions at the local, state, and national level—a first that strengthened the community's ties to the Roosevelt administration. It was also a time of advocacy and coalition building within the legislative arena and at the ballot box, where both Democrats and Republicans competed for the Latino vote. The era likewise demonstrated the value of powerful friends. U.S. Senator Dennis Chávez's relationship with Eduardo Quevedo provided many beneficial results. It elevated the role of Mexican Americans in California and throughout the nation in both the political and legislative arenas. So, too, did the appearance of Vice President Henry Wallace at the 1942 Mexican Independence Day festivities in Los Angeles. Still, two major objectives remained unfulfilled: enacting fair employment legislation and electing a Latino to the Los Angeles City Council.

These two goals would ultimately be advanced by developments largely outside the Latino community that corresponded, coincidentally, with changes inside the community. The dominant liberal Latino leader, Eduardo Quevedo, withdrew suddenly from politics and community life to raise his five children after the death of his wife. This created a void in the community; there was also a void on the left with the final collapse of El Congreso. At the same time, changes in civil rights politics in Los Angeles would also create new

progressive political space between the communist left and traditional liberalism. It would lead to a reengagement between Latinos
and labor and a more formal partnership with the liberal wing of
the Catholic church. For its part, the Archdiocese of Los Angeles
worked with Bishops' Committee for the Spanish Speaking, organized with a grant from President Roosevelt. Archbishop Cantwell
of Los Angeles served as titular head, but the committee operated under the guiding hand of Archbishop Robert Lucy of San
Antonio (who had begun his clerical career as a labor priest in Los
Angeles).[77] The archdiocese also established the Catholic Labor
Institute to replace the St. Ballantine Guild for Labor and Industry,
which had become inactive during the World War II years.

A second development was the beginning of the AFL's full-time
engagement in civil rights. Proposition 11, an ultimately unsuccessful effort to establish a state FEPC law in California, was placed on
the November 1946 ballot by the NAACP, the CIO, and leftists
who collected hundreds of thousands of signatures. Proposition 11
forced the AFL to act. The International Ladies Garment Workers'
Union now enjoyed one of the largest concentration of Latino
members. In the summer of 1946 the garment union helped establish a civil rights committee within the Los Angeles Central
Labor Council and staffed it at no cost to the council. The council's
new Labor Committee to Combat Intolerance operated under the
direction of Zane Meckler and the ILGWU-headed Jewish Labor
Committee (JLC), who formally employed Meckler. After the election, Meckler, a socialist from New York, continued to staff the
AFL Central Labor Council and to work with CIO unions loyal to
the national CIO leadership and in opposition to the communists
leading the Los Angeles CIO Council. This served to create an alternative, labor-based civil rights network. Moreover, the Jewish
and Latino members of the increasingly civil rights oriented garment union worked in downtown factories and lived in proximity
to each other in Boyle Heights.[78]

CHAPTER 3

EDWARD ROYBAL

AND

THE BIRTH OF THE
COMMUNITY SERVICES ORGANIZATION

The November 1946 election provided both continuity and transition. Despite a Democratic registration advantage, the electorate returned centrist Republican Governor Earl Warren, who won easily with the backing of the AFL California Federation of Labor.[1] The Republicans achieved a second victory as appointed U.S. Senator William Knowland, scion of the ultraconservative publisher of the *Oakland Tribune*, defeated former Congressman Will Rogers, Jr., the son of the cowboy comedian.[2] It was, however, a time of transition for Mexican American political activists. To fill the void left in Latino Los Angeles by Eduardo Quevedo's withdrawal from politics, and with the apparent demise of the Federation of Spanish-American Voters of California, two Latino businessmen stepped forward. Spanish-born theater owner Francisco "Frank" Fouce and Mexican-born attorney Philip Newman organized the Latin American Division of the California Democratic Party for the 1946 election. They ran a series of full-page ads in *La Opinión* and sponsored a pre-election rally at the Shrine Auditorium. "[Fouce] put on a great show," recounted Newman. "Packed it with people who had been going to the Mexican theaters." Newman's father was Bruno Newman, who represented the Mexican Consul in Los Angeles and had chaired the 1942 Los Angeles Mexican Independence Day celebration that feted Vice President Henry Wallace and Mexican Interior Secretary Miguel Alemán. Present at the 1946 rallies were such political notables as California Democratic Party Chairman James Roosevelt, Boyle Heights Assemblyman William Rosenthal, attorney general candidate Pat Brown, and congressional candidates Jerry Voorhis and Helen Gahagan Douglas.[3]

The Newmans took time from the fall 1946 campaign to plan for the spring 1947 municipal races in Los Angeles. They held a small meeting in their downtown law office with Frank Fouce and

Dr. Camilo Servin, who was a politically active physician long allied with Quevedo. All were "keenly interested in getting some Spanish-speaking person into public office," according to Roger Johnson, a liberal reformer who had worked for Mayor Bowron and Governor Olson. "One day he called me and said he had a young man that he and some of his friends had in mind to run for city council, and would I mind coming down to meet him, and if I like him, perhaps I would run his campaign."[4]

The young man was Edward R. Roybal, a health educator for the Los Angeles County Tuberculosis and Health Association. At thirty, he was more established in the community and in his family life than most other World War II veterans, who were in the throes of getting married and starting families or using the GI Bill to attend college or launch a business. Roybal, like Quevedo, was a native of New Mexico. His family moved to Boyle Heights in 1922 following a railroad strike that left his father unemployed. Graduating from Roosevelt High School in 1934, Roybal joined the New Deal's Civilian Conservation Corps and enrolled briefly at the University of California at Los Angeles. During difficult times, he worked in the garment industry. Upon discharge from the Army, he quickly jumped into politics. Roybal endorsed the Quevedo-organized Roosevelt "Good Neighbor" Rally in 1944 and that same year was the only Mexican American to win a place on the Los Angeles Democratic Central Committee. He joined several Latin American consulates in Los Angeles in supporting the Pan American Folk Festival at Hollywood High School. That event was organized by the popular front, the coalition of liberals and communists that enjoyed a partial revival during World War II. Finally, during the summers of 1945 and 1946, Roybal used his vacations to travel to Chicago to study community organization under the tutelage of social worker and independent radical Saul Alinsky. Roybal, his wife, and two children lived in "the flats," the multiethnic neighborhood on the southern edge of Boyle Heights.[5]

At the fall 1946 meeting in the Newmans' law office, Philip Newman encouraged Roybal to run for the ninth district council seat that was based in Boyle Heights. "Me, run for office? I'm a social worker. I'm not a politician," Roybal responded. The Mexican American business leaders persisted. "[Christensen] isn't going to run, we understand, so we need somebody to run for the city council in the ninth [district]." At the meeting Roybal spoke with Roger Johnson, who agreed to become his campaign manager. "I met with Roybal and something sparked," recalled Johnson, "We both seemed to like each other, and I liked what he had to say and apparently he liked what I had to say."[6]

"We held our first [campaign] meeting in a little broken down hall on East First Street and a small handful of people, about 20 or 30, showed up," Johnson recalled. "A good number of them were Roybal's relatives. We decided to launch the campaign. We took a collection, and our first collection was thirteen dollars. That started our campaign."[7] The meeting also attracted two experienced union organizers with political ties and campaign experiences—Jaime González and Anthony P. "Tony" Ríos. González, one of the highest-ranking Latinos in the Los Angeles CIO Council, had quit being a steel worker to become a youth counselor with the East Los Angeles YMCA. This decision reflected a personal interest in upward mobility and the belief that recreational activities would reduce "many of the evils of racial misunderstanding."[8] Tony Ríos was vice president of the United Steel Workers' Utility Foundry Local 1918. The self-taught Ríos had dropped out of school after the eighth grade to support his migrant-farm worker family. He had contacts with other unions through membership on the CIO-PAC, the political arm of the Los Angles CIO Council. Not only did they both come out of the steel union, but Ríos' sister and González's mother were activists in the ILGWU.[9]

Roybal was not the only person running for the ninth district council. Anticipating Christensen's departure, a myriad of ethnic, labor and political organizations met to identify possible replacements. Engineer Fred Shalmo eyed the post. Although a German American, he was closely associated with Quevedo. Shalmo had helped welcome Senator Chávez to Los Angeles in 1944 and in 1945 had managed Quevedo's city council campaign. Roybal, however, was a fellow Latino and closer ideologically to Quevedo. The two were progressives with an activist orientation who during periods of popular front legitimacy were open to working with individuals on the left in pursuit of mutual goals. In the 1947 local election, the first since the end of World War II, Roybal had the politi-

Friends and family gather for the first meeting of Edward Roybal's 1947
campaign.   *(Kenneth C. Burt)*

cal advantage over Shalmo by virtue of being a veteran, but neither
was a stranger to politics. Both had developed networks beyond the
Latino community. These prior relationships carried both positive
and negative baggage. After Quevedo lost during the first round of
the 1945 city council campaign, Shalmo ran the campaign for Mark
Allan, who positioned himself to Christensen's right. But in so opposing the progressive incumbent he earned the enmity of the labor-
left.[10] For their part, progressives sought a consensus candidate. The
CIO-PAC's records indicate "there is a feeling should [Christensen]
change his mind and run, he would be defeated." Citing a consensus
among CIO, AFL, and the [independent] Railroad Brotherhoods,
the CIO-PAC voted to "call upon [Assemblyman] Rosenthal to run
for Councilman in the 9th district."[11]

The 1947 New Year's Day *Eastside Journal* carried the news
that Councilman Christensen changed his mind and would run
again. For his part, Assemblyman Rosenthal decided not to challenge the aging incumbent, and thus missed an historic opportunity
to parlay support in the district to give the Jewish community their

long-sought representation on the city council. Organized labor responded by rallying support behind the incumbent despite their earlier misgivings. Community and political groups associated with the CIO Council also joined the bandwagon, including the newly organized Progressive Citizens of America.[12] Dorothy Healey, who married Los Angeles CIO Council head Philip Connelly in 1947, and was the head of the Communist Party in Southern California, argued that Christensen "had a long and vigorous record of support for the Left and it would have been ingratitude to reject him."[13]

Still, Roybal and Shalmo decided to challenge Christensen, as did two others—attorney Filmore Jaffe, a decorated war hero, and downtown public relations consultant Julia Sheehan, a Democratic Party official with ties to Governor Earl Warren. For Roybal, the political landscape presented few opportunities. The small Mexican American base was split and there were few identifiable pockets of voters upon which he could build an effective coalition to compete with the incumbent. Christensen had the backing of the unions and the progressives; Jaffe would do well among fellow Jews in Boyle Heights; and Sheehan would do well in downtown and among moderates. Shalmo would take his share of Latino votes and also appeal to moderates and conservatives. Yet against these odds, Roybal persevered.[14]

Each morning he boarded the streetcar that took people from their homes in Boyle Heights to the factories and offices downtown. Wearing a red, white and blue campaign button, he shook hands and distributed union-printed palm cards. The cards stressed Roybal's name, and the words "veteran" and "progressive." This placed him in the ideological center of the district and associated him with American victory over fascism. The veteran label had a particular resonance with the larger populace as well as the large number of Latinos who served in the military. Mexican Americans were awarded more Congressional Medals of Honor than any other ethnic group.[15] The campaign slogan, "Give A Young Man A Chance!" sought to tap into the respect for returned veterans while providing a contrast to Christensen's advancing years. According to Johnson, "We carried on a campaign of not very great intelligence. It was basically, 'we need better street cleaning, we need better street lights, we need protection from police brutality,' and that type of thing, rather than anything very lofty."[16]

Large Latino households where no one was registered to vote repeatedly frustrated Roybal. Typical were immigrant parents who had never become citizens and their adult children—living at home due to cultural expectations and the scarcity of housing—who were eligible to vote but had never bothered to register. Roybal was also frustrated by his inability to line up support from organizations. The only institutional endorsements came from a small Mexican American newspaper, *El Pueblo*, and, according to Roybal, "one local of the steel workers and one local of the International Ladies Garment Workers Union."[17]

In the final days, the two major newspapers split their endorsements. The liberal *Daily News* endorsed Christensen and the conservative *Los Angeles Times* endorsed Julian Sheehan, who sought to become the first woman on the council. The support by the *Times* helped to make her stand out as the primary opponent to

Edward and Lucille Roybal plan strategy with campaign manager Roger Johnson and other supporters at the campaign headquarters.
(Edward Roybal Papers, Kennedy Library, California State Library, Los Angeles)

Christensen.[18] As a result, Christensen received 8,948 votes, Julia Sheehan finished second with 3,783 votes, and Roybal missed the runoff by 433 votes and came in third. He finished just 249 votes ahead of Filmore Jaffe, and far ahead of Fred Shalmo.[19]

The reelection of Los Angeles City Councilman Parley P. Christensen in the spring of 1947 left Edward Roybal and his Mexican American supporters pondering what they would do next. Roybal and the young activists, meeting around a table at the Carioca Restaurant in Boyle Heights, decided to stay together. "In 1947, we tried what we thought was possible, but we found out that it wasn't that easy," declared steel worker Tony Ríos. "So we began to prepare ourselves for the long range goals instead of quickies."[20] They formed the Community Political Organization. The group sponsored a fiesta dance at Angeles Hall on Friday, June 27, 1947. Dance tickets proudly proclaimed sponsorship by the "Community Political Organization, formerly the Committee to Elect Ed Roybal."[21]

Roybal privately faced conflicting demands from his wife and campaign manager. The Roybals were planning to move into a new home in El Sereno that was outside the ninth district. "Mrs. Roybal, particularly, was looking forward to the new home. But I told them that if they moved into [Councilman Ernest] Debs' district, they'd never have a chance to get elected, because Debs was too strong a candidate and [Roybal] would never make it; that they should rather gamble by not moving into the house, staying where they were." Roybal, however, acceded to his wife's urging and the family moved out of the Boyle Heights-based city council district.[22]

Other developments would soon impact Roybal's ultimate career and family decisions. Saul Alinsky, the Chicago-based community organizer, serendipitously learned of Fred Ross. Ross had been hired by the American Council of Race Relations to study racial tensions in Los Angeles, but instead was using his time to organize politically through Unity Leagues. While Ross' proclivity to organize infuriated his boss, it was music to the ears of Saul Alinsky who contacted Ross and, in early June 1947, traveled to Los Angeles to meet the thirty-six-year-old organizer. Ross took Alinsky on a "trip through the East Side," stressing the need for improving the living conditions within Latino Los Angeles. Alinsky was impressed with Ross' natural abilities and offered him a job as a full-time organizer in the Midwest, where he had a number of ongoing projects. Ross refused, emphasizing his determination to assist Mexican Americans and to stay in Los Angeles.[23]

While in Los Angeles, Alinsky met with Edward Roybal, Carey McWilliams and a number of others, including Roger Johnson, who spent "several days" showing him around town on behalf of Mayor Fletcher Bowron. When Alinsky talked to Johnson about focusing on African Americans, he was told, "Blacks are relatively well organized. They have the NAACP, the Urban League, and other groups. Why not consider doing something among the Mexican American people? Because they really have no good organizations."[24] Before leaving town, Alinsky agreed to hire Ross to work with Mexican Americans in Los Angeles. He offered Ross $3,000 for the first year, which Alinsky would raise, and suggested that he could get another $1,000 from actor Melvyn Douglas and his wife, Congresswoman Helen Gahagan Douglas. Alinsky took Ross to meet the Douglases, who donated the money.[25]

Fred Ross had gained considerable insight during the previous couple of years while organizing Mexican Americans into Unity Leagues in small rural communities in Los Angeles, Riverside, and Orange Counties. In each area he found a shared common denominator: a powerlessness that translated into unequal treatment from government. Ross recognized the inherent ability to alter such power relationships through the ballot and ongoing civic engagement. He used voter registration drives to develop new leaders and to gain respect for the community with government officials.[26]

Mexican Americans represented a huge reservoir of potential voters. Unlike most of their parents, who had never gone through the naturalization process, members of this cohort were U.S. citizens by birth. "In the past ten years practically the entire United States-born second generation has come of voting age," observed Ross at the time. He added that "sizeable segments of this second generation, particularly the veterans, are possessed of a strong social will to bring about basic improvements in the neighborhoods so that at least their children can have a better life, a better place to live it."[27] Others had developed a civic awareness while working on the home front in unionized factories, particularly in the production of steel and garments.

Ross understood that if he wanted to organize Mexican Americans in Los Angeles, he had two choices. He could identify new leaders and develop a new group as he had done in the Unity Leagues or he could gain the confidence of Edward Roybal and the members of the Community Political Organization who could serve as the nucleus for an expanded organization. Ross spent six weeks courting Roybal and those around him. He met with them individually and collectively. "He came with his ideas. And how he had some financial support," explained Margarita Durán, a student at UCLA and the daughter of ILGWU leader María Durán.[28] While the activists agreed with Ross' analysis and proposed strategies, they remained suspicious. He was, after all, according to steelworker Tony Ríos, "an Anglo who wore cowboy boots."[29]

The Durán women represented an important political dimension. First, they were part of a small but growing number of Latinas with political skills and connections. And second, they were outside the Communist Party orbit. In general, politically active Latinas were union leaders, college students, or professionals. These women first emerged in Los Angeles politics with the formation of El Congreso, founded by union organizer Louisa Moreno and staffed by college educated Josephina Fierro de Bright. Other Latinas, most notably from the cannery workers, were active within the leftwing of the CIO.[30] At the same time, Latina garment workers were developing leadership skills. These women came up within an AFL union with a Socialist Party orientation although there were other progressive anti-Stalinists. (The term Stalinist was used by non-communists on the liberal-left to describe the followers of Joseph Stalin and is similar to referring to the followers of Stalin's rival, Leon Trotsky, who had been murdered in Mexico, as Trotskyists.) María Durán, for example, was an "independent socialist." Daughter, Margarita Durán, was close to the Trotskyists.[31] While these women of the liberal-left were politically sophisticated, the successful organization of the community would involve other active women. One of them was Alvina Carrillo who belonged to the Catholic Youth Organization (CYO). In the Latino community of the late 1940s, women generally prepared the food that was part of most gatherings, including fundraisers, and performed clerical tasks. Most important, they provided the social glue that was the key to the mobilization of overlapping family, religious, and union networks that operated in a blue-collar neighborhood.[32]

The Community Political Organization insisted Ross prove he was not a communist. Not knowing how to prove what he was not, a frustrated Ross called Alinsky in Chicago who instructed him to "sit tight for a couple of days." Alinsky then contacted Chicago Bishop Bernard J. Sheil. The auxiliary bishop served on Alinsky's board, headed the national CYO and had been instrumental in organizing the packinghouse workers in Chicago. Bishop Sheil called Bishop Joseph McGucken, his counterpart in Los Angeles, who had chaired Governor Warren's commission investigating the causes of the Zoot Suit Riots and shared Sheil's enthusiasm for the social gospel. As a result of the cross-country conversation, Ross received an audience with Bishop McGucken, who agreed to back the organizing effort.[33]

For the Community Political Organization, accepting Ross as their organizer also meant an affiliation with Alinsky and the removal of the word "political" from its name. Alinsky told Tony Ríos, "In order for me to give you any money, you have to change your name to the Community Service Organization [CSO]."[34] This was because Alinsky's organization was a non-profit foundation. There was also a tactical consideration in removing the word political from the group's name. "I remember very distinctly when we decided, well, we'll hang together under the guise of a service organization but we're really a political organization," recalled Jaime González. "We could cover more ground and recruit more people as a service organization because, after all, there was so much service that the community needed."[35]

Alinsky believed in demanding that the United States live up to its founding egalitarian ideals. He organized people around specific grievances to force those in positions of authority to become more responsive to the general needs of the community. The Industrial Areas Foundation was most famous for its Back of the Yards organizing in the Chicago neighborhood next to the meatpacking district. There Alinsky organized the multitude of community based groups—the two largest being the United Packinghouse Workers and the Catholic Church—into a powerful force to improve the lives of the often immigrant, working class residents. He would soon advance his reputation by writing a biography of CIO founder John L. Lewis (whose daughter sat on his board).[36]

One of the first tasks was to formalize CSO's structure. Roybal became chairman, in large part because he was widely known in the Mexican American community and represented the World War II veterans and the emerging middle class. The labor leader-turned-YMCA youth counselor, Jaime González, filled the slot of vice chairman. Immigrant María Durán, then a member of the executive board of the ILGWU Dressmakers Union, accepted the post of treasurer. The board included steel worker Tony Ríos and X-ray technician Henry Nava. The son of a barber, Nava grew up in a local Spanish-speaking Presbyterian Church. Most of the twenty people coming to the CSO meetings were, like Ríos and Nava, friends or co-workers of Roybal or, like Manuel Tafoya, Roybal's uncle, part of the extended family.[37]

Ross focused on broadening and deepening the organization's ties. He reached out to the business and professional leaders who had long served as Eduardo Quevedo's political base, particularly the three who had recruited Roybal to run in 1947. He sought their advice, contacts, and legitimacy. He linked them to the new organization by forming an Advisory Committee for the Mexican American Program. The five-member committee consisted of Dr. José Díaz, theater owner Frank Fouce, attorney Richard Ibañez, attorney Philip Newman, and Dr. Camilo Servin. The only member new to the Los Angeles scene was Ibañez, a law partner of former Attorney General Robert Kenny, and a board member for the Progressive Citizens of America.[38]

At the same time, Ross moved to obtain the institutional support from the two groups with the largest number of Latinos: organized labor and the Catholic Church. Bishop McGucken's interest in the CSO facilitated the incorporation of the clergy into the organization. The bishop was close to Monsignor Thomas O'Dwyer who served as the director of Catholic Charities in Los Angeles and was Archbishop Cantwell's representative on the national Bishops' Committee for the Spanish-Speaking. He also oversaw St. Mary's, the largest church in Boyle Heights, and the "mother church" to the surrounding Spanish-speaking missions and parishes. O'Dwyer

knew Alinsky and Bishop Bernard Sheil through the national social worker network and was predisposed to support any Alinsky
project—particularly one designed to address the needs of Mexican
Americans within the boundaries of his parish.[39]

O'Dwyer agreed to join the advisory committee but since he
was stretched very thin between his administrative and pastoral responsibilities, he turned to his parish staff for assistance. Father
William J. Barry recalled that O'Dwyer met with him and the other two assistant pastors. "O'Dwyer began to share his enthusiasm
for the Industrial Areas Foundation (IAF), for what they were trying to do with CSO." Barry stressed that O'Dwyer, whom they
all admired, suggested they take a look at the inchoate CSO. The
young Irish American and German American priests did just that.
"So we attended three or four meetings and reported back to him
that we liked the organization and the direction that it was taking,"
related Barry. "He was excited to hear that. He felt that if Mexican
Americans organized they would have a voice in society." Father
Barry accepted a seat on the CSO's executive board and shared his
work with fellow clerics in Boyle Heights. The strong support provided by Bishop McGucken, Monsignor O'Dwyer, Father Barry,
and the other parish priests in the area effectively elevated CSO to
the status of a church auxiliary.[40]

CSO recognized the strategic importance of organized labor.
Since the beginning of World War II, Latino membership had risen
in AFL unions and both the liberal and left wings of the CIO. A
study of twenty-eight unions in Los Angeles showed that in the AFL
building trades, Latinos comprised ten percent of plasterers, twenty
percent of painters, and half of cement finishers. Among AFL industrial workers, Latinos represented forty to fifty percent of workers producing brick and clay, garments, furniture, and slaughtering
meat. Thirty-eight percent of AFL dishwashers were Latino. The
pattern continued with CIO unions: roughly ten percent of auto,
rubber, and shipyard workers were Latino, as were twenty percent
of furniture, steel, and textile workers, thirty percent of packinghouse and nearly half of furniture workers. The number of Latino
union stewards, executive board members, and staff also continued
to rise—although it lagged the growth in the membership.[41]

CSO aligned itself with two strategically situated unions: the

AFL International Ladies Garment Workers' Union and CIO United Steel Workers. Each had ten to fifteen thousand members in Los Angeles and believed in organizing around labor and community issues. Moreover, rank-and-file leaders María Durán and Tony Ríos were part of the CSO leadership. The two unions also shared a progressive anti-Stalinist vision and had an independent relationship with the Catholic Church.[42]

The United Steel Workers had organized the bulk of the local steel plants during World War II. The war helped transform historically anti-union Los Angeles into a city where organized labor became an accepted part of business and politics.[43] Up to a third of the steelworkers' local membership were Latinos. Most Mexican American union members participated in their first national strike in 1946. The CIO union also had a base in the aluminum industry, where Latinos were replacing Italian Americans as the primary source of labor. The steel workers union played a leadership role in the Catholic Labor Institute.[44]

The ILGWU was in similar throes of growth.[45] "In '47 we had a big strike here and we organized the sportswear industry. The sportswear industry was 95 percent Latino at that time. And here were these Latino garment workers, men and women, particularly women, being led by a couple of Jews from New York," explained the ILGWU's Abe Levy, the son of the union's Pacific Coast Director, Louis Levy. "We tried to get connections from the community," stated Levy, "through Tony Ríos, through helping Roybal, through contacts with Spanish priests, and Irish priests, like Father Kearney and Monsignor O'Dwyer, and the Catholic Labor Institute."[46]

As a result of these shared efforts and a desire to strengthen institutional linkages at the local level, both the steel and garment unions assigned staff to work with CSO. United Steel Workers' International Organizer Gilbert C. Anaya and Business Agent Balt Yañez assumed key roles in the organization. Anaya joined the advisory committee with O'Dwyer and the Mexican American businessmen.[47] The ILGWU donated organizer Hope Mendoza, a World War II "Rosie the Riveter," who also served as Congressman Chet Holifield's point person on immigration issues. Mendoza, in turn, reached out to fellow AFL labor leaders such as J.J. Rodríquez, head of the butcherers' union.[48]

CSO likewise reached out to the business community and to non-Latinos, including Jews and other white ethnics. Dr. Konstantin Sparkuhl, a young Boyle Heights physician of Greek and Italian heritage, became a mainstay in the group, along with his spouse, Mary. She was an Irish American whose father was a member of the International Workers of the World, or "Wobblies," who had come to the area in the twenties following an unsuccessful miners strike in Arizona.[49]

CSO now had a leadership that represented some of the best young organizers and benefited from ties to key institutions within the Latino Eastside. But in order to succeed, the CSO needed to develop a popular base. Ross proposed a variation on the "home visits" used by union organizers and Catholic priests. "[Ross] introduced house meetings so that we could invite neighbors because it would be easier for neighbors to travel a half-a-block or a block to a house meeting than to travel two or three or five miles to a meeting place," explained CSO board member Henry Nava.[50]

At each meeting, Ross would ask the host and his neighbors about their grievances. They complained about discrimination in employment, housing and education, and unequal treatment received from the city public works, health and police departments. Ross then tried to show how they could change these conditions by joining under the banner of CSO. Interested individuals were asked to host a meeting in their home, to join a committee working on public health, civil rights, voter registration or social activities, and to participate in bi-monthly membership meetings. During the day, Ross worked to coordinate these committee activities and to plan the next nightly house meeting. The grueling schedule often lasted eighteen hours a day. It produced results, according to Hope Mendoza, only because the indefatigable Ross "lived and breathed CSO."[51]

While the building of CSO was driven by anger at discrimination, the social activities were central to creating a sense of community. "The social committee was the most popular committee," stated Margarita Durán.[52] This sentiment was echoed by Elisio Carrillo, a twenty-three-year-old World War II veteran, who had worked his way through East Los Angeles Junior College by building ships and making steel, and was now working on a City of Los Angeles survey crew. Carrillo expressed the view that young people often attended CSO meetings, in part, because it was a good place to get a date.[53]

Still, the organization benefited from a highly charged political atmosphere. On Labor Day 1947, 100,000 Los Angeles workers took to the streets to protest Congress' passage—over President Truman's veto—of the Taft-Hartley bill, restricting labor rights. The Catholic Archdiocese of Los Angeles used a newly established Labor Day Mass at St. Vibiana's Cathedral to call for its repeal.[54] The Catholic Church not only gave its imprimatur to labor's top political priority, but also invited unionists to see themselves in the image of a working class Christ. This powerful idea was captured in the Association of Catholic Trade Unionist's "The Prayer of the Worker," which was used by the Catholic Labor Institute. The archdiocesan-sponsored organization was charged with promoting the social gospel within the field of labor relations. This meant supporting workers' efforts to unionize, encouraging Catholics to become leaders in their respective unions, and recognizing employers who worked well with organized labor. The validation of unionism and blue-collar work was reinforced by Pope Pius XII's 1947 encyclical, *Mediator Dei*. It defined Christ's presence as in the "collective persona of the faithful," recalled Los Angeles labor priest Joseph Kearney. This meant that workers, as part of the Body of Christ, must be treated as human beings "and not as things or as slaves."[55]

These developments provided a powerful mix, particularly for blue-collar Latino Catholics living on the Eastside. The Church was encouraging them to overcome discrimination in the neighborhood through CSO and to work for higher wages and human dignity on the job through their individual unions and the Catholic Labor Institute. Father Barry and leaders of the steel and garment unions were involved in CSO and the Catholic Labor Institute. Their membership provided additional organizational linkages and an ideological cohesiveness between the unions and the progressive wing of the Catholic Church, which shared an enthusiasm for social justice and an antagonism towards communists.[56]

CSO also reached out to members of non-Catholic religious traditions. According to Father Barry, most of the Protestant churches on the Eastside were small and in terms of social action followed the Catholic lead.[57] CSO likewise reached out to the Jewish community. "[Jews] were very powerful," recalled CSO student leader Ralph Poblano. "They had a lot to say" about what happened in Boyle Heights. Moreover, "a lot of the Jewish guys were into liberalism, you know, extreme. I call it socialism."[58] It was a label proudly worn by many Jewish activists. The International Ladies Garment Workers' Union had supported the Socialist Party prior to the New Deal and there was still a great deal of sentiment for the idea even though most identified as Roosevelt Democrats. The garment union, which was seen by some in the Jewish community as the voice of its working class, was central to a network of allied groups that included the *Jewish Daily Forward*, the Workmen's Circle, and the Jewish Labor Committee. Individuals within this progressive fraternal network were also part of two new post-war initiatives designed to promote civil rights. The first was the Central Labor Council's civil rights committee and the second was the Jewish Community Relations Council (JCRC), which served as the organized Jewish community's connection with other minority organizations. JCRC executive director Fred Hertzberg agreed to become the ninth member of the CSO's advisory committee.[59] More generally, among Boyle Heights Jews, it did not hurt that CSO's patron, Saul Alinsky, was a well-known Jewish radical.

Fred Ross utilized CSO's expanding membership base and political network to set meetings with civic leaders.[60] When concern for a specific example of police brutality emerged out of one of the house meetings, Ross and Henry Nava arranged for the abused boy's mother, Mrs. Alessandro, to meet with Councilman Christensen and the Police Chief Clarence B. Horral. "You know, at first, I was pretty jittery sitting there in front of the big desk," Nava stated afterwards. "But, when [Chief Horral] begins sticking up for that damn cop, and running down the Alessandro kid in front of his mother, I just had to say something. Yeah, and then that old goat, Christensen: 'But, gentlemen, this boy had a record!' God! A helluva City Councilman he is!"[61] As frustrating as such meetings were, they represented progress: CSO had the ability at least to meet with important civic leaders even if the organization did not have the power to alter the behavior of the city officials or departments.[62]

After one particular house meeting, when the CSO leaders gathered for a late-night meal, Ross recalled "all of them seem to sense the beginning of a real Mexican American movement." Roybal provided the most tangible evidence. "As we're leaving, he asks if anyone would like to give him a hand over the weekend. It seems he's moving back into the District!"[63] The decision by Roybal was profound: he had decided to sacrifice his family's personal comfort and the status associated with economic upward mobility to dedicate himself to empowering the Mexican American community, a cause with a promising if uncertain future.

CSO believed that the politicians would listen more intently if more members of the Mexican American community registered to vote. "We had already had meetings with mayors, police chiefs, editors of the *Los Angeles Times*. We had special meetings with them to discuss a few problems, and we had seen [their respons-

Margarita Durán and Carmen Medina print flyers on a mimeograph machine at the CSO office. Women played an important role in the voter registration drive and in the larger organization.
(Los Angeles Daily News Collection, Department of Special Collections, Charles E. Young Research Library, UCLA)

es]," recalled Henry Nava, and "we had started to imagine how effective new voters would be. So we easily, quickly absorbed all the information, the enthusiasm that Fred Ross threw our way about becoming deputy registrars."[64] According to Roybal, "at that time, there were only two registrars of Mexican descent in all of Los Angeles."[65]

In January 1948, with CSO's activist base having reached several hundred, and house meetings bringing in still more, the organization (with the help of the AFL Central Labor Council) convinced the Registrar of Voters to come to the Eastside to conduct its first-ever swearing-in of Mexican American volunteer registrars. Election officer Marcus Woodward swore-in forty-nine registrars in the social hall of St. Mary's Catholic Church.[66] With missionary zeal, they began, in Tony Ríos' words, to seek out individuals eligible to vote in "churches, markets, and door-to-door."[67]

"All of us were voter registrars," recalled Margarita Durán. "That's how I met my husband. We registered people to vote. Fred [Ross] would pick you up at the house. He'd drop you off in a neighborhood. Then he'd pick you up after a few hours of work."[68] "At that time, we were amazed, as I am still amazed, how many people do not know about voting, do not know about becoming registered to vote, and do not know the value of voting," recalled Henry Nava. "We knocked on every door on every single street where there [was] a Spanish-speaking person. We [would] sign up four or five people, all in one house, and boy, that used to be about every other house."[69] Those who agreed to register had to decide which political party to join.

"Mexican Americans didn't really know the difference between the Democratic Party and the Republican Party," lamented ILGWU organizer Hope Mendoza. "They would ask, 'What was Roosevelt?' You'd say, 'Democrat.' 'That's what I want to be.' This was their identification . . . Because they saw him as the fellow who was bringing in social programs to fight the Depression." Mendoza, already a voter registrar by virtue of her union work, served as the liaison between CSO and the Los Angeles County Registrar. She regularly collected the books in which the volunteer registrars had signed up voters and returned them to the County for processing, replacing them with new books.[70]

The results were phenomenal. "In a 3 1/2 month campaign by the Community Services Organization, more than 11,000 voters were registered in Los Angeles' eastside communities," announced the *Belvedere Citizen* in April 1948. This effectively doubled the number of Los Angeles Latino voters. CSO celebrated its success in registering thousands of new voters in Boyle Heights and Belvedere by sponsoring a dance at St. Mary's Church. The social event honored the most prolific registrars: Matt Arguijo, who registered 2,200 persons; Mrs. Jerrye Overton, more than 600, and Mrs. Lourdes Tafoya and Mrs. Eliza Baker, more than 500. The influx of new registrants generated positive headlines in the daily press.[71]

CSO was now the most organized and politically connected grassroots group ever in Latino Los Angeles. Yet, its ability to transform its latent power into tangible influence at the ballot box and in public policy was still to be tested. There would be two statewide elections in 1948—a June primary and a November general—during the twelve months between CSO's celebration of its successful voter registration drive and the next election for the ninth district city council seat. These elections would provide an opportunity for CSO to inculcate the habit of voting into the newly registered. But there was also a huge downside since those who did not vote in 1948 would be purged from the voter rolls and thus not be able to vote in 1949 unless they reregistered.

CSO received a boost from an unexpected source. The Los Angeles CIO Council and groups around the Communist Party were then seeking to recruit Latinos to the Independent Progressive Party (IPP) formed around the presidential candidacy of former Vice President Henry Wallace. While CSO did not share the IPP's agenda, it did recognize that the increased interest in newly registered voters could be used to encourage them to vote for the first time. Frank López, the former CIO Council and El Congreso officer, led the third party outreach among Latinos. López was ideally suited for the task because he had a reputation as an able organizer, most recently as president of the Shoe Workers, where he recalled that he "negotiated the first citywide contract for the shoe industry in Los Angeles."[72] Even those at odds with López admired him. According to steel worker and CSO leader Tony Ríos, "all of us had a lot of respect for Frank" despite his being "with the

Independent Progressive Party and the Communists."[73]

The IPP's most notable inroads into Latino Los Angeles came with the recruitment of CSO member José Chávez and CSO advisor Richard Ibañez to run for elected office. José Chávez was a former New Mexico state legislator and a member of CIO Shipbuilders Local 9 during World War II, who had run for the state assembly in 1946. He was running again in 1948, challenging Assemblyman Elwyn Bennett anew for the right to represent the Eastside district that included the heavily Latino area of Belvedere. The incumbent had a 100 percent CIO voting record and had helped the Latino community by co-sponsoring the historic Quevedo-initiated legislation outlawing school segregation. Two years earlier, in 1946, the CIO and its leftist allies had backed Bennett against Chávez. Now, with Frank López serving as Chávez's campaign manager, the Los Angeles CIO Council did a complete flip.[74] John Allard, a member of the CIO Council's Political Action Committee and president of UAW Chrysler Local 230, added that CIO Council head Philip Connelly used the election to reach out to Latinos "with zest, with zeal" because "there was strength" in the developing community.[75]

Unlike Chávez, who lived in the Mexican colony in Belvedere, Richard A. Ibañez was part of the Latino elite. Ibañez lived in Hollywood where he was the law partner of former California Attorney General Robert Kenny and a close friend of Carey McWilliams. He graduated from UCLA and the University of California, Berkeley Law School. Prior to military service in World War II, he served as a city councilman in the small, conservative town of Upland in San Bernardino County. The Ibañez campaign also differed from Chávez's, in that he was running for a nonpartisan judicial post and he enjoyed a broad personal network. As a result, the popular barrister had supporters from every major faction in the Mexican American community, including CSO, the third party, and business leaders. He likewise had support in the African American and Jewish communities and received the nod by both the liberal and left factions within the CIO Council. Hollywood, seniors, academics and religious leaders rounded out his support.[76]

The two CSO-affiliated Latino candidates soon found themselves in the middle of the bitter struggle for control of the Los Angeles CIO Council. Unions loyal to the national CIO, like the United

Steel Workers, were challenging Connelly over the council's refusal to follow union policy that was to oppose the third party (which
was seen as helping the Republicans) and the Marshall Plan to rebuild Europe. In a new twist, the Los Angeles CIO Council raised
the issue of race. Seventy-five African American and Mexican
American CIO activists charged that members of the National CIO
PAC, of which the steel workers were leaders, "gave almost no
consideration to the aspirations of Negro and Mexican people for
representation in public office."[77] The facts were more complicated, however. The National CIO-PAC had endorsed Richard Ibañez
and African American Assemblyman Augustus Hawkins, the most
prominent minority candidates on the June 1948 ballot. But they
had not backed José Chávez or any third-party candidates running
for partisan office. This use of "race-baiting" demonstrated the in-
tensity in the no-holds-barred contest for control of the Los Angeles
CIO Council, the direction of post-World War II domestic politics,
and their links to foreign affairs.

On May 16, the Amigos de Wallace campaign hit a crescendo
when the former vice president made an historic visit to Latino
Los Angeles. The decision to address a Sunday afternoon rally
in Spanish at the Lincoln Park Stadium, on the northeast bound-
ary of Boyle Heights, touched veteran activists, ordinary citizens,
and the more staid members of the ethnic establishment. Ignacio
López, an Eduardo Quevedo associate who had worked briefly for
Roosevelt's Fair Employment Practices Commission, agreed to
serve as the master of ceremonies. La Opinión heralded the event
on its front pages. Wallace became the first presidential candidate
to personally court the Latino vote in Los Angeles, and did so in
Spanish, a symbolically powerful statement that underscored his
concern for the immigrant community at a time when children were
punished for using their native tongue at school.[78]

Ten thousand Latinos showed up to hear Wallace at an election
rally that transcended partisan politics. Henry Wallace spoke of his
role in the Roosevelt administration, beginning as secretary of agriculture. He outlined the "moral and material progress" made during
the New Deal, which his candidacy sought to extend. Then in an
almost professorial manner, Wallace laid out his vision and worldview, creating an historical context for the fight for freedom and

democracy and against discrimination and subjugation. Wallace concluded by emphasizing "importance of voting." He said that "Voting is a democracy breathing—it is a democracy in action. And only by voting can the people's voice be heard."[79] Wallace reemphasized the liberating power of the ballot, the importance of Latino candidates, and the historic nature of the Lincoln Heights rally in his *New Republic* column.[80]

CSO leaders and members were among the crowd at the Wallace rally. CSO president Edward Roybal said he "went to listen," but his presence could be interpreted as a deft move to gain visibility for himself and CSO and to reassure the left that he was accessible.[81] Outside the stadium, Sally González handed out leaflets inviting people to join the organization.[82]

CSO stayed above the partisan fray and focused its efforts on educating and energizing Latinos to take part in what was for most their first electoral experience. This included using borrowed voting booths to familiarize people with the physical process of marking their ballot. Then in the days preceding the election, CSO volunteers again went door to door.[83] Evoking anger at unequal treatment, CSO explicitly linked voting, respect, and government services in a widely distributed flyer:

REMEMBER—how we used to ask for street lights,
bus transportation, playgrounds, sidewalks, street repairs, for help
in getting equal treatment in housing and employment?
REMEMBER—how they used to cup their hands to their ears
and say, "Speak louder, please.
We only hear about one-fifth of what you are saying"?
That is because only one-fifth of us had registered and voted.
That is why we always ended up with one-fifth
of the neighborhood improvements we needed . . .

"BUT TIMES HAVE CHANGED! . . .
TODAY THE MAJORITY OF US IN THIS NEIGHBORHOOD
ARE REGISTERED, WE CAN . . . WE WILL . . . WE MUST
VOTE!"[84]

On June 1, 1948, thousands of newly registered Mexican American voters went to the polls. The result was electrifying. The two Mexican American candidates achieved a record number of votes in their ultimately unsuccessful campaigns. "[A] democratic development has taken place almost unnoticed," editorialized the *Daily News*, adding, it "hasn't taken place by accident but because a group known as the Community Service Organization has worked to encourage it." The paper added: "The fact that a pro-Wallace spirit may have animated some of the election interest nevertheless doesn't invalidate the deeper significance of what took place."[85]

During the summer and fall of 1948, CSO continued to organize its members to address specific inequalities and to ensure another massive turnout at the polls in November 1948. It also sought to expand its sphere of influence. Starting in the fall of 1948, CSO established an organizing committee in Lincoln Heights, north-east of Boyle Heights, where Latinos had started to move into a largely Italian neighborhood that also "included other ethnics, in-cluding Germans who came to the area to work at the East Los Angeles Brewery," according to public health nurse Henrietta Villaescusa.[86]

Fred Ross worked with Alinsky to ensure the group's continued fiscal solvency. The money raised to cover the first year's operation was now depleted and the Chicago organizer did not have funds to cover a second year. Alinsky sought to turn this negative into a pos-itive by raising money and expanding the group's political allies with an approach to self-made businessmen and Hollywood stars who shared his progressive politics and Jewish heritage.

Alinsky was the special guest at the Biltmore Hotel at a September 1948 luncheon hosted by former Judge Isaac Pacht and Ben Shapiro of Leroy's Jewelry Company. The twenty-five-person group included "several judges and many Jewish business and pro-fessional people," noted an aide to Supervisor John Anson Ford, who had long worked with Eduardo Quevedo and the Latino com-munity.[87] Supervisor Ford's office emphasized that "the number one problem that they feel exists in America is apathy, meaning that the minority groups are the hardest to convince in any number to improve conditions because they feel what's the use. They never have been taken into the body politic of the nation and feel that there is not much use attempting again after so many failures."[88] A few days later, the group held a second meeting with Alinsky at the Beverly Hills Hotel. This time Harry Braverman and Saul Ostrow joined Isaac Pacht and Leroy Shapiro in sending out the invitational telegram. Ostrow was the owner of the Sealy Mattress franchise and leading donor to Henry Wallace's third party.[89]

These meetings produced immediate and tangible results. Judge Isaac Pacht (who worked with Quevedo on civil rights during World War II) agreed to assume the chairmanship of the Industrial Areas Foundation's new Southern California Advisory Committee and within two weeks had obtained pledges of $10,000. In addition to support from well-heeled individuals, the business and civic leaders tapped into institutional Jewish resources. The Jewish Community Relations Council immediately issued a check for $1,000, the first installment on its $7,500 pledge. The check was made out to Alinsky's group in Chicago but "earmarked" for CSO.[90]

The CSO's Southern California Advisory Committee was also organized at this time. Supervisor Ford quickly agreed to have his name "used on the letter head to induce people of goodwill to join the organization." The committee soon included Sheriff Eugene W. Biscailuz, actor Melvyn Douglas, Rabbi Edgar F. Magnin, Monsignor Thomas O'Dwyer, business executive and Democratic National Committeeman James Roosevelt, Judge Thomas White, and Church Federation of Los Angeles head E. C. Farnham. CSO, a model grassroots organization, could now act with the imprimatur of some of the leading liberal civic figures in Los Angeles.[91] Ironically, even as Sheriff Biscailuz publicly embraced the largely Mexican American organization, the Sheriff's Department and the Los Angeles Police Department monitored its activities. The agencies paid informers and wrote down license plates of those attending CSO meetings.[92]

Most CSO members, and the larger Latino community, spent the fall focused on the 1948 presidential campaign. Of all the candidates, Henry Wallace stood out for his appeal to Latino voters: he campaigned in Spanish, emphasized Latino concerns, and ran Latinos on the Independent Progressive Party ticket. The third party effort helped animate Latino political activity around the state. Cries of "Viva Wallace" were part of large rallies in Oakland and

San Francisco, where the majority of Latinos were non-Mexican. The ILWU Ship Scalers included members from Central and South America, and refugees from Spanish fascism.[93] The third party promoted Spanish-speaking candidates in Fresno and San Diego that reflected the community's diversity. Josephine Daniels, an UCLA educated Latina married to an Anglo businessman, ran for Congress from the Fresno-Madera area. In San Diego, retired fire chief Alfredo N. Salazar ran for the assembly. He was a civic pioneer in that city, a leader within the Mexican colony despite his own father being born in Spain. According to his son, Salazar retained a progressive vision because of observed racism and his youthful experience in a Colorado coal mine.[94]

Wallace returned to Los Angeles' Eastside in October 1948. Accompanied by Progressive assembly candidate José Chávez, the former New Mexican legislator, Wallace spoke against the backdrop of the Mexican American Veterans Memorial, a powerful metaphor of the left's recognition of the importance that Mexican Americans placed on military service. Neither President Truman, the Democratic candidate, nor New York Governor Thomas E. Dewey, the Republican candidate, targeted Latino voters in California. This is not to say that Latinos were not involved in Truman's campaign. Hollywood star Desi Arnaz, a Cuban American, endorsed the president and Los Angeles-based National CIO PAC staffer Henry Santiestevan helped deliver a pro-Truman message to union members.[95] And to his credit, earlier in the year Warren's Lieutenant Governor, Goodwin Knight, keynoted an "I Am An American" celebration at the San Jose Civic Auditorium that feted Latinos and others eligible voters due to age or naturalization.[96] Most Latinos ultimately joined other liberal and progressive voters in backing Truman, according to Jaime González, even if Wallace's program "had a lot more appeal to the workingman and to minorities."[97] Truman won an upset presidential victory and carried California partly because 8,333 voters like González voted for him for two reasons: Wallace didn't have a chance and Thomas Dewey, the Republican candidate, was seen as a worse choice.[98]

A great deal had changed in the three short years since Edward Roybal had assumed the political leadership in the Latino community from Eduardo Quevedo. CSO emerged from the 1948 presidential election as a vibrant organization, with an expanded number of indigenous leaders (including women), and an animated membership that had twice exercised the right to vote. It also enjoyed a strong financial base and extensive political relationships. Only time would tell if these developments would profoundly change Latino politics. But it was clear that CSO represented a new model of Latino self-organization supported by some labor unions and the Catholic Church, and underwritten by the IAF, with assistance form the Los Angeles Jewish community. The immediate political challenge was to translate the growing block of Latino voters and the new found alliances into the election of the first-ever Latino council person in a district where Latinos represented a minority of the electorate.

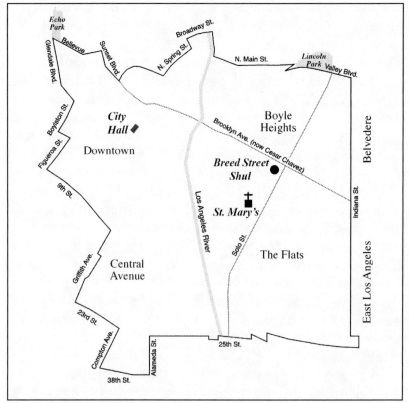

The expanded boundaries of Los Angeles' Ninth City Council District for the 1949 municipal election.

CHAPTER 4

ELECTING
"ONE OF OUR OWN"

Edward Roybal officially made the transition from CSO president to candidate for the ninth district city council seat at a meeting of 300 members in January 1949.[1] Roybal and the Latino community had gone through profound changes since his first campaign. Over the past eighteen months he had helped create and lead the first broad-based organization within the Mexican American community. The group had developed an independent political base that incorporated hundreds of activists, a thousand members, and 15,000 new voters. Moreover, CSO was near the center of the liberal-left ideological spectrum in the district with established ties to organized labor, the Catholic Church, the Jewish community, and individuals in both the Democratic and Progressive parties. It had benefited enormously from the steady hand, adroit skills, and tireless efforts of Fred Ross, who was proving to be one of the best organizers of his generation. The campaign would test CSO's ability to mobilize Latino voters and Roybal's coalition building skills—particularly since Councilman Parley P. Christensen had decided to seek yet another term.

The campaign team had been quietly put together in anticipation of Roybal's announcement. United Steel Workers' Business Agent Balt Yañez was tapped to serve as the campaign chair, further integrating his union into the campaign.[2] The politically connected Roger Johnson agreed to serve again as campaign manager and oversee such fundamentals as organization, endorsements, fundraising, and press. Fred Ross took the lead in running another voter registration drive and in setting up the structure necessary to ensure a nearly complete turnout by CSO registered voters, whose names he kept on 3 x 5 inch cards in a shoe box. For his part, the candidate met with groups, walked precincts, and helped raise money. According to his then seven-year-old daughter, Lucille, much of the volunteer-driven campaign, including the proverbial envelope stuffing, run out of the Roybal home.[3]

To add to the challenge, much of Roybal's political strength was illusory. Only Roybal's closest friends knew that his employer, the T.B. and Health Association, had required him to resign his post prior to undertaking his campaign. Moreover, CSO President Henry Nava and the majority of its new officers, along with a significant portion of its membership lived in Belvedere where CSO had run its most successful voter registration drive and where José Chávez had run for the Assembly on the Independent Progressive Party ticket. But these newly organized Latinos were not eligible to vote in the upcoming council election because Belvedere was outside the Los Angeles city limits. Likewise, only a few of those in the new Lincoln Heights CSO chapter lived within the ninth district. The ninth district was, by best estimates, twenty percent Latino.[4]

Because Latinos were a numeric minority in the polyglot district, Roybal could win only through the skillful mastery of coalition politics. So the Roybal partisans worked their networks. According to Cass Alvin, the western editor of *Steel Labor*, the steel workers brought in the auto and rubber unions. Sometimes this reinforced existing relationships, such as when CSO activist James Méndez, an autoworker at the Ford Motor Company, introduced Roybal to his union, Local 216. Help also came from UAW North American Local 887, whose members made airplanes. Paul Schrade, the Yale educated union leader, who shared a leftist but anti-communist outlook during this period, recalls that "we did special things for special people, and Ed was one of the best."[5]

The steel workers also brought in the National CIO PAC. "I remember doing door-to-door voter registration in Boyle Heights for the Roybal campaign as a CIO-PAC person working under the guidance of Fred Ross and his CSO direction," recalled Joyce L. Kornbluh, then at the UCLA Labor Center. "We would meet at Ross' house and fan out in teams." She added "His astuteness as a strategist and low-keyed interpersonal style helped win over CIO officials who were non-Hispanic." At the same time, Kornbluh stressed that the Roybal campaign strengthened the Latino-labor alliance, and resulted in "more Hispanic visibility and awareness with labor unions."[6]

The National CIO-PAC donated the services of Henry Santiestevan. Experiences at Occidental College a decade earlier shaped the Mexican-born journalist and organizer's life. There the college president introduced him to the work of alumnus Ernesto Galarza, whose progressive politics and commitment to the working class he would emulate. On campus at the time of the Hitler-Stalin pact, he would forever be suspicious of communists. Santiestevan received his citizenship for service in World War II. Upon discharge, he pursued a career at the *Hollywood Citizen News*, making him one of the state's first Latino journalists. The national CIO hired him to edit the California edition of the *CIO News,* which expanded in scope and circulation to compete with the leftist California CIO *Labor Herald.*[7]

Roybal and CSO had tapped into the "intelligentsia of the Latinos," according to UCLA student Margarita Durán. "The few Mexican American attorneys, like Richard Ibañez, and the Newmans, and the few Mexican doctors that were around were contributing."[8] Eduardo Quevedo briefly came out of retirement to work on the campaign.[9] Three unions with a large Latino member-ship, the AFL Laborers Local 300, the CIO Amalgamated Clothing Workers, and the independent railroad union, the Brotherhood of Maintenance Way Employees, also joined the campaign.[10]

Roybal supporters pursued multiple connections with the high-ly organized Jewish community, which had a mixed relationship with incumbent Christensen. Key individuals in the Jewish com-munity had repeatedly sought the council seat for one of their own, while others had strongly supported Christensen because of his re-lationship with labor and the left. Christensen's missed votes due to illness hurt him, including the symbolically potent 1948 reso-lution urging Truman to arm Jewish freedom fighters in what be-came the State of Israel.[11] CSO worked with the B'nai B'rith and the Southland Jewish Organization to jointly sponsor community events, as way of getting Latinos and Jewish residents in Boyle Heights to get to know each other.[12]

According to garment organizer Abe Levy, the ILGWU helped activate allied Jewish organizations such as the Jewish Labor Committee and the Workmen's Circle, which operated out of the Vladeck Educational Center on North St. Louis Street in Boyle

Heights.[13] "We were active in the Roybal campaign," recalled Workmen's Circle youth leader Sam Margolin.[14] "We were involved because he was the underdog, essentially because he was against the establishment." Roybal was "good for the people" echoed Ed Buzin.[15] Support came from the Boyle Heights-based AFL Jewish Carpenters and Painters unions, which were in the process of moving from left to liberal, and were among the first craft unions to admit Latinos.[16]

The campaign reached into the Jewish business and professional ranks. Bill Phillips of Phillips Music Company on Brooklyn Avenue organized support among fellow merchants. Attorney Filmore Jaffe, the Jewish council candidate two years earlier, gave Roybal $100 and agreed to serve as finance chair. The largely ceremonial post still sent a powerful signal: "When I endorsed him, all the people that supported me supported him," including theater owner Jack Y. Berman and *Eastside Journal* publisher Al Waxman.[17] Jewish labor leaders and business owners helped with fundraising. "Ed and his people were reaching across town for Jewish money from the Westside, but that was facilitated by the approval and support of the Jews in Boyle Heights," remembered Philip Newman, who was part of Roybal's fundraising network centered in the Jewish community, organized labor, and Hollywood.[18] According to Roybal, Congresswoman Helen Gahagan Douglas brought glamour to one of his grassroots events: "We charged a dollar and a half for a banquet [with] spaghetti and meatballs."[19] According to the candidate's wife, Lucille Roybal, the food for such fundraisers was usually donated and prepared by women within the CSO; "If we were not registering [voters], we were cooking."[20]

Concurrent with fundraising and gathering endorsement, Johnson and Ross worked feverishly to reduce the number of candidates who would draw support away from Roybal or split the anti-incumbent vote. This effort was successful in talking two Latinos out of the race and in persuading a number of candidates, from the numerically large Jewish community and the communist-influenced left, not to file. In all probability, the Independent Progressive Party and Los Angeles CIO Council were reluctant to oppose both a friendly incumbent and the Latino and Jewish communities, which had provided key pieces of the 1948 Wallace cam-

International Ladies Garment Workers' Union organizers Hope Mendoza and Abe Levy dine with John F. Aiso and other Japanese American leaders. The union built coalitions to promote organizing and political action.
(Kenneth C. Burt)

paign. At the same time, there was no practical way that a leftist candidate could win in a multi-candidate race where support for both Christensen and Roybal overlapped their own base within the minority-liberal-labor-left.[21]

Despite multi-pronged efforts, however, a number of individuals did initially enter the historically crowded race: Isabel García Rodríquez, Amos Black from the African American community, and Assemblyman Edward Elliot, who represented the downtown portion of the council district. "[But] we talked them out of the campaign," recalled Tony Ríos.[22] As a result, when the City Clerk announced on February 25, 1949 who had had qualified for the April 5 election, there were only four: incumbent Christensen, Roybal, Julia M. Sheehan (who had edged out Roybal for the second spot in the council race two years earlier), and Daniel A. Sullivan, an Irish American.[23]

The Roybal campaign was optimistic, with a progressive base

in the Latino and Jewish communities and with the active support of the garment and steel unions. Yet challenges and dilemmas remained. Roybal's base, while significant, did not necessarily translate into an electoral majority. What could his campaign do to obtain the support of key pieces of Christensen's base? Such defections, could they be achieved, would deny the incumbent support while ensuring that Roybal remained the principle challenger.

There were three general (and often overlapping) areas to target: organized labor, racial and ethnic minorities, and the forces around the Communist Party left. Appealing to these leftist factions was complicated by the fact that Roybal's closest labor supporters were seeking to root out the communists from their respective organizations. Roybal could use CSO's general approach of welcoming all who wished to support the goals of the community (without letting them take control of the organization). But would this work? Would the left be willing to support Roybal knowing that his closest allies were their archenemies? Would the anti-communists within the progressive union movement tolerate a coalition with those they were seeking to discredit? Roybal had to try because the left controlled institutional resources within the labor movement and the minority communities, which could be used to influence a large number of voters. At the same time Roybal sought to avoid formal support from the Communist Party.

The other concern was the AFL. Most of the AFL unions were less progressive than Roybal and inclined to back the supportive incumbent. Finally, could Roybal garner the support of African Americans, Japanese Americans, and the myriad of white ethnics? Navigating around these potential landmines would be difficult. Fortunately, Roybal had the benefit of two men who understood the political terrain in campaign manager Roger Johnson and CSO organizer Fred Ross.

Three important institutions in the district stayed with Councilman Christensen. The first was the weekly *Eastside Sun*, which competed with the *Eastside Journal* for readers and advertisers. The second was Assemblyman Elliot. The third was the AFL Central Labor Council, which rewarded the incumbent for his pro-labor voting record. The AFL used its weekly paper, the *Los Angeles Citizen*, to advance the Christensen candidacy. In this effort it was joined by two other important labor groupings, the AFL Building and Construction Trades Council and the Railroad Brotherhood.[24]

The Los Angeles CIO Council had a more difficult decision. They could do as they did in 1947 and join with the AFL to back an old friend, Councilman Christensen. If so, could they win? And at what cost? Or they could back a challenger with whom they shared progressive allies. Of the challengers, Roybal was clearly the best ideological and demographic fit. He was a progressive who had demonstrated that he could work with the left and he was the titular head of the Latino community upon which the Independent Progressive Party and the CIO Council had increasingly lavished attention.[25]

The Communist Party press had taken notice of Roybal even before he announced his intentions to CSO. "Roybal is an outstanding Mexican American leader and many think the day is long past due when Mexican Americans got a voice on the city council," pontificated the *People's World* political columnist. "Running as an unknown without much support, Roybal ran third against Christensen in the primaries of 1947. The word is that this time Roybal will have plenty of support."[26] Still, nice words in the *People's World* did not necessarily mean a CIO endorsement.

The key decision-maker was CIO Council head Philip Connelly. His options in the council race were reduced by decisions made the previous year during the 1948 presidential contest and the battle for control of the Council. The Council, in its efforts to make inroads into the Mexican American community and to gain a competitive advantage over its rivals loyal to the national CIO, had set a precedent of deviating from the general practice of backing pro-labor incumbents. They went further and accused the National CIO-PAC of being racist for not supporting José Chávez's third party assembly campaign, thus making support for a Mexican American candidate virtually a litmus test of one's progressive credentials. A decision not to support Roybal would risk exposing the Council to race-based attacks from the National CIO-PAC, which was deeply involved in the Roybal campaign, as well as isolating the Council from the most dynamic social force in Los Angeles, the Roybal coalition.

"So by 1949, Phil Connelly knew that things had changed a lot," quipped Tony Ríos. "It was an exciting flip," stated James

Daugherty, describing the CIO Council's decision to back Roybal. A long-time confidant and communist comrade, who in the late-1930s had helped force the Los Angeles utility companies to hire Latinos, Daugherty was now head of the California CIO Council. He added that the decision was not universally supported. "There was a lot of criticism," both from Connelly's "enemies" and from longtime "Christensen supporters" in the Council.[27]

The Independent Progressive Party followed the CIO Council's lead. "Roybal, more than any other candidate in the field, meets the needs of the community," announced Eastside Independent Progressive Party leader and open Communist Jack Berman. He promoted Roybal: "for the first time in the history of Los Angeles will give a voice to the thousands of Mexican American residents of this area."[28]

The pragmatic considerations of the Independent Progressive Party, Los Angeles CIO Council, and the Communist Party dovetailed with a new ideological construct. Progressive Citizens of America board member Leroy Parra believed "the only way to combat racism" was "to support minority candidates," even against "more progressive" or "better prepared" white candidates, because minorities had fewer opportunities to develop their skills in a racist society.[29]

The Communist Party's daily paper, the *People's World*, emphasized the CIO Council's affinity with minority groups. "The CIO endorsed George E. Bryant, the only Negro, and Edward R. Roybal, the only Mexican-American, in the city council races." The CIO also backed the Jewish candidate, Isaac Kushner. The top council priority, however, was the insurgent mayoral campaign of former Lieutenant Governor Ellis Patterson. He was running against Mayor Fletcher Bowron, who was also being lambasted by a candidate to his political right.[30]

The CIO Council, in a letter from Legislative and Political Action Committee Chair John Allard, a UAW official, urged its affiliates to "give full and immediate consideration" to the endorsed candidates.[31] The Independent Progressive Party, the leftist Latino CIO unions, and the African American *California Eagle*—all of whom had campaigned for Christensen two years earlier—joined the CIO Council in backing Roybal. The *Labor Herald* later stated that Roybal "was vigorously supported by several CIO local unions with heavy membership in his district, namely Furniture Workers local 576, ILWU Warehousemen's local 26, Electrical Workers local 1421, FTA local 25 and Mine-Mill local 700."[32] This decision to back Roybal also increased enthusiasm within leftwing AFL locals with members in Boyle Heights that included the Jewelry Workers, with a significant Jewish membership led by Adolph González.[33]

The CIO Council and its allies, however, did not join the formal Roybal campaign. They chose instead to help in their own way and participated in an independent pro-Roybal campaign in conjunction with the third party. This allowed third party activists to campaign for "Roybal and Patterson," the mayoral candidate who had addressed the 1939 Congreso. Communist Party chief Dorothy Healey defended the practice, saying: "The CIO always ran its campaigns independently."[34]

Roybal appreciated the help but remained cynical about their motives. "Connelly and company" joined the campaign only after Monsignor O'Dwyer and "everybody else was in there," according to Roybal. "They didn't want a pro-Roybal campaign as such. They wanted to use my name and the CSO as a vehicle to build [the Independent Progressive Party]."[35] Regardless of motive, campaign manager Roger Johnson astutely recognized the importance of the CIO Council's support in both filling out the Roybal coalition and denying the incumbent one of the most activist elements of his political base. At the same time, Roybal's acceptance of the CIO Council's support stirred strong feelings in Tony Ríos and other anti-Stalinist CIO union leaders, who sought to deny Connelly legitimacy and to topple him as council executive. Despite such passion, and a few heated arguments, cooler heads prevailed, and Roybal's core supporters never let such personal feelings divide what they saw as a winning coalition.[36]

While accepting support from a myriad of Communist Party-influenced organizations, Roybal was wary of the negative reaction if the party itself endorsed his campaign. Roybal approached Alice Greenfield, who had staffed the Sleepy Lagoon Defense Committee, and asked her to relay the message to the communist leadership that he didn't want their endorsement. Greenfield told him that she was just a member and lacked access to the top party leaders. She did not pass on the message.[37]

The issue of the Communist Party's role in the election soon surfaced. The AFL Labor League of Hollywood Voters, a federation of twenty-odd Hollywood unions, issued a statement two weeks prior to the March election that lauded Christensen and attacked Roybal for accepting support from the CIO Council and its allies in the community. "It is the position of the League of Hollywood Voters that 'Stalinists' constitute the main menace to full democracy and complete civil rights at home and abroad, and any candidate who accepts their support is automatically an opponent of free labor and good citizens alike."[38] The strong statement was likely a reflection of the transformation of its chairman, actor Ronald Reagan, from a popular-front leader to a strident anti-communist liberal during the 1946 studio strike.[39]

The final effort of Roybal's campaign was to reach beyond his now rock-solid Latino and Jewish base in Boyle Heights. His courting of the Central Avenue-based African American community paid dividends when the campaign announced support from a newly formed Committee for Equality in the City Council. Loren Miller, a liberal African American attorney, NAACP leader and *Los Angeles Sentinel* publisher, led the group. Shortly after the announcement, the liberal African American *Sentinel*, which had previously not endorsed any candidate in the ninth council district, joined the leftist *California Eagle* in backing Roybal. Miller's high profile role—combined with support from CIO activist Gilbert Lindsay, Dr. Claude Hudson, a prominent businessman and community leader, and Edward Hawkins, the assemblyman's brother—sent an important message to African Americans that Roybal would stand with them. The word traveled to the smaller Black community in Boyle Heights, according to resident Albert Johnson, Sr.: "Whoever they endorsed, we endorsed."[40] Young African American activists such as police officer Tom Bradley also volunteered for the campaign.[41]

The thirty-nine-member Committee for Equality's influence, however, reached way beyond the African American community. The Black-led group was diverse in terms of race, class, and geography. It included Black, Jewish, and Latino labor and community leaders. The committee included John F. Aiso, the Harvard-educated Japanese American attorney who worked with the ILGWU, and Beatrice Griffith, author of *American Me*, which chronicled the plight of Mexican Americans in the thirties. Other supporters had Irish, Italian, German, Greek, and English surnames. The committee said Roybal was committed to "a municipal Fair Employment Practices Commission ordinance, equal health facilities, improved police practices, and better education facilities."[42]

Ten days before the election, the campaign sponsored a Friday night rally and dance at the Paramount Hall on Brooklyn Avenue in Boyle Heights.[43] On the final Wednesday before the election, the campaign published a full-page advertisement in the *Eastside Journal*. This was a rare expenditure for the low-budget organization and volunteer-driven campaign. Titled, "Let's Get Things Done," the promotion focused on the issues of fair employment, health, housing, civil liberties, transportation, traffic, labor, and racial tolerance. It listed some fifty members of the Committee to Elect Edward Roybal. There were greater numbers of Latinos, Jews, and other white ethnics—particularly the Irish (which undercut support for candidate Sullivan)—and smaller numbers of African Americans and Japanese Americans.[44]

The presence of CSO members among the endorsers was impossible to miss as was the participation of more established Latino business and professionals, including the three "ringleaders" who had recruited Roybal to run two years earlier—theater owner Frank Fouce, attorney Philip Newman, and Dr. Camilo Servin. Of particular significance was the presence of Monsignor Thomas O'Dwyer. As CSO's patron, he spoke with the authority of the archdiocesan chancery and served as pastor to the white ethnics and English-speaking Latinos attending St. Mary's. "The Irish built St. Mary's" and lived "south of 4th street" in Boyle Heights according to parishioner and Roybal volunteer Connie Meza, who worked for the Los Angeles City Health Department.[45] It worked with the surrounding Mexican parishes and missions that served the primarily Spanish-speaking residents. It was clear for all to see that Roybal's election was now the top priority of the "nonpartisan" CSO.

The final weekend before the election, the liberal, multiethnic Roybal campaign, which had moved from the candidate's home to a headquarters on Whittier Boulevard, focused on walking as many precincts as possible and talking directly to voters. The steel workers sent pro-Roybal mail directly to their members in the district and featured Roybal in the union's newspaper. The "independent campaign" being waged by the CIO Council in conjunction with the Independent Progressive Party and the *California Eagle* augmented these efforts. The passionate doorway conversations—by women and men—were reinforced by a union-owned sound truck. Roybal, riding in the truck, would talk to the hundreds of voters who came out of their home to hear him.[46] The last institutional players to announce their preferences were the daily newspapers. They failed to alter the election dynamic by not weighing-in for either Christensen or Roybal. The liberal *Daily News* endorsed Sheehan and the conservative *Los Angeles Times* stayed neutral.[47]

On Election Day, fourteen of the fifteen city councilmen easily won reelection. Only Christensen failed to win outright. Not that he had lost support in the district; he had actually gained more than seven percent over his previous total. The big change was Roybal. His support increased almost four-fold, due in large measure to the successful CSO voter registration and get-out-the-vote drive, and overwhelming support from the Jewish precincts in Boyle Heights. As a result, Roybal out-polled the incumbent by close to two thousand votes and received a psychological lift going into the runoff.[48]

Roybal's vote tally attracted attention in a number of quarters. Ross remembered a call from Mayor Fletcher Bowron's office "the day after the Roybal victory in the Primary." The mayor's public relations person said: "The Mayor's been hearing a number of good things about the CSO recently, and he'd like to come out and talk to some of the leaders. You know, get a little insight into some of the East Side problems." For the first time during his twelve years in office, Mayor Bowron wanted to come to Boyle Heights to meet with Mexican Americans. Instead of the hoped-for private meeting with CSO leaders, however, the organization sponsored a forum at Euclid School one week before the runoff election. They also invited Lloyd Aldrich, the more conservative mayoral candidate who had made it into the runoff, to address the group. This event provided a real informational service and demonstrated CSO's ability to bring both candidates to meet with members of the Latino community.[49]

The Communist Party, fulfilling Roybal's worst nightmare,

openly associated themselves with the candidate and his coalition. The *People's World* ran the following:

> Around the candidacy of Roybal, youthful WWII veteran, a coalition has been developed based on support from both [the so-called] left-wing and right-wing CIO, local AFL unions, elements of the Catholic Church, Jewish mass organizations, Mexican organizations, the Independent Progressive Party, the Communist party, and outstanding community people representing all sections of the population.[50]

Roybal had courted mainstream organizations with a communist influence, such as the Los Angeles CIO Council, but wished to avoid any formal linkage—a message he had sought to transmit through former Sleepy Lagoon Defense staffer Alice Greenfield. But the communists, having invested heavily in courting Latinos through a number of fronts, including Amigos de Wallace, apparently wished to get credit for their support. The brazen communist effort to gain legitimacy left Roybal vulnerable to attack.

For their part, the Roybal campaign leaders worried about overconfidence as new volunteers joined the bandwagon. It also sought out the supporters of the former candidates running against the incumbent and focused renewed attention on the non-Boyle Heights sections of the district where support was weakest. One of those areas targeted was Temple Street, an area downtown dominated by long-time residents down on their luck and new arrivals en route to a nicer area. "We were all children of immigrants—whether Latino, Japanese, Jewish, whatever—and everyone was struggling," stated Rebecca Tuck, then a Belmont High School student living with her family in the back of a small grocery store. "[Roybal] came around to every person's door and talked to us," she said, adding that her family "voted for him and we loved him" because of his desire to help all people, regardless of race or creed.[51] The campaign targeted voters in Little Italy utilizing an Italian American committee led by Joseph Bozzani. And on Bunker Hill, Daniel Sullivan urged his former supporters to back the "vigorous" Roybal campaign.[52] There was also a redoubled effort to reach African Americans in Central Avenue.[53] The Roybal campaign approached working-class voters of all backgrounds through the unions. With the other city council races settled, groups like the National CIO-PAC, with its base among steel and autoworkers, was now able to direct new resources into the ninth district.[54] So, too, did the Independent Progressive Party whose mayoral candidate had lost in the initial election. Art Takei oversaw the third party's "mobilization points" on Brooklyn Avenue in Boyle Heights, on West Sixth Street in downtown, and on East 41st Street in Central Los Angeles.[55] With the infusion of additional activists, according to campaign manager Roger Johnson, "we actually covered every house in the district, personally, by some worker"—a huge achievement in a city as large as Los Angeles without a partisan political machine.[56]

The momentum was clearly in Roybal's favor despite last minute efforts to derail the campaign. The most serious threat was a dirty trick that portrayed him as a communist. This anonymous attack came in the form of postcards mailed to voters' homes shortly before the election. Progressive anti-Stalinists like the National CIO-PAC defended Roybal.[57] More important in countering the threat was CSO's call to action, which generated a massive response from activists angry at the attack and energized by the promise of electing one of their own to the City Council. According to Ross, the group organized its members to make "close to forty-thousand phone calls to offset that attack and explain its purpose to the people in the area."[58] Thanks to an extraordinarily tight organization and a large volunteer base, these last-ditch efforts to preserve the status quo were effectively countered. The *Daily News* and the *Belvedere Citizen* (whose circulation included the western edge of Boyle Heights) also provided credibility and endorsed Roybal for the first time.[59] Roybal and the Latino community were not standing alone. Liberals, progressives, and the left, Catholics, Jews, and Protestants, organized labor, social clubs, and veterans' organizations—all pulled together in what had become a "holy" crusade with strong ethnic and class overtones.[60]

On Election Day, with emotions among Latinos in Boyle Heights hitting a feverish pitch, the Roybal campaign worked to get every identified supporter to the polls. CSO focused its organizational efforts on newly registered Latinos in what was now its fourth get-out-the-vote operation in twelve months. Paired volunteers knocked on their neighbors' doors with the simple message that "today is the day." Through voting, residents could achieve a new level of dignity while improving their lives materially. The message was clear—and it was delivered again and again.[61]

When the polls closed and the votes were counted, the extent of CSO's operation and the larger Roybal campaign became clear for all to see. Roybal received over 20,000 votes, twice his primary total, and more than double the *total* votes cast in the entire 1947 election. Roybal's margins were once again greatest in the Latino and Jewish sections of Boyle Heights.[62] According to CSO, the newly registered voters had turned out at the unbelievably high rate of eighty-seven percent.[63] While there is no detailed accounting of how Roybal spent his funds, contemporary news reports placed the amount raised at $5,500, which represented about a third of the average campaign budget.[64] Voters in Los Angeles had elected its first Mexican American councilman since 1881.

Roybal's activist orientation was clear even before he took

Fred Ross and Lupe Castro. The Spanish-speaking Ross oversaw CSO's get-out-the-vote operation for the city council election in 1949.
(Los Angeles Daily News Collection, Department of Special Collections, Charles E. Young Research Library, UCLA)

the oath of office. So, too, were the signals from the city departments that they would be responsive. In the time between Roybal's
election in May and swearing-in in July, the Los Angeles Police
Department sponsored a series of high level meetings designed to
improve police-community relations. The meetings involved the
new Police Chief, W. A. Warton, along with Spanish-speaking Police
Commissioner Bruno Newman, Roybal, representatives from the
CSO, and Monsignor Thomas O'Dwyer. The LAPD agreed to appoint a liaison to the Latino community, provide cultural sensitivity
training to officers, and to work more closely with area churches, social workers, and community groups to tackle youth crime issues.[65]

On the morning of his swearing-in, July 1, 1949, the *Daily News*
praised the incoming councilman in an editorial, "The Latin One-
Eighth." It signaled that the city's liberal community was finally
beginning to grasp the significance of the social revolution underway on the Eastside. Further, it focused on the role Roybal and
CSO played as the collective voice and organizational vehicle for
Mexican Americans who, "after nearly a century of civic silence,"
were "learning to make use of the most effective channel open to
democracy's cultural minorities—the ballot."[66]

The *Daily News* expressed the hope that this use of the vote and
"rising political consciousness" would "succeed in drawing attention of the rest of the community to the needs of their neglected
neighborhoods." It also expressed the desire that the nascent CSO
would serve as "the beginning of a valuable bridge-building" process leading to the integration of Mexican Americans into the larger American society. Congressman Chet Holifield underscored the
new political reality by incorporating the editorial into a glowing
statement, "Election of Roybal—Democracy at Work," which he
placed in the *Congressional Record,* and then distributed to constituents.[67]

Roybal made history as a Latino. He acknowledged this at his
swearing-in when he said, "This is the first time in 70 years that a
Mexican American has taken office in this city hall." Roybal's use
of the self-identifying term Mexican American, however, signaled
a significant shift. From the late thirties to the mid-1940s, the politically oriented activists used pan-Latino terms such as Spanish-
speaking, Spanish American, and Latin American. The change

away from a pan-Latino orientation in Los Angeles reflected several trends. First, the numerically dominant Mexican American heritage community sought an affirmation of their importance. Moreover, these children of immigrants were playing an increasingly important role within the community. This was in contrast to El Congreso, which enjoyed a largely Mexican and Mexican American membership but was founded by Luisa Moreno from Guatemala, and led by Eduardo Quevedo, a Hispano from New Mexico. Second, the creation of local, largely homogeneous groups like CSO meant that the diversity came largely from non-Latino members. This differed from being a local affiliate of a national organization such as El Congreso or Amigos de Wallace, or even the League of United Latin American Councils, that required a name that would be inclusive of Puerto Ricans, Cubans, Hispanos, and Spaniards. Finally, in Southern California the relatively small number of Latinos from places other than Mexico were being integrated into the dominant Mexican-oriented culture, although San Francisco remained noted for its residents from Central and South Americans. The New Mexico born Roybal, a Hispano who traced his ancestry to the Spanish founding of Santa Fe, publicly identified himself as Mexican American.

Roybal's assumption of power at City Hall was significant for other reasons. Roybal and CSO had created and used a social movement to bring new voters to the polls and to realign existing voter blocks. Latinos had turned out to vote in percentages never before seen in California. Moreover, Roybal formed powerful alliances based on race, class, and ideology. His campaign adroitly navigated deep divisions within labor and the community against the backdrop of the failed 1948 Wallace campaign and the emerging Cold War with the Soviet Union. To his credit, Roybal succeeded in gaining support from the broad liberal-left even as key backers were simultaneously engaged in a life or death struggle against each other.[68] This remarkable achievement reflected, in part, the skill of CSO organizer Fred Ross and campaign manager Roger Johnson; but it also revealed the profound respect that people of diverse ideologies and background had for CSO's independent political base. In joining a city council with thirteen white Protestant men and one Irish Catholic man, Roybal would serve as the voice for Latinos, as well as other groups, particularly Jews, Blacks, Asians, Catholics, unionists, and progressives. Or, as Roybal stated at his swearing-in ceremony, he would "represent all the people in my district—one of the most cosmopolitan in our city."[69]

CHAPTER 5

CIVIL RIGHTS
AND COALITION POLITICS

Los Angeles City Councilman Edward Roybal instantly became an important statewide ethnic symbol in 1949 as the only Mexican American to hold a major elective office in California. He was also among a select number of politicians whose post represented a full time job. State legislators, for example, only worked a few months' every other year, unless called into special session, and most other city councils in the state were seen as community service rather than a career. For the thirty-three-year-old councilman, the challenge was to present a progressive agenda to an increasingly conservative council while consolidating his power in the district to ensure his reelection two years later. This required that he maintain the strong support of Mexican American voters and his multiethnic and multiracial working class base. To this end, he focused on delivering tangible neighborhood improvements, such as streetlights and sidewalks in a city with an increasing number of automobiles. Achieving such family safety issues became "almost routine," reflected Henry Nava, CSO's second president, after the "various city departments saw that we were able to elect somebody."[1] The focus on such "women's issues" reflected the ability of Latinas with the Community Service Organization to set the agenda.[2] Roybal also decided to champion issues that resonated with his activist Latino base while also cutting across the multicultural district.

The first and most important political issue was fair employment. Despite his freshman standing, Roybal was a natural to take the lead on the council and to work with a broad array of community-based organizations. He was the only identifiable "minority" on the council. Roybal also had more freedom to focus on such an issue because voters in his district supported civil rights and expected its representatives to fight for social justice. Still, it would be a challenge because Roybal needed to establish rapport with his colleagues while he asked for help on a controversial measure in which the councilmen had already staked out clear positions, voting eight to seven against a similar Fair Employment Ordinance the previous year. The proposal went beyond the state law signed by Governor Olson in 1939 and President Roosevelt's executive order during World War II that had prohibited discrimination on jobs resulted from government contracts. This ordinance was more universal—and some saw it as intrusive—because it would prevent individuals and companies from discriminating in cases where the government's only interest was that of fairness.[3] The issue was once again before the municipal government because a coalition of conservative Republicans and conservative Democrats had blocked a fair employment measure in Congress and in the state legislature. State representatives even defeated a bill by Republican Governor Earl Warren to study the issue.[4]

Roybal quickly agreed to introduce a new Fair Employment Ordinance and to work with an emerging liberal minority coalition that had drafted language for a law based on measures adopted in other cities and states. The new coalition was known as the Council for Equality in Employment. Milton Sean, director of the Anti-Defamation League, served as the temporary chair, and the group included the Jewish Community Relations Council, the AFL Central Labor Council, and the Los Angeles CIO Council—which had recently swept aside its longtime communist-friendly leadership and elected men loyal to the national CIO.[5] The Council for Equality in Employment recognized the need to alter the political dynamic on the city council if the proposed ordinance were to get the eighth vote it needed to pass.[6]

The most likely councilman to switch his position on the issue was Councilman Edward Davenport, the lone Irish Catholic on the council. He was a complex figure, troubled by alcohol, and moving politically from left to right. The Pennsylvania-born advertising executive represented a liberal district that included much of central Los Angeles. He had been elected in 1945 on a platform that included a commitment to "fair and full employment." However, in 1947, he voted against fair employment when opponents portrayed the issue as part of the communists' agenda to create divisiveness within the United States.[7]

Roybal and six colleagues introduced the Equal Opportunity Ordinance on August 9, 1949. Outside the council chambers, the Council for Equality in Employment sought to advance the ordinance by positioning itself as a "constructive voice" and sought to marginalize those on the racist right and the communist left. "The evils and injustices arising from discrimination in employment because of race, creed, color, or national origin form a fertile breeding ground within our City for communistic influences," wrote the liberal civil rights coalition. "To fail to take constructive action now will give further credence to the belief that racial and religious discrimination is too thoroughly established in our economy to be outlawed."[8] With this position, liberals sought to limit the ability of conservatives to use the fear of communism to oppose civil rights. The framing of social justice as the antidote to the totalitarianism also reflected a desire to get Davenport's vote and the tactical needs of coalition members battling communists within their own groups. The Council for Equality in Employment likewise emphasized that Chicago, Phoenix, Philadelphia, Milwaukee, and Minneapolis had all enacted similar measures to good effect.[9]

While Roybal focused on pushing the fair employment ordinance, CSO organizer Fred Ross quietly dealt with the CSO's Achilles heel: money. The public image of CSO as a confident, robust, and even aggressive organization masked the private reality that the organization was unable to meet Alinsky's goal of becoming financially self-sufficient. So Ross went back to those who had demonstrated their generosity in the past, most notably the Jewish Community Relations Council, hoping that it would once again underwrite the operation of the Latino-oriented organization. He met with key decision-makers that included organizational representatives, major donors, and Judges Benjamin Rosenthal and Stanley Mosk. Jewish Community Relations Council executive Fred Herzberg supported providing CSO with additional funds. He emphasized that the "subvention was used to establish an organization among the only heretofore totally unorganized minority group in the city." This led to a reduction in inter-ethnic violence and enhanced inter-group cooperation, including "CSO requesting material on Israel without any prompting on the part of the Jewish organizations."[10] The organized Jewish community voted to fund CSO for another year, but stressed to Ross the importance of developing financial support from within the Latino community.[11]

The Jewish community's financial backing of CSO served to further cement its already strong alliance with Roybal, for whom bitter personal experiences served to reinforce his identification with societal underdogs. Shortly after his election, Roybal sought to buy a new home. He found one advertised for veterans, however, the realtor refused to sell it to him because he was "a Mexican." Once the realtor learned that Roybal was the city councilman, he offered to make an exception, but by then it was too late. Roybal refused on principle to buy the home and CSO moved quickly to use the case to underscore the larger problem of discrimination. CSO activists set up a picket line around the development, which lasted until the developer agreed, in the words of the *CSO Reporter*, to "make this [housing] available to all [former] GIs regardless of color or creed."[12]

Despite such distractions, Roybal and CSO remained focused in late summer 1949 on the councilman's proposed fair employment ordinance. Meanwhile, the Council for Equality in Employment formalized its structure with Judge Isaac Pacht, who had previously worked with Quevedo on fair employment issues, agreeing to serve as chair of the new group. The functioning steering committee included representatives from every sector of the city, including CSO President Henry Nava, and the leaders of the Japanese American Citizens League and the NAACP, and the AFL and CIO. The group sought and obtained a list of prominent "sponsors." These included James Roosevelt, the late president's son and a prominent political and business figure in Los Angeles, and Will Rogers, Jr., a former member of Congress and the son of the famous cowboy comedian. The Council for Equal Opportunity then established an organization within each of the fifteen council districts and began lobbying the respective councilmen. Almost all of the full time organizers loaned to the coalition came from organized labor or the Jewish community.[13] The fight for fair employment was particularly intense in two districts, although for different reasons.

In Roybal's district, the Council for Equal Opportunity assigned three organizers to direct and help keep control of the debate. CSO organizer Fred Ross was assigned to oversee the campaign in Roybal's political base of Boyle Heights. He achieved what no other Council for Equal Opportunity designated coordinator dared try: the integration of the communist left and their allies into a united front. This was finessed by the creation of a new organization, the 9th Independent Citizens Council for a FEPC Ordinance. According to Ross, "we have been able to persuade the leadership in every group to make compromises in the interest of united action for FEP." This effort reflected CSO's non-sectarian approach and met Roybal's political needs. [14]

The most important district in terms of the final council vote was the twelfth, home to Councilman Davenport. The campaign reached out to labor, church, minority, civic, and veterans groups within the district. Opinion leaders in the district were encouraged to contact the councilman and editors of neighborhood papers were requested to publish informational articles. Organizations were asked to pass a supportive resolution and to hand out postcards for members to fill out and sign. The cards were then collected, stamped, and mailed to Councilman Davenport. [15]

Labor Day 1949 celebrations provided an ideal setting to garner support for the proposed ordinance. The first major event of the day was the Catholic Labor Institute's annual Mass where afterwards CIO Director Irwin DeShetler shared the stage at the breakfast with Archbishop James Francis McIntyre and AFL Council President Thomas Radford. This was followed by the Los Angeles CIO Council's citywide picnic for 7,000 at Streamland Park in the Eastside community of Pico Rivera. [16]

With the vote nearing, the Council for Economic Equality asked Councilman Roybal to speak at the September 16 Mexican Independence Day celebration in Davenport's district. Roybal's appearance signified his appeal to Latinos throughout the city and his willingness to venture into a colleague's district for the purpose of generating support for an upcoming vote. Roybal and the liberal civil rights coalition were going all out to pressure Davenport. [17]

On September 23 the *Los Angeles Times* weighed in, editorializing against the proposed ordinance. The paper argued such a measure "tends to rob an individual of his freedom to choose his associates in work, as business partners or employees, and stirs up a train of resentments and conflicts." It reiterated the charge that the communists supported the measure. Then came a new argument. The *Times* extrapolated data from the failed 1946 fair employment initiative to show that voters in fourteen of the fifteen council districts opposed a fair employment law. Only voters in the ninth district backed the initiative. It dryly acknowledged that "[Councilman Roybal] apparently supports the wishes of a majority of the people whom he represents."[18]

Four days later, on September 27, the Council held a five-hour hearing. Speaking for the Roybal authored ordinance was Rabbi Edgar Magnin, Catholic labor priest Joseph Kearney, and leaders from the unions and the Japanese American and African American communities. Opposition came from former Chamber of Commerce president Frank P. Doherty, who called the FEPC "un-American and Communist" and Alfred E. Herbert of the Christian Nationalists who said "this is a white man's country and we will keep it that way." The council ultimately voted eight to six against the ordinance.[19]

The disappointing defeat was still a victory for Roybal and CSO. The campaign elevated Roybal's political profile and hastened CSO's integration into the city's developing minority-liberal-labor-religious alliance while protecting itself from criticism from leftists. The annual report of the Japanese American Citizen League stressed its membership in the Council for Economic Equality and their work with Roybal and CSO in the fight for fair employment. More importantly, the report suggested a newly institutionalized dialogue between minority and labor groups, through membership in the Los Angeles County Conference on Community Relations.[20] CSO also cemented its relationship with the unions by forming a CSO Labor Advisory Committee.[21]

Governor Earl Warren invited CSO representatives to Sacramento to participate in his Unemployment Conference in December 1949. María Durán, the immigrant garment worker, served as CSO's delegate and Roybal served as the consultant to the minority concerns panel.[22] This, combined with his appointments of Manuel Ruiz to the California Youth Commission, Leo Carrillo to the Parks Commission, and Ernest Orfila to the Veterans Welfare Board, meant that Warren was continuing the engagement of Latinos as he sought to find the center of post-war California politics.[23] He was

Actor Leo Carrillo and Governor Earl Warren enjoy a rodeo sponsored by Los Angeles Sheriff Eugene Biscailuz. Carrillo served as a Warren campaign spokesman and represented the governor on the commission investigating the Zoot Suit Riots and on the State Parks Commission.
(Earl Warren Papers, California State Archives)

also making history as the most inclusive Republican governor, although years later he stated, "I never went to the Chicanos and asked them what they thought."[24]

Over the next year, Roybal and CSO would continue to expand their influence in the electoral arena and would use their organization and coalition partners to fight for a variety of social justice issues. One of the most important revolved around the high school in Boyle Heights. "The Board of Education was planning to make Roosevelt High School a trade school," stated Father William Barry, head of CSO's Education Committee. A number of high school students, "who wanted to have the incentive to go on to junior college and on to college to get academic degrees, to move ahead," approached him. Barry worked with CSO Youth Committee chair

Ralph Poblano to assemble a delegation that met with the school administrators and the school board. As a result, the school district backed down and Roosevelt retained its academic orientation. "That was a victory," recalled Father Barry. "We never would have done it had CSO not taught us how to confront people who have authority with the values of truth."[25]

CSO used its increased clout to geographically expand its political base beyond the adjoining communities of Boyle Heights, Belvedere, and Lincoln Heights. In the year after Roybal's election, CSO took its basic message—that voting makes a difference—to isolated and marginalized Latino neighborhoods around Los Angeles County. This produced ten thousand new voters and created a Mexican American political presence in a number of Anglo dominated districts and smaller cities for the first time.[26]

The most dramatic election was in the City of San Fernando, northwest of downtown Los Angeles. The city had grown up around a Spanish Mission, but was now part of the developing suburbs. Led by garment worker Hope Mendoza, CSO activists went door-to-door and registered hundreds in the segregated Latino sections of town. Then in April 1950, Latino activists turned out the Mexican American vote for businessman Albert G. "Frank" Padilla. Padilla not only became that city's first Latino councilman, but he came in first in a multi-candidate field for two open seats.[27]

As a result of this new political dynamic—particularly the presence of a large block of Mexican American voters—state and national Democratic candidates added new stops to their schedule. In May 1950, Governor Earl Warren and his Democratic opponent, James Roosevelt, made separate pre-primary stops at the Mexican American Veterans Memorial, at the border of Boyle Heights and East Los Angeles, where Councilman Roybal met them.[28] So, too, did Helen Gahagan Douglas bring her U.S. Senate campaign against Richard Nixon to the Eastside. One of her stops was at the Carioca Café in Boyle Heights, where she was introduced at an outdoor rally by CSO's third president, steelworker Tony Ríos.[29]

Despite the presence of Councilman Roybal and CSO leaders such as Hope Mendoza and Tony Ríos in partisan politics, the organization remained strictly nonpartisan. Fred Ross and Saul Alinsky successfully argued that CSO had effectively used the Roybal campaign to empower the community and as a result there was now an effective network of political activists. CSO's job was to keep the politicians honest and to address unmet needs in the community. This was also in keeping with what Jews and Blacks had done in forming nonpartisan civil rights groups such as the Anti-Defamation League and the NAACP. According to Hope Mendoza, "You have to set up separate organizations."[30]

Helen Gahagan Douglas sought Latino help in her 1950 U.S. Senate campaign against Richard Nixon. CSO's Tony Ríos looks on.

(Kenneth C. Burt)

To fill the political void, Hope Mendoza, Balt Yañez, María Durán, Tony Ríos and other CSO leaders joined allies in labor and the Jewish, Anglo, and Japanese communities to create Citizens For Democratic Government prior to the June 1950 primary. She recalled "We were all trying to pull together a slate to maximize the vote." This group endorsed a slate of "liberal Democrats—Democrats with a long record of working for the 'common man.'" The slate worked because Mexican American voters looked to

CSO leaders for cues on which politicians best represented community interests, a responsibility enhanced by Roybal's decision not to endorse candidates in many races. The group rewarded friends, established new alliances, and settled old scores. It supported Edmund G. "Pat" Brown for California Attorney General and helped to oust Supervisor William Smith, who had first angered Quevedo and El Congreso in 1939 by his suggestion that non-citizens on relief leave Los Angeles. The group also backed the State Senate campaign of Assemblyman Glenn Anderson, a liberal recruited to oppose the candidacy of former Attorney General Robert Kenny, who was supported by the remnants of the Independent Progressive Party. This ad hoc committee represented an effective short-term solution to CSO's decision to remain nonpartisan; but the Latino community needed a permanent, year-round political organization. Brown was the lone statewide Democratic candidate to win in 1950; Governor Earl Warren won reelection because he better filled the nonpartisan image that voters rewarded.[31]

Under the direction of Henry Nava, CSO continued to focus on issues, including relations between Mexican Americans and the Sheriff's Department—still headed by Eugene Biscailuz—in the unincorporated sections of the county. The group also met with the Los Angeles Police Department. On June 7, 1950, three ranking policemen—Captain Ben Stein, Lieutenant Tony Ruiz, and Sergeant Lenwood Rottier—addressed a CSO membership meeting where they asked those present to fill out a questionnaire sponsored by the department's public affairs unit. It included a question of identity: were CSO members American Mexican, American Spanish, or American white? The survey also asked residents to judge the appearance of police officers. In response, one person stressed that everyone was part of the "human race" while another stated "it's (the officers') actions we're interested in—not how they look."[32]

Unknown to CSO, the organization was about to receive increased scrutiny. An internal FBI memorandum dated August 1950 raised the specter of communist infiltration within the civil rights organization.

> In view of the belief on the part of the Sheriff's Office that the Community Service Organization is on the verge of being infiltrated by the Communists as in the case of the National Association of

Mexican-Americans, it is recommended that a dead file be opened on the captioned organization for the purpose of channeling any further information coming to the attention of this office. It should be noted that none of the current officers in the organization are known to be members of the Communist Party.[33]

The FBI cross-referenced information gleaned from CSO and other sources, including informers with the Mexican Commission of the Communist Party. Ultimately, it was more a story of leftist maneuvering for influence than exercising real power.[34]

The pervasive fear of communism in late 1950 and early 1951 influenced CSO's public posturing. The organization, which remained open to all, nevertheless placed itself within the liberal civil rights paradigm that stressed reductions in poverty and discrimination would reduce the appeal of communism. CSO published its history and program in a booklet, *Across The River*. The cover featured Roybal and included a single quote, which is attributed to him: "To drive out Communism we must strike at conditions which foster its growth." This served to highlight the differences between liberal and conservative anti-communists. Where conservatives had attacked Roybal's proposed fair employment ordinance in 1949 as advancing the communist agenda, Roybal and CSO argued that economic and social justice would have the opposite effect—it would reduce the influence of the Communist Party. Such an argument played well with CSO members as well as its liberal and labor benefactors.[35]

CSO exercised increasing influence within the political arena. This newly found power at the ballot box was infectious and exhilarating. The palpable change in politics was being felt across Los Angeles County as the number of newly registered Latino voters reached 35,000 prior to the November 1950 election. CSO's influence now reached way beyond the Eastside, into the San Fernando Valley, the San Gabriel Valley, the southeastern portion of the county, and the Westside. There, CSO activists walked precincts for Frank Mankiewicz, a liberal Jew running for the state assembly in Republican dominated Santa Monica, which still had a Mexican colony and large celery fields.[36] This new sense of ethnic empowerment was captured in the refrain heard at CSO gatherings: "Now the politicians come to us."[37]

The biggest pre-election event was for an elected official not on the ballot: Councilman Edward Roybal. More than 700 gathered the Sunday night before the November 7, 1950 election for a testimonial dinner and fundraiser for CSO. President Henry Nava welcomed the crowd and Rev. Carmelo Santiago provided the innovation. The list of speakers and honored guests demonstrated how Roybal, in less than a year and a half on the council, had become the city's leading liberal and master at coalition politics. County Supervisor John Anson Ford, Congresswoman Helen Gahagan Douglas, and author Carey McWilliams extolled Roybal in their praises. So, too, did Monsignor Thomas O'Dwyer, Judge Isaac Pacht, African American *Sentinel* publisher Loren Miller, and Leslie Claypool, the political editor for the *Daily News*. Honored guests included attorney general candidate Pat Brown and businessman Edward Mehren, from the Los Angeles County Conference on Community Relations.[38] Labor was likewise present. In fact, the Los Angeles CIO Council had recently voted to "pledge complete physical and moral support to the Community Services Organization."[39]

The accolades for Roybal and CSO continued to pour in. In mid-November 1950, *Fortnight*, a statewide liberal magazine, named Roybal as one of the outstanding elected officials of the year.[40] Then on Christmas Day, 1950, the *Daily News* started a five-part series extolling CSO's virtues and successes, followed by an editorial stressing the urgency of CSO's raising money to address uncompleted tasks.[41]

Meanwhile, the city's conservative anti-Roybal forces were not idle. Councilman Davenport and the Small Property Owners League were conspiring to defeat the progressive incumbent. The landlord lobby was reportedly prepared to spend $5,000 to defeat Roybal. Key to their strategy was to splinter the Roybal coalition. A civic leader boasted: "If Roybal runs on that unification of minorities claptrap again, we'll hang him with it. We'll buy ourselves a Negro, a Mexican, and a Japanese for a thousand bucks each, and we'll run them all. We'll split that vote so wide [notoriously racist] Gerald L. K. Smith could get through."[42]

These conservative forces failed to recruit a Latino, Black, or Asian challenger, but they did recruit a former cop, John Kenneth

Harvey, and a Jewish businessman, Irving Rael. Harvey died soon after announcing his candidacy, making it a two-person race. The anti-Roybal forces now sought to split the Latino-Jewish coalition at the core of the Roybal's political base in Boyle Heights. Irving Rael was the proprietor of the Great Western Furniture Store and president of the Brooklyn Avenue Businessmen's Association. In the one-on-one race, Rael hoped to pick up Jewish votes on the basis of shared heritage and then to capture voters to Roybal's right by portraying himself as more "American."

Rael's campaign gained the backing of the *Eastside Journal*, an important piece of the 1949 Roybal coalition, probably because his furniture store was the paper's largest advertiser.[43] Despite the *Journal's* support, Rael failed to gain traction among fellow Jews. This was due in large measure to the strong bonds that Roybal and CSO had developed with the various sectors of the Jewish community, the liberal-left ideological orientation of the district's voters, and Rael's earlier efforts to obscure his ethnicity. "He caught hell from the Jewish community because he wanted Jewish support but at the same time he shortened his name [from Israel to Rael]," recalled educator Stanley Bunyan.[44]

The 1951 election was more politically sophisticated, better financed, and felt more like a traditional campaign than the cause that had characterized Roybal's 1949 victory. Roger Johnson served again as the campaign manager. The big difference was that Roybal now had a record to talk about and could use the power of incumbency to gain institutional support. This included two of the most important pieces of the last Christensen campaign: the AFL Central Labor Council, with its weekly *Los Angeles Citizen,* and the *Eastside Sun.*[45]

Unlike two years before when the CIO Council gave him late and qualified support, Roybal now enjoyed the early and total support of the new leadership of the Los Angeles CIO Council.[46] He received the assistance of CIO Council political director Henry Santiestevan, the first Latino to hold such an important post in the local labor movement. For its part, the campaign used multiple support committees, endorsements, mailers, signs and public events in a reelection drive that strategically consolidated support on the left and then moved to the center.[47]

The Citizens Committee to Re-Elect Roybal sponsored a multi-ethnic, liberal-left campaign kickoff at the San Kwo Low restaurant in Little Tokyo, attended by more than 200. Bill Phillips presided. The proprietor of the music store in Boyle Heights also served as the vice president of the Soto-Michigan Jewish Community Center that offered multicultural programs and had become controversial in the larger city because it reflected the Eastside's radical political tradition. It worked, for example, with Roybal and both CSO and the National Association of Mexican-Americans (ANMA), the successor of Amigos de Wallace.[48] Dr. E. I. Robinson, chair of the Central Los Angeles-based NAACP, served as the master of ceremonies. Assemblyman William Rosenthal attended. He was elected in 1948 by running on both the Democratic and Independent Progressive Party tickets. The group also included Jack Berman, Art Takei, and Alfredo Montoya, leading figures in the Jewish, Japanese and Latino left. Montoya had come out of Mine-Mill and now served as ANMA's national executive director.[49] This led the Communist Party's *People's World* to call the committee the "broadest that has been seen in many a political moon"—and resulted in the FBI monitoring the fundraiser.[50] The group opened its own headquarters on Brooklyn Avenue in Boyle Heights.[51] Many of these same activists helped organize the annual Festival of Friendship in Boyle Heights that featured Latino, Jewish, Japanese, Filipino, and African American food and entertainment.[52]

The formal Roybal campaign, the Committee to Re-Elect Councilman Roybal, operated out of a headquarters on East First Street, with additional offices on South Broadway and Sunset Boulevard.[53] The campaign bulk-mailed an issue-oriented piece that served as an anchor for his reelection. Entitled, "Get Things Done in '51!," it stressed, "Vote For Roybal—He Votes For You!" It listed "20 Reasons Why You Should Keep Roybal," an impressive list of achievements, including "22 new traffic signals, 23 new pedestrian crosswalks, and 18 boulevard stops." The mailer also stressed Roybal's work to open public libraries, to increase the number of streetcars, to fight for rent control and public housing, and to oppose employment discrimination and the curtailment of civil liberties. He also had led the first effort to address the city's growing air pollution problem.[54]

The mailer included the following tag-line: "Councilman Roybal says: 'To drive out Communism, we must strike at the conditions which foster its growth.'" This slogan is the same as the one attributed to Roybal on the CSO's *Across The River*, and which the councilman attributed to Bishop Sheil in his stirring City Hall defense of the right of communists to hold unpopular views. Roybal's campaign may have found the tactic necessary to blunt Rael's repeated insinuations that the councilman was unAmerican because of his liberal policy stands and political ties to the left. This was because the Red scare gained additional legitimacy with the attacks on communists in Hollywood, President Truman's imposed loyalty oaths for federal employees, and the start of the Korean War. North Korea, with the assistance of China and the Soviet Union, was fighting U.S. and United Nations troops. Locally, the left-led unions had been thrown out of the CIO and communists purged from liberal unions, suspected communists faced deportation, and the Jewish People's Fraternal Order was banished by the organized Jewish Community for its political leanings.[55]

Yet another group, the Non-Partisan Committee to Re-Elect Ed Roybal reinforced the twenty reasons to support Roybal, including the aforementioned tag-line, in a piece that sought to demonstrate the breadth of the Roybal coalition. It featured a letter by African American Assemblyman Augustus Hawkins and listed Jewish, Latino, and ethnic Catholics as endorsers, including religious leaders such as Rabbi Morton Kaufman and Monsignor Thomas O'Dwyer. The group's focus, however, was placed on labor unions, which cut across ethnic lines, as well as the smaller minority groups within the district. The list included John E. Aiso and Harry Honda from the Japanese community, Sam Wong from the Chinese community, and a number of white ethnics, including Armenians.[56]

Organizing along ethnic and neighborhood lines reinforced the broader issue-oriented appeals. This allowed the campaign to go deep into specific communities which was particularly important in the Jewish community where Roybal employed policy differences and personal relationships to trump Rael's shared ethnic heritage. Special committees were established in the Wabash and Brooklyn areas. These two business districts in Boyle Heights were surrounded by thriving Jewish neighborhoods. Community leaders asked fellow Jews to place Roybal signs in their front lawns and shop windows, and prominent small business proprietors joined pro-Roybal committees.[57] One of the retailers supporting Roybal was Harry Block of Block's Bakery. According to spouse Clara Block, the family-run, five-person bakery staff generally avoided politics, except when there was "a good Jewish candidate." This time, however, the Blocks joined with their fellow merchants to back Roybal.[58] The Wabash Area Committee to Re-Elect Ed Roybal, of which the Blocks were part, sent out a "Dear Neighbor" flyer that featured twenty-four business leaders.[59]

The decision to highlight Roybal's support from Jewish merchants—and not from the Jewish unions or other more radicalized sectors of the community—sent a powerful message to voters on several levels. First, well-known and respected neighborhood leaders supported Roybal. Second, having the support of those who embodied free enterprise undercut Rael's message that Roybal was somehow a communist or anti-business. Third, this was a powerful repudiation of a fellow businessman that everyone knew and liked. It underscored the fact that Jewish leaders were putting coalition politics ahead of ethnic solidarity.

As the campaign approached Election Day, the *Daily News* endorsed Roybal, calling him "our favorite councilman." The paper gushed that "Roybal has demonstrated not only great ability and deep sympathy with the needs of the people but he has proved his courage on many occasions by standing for principle when it was unpopular and politically dangerous." In so doing, the paper reinforced the campaign's work on the ground and in the mail.[60] So, too, did all four of the state assemblymen whose districts overlapped the council district. The four—two Anglos, a Black, and a Jew—shared a commitment to liberalism, had similar institutional supporters, and enjoyed a relationship with Roybal and the CSO.[61] The *Los Angeles Times* remained neutral.[62]

Desperate, Rael sought to make inroads into Roybal's base by implying support from key political and community leaders. He used photos of himself with Attorney General Brown, Assemblyman Rosenthal, and Monsignor O'Dwyer. The Roybal campaign quickly turned this act of deception against the challenger. Monsignor

O'Dwyer denounced the tactic and stated "Councilman Roybal has my full support in his present campaign."[63] Brown's office released a non-endorsement endorsement. "The Attorney General of California does not participate in politics, local or otherwise," wrote his assistant in charge of the Los Angeles office. He continued, adding "but if Attorney General Edmund G. 'Pat' Brown were to lend his support for the candidate for public office, he would wholeheartedly endorse and lend his support to men such as Councilman Edward R. Roybal, an outstanding and devoted public servant."[64] At the same time, the Roybal campaign went after the challenger's supporters, forming the Republican Committee to Re-elect Roybal, which sent out a mailing to GOP registrants.[65] Then, in the final days of the campaign, the Los Angeles Fire and Police Protective League—representing the city's cops—joined in praising Roybal, calling him "the most pleasant surprise ever sent to the City Council" and saying that "Spanish-speaking people, and all other citizens, need men like Roybal."[66]

Roybal ended the 1951 campaign with an evening rally designed to motivate his core supporters. The rally was held at the Jewish Folk Schule on North Soto Street in Boyle Heights that had once served to promote Henry Wallace. *Eastside Sun* publisher Joseph Kovner served as master of ceremonies. Jewish businessman and Michigan-Soto Community Center official Bill Phillips and Latino labor and CSO activist María Durán joined Roybal at the podium. Leaders of the Non-Partisan Veterans Committee for Roybal made the flag presentation, underscoring Roybal's own service in World War II and by extension, his patriotism.[67]

On Election Day, Roybal achieved a landslide reelection unparalleled in the history of the cosmopolitan district, besting his opponent by more than three-to-one. Roybal received 17,967 votes to Rael's 5,864.[68] Through his leadership as a councilman and a candidate, Roybal, had once again demonstrated that votes count and coalitions matter because he achieved victory in a district where Mexican Americans remained a minority of the voters and CSO did not conduct a get-out-the-vote effort. As a result, Roybal won over a larger share of the voting electorate, including overwhelming support in Latino and Jewish precincts, even as total turnout dropped from the previous election's historic high level.[69]

Roybal's 1951 victory was emblematic of the position of Mexican Americans in Los Angeles. CSO activist and later political scientist Ralph Guzmán emphasized that CSO "placed the Mexican American people, for the first time in their history, in a position where they could learn from American society by interacting with it and induce social change by manipulating its political institutions."[70] The Roybal coalition had been built in a three-stage process through four years of tireless organizing. CSO had established a powerful Latino voter base by sponsoring voter registration and get-out-the-vote campaigns. The group then found ways to coalesce with Jews, labor, and other minority groups to achieve an electoral majority to elect Roybal to the city council. Finally, Roybal used the power of incumbency, along with mobilizing activists, to deliver for specific constituent groups while focusing on issues, such as fair employment, that cut across ethnic and racial divisions and appealed to progressive Anglos. This strategy served Roybal and CSO well. Roybal won big in 1951 and never again faced a serious campaign for reelection.

The 1951 campaign also reflected power shifts within the liberal-left and the larger society during the Cold War, most specifically the interjection of growing U.S.-Soviet tension into the most progressive council district in Los Angeles. Roybal, the New Deal Democrat, found it necessary to repeatedly state his opposition to communism. The enthusiasm on the liberal-left for Roybal no doubt reflects his role in founding CSO, his successful efforts to deliver for the neighborhoods, and his inclusive style of working on issues such as fair employment with racially and ideologically diverse groups. The Roybal vision included advancing the interests of workers and minorities as well as defending civil liberties of people who belong to unpopular groups. This helps account for Roybal's coalition building skills, particularly his ability to retain Jewish support against a Jewish opponent. But it also reflected a larger trend. Ironically, Boyle Heights was becoming more radical and more multiracial in its politics even as it was becoming more Latino in population and as Los Angeles and the nation moved right. The area served as a haven for radicals who felt increasingly isolated or under assault. It likewise provided a unique immigrant and multicultural feel that was absent in the rest of the city.[71] At the same time, Roybal and CSO utilized powerful symbols such prayers and flags to associate their progressive agenda with God and Country. This, and an absence of any ties to foreign governments hostile to the U.S., exempted them from the worst abuses during the McCarthy era.[72] In terms of identity, CSO used the term "Spanish-speaking people" in *Across The River*.[73]

Further north, in San Francisco, the more diverse Spanish-speaking community came together under the aegis of the United Latins of America in its search for a civic voice. Manuel Maldonado testified on the group's behest before the Board of Supervisors, endorsing a proposed Fair Employment Practices ordinance there. The argument based in World War II service echoed the manta in Los Angeles. "We are proud of the great number of Americans of Latin American extraction who have served their country well," extolled Maldonado before stating that "only by Fair Employment legislation will this racial barrier that we all know exists be removed."[74]

Despite the increased visibility of the Latino community in California, and Roybal's huge role in Los Angeles area politics, the newfound influence did not yet reach into the inner circles in Sacramento, and particularly among the Republicans who controlled the Office of the Governor and the State Legislature. This reality was made apparent when Councilman Roybal sought to have an assembly seat created that a Latino would have a good chance to win following the 1950 reapportionment. Under the existing formula, Latinos were an organized force in two districts, the Boyle heights-based 40th, which Roybal represented on the city council, and the Belvedere-based 51st, where José Chávez had done well in the 1948 primary. The state's tremendous growth in the suburbs and smaller towns during the preceding decade required that these old urban districts grow in size. It was possible to construct a Latino heavy district in Los Angeles County by combining the adjacent neighborhoods of Boyle Heights with the Belvedere and East Los Angeles areas. There was no apparent support for the idea among those people who controlled the process. "[O]ne of the Assemblymen . . . said that he believed that the Spanish-speaking were not participating sufficiently in civic affairs," said Roybal. "I tried to convince him at that time that he was very wrong."[75]

In the end, partisanship and the desire to protect incumbents dominated the process. Assemblyman Edward Elliot, the down-town-based liberal who had agreed not to run against Roybal in 1949, was given new territory in Boyle Heights. Belvedere was combined with additional Anglo areas farther east. The Legislature clearly missed an opportunity to create a Latino friendly seat, but did the process reflect anti-Latino sentiment? Roybal's exchange indicates a lack of awareness of the dynamic changes within Latino Los Angeles. And the process placed a priority on protecting in-cumbents, most of whom were Anglo, and maximizing the number of Republican-controlled seats. So how did the other two "minori-ty" groups do? African American Augustus Hawkins got to keep his Central Avenue seat. The Jewish community lost its seat in Boyle Heights but received one that they could win in the mid-city area. To its credit, the Democratic Party protested the process. The 1952 California Democratic Party Platform condemned the "Republican Reapportionment Bill of 1951" for its "UnAmerican gerrymander-ing" that "denied many citizens equal representation."[76]

The issue of Latino representation in state government raised by Roybal would have to wait for another ten years. That same year, 1951, Congress in Public Law 78 institutionalized the brace-ro program, to import Mexican farm workers to the United States, leading to the importation of hundreds of thousands of Mexicans into California.[77] For now, the focus of Latino political ambitions remained on Los Angeles. Through Roybal and CSO Latinos had developed strong ties to the liberal civil rights movement and to the liberal wing of the Democratic Party. CSO operated as the of-ficially recognized Latino organization within the AFL, CIO, and the organized Jewish community, and developed relationships with the NAACP and the Japanese American Citizens League. In this regard, the changes within groups such as the Los Angeles CIO Council proved beneficial. Instead of fighting Philip Connelly and other communists, CSO leaders like steel worker Tony Ríos en-joyed personal and organizational ties to steel worker John Despol and other leaders within the new liberal CIO leadership.

CHAPTER 6

THE TONY RÍOS
AND
BLOODY CHRISTMAS POLICE BEATINGS

Christmas Eve is a traditional time spent with family and friends, and Christmas Eve 1951 was no exception. The smell of tamales wafted through the air as women prepared the customary meal while making sure the children had on clean clothes for Midnight Mass. The safety of loved ones thousands of miles away fighting communist aggression in Korea was on the minds of many. Despite such concerns, daily life in Mexican American neighborhoods had improved. Local government was becoming more responsive due to the efforts of Councilman Roybal. The new East Los Angeles Junior College had made higher education more accessible and the GI Bill of Rights made it more affordable for veterans. Rising wages in the heavily unionized economy provided stability and allowed Latinos and other Angelenos to purchase automobiles, refrigerators, and televisions on payment plans. A number of young Latinos joined their Anglo counterparts in buying homes or starting businesses. Yet other problems persisted. These included discrimination, housing shortages, economic dislocations, and relations with law enforcement, most notably the Los Angeles Police Department. The Latino community's ability to condemn police brutality at the height of the Cold War demonstrated its growing political influence, which rested on Councilman Roybal's leadership, CSO's organizational prowess, and labor and liberal coalition partners.[1]

In this atmosphere, a coterie of friends left a family gathering in Boyle Heights seeking a nightcap at the Wagon Wheel, a bar on Riverside Boulevard, in neighboring Lincoln Heights. Blood, marriage, and friendship connected the seven young men—four Latinos and three Anglos. Most were veterans and family men who were working full time in a mix of white and blue-collar jobs; two were employed by the city, and one was still in the U.S. Marines. They were "good citizens" with secure futures, according to Aurora

Hernández, a hospital worker and the spouse of one of the men. Along with thousands of other Latinos, she voted for the first time in 1948; her husband had missed Roybal's initial election because he was a military policeman still in the service.[2]

"I hadn't even been served a drink when I noticed a policeman taking one of my friends toward the back door," recounted city structural engineer Eddie Nora shortly thereafter. "There was some kind of a fight. When it was over we all went to the home of my friend, Danny Rodela, on Glen Elen St. We were there only a short time when the police arrived and ordered all of us to come out with our hands up."[3]

At the Central Police Station the situation turned ugly. Police officers were in the midst of an alcohol accented holiday celebration and responded to a false rumor that the men had beaten a fellow cop. Dozens of uniformed officers took turns entering the jail cell to mercilessly beat the young men. The men were taken to the hospital and "cleaned up," according to victim Manuel Hernández, and then moved to the Lincoln Heights Police Station, where they were paraded before police beat journalists. The beatings continued at the Lincoln Heights Station.[4] Nora described the nightmare. "As I lay on the floor in a pool of blood a man with a pistol stood over me. He said, 'I'll shoot this—and I begged him to 'go ahead.'"[5] The worst beating was inflicted upon Danny Rodela, who was not at the house when the officers picked up the others. When the officers arrested him in the early hours of Christmas morning they took him to Elysian Park where they beat him.[6]

The city's five daily papers—the *Times, Mirror, Examiner, Herald and Express*, and the *Daily News*—reported the story as the police provided it. According to LAPD, the young men had threatened a tavern owner and then attacked the cops who responded to the scene. The *Daily News*, the city's only liberal paper, followed the pack, running a photo of the alleged ruffians against a wall at the police station, with the headline: "Celebrate Christmas Eve By Beating Up Two Cops."[7]

Unlike the city's papers, Councilman Edward Roybal was disinclined to take the LAPD's pronouncements at face value despite having publicly minimized the problem of police brutality and having been supported politically in his reelection by the Los Angeles

Fire and Police Protective League.[8] Concerns about brutal cops and a biased judicial system was an ever-present issue in the Latino community. Problems dated back to the arrival of the Mexican immigrants, although few incidents attracted attention outside the community.[9] The more notorious incidents included the finding of institutional brutality stemming from the El Congreso inspired investigation into the death of Benny Moreno and another boy, and the Sleepy Lagoon case, where multiple false convictions were reversed on appeal. Daily problems with police in the neighborhood had emerged as an issue in CSO's house meetings in 1947. It was a concern that CSO had tried to address by meeting with LAPD Chief Horral and joining with a left-led coalition in 1948 seeking justice for seventeen-year-old Augustin Salcido who had been shot in the back.[10] Then in 1949, Roybal and CSO brought up the topic of brutality with the Chief W. A. Worton. Conditions improved. But now there was another chief, William Parker, the third in a five-year period. He placed a priority on the elimination of corruption within the police force and was less concerned than his predecessor with minority group relations.[11]

When CSO heard an account of the arrest and beating that contradicted the official police record, they responded. CSO board member, Dr. Konstantin Sparkuhl, provided emergency medical care at the police station that may have saved the life of one of the victims.[12] CSO President Tony Ríos met with the young men. He urged them to talk publicly about their police beating, and to work with CSO Civil Rights Committee chair Ralph Guzmán. Two weeks after their arrest, CSO voted to "support the case."[13] The defendants were becoming known as the "Christmas Seven" and the incident as "Bloody Christmas."

The young men obtained James O. Warner as their legal counsel through the Southern Pacific Railroad, where two of the men worked. The high quality legal services came thanks to the efforts of defendant Jack Wilson's father, an English railroad welder, who went to his union for help. Warner did not share CSO's desire to make his clients' case a cause célèbre. "We had a lot of people wanting to help, from the Communists to Community Service Organization," stated the younger Wilson. "Warner said, 'no, I won't get involved unless we play it straight. Forget about being a Mexican, an Anglo.'"[14] Their attorney also shared his approach with CSO's Fred Ross. "I'm only interested in one thing, keeping these kids out of jail," said Warner. "The second the Chief and the prosecution got wind we're going to blast the cops, they'd use every trick in the trade to get a conviction on these boys."[15]

The Christmas Seven entered the judicial system as just another case. It differed from most other cases only in that the defendants had an attorney. In deciding not to confront the LAPD, Warner was playing the odds. To underscore this point, Fred Ross recalled CSO's own failure in its recent bid to aid two young men it felt were mistreated at the hands of law enforcement.[16] Unforeseen events, however, were about to propel the case into widespread public attention and put unprecedented focus on the all too routine treatment by police officers of members of the Mexican American community.

On the evening of January 27, 1952, Tony Ríos visited the Carioca Café, which "was a *real* meeting place," noted social worker and CSO leader Margarita Durán Méndez, and the birthplace of the organization some five years earlier.[17] Ríos talked with the proprietor, Margaret Torres, who was selling tickets for an upcoming CSO fundraiser. While there, Ríos noticed two inebriated men drinking at the bar. After a while, the two men followed Joe Betance, a twenty-nine-year-old laborer, to the parking lot. They proceeded to strike him repeatedly. Ríos called out for the men to stop and yelled for someone in the café to call the police. One of the men then pulled out a gun and threatened to shoot Ríos and another man, Alfred Ulloa, when he sought to write down the license plate of the car into which they pushed Betance.[18]

When a police squad car arrived, Ríos requested the arrest of the inebriated men. To his surprise, the men turned out to be Officers Fernando Najera and George Kellenberger, plainclothes vice cops. The officers were not arrested. Instead, they arrested Ríos and Ulloa for "resisting, delaying and obstructing officers in the official performance of their duties."[19] At the Hollenbeck police station, the two men were stripped and beaten. "Most people try to cover their face when they are beaten, but I covered my body," recalled Ríos, "I wanted people to be able to see what the police had done."[20] Bravado aside, the incident was very serious.

CSO activist and city employee Joe Carlos was at the café at the time and he immediately called Councilman Roybal at home. He told Roybal that his "compadre" was in jail and might be in trouble given the circumstances surrounding his arrest. Roybal called the police station, at which point the officers stopped beating Ríos. Carlos then drove to pick up Roybal and Ross. The three friends bailed out the bruised but defiant Ríos. The thirty-nine-year-old self-taught firebrand believed that the only way to end police brutality was to expose it.[21]

Roybal shared Ríos' anger, but was more cautious in his approach. Police Chief William Parker, who ran his department out of the basement of City Hall, had rapidly consolidated his power, which now rivaled that of Mayor Fletcher Bowron and the fifteen-member city council, who could not directly remove him. Parker also courted civic leaders, his efforts buttressed by the department's practice of keeping files on prominent citizens and even city council members. Los Angeles' rich and famous found in illegal or embarrassing situations would be told not to worry, while the information was placed in a file, according to LAPD records officer Alice Soto. The department could later collect on the favor. "It was all about power," she added.[22]

Roybal decided to talk to Parker about the specifics of the Ríos case—but not about Bloody Christmas or police brutality more generally. "The Ríos beating was more of a blatant case, and Roybal knew that Tony Ríos would never attack or threaten to attack a policeman," stated past CSO president Henry Nava.[23] "They beat up the wrong guy, because Ríos was a real good guy and a well known guy," added William Barry, the priest who had served on the CSO board during its formative years.[24] Larry Margolis, a Boyle Heights-born Westside activist who served with Ríos on the Los Angeles County Democratic Central Committee, added: "Tony Ríos was considered solid and a representative of Mexican Americans, labor, and liberals."[25]

With Roybal seeking an appointment with the police chief, Ríos looked for an attorney willing to risk his legal career by directly challenging the Los Angeles Police Department. Ríos approached the group he thought was the most likely to help, the American Civil Liberties Union of Southern California.[26] To his disbelief,

CSO President Tony Ríos.   *(Kenneth C. Burt)*

"the ACLU at that time didn't consider police brutality cases as civil liberties cases," stated Ríos. He turned to Saul Ostrow, owner of the Sealy Mattress franchise and one of the progressive Jewish businessmen who served as CSO's financial patrons. The philanthropist went to work on the ACLU. "Ostrow told them very bluntly that if my case is not a civil liberties case he wasn't going to give them any more money," emphasized Tony Ríos. "So they changed their policy and provided an attorney."[27] The ACLU turned to Wirin, Rissman, Okrand & Nutter, a firm it had on a modest retainer.

It was more than pressure from a client, however, that led the firm to accept Ríos' case *pro bono publico*. Thirteen years earlier, the firm's senior partner, Al Wirin, had been a partner with Leo Gallagher when the latter chaired the El Congreso-selected and Olson-appointed state committee investigating into the death of Benny Moreno. Wirin's newest partner, Ralph H. Nutter, was a thirty-two-year-old decorated hero of World War II, who possessed an abiding interest in civil liberties and an affinity for societal underdogs.[28]

While Nutter approached the case in terms of civil liberties, Roybal and CSO saw the upcoming trial in a more political context. They saw this as their opportunity to expose police brutality. Likewise, a conviction of Ríos, the CSO president, would serve as a powerful setback to both the city councilman and the community organization, and to the empowerment of Mexican Americans. With the stakes high, CSO and Roybal moved to mobilize their Eastside political base and to involve the Democratic Party and the citywide civil rights coalition. In the process, they elevated the trial of Tony Ríos to that of a cause célèbre. CSO also reached out to the press and obtained a meeting with the *Daily News*. Up to this point, the paper had refused the organization's request to write about the problem of police conduct in relation to Latinos even as it ran a laudatory five-day series on the organization's work in other fields.[29]

Soon thereafter, the *Daily News'* political editor, Leslie E. Claypool, used his column to provide the first favorable coverage for the defendants. "Chief of Police William H. Parker has the matter of police brutality right smack in his lap today and the general view is that he had better make it look better than the available evidence seems to make it, or else," he wrote.[30]

Meanwhile, members of the LAPD sought to undermine Ríos' case by intimidating witnesses at the café, including owner Margaret Torres.[31] They also went after the defendant. One morning, Ríos opened his front door to find two officers on his porch. They demanded that he look outside. There on the street stood a row of uniformed officers. One of the officers then told him: "There are 4100 just like those, and we'll get you sooner or later."[32] To make matters worse, according to Ríos, the two men on his porch were the very officers assigned by the department's Internal Affairs unit to investigate the handling of his case.[33]

Ríos and Roybal refused to back down. They found solace in knowing that Ríos was innocent of the police charge against him and was, in fact, the victim of a police beating. They also gained strength from support they were getting from CSO members and political allies throughout Los Angeles.

The Tony Ríos and Alfred Ulloa trial opened on February 26, 1952, with an all-white jury of eleven women and one man. The prosecutor immediately employed racist stereotypes and charged that the defense was linked to communism. The defense fired back. "I was the first lawyer in Los Angeles, in my opening statement, to accuse the police department of police brutality," stated Nutter. He also sought to inoculate himself and his clients against the charge of a communist affiliation. He shared his own World War II service record and his status as a Lieutenant Colonel in the Air Force Reserve. He then stated, "If I were a Communist, I think the Air Force would kick me out." The prosecutor claimed Nutter's argument was "prejudicial," but he responded by saying, "You raised the issue [of communism]. I'm just replying," and the judge let it stand.[34]

That same day at City Hall, Councilman Edward Roybal charged for the first time in an open meeting that a number of police officers brutalized Mexican Americans. Roybal talked specifically about the Ríos-Ulloa case and charged that roughly fifty cases of abuse had been reported to his office in the last month alone. He added, "We already have the facts to prove the charges in at least six of the cases." Roybal then announced that he would lead a delegation to meet with Chief Parker to discuss corrective measures, including the establishment of citizen-police committees to increase communication. Among those who planned to join him were Monsignor Thomas O'Dwyer, Los Angeles CIO Council head Albert Lunceford, and AFL Central Labor Council leader W.J. Bassett.[35]

When Roybal finished, a number of his colleagues immediately rose to defend Chief Parker and the honor of the police department. Most of the daily papers supported the police department and Parker was quoted as saying that the "over-exertion of authority by police officers is definitely on the decline."[36]

The *Daily News* and the *Mirror* ran the story. Roybal's accusation coincided with the Ríos-Ulloa trial and the bizarre police shooting of a Latino physician in the Hollywood Hills. If that was not enough, a fourth event added legitimacy to the charges and worked its way into the news: the Los Angeles Conference on Community Relations mentioned the beating of CSO President Tony Ríos and the problem of police brutality in its newsletter. Some sixty minority, labor, and religious groups, including CSO belonged to the conference, which facilitated a regular dialogue between liberal civil rights-oriented groups and provided a collective voice in dealing with local government.[37] The Conference on Community relations complained in its report that the "LAPD's Internal Affairs Division took fifty-four days to conclude its report, and had taken no action at all until Judge Call demanded a grand jury investigation.[38]

Chief Parker moved rapidly to distance himself from the controversy and frustrated further investigations by stating that the duty to take corrective action rested with the City's Police Commission. Thus, he publicly asserted, it would not be appropriate for him to meet with Councilman Roybal or concerned individuals. "Cop Chief Steps Away From Heat" and "Chief Ducks Out of Brutality Quiz: Parker Passes Buck to Board," ran headlines in the *Daily News*.[39]

Roybal's decision to criticize the police put him on a collision course with the LAPD. "[Joe] Carlos spent a lot of time riding with [Roybal] so there would be a witness because they were trailed by the cops," recalled the newly married Hope Mendoza Schechter. The police officers reportedly wanted to catch him in a traffic violation "or God forbid," according to the CSO leader and garment union organizer, "he should be with a woman or something. So he was very, very careful about everything he did."[40] Harvey Schechter, Hope's new spouse, and the assistant director of the Anti-Defamation League, bluntly added: "They were ready to frame him."[41] Nutter, the defense attorney, feared for his own safety. "When I drove to court every morning I was careful not to violate any speed laws, because I figured if I was in jail they would have beaten the hell out of me."[42]

On the opening day of the trial, the *CSO Reporter* carried a front-page editorial, "Ríos-Ulloa Trial Opens." It captured the group's anger at prosecutor Marshall Morgan's attempt to smear Ríos by associating him with anti-social behavior and communism. It also underscored the importance of the trial to Latino Los Angeles.

> We who belong to the CSO know that we are not Communists. The Communists know that we are not Communists. And Mr. Marshall Morgan, the prosecutor, is too astute and intelligent a lawyer not to know that we are not Communists.
>
> Mr. Morgan, who seems to be more interested in winning at any cost than in the administration of justice, could better consider how the miscarriage of justice and his remarks serve any enemy of our country who is looking for propaganda to use against us.
>
> The Ríos case is the most important case ever to come before the courts with regards to the Mexican-American community.
>
> If Tony Ríos, a respected member of the community, a leader in the political affairs of the district, an outstanding member of the CIO, a life-long devout Catholic, a delegate to the Democratic County Central Committee, a deputy-registrar of voters, and one of the staunchest anti-Communists of the community; if Tony Ríos cannot secure justice in the courts of this city, then no Mexican-American can expect or hope for justice.[43]

The newsletter carried an appeal to members to attend the trial.[44]

Everyone in CSO knew Ríos. And everyone knew how difficult it was for Mexican Americans to get justice in court. Thus the statement—"If Tony Ríos cannot secure justice in the courts of this city, then no Mexican-American can expect or hope for justice"—echoed in the collective consciousness. According to CSO college student leader Ralph Poblano, "Ríos was definitely a leader, no question about it. He was doing what had to be done. Stand up and fight."[45]

The two officers, for their part, stuck to their original story, although new details emerged over the course of the trial. They accused Ríos and Ulloa of not only personally interfering with their police work, but trying to incite a crowd to free the prisoner, claiming that this required the officer to draw a gun to maintain control of the situation.[46] Officer Fernando Najera "testified that (Ríos and Ulloa) were stripped because he and Kellenberger were looking for hypodermic needle scars."[47]

Judge Ben S. Beery refused to allow testimony about the police beating, saying that was an issue to be settled in a counter suit by Ríos and Ulloa against the LAPD. The information made it into the newspaper stories about the case anyway.[48] For its part, the CSO helped to focus Mexican American interest on the trial. Fred Ross arranged car pools to take "CSO housewives" to the courthouse. African Americans, unionists, and other supporters joined them in filling the chamber. Tony Ríos took the stand in his own defense and his attorney produced witnesses to corroborate his story. Under cross-examination, Officer Najera admitted that he drank at the bar while on duty and paid for the drink with police department funds.[49]

Slowly the trial attracted greater coverage: "Drunken Cop Beat Them, Say 2 Men on Trial Here." "Cops Flashing Guns in Row Over Beating Testifies." "'Toughest Cop' Brutality Quiz Gets Court Ban." "Cops in Ríos Case Admits Taking Drink." "Ríos Takes Stand Again in Row Trial."[50] The articles began to have a cumulative impact within the civil rights community, at city hall, and among the citizenry. Tony Ríos sought every opportunity to publicize his case and to increase its saliency for CSO's community allies.[51]

Ríos obtained an invitation as the CSO president to appear as a guest on a Friday night public affairs television show, "The World In Your Hands," sponsored by the County Conference on Community Relations to discuss improving police-community ties. TV was a new technology and its political impact was only starting to be understood. The newness of the medium helped attract relatively large audiences for the limited number of programs that ran in black and white on only a few stations.[52]

The police lieutenant on the show admitted there might be a few "bad apples" on the force. Apparently unaware of Ríos' case, the policeman turned to the CSO president, and asked: "But how do you know, Mr. Ríos, that what those alleged victims say is true? Have you ever actually seen any of them being beaten?" This provided the opening Ríos was looking for to talk about his own case. The lieutenant then suggested Ríos report the incident through proper police channels. Ríos related that he had, only to have the investigators come to his house and threaten him. Before he was through, Ríos mentioned the Bloody Christmas beatings.[53] Ríos had effectively used television in the early fifties to circumvent the conservative papers in the same way that President Roosevelt and Governor Olson and other liberal politicians in the thirties and forties had used the radio to speak to the public.

The Ríos beating story was now in the public domain. Shortly after the broadcast, the Los Angeles County Conference on

The Christmas Six defendants were (l to r) Danny Rodella, William Wilson, Raymond Marquez, Jack Wilson, Manuel Hernández, and Elias Rodella.
(Los Angeles Daily News Collection, Department of Special Collections, Charles E. Young Research Library, UCLA)

Community Relations sought a meeting with Mayor Fletcher Bowron and called upon the Police Commission to hold public hearings. On March 6, 1952, with the Ríos trial in its second week, the Police Commission voted to hold a public hearing on March 17 at city hall to look into alleged misconduct, and formally requested the attendance of Mayor Bowron and Chief Parker.[54]

On Friday, March 11, after two weeks of testimony, the prosecutor and the defense made their summations. On Monday, the impaneled jury deliberated and found Ríos and Ulloa not guilty. After the decision was announced, jury foreman John K. Kissane said, "We were practically unanimous as to their innocence from the start."[55] The decision of a non-Latino jury to find two Mexican Americans more credible than two police officers helped shatter the aura of invincibility that surrounded the LAPD. Sensing such a shift in attitude, and no doubt influenced by the growing media coverage, James Warner, the counsel for the Bloody Christmas defendants, then nearing the end of their own trial, agreed to allow his clients to talk about their police beatings.[56]

Municipal Judge Joseph L. Call presided over the trial of the Christmas Six, who were charged with beating officers J.L. Trojanowski and N.L. Bronson outside the Wagon Wheel. Four years earlier the judge had played a minor role in the Salcido shooting case when he dismissed the disturbing the peace charges against a woman who had contradicted the police officer.[57] In the current case, the prosecution began by filing a felony charge and labeling the group the River Rat Gang. The court soon discovered that the defendants were each part of an extended family, with military records and good jobs, and that the evidence against them was weak. The prosecution dropped the felonies to misdemeanors. The prosecution also dropped the charges against one of the men, who had a relative working for the mayor.[58] "In instructing the jury," the *Los Angeles Times* reported, "Judge Call told them the brutality charges were not at issue." The jury convicted the six men of disorderly conduct.[59]

Judge Call, however, was so affected by the testimony of police misconduct in his court that he set aside the punishment and asserted that the officers had violated five different sections of the penal code. He then demanded an immediate Grand Jury investigation. "The record in this case is permeated with testimony of vicious beatings and brutality perpetuated without cause of provocation long after these defendants were taken into custody," averred Judge Call. "This testimony stinks to high heaven and all the perfumery in Arabia cannot obliterate its stench."[60]

Judge Call's very public demand for justice forced the hand of those throughout the criminal justice system who had done little, hoping the issue would resolve itself. For the next forty-five days, the daily papers were replete with dramatic updates on the widening police brutality scandal, eclipsing the furor around the ongoing trial of communist leaders and the fight over public housing.[61] In addition to the Grand Jury investigation, the Police Commission began to investigate and hundreds of citizens, including representatives from the County Conference on Community Relations, packed the City Council chambers demanding that law enforcement be held accountable for their actions. In response, Bates Booth, the attorney-president of the Los Angeles Police Commission, declared that the brutality had to stop. "We will not tolerate in the department a police officer who abuses his authority to infringe the constitutional rights of any citizen, no matter how lowly or friendless," he said.[62] The California State Legislature also took up the issue as Assemblyman Vernon Kilpatrick, chair of the Interim Committee on Crime and Corrections, and a CIO political ally, announced he would introduce a resolution instructing Attorney General Brown to investigate and to report back the following month.[63] The Tony Ríos case and Bloody Christmas Beatings became Exhibits A and B in the first widespread public discussion of police brutality against minorities in Los Angeles.

Finally, after eleven days of vivid, even spine-tingling testimony, the Grand Jury indicted eight cops, including Radio Officer Robert Sánchez. This set off months of high profile trials, each of which was widely covered in the *Daily News* as well as the *Los Angeles Times*. In the end, six policemen were convicted, while two were kicked off of the force and spent time in jail. Another thirty-six officers received official reprimands.[64]

CSO praised "those Lincoln Heights boys who swallowed their fears of future reprisals and renewed beatings and went on to testify." According to an editorial in the *CSO Reporter*, "They deserve lasting appreciation from the rest of the community who will profit from their quiet heroism." The organization used the incident to illustrate the value of civic engagement: "The lesson to be learned is not a new one. But a hard one. It is a lesson that people get that degree of attention and courtesy from their public servants that they put into civic duty and constant scrutiny of public officials' acts."[65]

CSO had helped achieve what seemed impossible: it had exposed the all-too-common police mistreatment of Mexican Americans. But they had not done it alone. The victory in the Tony Ríos case and the indictment of the police officers for abusing the Bloody Christmas defendants was due to a convergence of interests, good timing, some luck, and an incredible amount of legal, political, and journalistic work. City Councilman Edward Roybal, philanthropist Saul Ostrow, defense attorney Ralph Nutter, Judge Joseph Call, the *Daily News*, the Grand Jury, and civil rights allies all played pivotal roles at critical junctures in the unfolding drama. The timing of these events was fortunate for yet another reason. The *Daily News* ceased publication in 1954, eliminating the lone liberal voice among the daily newspapers.[66] Seen with an historical eye, these legal victories went beyond that achieved in the Sleepy Lagoon case. In that case the wrongfully convicted won on appeal and were released from jail; here, neither Ríos nor the Bloody Christmas defendants had to spend months in jail. In the Bloody Christmas case the cops who violated the rights of the young men were punished, and five went to jail themselves.

Against the backdrop of the Cold War, the issue of communism was interjected into the struggle over police brutality. The first incident occurred when the prosecutor in the Ríos case raised the subject in an effort to reduce the credibility of the CSO leader. With the increased attention on the Bloody Christmas beatings, Mayor Bowron and Chief Parker raised the specter of communism to discredit those seeking to end unequal treatment by his officers.[67] To their credit, communists had long raised the issue of police brutality, playing a key role in setting up the Sleepy Lagoon Defense Committee and they sought to involve themselves in the present controversy. Yet times had changed both in terms of Latino political development and the larger political environment. In 1942-

43, the dominant Mexican American organizations led by Eduardo Quevedo and Manuel Ruiz lacked the resources to assist the youth captured in mass arrests. This provided a political opening for the labor-left, marginalized since the Hitler-Stalin pact but enjoying a resurgence of legitimacy with the post-1941 wartime unity between the U.S. and Russia. The labor-left had filled an important role by providing labor attorneys for Sleepy Lagoon defendants. By 1950-51, the Roybal and Ríos-led CSO enjoyed access to a previously unknown level of legal and political resources; while the Bloody Christmas defendants ultimately found their own employer provided counsel.

Ríos generated headlines by attacking a communist "front group," the Committee to Preserve American Freedom, for the unauthorized use of his name and for seeking "to exploit police abuses for their own totalitarian ends."[68] For Ríos, the militant union leader with good relations with much of the non-communist left, the incident reflected genuine antipathy towards "Stalinists." The incident reflected the need for progressives such as Roybal, Ríos, and CSO, who were left of center, to avoid association with the marginalized communists. Roybal expressed this concern the previous year by adopting the campaign tagline, "To drive out Communism, we must strike at the conditions which foster its growth." After his successful defense effort, Ríos reluctantly assumed control over a CIO-led union organizing drive designed to prevent the communist-led United Electrical Workers Local 1421 from taking over a large plant on the Eastside. He was successful due, in part, to his new celebrity status as well as to long established relationships with labor priests and union officials supportive of CSO. The union election campaign enjoyed Roybal's informal support.[69]

Unfortunately, the highly publicized trials did not end the tension between the Mexican American community and the Los Angeles Police Department, although conditions temporarily improved, according to defendants Manuel Hernández and Tony Ríos.[70] The LAPD continued to insist on its autonomy from outside review and to place a higher priority on combating corruption than eliminating brutality. In weathering the storm of public criticism, it adapted its practices to reduce the probability of a future scandal.[71] In 1953, Chief Parker moved Officer Julio Gonzales into the department's public information division and then in 1955, Gonzales was paired with Lieutenant Tom Bradley, an African American, to staff the nation's first community relations office.[72] Roybal and CSO worked with Gonzales and Bradley, but also monitored LAPD activities. In 1956, CSO and the ACLU took up the cause of thirteen-year-old David Hidalgo, a case in which the jury in a civil suit found two Los Angeles deputy sheriffs guilty of brutality.[73] That same year CSO's Eliseo Carrillo joined the ACLU board and served as a liaison between the two groups. The ties were formalized in 1956 when Roybal helped establish an East Los Angeles chapter of the ACLU that focused on police-community issues.[74]

Councilman Roybal's public criticism of the LAPD for beating Ríos in 1952 and his help in establishing an ACLU chapter in 1957 reflected both his desire to challenge the status quo and the realization that he lacked the votes to make legislative changes within city government.[75] This made the trials and exposés all the more remarkable. Forcing the city to grapple with police conduct in the Latino community was the only notable liberal victory in a city where the council voted against fair employment, mandated communist registration, ended rent control, and was in the process of withdrawing from federally-funded public housing. Equally important, all of this was occurring at a time of rightward shift in state and national politics. In November 1952, California went the way of the nation, voting Republican in a presidential race for the first time since the beginning of the Great Depression. The victor was Dwight D. Eisenhower, Commander-In-Chief of the Allied Forces in World War II and a nonpartisan moderate in the tradition of Governor Earl Warren.

Ironically, CSO's greatest victory also coincided with the most fundamental change within the organization since its founding. With financial assistance from local labor and liberal allies, CSO was able to maintain an office and a secretary, but not an organizer. Fred Ross, for his part, needed to support his family. So, with a sad heart he accepted a part-time position as the executive director of the California Federation for Civic Unity, a San Francisco-based civil rights group. Councilman Roybal hosted the send-off celebration in his home. The fete included leaders from the three Los Angeles CSO chapters and special guest Ernesto Galarza, now

Director of Research and Education for the AFL National Farm Labor Union, who had used his position to urge Mexican Americans to become more politically engaged.[76] Before leaving Los Angeles, Ross helped organize CSO's fourth chapter, the Los Nietos CSO, in southeastern Los Angeles County. Leadership for the chapter came from CSO members who had recently moved from East Los Angeles to the developing suburbs.[77]

CSO was well positioned to extend its influence despite its financial problems and the growing conservatism of the times, as success in the Tony Ríos and Bloody Christmas beating trials bred new interest in the organization outside of Los Angeles. So powerful were these legal achievements that news about the case spread like wildfire by word of mouth throughout the state's barrios, and even throughout the greater Southwest. It was time for CSO to expand beyond Los Angeles and to strengthen its alliances with Latinos in other states. Success would result from addressing unmet community needs. As in Los Angeles, the Catholic Church, labor unions, and liberal groups would play a significant role in the CSO's growth.

CHAPTER 7

STATEWIDE CANDIDATES
AND
STATEWIDE NETWORKS

The prosecution of Los Angeles police officers for their role in the Bloody Christmas beatings served to illustrate the ability of the Mexican American community to achieve justice in an increasingly conservative era. This facilitated the expansion of the Community Services Organization (CSO) beyond the borders of Los Angeles County. Its growth occurred in tandem with new statewide initiatives by liberal Democrats and civil rights advocates. CSO members participated in the formation, in 1953, of both the California Democratic Council (CDC) and the California Committee for Fair Employment Practices. For Californians, 1953 represented a political transition for yet another reason: President Dwight D. Eisenhower appointed Governor Earl Warren as Chief Justice to the United States Supreme Court, removing the popular Republican moderate from state politics.[1] In this political environment, his successor, Republican Governor Goodwin Knight, would partner with President Eisenhower and Republican U.S. Senator Thomas Kuchel in reaching out to the growing number of Mexican American voters.

California in the mid-1950s was less contentious and less polarized than any time since the 1930s, despite Republican control of a state in which Democrats constituted a majority of registered voters. Knight governed from the political center, continuing the practice established by Governor Warren. In so doing, he demonstrated a link to the populist tradition of progressive Republicans such as Hiram Johnson, whose reforms included the voter initiative and Workers Compensation for those injured on the job. If Knight represented the most liberal wing of the Republican Party, Vice President Richard Nixon represented its center, and U.S. Senator William Knowland, whose family owned the *Oakland Tribune*, spoke for the party's rightwing. At the same time, the left's influence in state politics had been eclipsed with the end of the New Deal, the routing of the communists and their allies from their leadership posts in the CIO and other liberal organizations, and the severed relationships that resulted from the failed Wallace campaign. In this environment, the AFL, representing about a fourth of the workforce, assumed new prominence as pragmatic liberals who were willing to work with moderate Republicans.[2]

In yet another political development important to Latinos, Congress passed legislation making it easier to become a citizen. This CSO-led legislative victory belied conventional political alignments while speaking volumes about the group's interpersonal relationships and political sophistication. As part of his crusade against communism, Nevada's U.S. Senator, Pat McCarran, a conservative Democrat, undertook the most fundamental reform of immigration laws since 1924. The 1952 Walter-McCarran Act attacked the civil liberties of immigrants by making it easier to deport people the government perceived to be radicals.[3] Though CSO and most liberals opposed the measure, CSO leaders sought to use it as a vehicle for long sought reform. Hope Mendoza Schechter, Congressman Chet Holifield's Latino liaison, had the East Los Angeles representative ask Senator McCarran to change the bill to expand citizenship eligibility and to allow long-term residents to take the exam in their native language. Schechter recalled that Holifield used the phrase "it's politically important" to McCarran. Holifield also "flattered" McCarran, remembered Harvey Schechter, himself a Jewish civil rights leader, telling the senator that he "would go down in history and this doesn't change the essence of the Act."[4] The result was a small but dramatic change in immigration policy. According to a contemporary CSO history, *American Democracy Is Not A Fake*, "for the first time, Spanish-speaking aliens who met the minimum requirements of being, at that time, over fifty years of age and having resided continuously in the U.S. for over twenty years, could have their citizenship examination in Spanish rather than English."[5] The new citizenship rules shaped CSO's statewide strategy for a decade, allowing it to simultaneously focus on both voter registration and citizenship classes.

The Community Services Organization continued to be the most important vehicle for Latino empowerment. Fred Ross' efforts in Los

Angeles had been so successful that he could not stop organizing for the group after his mid-1952 move to the San Francisco Bay Area to work for another organization. Soon, Ross set his sights on San Jose, home of a large Mexican American community. Quevedo had spoken there under the aegis of the San Jose Coordinating Council for Latin-American Youth during World War II and the left had tried to organize cannery workers, losing to the Teamsters in 1945—due in part to opposition of the AFL and the Catholic church. Utilizing the tactics that he had honed in organizing the first four CSO chapters, Ross began to talk to barrio priests, labor leaders, social workers, and public health nurses in San Jose in search of indigenous leaders. Alicia Hernández, a public health nurse, assumed the duties as temporary chair of CSO's San Jose chapter.[6]

Father Donald McDonnell, founder of Our Lady of Guadalupe Church in San Jose, was most receptive to Ross' ideas. Like Monsignor Thomas O'Dwyer in Los Angeles, he was to play a critical role in the organization's success. McDonnell headed the Mission Band, formed in 1950 to minister to migrant farm workers and Mexican Americans living in urban barrios throughout Northern California. This ministry, which included a strong dose of social action, emerged from the fourth annual conference of the Bishops' Committee for the Spanish Speaking. Archbishop Robert Lucy led the Bishops' Committee, with whom McDonnell remained in contact even after the Mission Band affiliated with the National Catholic Rural Life Conference. The Latino-oriented clergy also linked themselves to the National Catholic Welfare Council and the bishops' National Catholic Social Action Department, led by Monsignor George G. Higgins, who worked with Archbishop Lucy and the Los Angeles based Catholic Labor Institute. Father McDonnell also developed ties to AFL farm worker organizer Ernesto Galarza.[7]

Father McDonnell referred Ross to César Chávez to whom he had been teaching the social gospel. The twenty-five-year-old World War II veteran had become a migrant worker after his family lost their farm in Arizona during the Depression. Chávez moved to San Jose with other members of his extended family to work in the fields but now, with agricultural work slow, he labored part-time in a lumberyard. Chávez was initially dubious of Ross' intentions but agreed

to host a house meeting where Ross focused on neighborhood ir-
ritants, such as poor drainage. He then used the Los Angeles CSO
story to demonstrate the power of organization. "He talked about
the CSO, and the famous Bloody Christmas case in Los Angeles,"
said Chávez. "I didn't know what CSO was, or who this guy Fred
Ross was, but I knew about the Bloody Christmas case, and so did
everybody in that room. Five cops actually had been jailed for brutality. And that miracle was the result of CSO efforts."[8]

"[Ross] did such a good job of explaining how poor people could
build power that I could even taste it. I could really feel it," recalled
Chávez.[9] He volunteered to help register voters in the San Jose area.
But the drive got off to a rocky start when Santa Clara County initially refused to deputize a Mexican American as a registrar, before
finally agreeing to deputize the son of the local Mexican grocery
store proprietor. Chávez acted as "bird dog," going door-to-door
identifying people who wanted to register. The lone registrar followed behind, signing up the identified individuals. After a while,
Ross appointed Chávez to head the registration committee, and
the youthful leader began to recruit his friends to help with voter
registration, but there were limits to how many people one person
could register. "At this point the Los Angeles CSO was solicited for
help," recalled Josephine Duveneck, a Quaker who hosted Ross in
her home and who debriefed him every morning. CSO went to their
allies within the Los Angeles Central Labor Council who, in turn,
placed "pressure on the AF of L Central Labor Council in Santa
Clara" to persuade the local registrar to add additional deputy registrars. CSO proceeded to sign-up 6,000 new voters in Santa Clara
County, making Mexican Americans a potential force in San Jose
politics for the first time.[10]

The San Jose CSO's first experience with voting in November
1952 was a "disaster," according to Chávez, because "the Republican
Central Committee decided to intimidate the people that were voting for the first time." CSO agreed to contact the U.S. Attorney
General with a complaint, but Herman Gallegos, the chapter president and a county social worker just out of college, declined to sign
the telegram out of fear it would jeopardize his job. Chávez volunteered to put his name on the message and it became news.[11]

"[T]he Republicans accused us of registering illegals and dead people. We called them racists," said Chávez. The Federal Bureau of Investigation then visited Chávez at the lumberyard where he was working and, seeking to resolve the case, took him to a mediation session with the Republican Party leaders. Chávez quoted an FBI agent as telling the GOP leaders, "Well, we have enough of these problems in Mississippi and the South, and we don't want to have any of this nonsense here in California."[12]

Told by the FBI to stop intimidating Mexican American voters, the Republicans switched tactics, accusing Chávez and CSO of being communists. Chávez responded by organizing the clergy. "I got some of the Catholic priests in town together with the help of Father McDonnell, and they put out a statement that we weren't communists," said Chávez. The rightwing attack on CSO attracted the attention of area liberals, with whom Chávez developed a lasting friendship. "From then on, every little place I went, I met the liberal lawyer, the liberal teacher, the liberal social worker."[13]

The success of the San Jose experience led Saul Alinsky to raise the funds to hire Ross and Chávez to organize CSO statewide in 1953. The duo started in the San Francisco Bay Area cities of Decoto (now part of Union City) and Oakland, in Salinas, and in the Central Valley towns of Madera and Merced.

"Red-baiting in Madera was the worst I ever experienced," according to Chávez. This was because Latina Josephine Daniels had run for Congress in 1948 on the Independent Progressive Party ticket. As a result, people "assumed anyone starting a registration drive must be a Communist." Despite the difficulty, CSO built a strong chapter, registering 300 new voters and conducting citizenship classes for another 300. When older people attempted to take the naturalization test in Spanish as the law allowed under the Walter-McCarran Act, the examination officer in Madera attacked CSO as subversive. CSO challenged the behavior of the Madera hearing officer by going over his head. The group convinced Bishop Aloysius Willinger of Fresno to write General Joseph Swing, Eisenhower's chief of the Immigration Naturalization Service, and vouch for CSO. After Willinger arranged for the group to meet with the examiner's supervisor in Fresno the examiner developed a much more cooperative attitude. Mexican Americans in Madera had never seen such a political accomplishment by a Latino organization.[14]

The lengths that CSO went to promote its citizenship classes, and to insist that government officials follow the law, demonstrated anew that access to national political leaders and institutions could be vital to succeeding in local communities. The Madera incident also underscored the centrality of citizenship to the organization's mission. CSO differed from GI Forum and LULAC in their outreach to non-citizens. "We are endeavoring to have these potential citizens participate actively on our many committees," stated Roybal in 1953. "This, we think, will give them first hand knowledge of the many civic problems that confront the [city council] district and will help them become better Americans."[15]

In addition to voter registration and citizenship classes, each CSO chapter lobbied their state legislators to support legislation to make long-term non-citizens eligible for state Old Age Pensions.[16] The bill, A.B. 2059, was first introduced in 1953 by Los Angeles Assemblyman Vernon Kilpatrick, who had spoken out on the issue of police brutality during the Tony Ríos and Bloody Christmas cases. The issue of benefits for elderly immigrants, many of whose children fought and died in World War II, had surfaced during CSO's house meetings in 1947. At the time the CSO was not in a position to pursue the issue, but now, with CSO's growing statewide presence, it made strategic sense to pursue the issue in the state legislature.[17]

Even as CSO projected its power statewide, however, politics in Los Angeles were changing. The biggest shift occurred in 1953 when conservative Republican Congressman Norris Poulson rode the wave of anti-public housing sentiment to defeat Mayor Fletcher Bowron, a nonpartisan, reform-minded Republican close to Roybal and CSO. Public housing was a popular New Deal program that provided livable space for families of modest means. Roybal joined organized labor and the faith community in supporting the expansion of public housing. Catholic, Protestant, and Jewish leaders published an ad in the *Los Angeles Mirror* advocating "Decent Homes for all the children of God." On the other hand, realtors attacked the program as communistic, using the slogan "Don't pay someone else's rent" on billboards. As a result, public housing construction stopped and the city's politics shifted right as the ethos of individualism and market capitalism replaced the New Deal emphasis on the common good and improving the lot of working families. Los Angeles Latinos lost out on the opportunity to benefit from the creation of high quality affordable housing. The mayoral election also had an immediate consequence: Latinos placed on city boards and commissions by Mayor Bowron lost their posts.[18]

The role of CSO within Boyle Heights also continued to evolve, in part because the mother chapter had achieved most of its initial goals. Moreover, its founding members were moving on to other aspects of their lives—starting families, attending college, and buying homes, usually in developing suburbs. The general movement out of old neighborhoods had been in process since the end of World War II, even as Roybal emerged as a political powerhouse. The two leaders to share the stage at Roybal's final 1951 rally, Bill Phillips and María Durán, were emblematic of this transition. María Durán remarried, retired from the garment industry, and moved east into the desert to open a Mexican restaurant. Music store proprietor Bill Phillips moved his family to the westside, settling near the Fairfax district, while retaining his shop in Boyle Heights. Other key allies also moved out of the neighborhood. Father William Barry was promoted to run Catholic Charities in Long Beach and in growing

Councilman Edward Roybal, CSO leader María Durán, Los Angeles Mayor Fletcher Bowron, and Eastside Sun *publisher Eli Kovner. Mexican Americans supported the mayor in his unsuccessful reelection campaign in 1953.* (Kenneth C. Burt)

communities in Orange County. The Latino, Jewish, and Irish residents who left Boyle Heights were generally replaced by Latinos from other parts of Los Angeles County (for whom Boyle Heights represented upward mobility), or by farm workers brought into the country as braceros that then decided to blend into the urban environment instead of returning to Mexico.[19]

Other CSO leaders and members followed María Durán out of their old neighborhoods and into largely Anglo areas. "Housing was real scarce," recalled her daughter, Margarita Durán Méndez, the social worker who married autoworker James Méndez and moved to Norwalk. "We had thought we'd buy a house in the City Terrace or East Los Angeles and stay close to the neighborhood. We couldn't find anything. And these houses came really cheap. A $100 down. Naturally we moved down here."[20] She added that her situation was similar to many of her friends. Henry Nava bought a house in Monterey Park. Hope Mendoza Schechter moved to the San Fernando Valley, as did Julian Nava. Margarita Durán Méndez also reflected a second social trend. Among the first Latinas in Los Angeles to attend college and obtain a professional job, in the early fifties she also joined the millions of women who left the workforce to raise their children. She referred to it as a "nesting instinct" consistent with the times. By contrast, Hope Mendoza Schechter adopted a less common approach; she chose not to have her own children, and this (along with a supportive husband) provided the opportunity to remain politically and professionally active on a full-time basis.[21]

Initially, this movement to the suburbs made little difference within the Los Angeles CSO because the activists returned to the Eastside for political activities and new activists stepped forward to assume leadership roles. In Lincoln Heights, public health care nurse Henrietta Villaescusa became the first woman president of a Los Angeles area chapter. She decided not to marry and to devote her life to her career and community. Such a highly personal decision reduced the challenge of juggling family responsibilities and allowed her to devote more time to community activities and to her political passions. The momentum within CSO in Los Angeles also continued because the group adopted new projects with community allies. For example, CSO partnered with the International

Councilman Edward Roybal, Monsignor Thomas O'Dwyer, and Father John Birch at a Catholic Youth Organization-sponsored event. Roybal remained close to church leaders, working together on a variety of issues and programs important to Latinos. *(Kenneth C. Burt)*

Institute and the Catholic Labor Institute to offer citizenship class-es. Over the next few years, however, with participation waning, CSO consolidated its chapters in Boyle Heights, Lincoln Heights, and Belvedere into one strong unit.[22]

CSO also took up a cause first advocated by Eduardo Quevedo more than a decade earlier—the appointment of a Latino judge in Los Angeles. (The recent death of Judge A.P. Molina in San Diego, the Olson appointee, meant that there was no longer a sitting Latino judge in California.)[23] While CSO was unsuccessful in obtaining a state judicial appointment, the organization did obtain a number of slots on local boards and commissions. One of the most important in the long-term development of Los Angeles County was Tony Ríos' tenure on the five-member Los Angeles County Park Commission. As the representative of Supervisor Herbert Legg, whom Mexican Americans had helped elect in 1950, Ríos secured funding to ex-pand and develop a number of parks in East Los Angeles and the Whittier Narrows Recreation Area regional park.[24]

More partisan activists also joined Democratic clubs affiliated with the California Democratic Council. CDC grew out of the 1952 Adlai Stevenson presidential campaign. It articulated a broad lib-eral vision and sought to organize along partisan lines to regain political control of the state. In November 1953, the group elected realtor Alan Cranston as its president. He had helped stop the Zoot Suit Riots at the behest of President Roosevelt and had more re-cently donated furniture to the upstart CSO chapter in San Jose.[25] "[M]ost of the Negroes and Mexican Americans who were active in California Democratic politics were in attendance," according to CDC's Fredrick Tuttle.[26] Most Latinos in CDC were college-educated professionals, entrepreneurs, or union leaders. A number bore the imprint of CSO training, such as social worker Henrietta Villaescusa, the past president of the Lincoln Heights CSO.[27] The CDC also included leftists like Bert Corona, the former Los Angeles CIO leader, who moved to Oakland to work in his father-in-law's jewelry business, where he joined the CSO. Corona was representa-tive of many activists from the old popular front milieu who in the early fifties joined the new liberal-led social movements following the demise of the Independent Progressive Party and the National Association of Mexican-Americans. In doing so, they contributed their leadership skills and helped infuse new energy into both grassroots organizing and coalition politics.[28]

The third statewide group to form in 1953 was the California Committee for Fair Employment Practices. This group was an outgrowth of the Los Angeles-based Council for Equality in Employment, the coalition formed in 1949 to back the Roybal-introduced Equal Opportunity Ordinance. These organizational representatives merged with a similar network in Northern California to more effectively advocate state legislation. The group selected as its chair C.L. Dellums of Oakland who was the West Coast head of the AFL Brotherhood of Sleeping Car Porters and the regional leader of the NAACP. Dellums personified the long struggle for fair employment. A close associate of A. Philip Randolph, he participated in the campaign that resulted in Roosevelt's 1941 executive order banning discrimination in the production of war materials. Like Randolph, Dellums was a progressive with old Socialist Party ties. Another socialist, William "Bill" Becker, who had organized California farm workers with Ernesto Galarza, became the civil rights group's chief lobbyist.[29]

Councilman Roybal and CSO fit well within this progressive milieu. Roybal was named as a co-chair of California Committee for Fair Employment Practices along with old allies from the CIO, Catholic Church, and the Jewish community. The group also drew leadership from Northern California, including C.J. "Neil" Haggerty, the head of the AFL California Federation of Labor. Josephine Duveneck, the Quaker leader who provided Ross a room in her home near San Jose, became the group's treasurer. CSO president and steel worker Tony Ríos represented Mexican Americans on its board, which served to further extend his already extensive political network. Herman Gallegos in San Jose and Margaret Cruz in San Francisco provided invaluable linkages between CSO and the fair employment advocates in Northern California.[30]

Popular within labor and minority circles, Roybal won praise from grassroots Democratic activists who met in 1954 under the aegis of the newly organized California Democratic Council to endorse a slate of statewide candidates. CDC's immediate objective was to ensure a full compliment of Democratic candidates on the November ballot by defeating the cross-filing Republicans in the primary. This would be easier than in past years because, due to a voter-passed initiative, the ballot would list each candidate's party in legislative and constitutional offices for the first time in years. The larger goal was to use the election to strengthen the Democratic Party so that it would be able to complete with the entrenched Republicans four years hence.[31]

Attorney General Edmund G. "Pat" Brown, the lone Democrat to hold statewide office, declined to confront an uphill campaign for governor and CDC backed him for another term as the state's top law enforcement official. The delegates endorsed Richard Graves to run against Governor Knight. He was the executive director of the League of Cities, and until recently a nonpartisan Republican in the Warren tradition. For U.S. Senate, the body backed Congressman Samuel Yorty against Thomas Kuchel, a moderate appointed by Warren to fill the seat left vacant by Richard Nixon's elevation to the vice presidency. An AFL favorite, Yorty generated passionate responses because of his political evolution from a popular front leftist to an ardent anti-communist labor-liberal. The endorsement of Graves and Yorty upset the more liberal delegates who wanted to run an unapologetic progressive campaign instead of promoting centrists and focusing on the arduous task of party building.[32]

This feeling of rebellion among the rank-and-file delegates corresponded to the lack of an identified frontrunner for the post of lieutenant governor. Graves and the state party chair, George Miller, pushed Assemblyman William Munnell from East Los Angeles, and California Democratic Council leaders backed attorney Steve Zetterberg, past president of the Los Angeles Democratic Club. Liberal and progressive elements championed Roybal, whose name had been mentioned prior to the convention but who had not planned on a statewide campaign. His acceptance of the nomination and convention victory "excited everybody," according to Roybal campaign manager Roger Johnson, "because he was going to be . . . the first Spanish-speaking person to run for the office."[33]

Fred Ross, the Industrial Areas Foundation's West Coast Director, was among those most excited by the prospect of the Roybal candidacy. In a letter Ross expressed how the Roybal campaign would animate CSO organizing efforts and would in turn help his campaign.

> I don't have to draw a picture for you of the importance of this de-
> cision both with regard to the morale-heightening effect it will have
> on the Spanish-speaking people of California, facilitation of CSO's
> program of voter registration and membership, as well as the oppor-
> tunity the campaign will provide for establishing the name of Roybal
> as a household expression throughout California . . . . CSO members
> have been spreading the good word all through the Salinas Valley, the
> Santa Clara Valley and Southern Alameda County.[34]

Ross added that he and CSO's newly hired third organizer, Gene Lowrey, would soon be talking up Roybal in Fresno and San Bernardino. The new San Bernardino County CSO signed-up prospective voters and recruited 700-750 people to take the English and citizenship classes it had organized in supportive churches.[35]

The symbolic convergence of these forces—Roybal as candidate for lieutenant governor and CSO as a growing organization—came together over the weekend of March 20-21, 1954 when the candidate and founding CSO president addressed CSO's National Founding Convention.[36] The ethnic leaders held the historic event at the conference center at Asilomar, in Monterey County, where Roybal and others had launched CDC the previous year. CSO elected steel worker Tony Ríos, police beating victim and the past president of the Los Angeles CSO, as its first state and national president (the group had designs on moving into other states).

In addition to Mexican Americans, Roybal's low budget campaign for lieutenant governor "relied pretty heavily on organized labor and organized CDC groups, and other Democratic groups," according to Roger Johnson. Support was strongest from CIO and progressive AFL unions, like the needle trades—the constellation of groups that proved central to Roybal's defeat of City Councilman Parley P. Christensen in 1949.[37]

As in the 1949 Los Angeles City Council election, in 1954 the AFL played it safe, choosing to support an incumbent with whom it enjoyed a positive relationship. Governor Knight paid particularly close attention to the AFL concerns. He had appointed AFL officials to state posts, raised unemployment benefits for the first time in six years, and promised to oppose any effort by his party's right-wing to enact a so-called Right-to-Work law to undercut collective bargaining. As a result, the AFL not only endorsed Knight's election but also his choice for lieutenant governor—Harold Powers, a Modoc County cattle rancher—against Roybal. A vocal minority within the AFL in Los Angeles formed a "Southern California Committee for Graves-Roybal."[38]

In the June 1954 primary, Roybal won his party's nomination as did all of the California Democratic Council-backed candidates. Roybal continued to use his city council seat to generate publicity as well as to maintain and build relationships. A case in point was his council resolution, co-sponsored by Rosalind Wyman, a Jewish councilwoman elected in 1951, praising the Friendship Day Camp. The interracial children's summer camp had grown out of the Friendship Festival in Boyle Heights. CSO's Tony Ríos was one of three directors who incorporated the camp in May 1953. The board then expanded to include steel worker and CSO leader Gilbert Anaya and Los Angeles Police Department Lieutenant Tom Bradley. Ezra Weintraub, the son of *Jewish Daily Forward* editor and a garment union ally, served as camp director. The Friendship Day Camp thus served an important secondary purpose: networking multicultural progressives who worked and lived in different parts of Los Angeles but shared a common dream.[39]

For the November 1954 election, Roybal traversed the state by automobile, campaigning before a variety of audiences. In San Diego, Roybal "was very strongly supported by the community," said educator Armando Rodríguez, a World War II veteran inspired by Saul Alinsky's vision for Latino self-empowerment.[40] The campaign also used technology to reach beyond the ethnic organizations. "We had a secret weapon. Every time we would go into a town, a small town, no matter how small, we would have access to the [Spanish language] radio," said Roger Johnson. "This was a very important thing in getting people to be interested in Roybal, and also to get active."[41] Many of those hearing about Roybal over the radio were newly registered voters. This was particularly true in places like San Jose where Eduardo Quevedo introduced Roybal to a bilingual crowd at a rally at the Civic Auditorium.[42] The excitement over having a Mexican American on the ballot likewise reached into the Central Valley, according to Richard Chávez, who helped organize CSO in Kern County.[43] Alvina Carrillo and other Latinas in CSO provided much of the clerical support in Roybal's Los Angeles headquarters.[44] Roybal also received help from Californio Lucretia del Valle

Grady. The state's former Democratic National Committeewoman headed the state women's committee for Roybal.[45]

Despite these efforts, Democrats lost the statewide elections, with Republicans—led by Governor Goodwin Knight, the AFL endorsed moderate—winning all but one statewide office and maintaining control of the state legislature. Attorney General Pat Brown's reelection provided the lone exception to the Republican sweep. However, Roybal emerged from the process with enhanced stature because of his energetic campaigning and his receiving more votes than the party's gubernatorial candidate. "GOP Knight, Dem Roybal Strong Men," read the post-election headline in the *Los Angeles Mirror*.[46] A more general result of the 1954 campaign was the stimulation of Latino voter participation in urban and rural areas around the state. "I know in my area, as a direct result of [his] campaign in 1954, the increased activity among the Spanish-speaking community was just phenomenal," stated Phillip Burton, a CDC activist in San Francisco.[47]

While Roybal and CSO were extending their influence in California, they were also networking with activists throughout the Southwest. The American Council of Spanish Speaking Organizations served as the primary vehicle. New Mexico Lieutenant Governor Tibo Chávez headed the council, which was at its core a collaboration of four organizations: the California-based CSO, the Arizona-based Hispano Americano Alianza, and the Texas-based LULAC and GI Forum. The council's members shared a positive post-war optimism and strong identification with their Latino roots and their U.S. citizenship. However, the Californians were the only ones to favor the term "Mexican American," according to founding delegate Hope Mendoza Schechter of Los Angeles. Representatives from other states preferred terms such as Latin, Spanish-American, or Hispano. Two Californians—CSO President Tony Ríos and Pomona-based *El Espectador* publisher Ignacio López—were elected to the board of the American Council of Spanish Speaking Organizations.[48]

The GI Forum, like CSO, was young and dynamic. The Forum was founded in Texas in 1949, the same year Roybal was elected to the Los Angeles City Council. It grew out of the successful use of political power to right an injustice. In January 1949, the body of Pvt. Félix Longoria, who had died fighting for the liberation of the

Philippines in World War II, was returned to Texas. His hometown cemetery refused to bury him because he was a "Mexican." Dr. Héctor P. García, a captain in the war, heard about the incident from the young man's mother and sought to reason with the mortuary but to no avail. Dr. García appealed for help to a number of politicians, including U.S. Senator Lyndon B. Johnson, who had won a razor thin race in Texas in 1948 with Latino support. In his communications with Johnson and others, Dr. García sought to use patriotism to trump racial prejudice, emphasizing the man had died in uniform. It worked. Senator Johnson went to the White House, and President Truman approved Longoria's burial at the National Cemetery in Arlington, Virginia, among the nation's military heroes.[49]

This regional expansion in political power led individuals outside the Governor Knight wing of the Republican Party to look more seriously at the Latino vote. In late 1954, Murray Chotiner, a Los Angeles advisor to Vice President Nixon, suggested that he use his office to attract the Spanish-speaking. "[T]here is a feeling that we are overlooking our friends to the South" with the post-World War II focus on Europe, stated the advisor. "This is, in the opinion of many, affecting our ability to win the votes of the people of Mexican descent for our candidates . . . . We cannot win [their votes] by appointing a Chairman of a Latin-American Committee four weeks before each election."[50] Shortly afterward, Nixon toured Mexico, where he met with President Adolfo Ruiz Cortines, as well as other nations in Latin America.

Despite courting from the Republicans, the Latino community remained largely Democratic in orientation and nonpartisan in organization. For its part, CSO strengthened its ties to the Catholic Church, the only organization with an organic relationship to the Mexican American community and a presence in every city and town with a barrio. After the American Council of the Spanish Speaking Organizations died as a casualty of insufficient funding, the Bishops' Committee for the Spanish Speaking stepped forward and helped maintain the multi-state and multi-organization network. In 1954 the Bishops' Committee used its newsletter to praise CSO, noting with pride that Rudy Ynostrosa had won a city council seat in Soledad and Camilo Díaz had won a seat in González, two agricultural communities east of Monterey.[51]

CSO also received a big boost from the National Conference of Catholic Charities, which vouched for the organization to local priests when necessary. The Right Reverend Monsignor John O'Grady toured the state in early 1955, meeting with hundreds of CSO members in twelve urban and rural chapters. O'Grady summarized what he had heard from CSO members in the *Catholic Charities Review*:

> For years we have lived in fear—fear of government, fear of the big growers. We are ready to stand up and be counted.
> Many thousands of our people have been registered as voters in all the areas in which the Community Service Organization has been set up. They are not only registering, they are actually going to the polls. In the last election the percentage of people of Mexican extraction voting was well above the State average. Since our people have been registering and going to the polls, local officials are beginning to pay attention to us. They are cooperating in the setting up of citizenship classes. . . . They are attended not only by young people but also by those well along in years.

Monsignor O'Grady underscored the role of the clergy in CSO's success by noting that Father Thomas McCullough from the Mission Band spent five weeks helping CSO conduct house meetings in Stockton, an agricultural town south of Sacramento, where school teacher Dolores Huerta was emerging as a natural leader.[52]

The national CSO, led by President Tony Ríos, had fifteen chapters in California and ten in Arizona by July 1955. The five newest California chapters included two in Los Angeles County (San Fernando and West Los Angeles), two in the Central Valley (Stockton and Kings County), and one on the central coast (San Benito). While extending its base geographically, CSO continued to run registration drives and citizenship classes, and—through Tony Ríos and others—maintained relationships with African American leaders, the Jewish community, and trade unionists. CSO made former newspaperman Henry Santiestevan of the Los Angeles CIO its director of publicity.[53] Moreover, the Los Angeles CSO chapter's fifth president, Butchers union president J.J. Rodríguez, continued to provide statewide leadership because the group did things on a grand scale. For example, in the fall of 1955, CSO sponsored a mass swearing-in of 3,000 new citizens at the Hollywood Bowl.[54]

Women taught many of the citizenship classes in Los Angeles and Pauline Holguín served as the local CSO treasurer. The former secretary-treasurer of ILGWU Local 384, she represented the continuing influence of the garment union in the CSO.[55]

While CSO was a perfect vehicle for working class and emerging middle class individuals around the state, it was not the ideal organization for everyone, particularly in Los Angeles, where returning veterans from World War II and Korea had helped to create a new, expanded middle and upper-middle class. As a result, a number of new organizations arose to address the needs of emerging professionals and small business owners, many of whom lived in the developing suburbs but maintained cultural and political ties to the Eastside. The most important group in Los Angeles was the Council on Mexican-American Affairs (CMAA). It included attorneys, union leaders and small businessmen, as well as a number of elected and appointed officials. A few former CSO members joined, including student activist-turned-teacher Ralph Poblano. CMAA thus served to network middle class activists and groups, took positions on issues such as police brutality, and advocated political appointments that they saw as both individual advancement and achievements for Mexican Americans as a group.[56]

For his part, Roybal remained the liberals' liberal. He was an important source of ethnic pride and a skilled practitioner of coalition politics. In 1955, he again authored a fair employment city ordinance, which lost on an eight to seven vote. Roybal was one of the brightest stars at the Los Angeles County Conference on Human Relations' tenth anniversary banquet.[57] He gained national notoriety in a *Readers Digest* story on Mexican Americans in 1956.[58] That year civil rights forces introduced yet another fair employment ordinance at the county level. United Steel Workers' official and past CSO president Gilbert Anaya served as co-chair of the Los Angeles Committee for Equal Opportunity with NAACP leader Loren Miller.[59] The years 1955 and 1956 culminated in a highpoint of multiculturalism as measured by the attendance of 25,000 each year at the Friendship Festival in Boyle Heights.[60]

The liberal networks overlapped into the electoral arena. In terms of issues, CSO joined Republican Governor Goodwin Knight and Democratic Attorney General Pat Brown in backing Proposition 13.

This proposition repealed the anti-Asian Alien Land Law, which was not only important to the Japanese Americans with whom CSO worked, but also raised CSO's visibility as the organization was listed as an initiative proponent in the state's official ballot arguments mailed to every voter.[61] In terms of partisan politics, Roybal became the first Los Angeles Latino to attend a Democratic National Convention as part of the 1956 Pat Brown-led Stevenson delegation. (Lucretia del Valle, from Berkeley, attended several times for Roosevelt).[62] Neither Stevenson nor the Democratic Party targeted Latinos as had Roosevelt or the Progressive Party's Henry Wallace. A chagrined Roybal publicly stated that a "mere 100,000 minority votes either way might spell victory or defeat for our party in the close election coming up." He pointed out that Republican U.S. Senator Thomas Kuchel had organized a statewide organization targeted towards minority voters.[63] Spanish-speaking voters were positioned to decide a close election in 1956 because, according to CSO, the voter rolls included 166,000 Latinos, who comprised 2.5 percent of potential voters.[64]

The effort by Republican candidates to court the growing number of Latino voters was truly historic in its proportions, and was organized to support both Senator Thomas Kuchel and President Eisenhower. The timing for such an effort was ideal from the standpoint of the GOP. A good proportion were World War II veterans who had taken advantage of the GI Bill and had moved into the middle class. Eisenhower, as a war hero and political moderate, had natural appeal. Moreover, far reaching civil rights advancement had come two years earlier when the Supreme Court's Chief Justice Earl Warren had led an unanimous opinion in *Brown v. Board of Education* that outlawed segregation in public education. Kuchel pleased CSO by promising to investigate alleged discrimination on the part of the federal immigration officer in Madera.[65] He also worked with the Latino business community, arranging for President Eisenhower to send a greeting to the 1954 Mexican Independence Day celebration sponsored by the Mexican Chamber of Commerce in Los Angeles.[66]

For the 1956 general election, Latinos formed a Latin American Division within both the Eisenhower-Nixon and the Kuchel campaigns. The group received support from small businessmen and professionals, veterans, and pastors of Spanish-speaking Protestant congregations. The business leaders included a number of those who had operated around Eduardo Quevedo, including Dr. José Díaz, Dr. Camilo Servin and Armando Torres, who headed up the "Democratic Committee." This title reflected the fact that "80 percent" of the committees' work was directed at Latino Democrats.[67] Senator Kuchel personally courted Los Angeles Latinos by rallying supporters at Hollenbeck Junior High School in Boyle Heights.[68] The Republican campaigns reinforced the organizational activities with pro-Kuchel and pro-Eisenhower advertisements in *La Opinión*.[69]

President Eisenhower won a landslide reelection, with Stevenson carrying only six Southern states. No statistics exist on how the Latino community cast its vote, but it is fair to assume that a significant number voted for a Republican presidential candidate for the first time in their life. This is based on the unprecedented Latino outreach and Eisenhower's inroads among other core Democratic constituencies, particularly African Americans and union members. However, the Latino community received little in terms of immediate rewards for its unprecedented efforts and increased vote totals for a Republican president and a U.S. senator.[70]

The increased Republican Latino activity coincided with the establishment and growth of the GI Forum in California. First generation professionals or proprietors of small businesses comprised much of the membership. The first chapter was based in East Los Angeles. Early members included Councilman Roybal, and attorneys Leopoldo Sánchez and Carlos Terán. Soon chapters developed in Southwest Los Angeles and in the eastside community of Pico Rivera. Frank Pax, a civil engineer working for the City of Los Angeles, was elected as the first president of the California Forum. Over the next couple of years, Raúl Morín and George Sotelo took the lead in organizing GI Forum chapters throughout the state and in Las Vegas.[71]

The GI Forum chose as its first major project a campaign for the appointment of a Mexican American to the state judiciary, an issue the CSO raised earlier with Governor Knight. According to Boyle Heights pharmacist Edward Ramírez, the Forum decided to target the three-member East Los Angeles Municipal Court because "99.9 percent of the people who went before the court were

Mexican or Mexican American."[72] The Forum supported three candidates: Henry P. López, F. Fernández Solis, and Carlos M. Terán. It then undertook a petition drive to demonstrate to the governor that Latinos cared about their lack of representation.[73] The petition drive was supplemented by the lobbying of Latino and Anglo Eastside businessmen active in the Republican Party, such as mortuary owner Manuel Vega.[74]

The campaign culminated in Knight's decision to act. His ascribed motive, according to several activists close to the campaign, was that politically the time had come to appoint a Latino. Instead of making a selection based on a staff recommendation, Governor Knight personally interviewed the dozen eligible individuals.[75] He selected Carlos Terán. The young barrister had been an Army

Civil rights leaders with the California Committee for Fair Employment Practices meet with Governor Goodwin Knight (center) to talk about CSO's legislation for Old Age Pensions for Non-Citizens. Tony Ríos (ninth from left) and Gilbert Anaya (on right side) spoke for CSO and the United Steel Workers. Other key allies from the period are Rt. Rev. Monsignor Thomas O'Dwyer (in collar), and Max Mont (second from left) and Bill Becker (eighth from the left) from the Jewish Labor Committee. The lone woman was Josephine Duveneck, the Quaker leader who provided Fred Ross housing as he organized CSO in San Jose. (Kenneth C. Burt)

company commander in World War II before graduating from the University of Southern California Law School and becoming involved community affairs. Terán served as President of the Board of Directors of the Council of Mexican-American Affairs and as a member of the GI Forum.[76] That year, Knight also demonstrated an interest in civil rights by meeting with CSO leaders Tony Ríos and Gilbert Anaya as part of the California Committee for Fair Employment Practices delegation.[77]

About the same time as Terán was being promoted, CSO focused its statewide attention on advancing its bill for Non-Citizen Old Age Pensions, which was reintroduced in the 1957 legislature. Each chapter organized a series of lobbying activities. These included a delegation meeting with the local legislator, a letter writing campaign, and circulating petitions supporting the bill. "Petitions are now being circulated in Redlands, Colton, Fontana, as well as San Bernardino," announced the Inland Empire chapter. The Monterey chapter reported: "We received confirmation from our two representatives, Senator [Fred] Farr and Assemblyman [Alan] Pattee that they will fight for the *Pensiones*. Pattee informs us he is the co-author of the Bill." In addition to demonstrating the bill's importance to Latinos, CSO worked to obtain support from non-Latino groups, including "the Los Angeles County Board of Supervisors through the Board Chairman John Anson Ford."[78]

Later in 1957, the organization, now with twenty chapters in California, voted to engage the farm worker issue. State and National CSO President Tony Ríos worked closely with Ernesto Galarza, who had organized California's fields in the late forties and early fifties and who enjoyed a long association with CSO.[79] Galarza sensed that it would be possible in the years ahead to defeat the bracero program in Congress, which he saw as a precursor to effective unionization. He sent a copy of his book, *Strangers in the Fields*, to each CSO chapter president. Ríos assembled a panel to discuss the bracero program at the group's July 1957 board meeting at the Biltmore Hotel in Los Angeles. The Galarza-headed panel included labor leaders and Catholic priests from around the state. Father Donald McDonnell, Chávez's mentor, traveled from San Jose. Father Thomas McCullough, who taught Huerta the social gospel, drove from Stockton, where he joined with John

Henning, the San Francisco-based research director for the AFL California Federation of Labor, himself a product of the Catholic Worker movement. The two Los Angeles panelists were Bud Simonson, Los Angeles organizer for the United Packinghouse Workers, and Max Mont from Jewish Labor Committee. After the discussion, CSO named Galarza chair of a new committee to work on the issue. The Texas-based GI Forum also made fighting the bracero program a priority. These Latino activists were of much help to the national labor and religious led coalition because they linked the federal program to Mexican American poverty.[80]

For the first time, in the mid-1950s Latinos were beginning to achieve a civic voice at a state, local, and federal level. Latinos were voting in record numbers, seeking out elected and appointed office, and working in statewide coalitions. Edward Roybal served as the 1954 Democratic nominee for lieutenant governor and Latinos played a role in the era's two most important liberal networks, the California Democratic Council and the California Committee for Fair Employment Practices. CSO boosted the most impressive grassroots organization in the state; its twenty chapters in California strongly promoted state legislation creating old age pension for non-citizens and opposed the extension of the federal bracero program. These state and federal initiatives were based upon expanding political networks with non-Latinos and dynamic chapters that shifted the contours of local electoral politics. Using the model pioneered in Boyle Heights and repeated in the City of San Fernando, CSO conducted impressive get-out-the-vote campaigns to elect Mexican American city council members in the rural communities such as Soledad and Gonzalez. The community had even greater success in getting the attention of incumbent politicians who previously ignored Latino concerns. "In the last election the percentage of people of Mexican extraction voting was well above the State average," proclaimed a national Catholic Church official. Monsignor O'Grady also repeated CSO's mantra: "Since our people have been registering and going to the polls, local officials are beginning to pay attention to us."[81] It was a powerful message for a community enjoying the first taste of power. "We started a revolution," stated Richard Chávez, looking back on this era.[82]

Women contributed much of the unglamorous, behind-the-scenes work needed to propel the organization forward, from printing flyers to writing letters to preparing food for fundraisers. A number assumed high profile leadership roles. Mildred Serrano, for example, chaired the CSO convention in Fresno in 1957.[83] However, some of the most important early Latinas within CSO left the organization, changed jobs, and chose to focus on partisan politics. Hope Mendoza Schechter resigned her post as an ILGWU Business Agent to become a court reporter. Among CSO's first board members, she helped run the historic 1948 voter registration drive and played the critical role in convincing Congressman Chet Holifield to ask Senator McCarran to amend his immigration bill to ease citizenship requirements. Schechter remained close to Roybal, Holifield, and others associated with the early CSO, but her ever-expanding rolodex was increasingly centered on the Westside of Los Angeles. She immersed herself in the California Democratic Party, then controlled by elected officials, where she emerged as the best known Latina.[84] Other Latinas, such as social worker Henrietta Villaescusa, the former president of the Lincoln Heights CSO, assumed a prominent role in the California Democratic Council, the voice for the party's more liberal elements.[85]

At the same time the Republican Party in California continued to demonstrate an openness to Mexican American voters. Governor Knight appointmented Democrat Carlos Terán to the Municipal Court, and a number of Latino Democrats backed Eisenhower, Knight, and Kuchel through supportive "Latin American Committees." Even Vice President Nixon, from the center of the state Republican Party, reached out to Latinos and undertook a symbolic trip to Mexico and Latin America. Negating some of this goodwill, however, was the memory of Republican efforts to prevent Mexican Americans from voting in San Jose in 1952. Overall, a contemporary journalist concluded that "a significant number" of Mexican Americans remained open to persuasion by either party.[86] The 1958 elections would prove pivotal in Latino relations to both the Democratic and Republican parties.

CHAPTER 8

HENRY LÓPEZ
AND
THE MEXICAN-AMERICAN
POLITICAL ASSOCIATION

Major fault lines in the seemingly stable Republican majority coalition began to appear in mid-1957 as activists within both political parties began to focus on the 1958 statewide elections. The
major development occurred within the Republican ranks. William
Knowland, the ultraconservative minority leader in the U.S. Senate,
decided to run for governor believing it represented a better spring-
board for an ultimate campaign for the White House. He did this
without consulting Governor Goodwin Knight, the popular incumbent, whose pragmatic and moderate politics fit well in the state.
After months of vacillation, a very unhappy Knight was forced to
shift his sights to the U.S. Senate to avoid a devastating intra-party
primary. About the same time, Knowland decided to inject conservative energy into his campaign by promoting a voter initiative to
make California a so-called "Right-to-Work" state. Among other
provisions, the initiative eliminated the right of unions and employers to agree that employees become union members and pay dues.
Voters had previously turned down anti-labor initiatives in 1938
and 1944. For Knight and other moderate Republicans, an all-out
attack on organized labor represented both bad policy and bad politics, for AFL support had enabled Republicans to win repeatedly in
a state where the majority of registered voters remained Democrats.
In this volatile environment, Latino leaders sought to protect the interests of their largely working class community, while seeking to
promote a statewide candidate.

The outlines of the year's titanic struggle became clear with
a poll showing Attorney General Pat Brown comfortably leading
Knowland in the race for governor, but another survey revealed the
Knowland-backed anti-labor initiative winning. The basic political
question was thus: could Knowland ride the initiative to victory or

would organized labor be able to demonize the initiative and thus seal Knowland's fate?

In January 1958, after the right-to-work advocates submitted their proposed initiative to the attorney general for title and summary, the AFL California Federation of Labor held a number of emergency meetings. The AFL began educating its membership as to the threat posed by the anti-labor initiative and undertook the daunting task of fundraising to run a campaign. The AFL also convened the central labor council leaders from around the state. These municipal bodies were central to any campaign; many operated their own weekly newspapers for regular communication with the rank-and-file and they also oversaw an extensive organization that cut across craft or industry line to bring together workers by neighborhoods. In what they perceived as a life and death struggle for the labor movement in California, issues would subordinate candidate concerns, although the two would become intertwined in a powerful way. The AFL reminded the Republican Party that having its gubernatorial candidate attack unions could prove fatal: "Governor Culbert L. Olson became California's only Democratic governor of the century" by defeating the incumbent who supported an anti-labor voter initiative.[1]

The California Democratic Council, with its partisan goal of electing Democrats to constitutional and legislative offices, met in January for its pre-primary endorsing convention as organized labor prepared to fight a voter initiative headed for the November ballot. The top of the ticket was set because Attorney General Pat Brown agreed to run against Knowland for governor, but candidates for the other races were less obvious. Party leaders and activists spent much of late 1957 seeking to decide whom to support at the CDC convention, which had become the party's de facto nominator. Candidates considered it futile for non-CDC-endorsed candidates to run in the June primary election that formally selected the party's nominees for the November election. There was also a tactical consideration. Because of the state's cross-filing system, the primary served as the first round of the general election, with candidates seeking to maximize support for their campaign in their own and in the opposing party.[2]

The expanding Spanish-speaking political network, Governor Knight's appointment of Judge Carlos Terán, and a historic breakthrough in Texas—where Raymond Telles was elected mayor of El Paso—raised expectations for new firsts in the electoral arena in California. Mexican American activists across the state looked to Los Angeles City Councilman Edward Roybal. He had a statewide reputation and had run ahead of others on the ticket in his 1954 campaign for lieutenant governor. Roybal was a strong leader who had mastered the art of coalition politics in the community, despite being on the minority side in the fights over development and discrimination in the city council. Despite remaining one-vote short for a municipal FEPC ordinance, Roybal did convince the city council to outlaw discrimination in the redevelopment of Bunker Hill. Even as he worked with a wide range of groups and individuals, Roybal remained the titular head of CSO. He attended the 1957 CSO Convention in Fresno, along with Saul Alinsky and Franklin Williams, the West Coast regional counsel to the NAACP. Roybal told the 200 delegates that Mexican Americans were progressing politically. "The sleeping giant is beginning to awaken, and it will not be long before his strength begins to be felt in the state and local elections."[3]

Seeking the number two spot on the Democratic ticket, Roybal met with Brown, who quickly dashed Roybal's hopes and aspirations. "Attorney General Brown felt that it would be detrimental to the Democratic Party to have two candidates who are Catholic running on the same ticket," said Roybal. "Well, the truth of the matter was he didn't want me as a running mate."[4] Roybal acquiesced and decided to run for the Los Angeles County Board of Supervisors with the backing of outgoing Supervisor John Anson Ford, who stated that Roybal's "diligence and integrity did much to increase the community's appreciation of its Mexican-American population."[5]

The campaign would be very tough. The expansive third district included the downtown area, Boyle Heights and Montebello to the east, Bell and Maywood to the south, Hollywood and Wilshire district to the west, and Silver Lake and Echo Park neighborhoods to the north. The cosmopolitan district included major financial businesses and shopping districts; movie production; and steel, rubber, and auto factories. Latino voters were concentrated in Boyle Heights and the Belvedere section of East Los Angeles in the de-

mographically diverse district that included a variety of white ethnics, Anglos like Ford from the Midwest, Dust Bowl refugees
from the South, and racial minorities such as Japanese Americans.
Moreover, numerous politicians coveted the seat. In addition to
Roybal, the race attracted Councilman Earnest Debs, whose district included Lincoln Heights; and Councilman Harold Henry, representing the Wilshire District with its office towers and expensive
homes. There was also an ideological overlay among strongest candidates: Roybal was the progressive, Debs represented pro-growth
liberalism, and Henry was the most conservative.

"My first choice as my successor is Ed Roybal. He, like myself,
can be described as a progressive," announced Supervisor Ford,
who had worked with Roybal and Quevedo before him, going back
to the founding of El Congreso. Roybal's coalition reflected his progressive values.[6] Many of his supporters came from the civil rights
coalition that united behind him in 1949 and an expanding network developed through participation in the California Committee
for Fair Employment and California Democratic Council. Roybal's
"Committee of 1,000" included Judge Isaac Pacht, Jewish community leader; Joseph Wyatt, CDC leader; Samuel Otto, ILGWU;
Mary Workman, an Irish American and liberal Catholic lay leader;
and Assemblyman Vernon Kilpatrick, who sponsored the first Non-
Citizen Old Age Pension bill. Crooner Frank Sinatra provided glamour to the Roybal campaign and appealed to Italian Americans.

A broad segment of the Latino community rallied behind Roybal.
Supporters included liberal and labor Latinos such as J.J. Rodríguez,
Los Angeles CSO president. Supporters likewise included promi-
nent businessmen such as Manuel Vega, the Republican mortuary
executive who had successfully lobbied Governor Knight to appoint Terán to the bench, and Armando G. Torres, who headed the
Democratic Committee within the Latin American Division of the
Eisenhower-Nixon and the Kuchel campaigns in 1956. Women also
played a prominent role. Lucille Roybal ran the headquarters in
Boyle Heights and Henrietta Villaescusa oversaw the operation in
Lincoln Heights. Las Madrinas Club, a nonpartisan women's organization, endorsed Roybal; the club hung a twelve-foot high portrait
of Roybal at the Casa del Mexicano. Manuel Toapato, an Ecuador
born painter and muralist, created the image, another example of
the diversity within the Latino community in Los Angeles.[7]

The Roybals pack the family car for a picnic. The campaign photo highlight-
ed the candidate's attractive family and demonstrated the urban politician's
comfort with the developing car oriented suburbs of the 1950s.
(Edward Roybal Papers, Kennedy Library, California State Library, Los Angeles)

With Roybal refocused on securing the supervisorial district, Henry P. López set his sights on running for secretary of state. López was a liberal's liberal who typified the self-made, issue-oriented professionals who drove the California Democratic Council. Born into a beet picking family in Colorado, López served in World War II and graduated from Harvard Law School. He moved to Los Angeles, worked briefly for the National Labor Relations Board before going into private practice and channeling his energy into a wide range of organizations. López served as Legal Counsel for CSO and on the Board of Directors of the GI Forum and in various posts within his Democratic club. López's campaign took off in the fall of 1957 when the Southern California CDC Caucus overwhelmingly endorsed him. Pat Brown responded by recruiting Roybal's ally, Supervisor Ford, to run against López.[8]

Support for Henry López was still strong in early 1958 when CDC convened its convention in Fresno. The group had grown to nearly 500 clubs and almost 40,000 members. This was nothing short of a political phenomenon in the historically disorganized and weak state Democratic Party. The growing number of activists were held together by ideology and partisanship. This provided the political space for activists such as López—and Roybal in 1954—though not without a struggle. Party leaders put pressure on López to withdraw from the race. When that failed they pressured Roybal to nominate Ford at the CDC convention since he was then running with the support of Ford for his vacant seat on the board of supervisors. Roybal refused, as did López's campaign manager, Lionel Steinberg, a liberal grower. Vaino Spencer, an African American female attorney, nominated López. In the end, López won the CDC endorsement and Supervisor Ford graciously withdrew from the race.[9]

In his gubernatorial campaign, Pat Brown announced that he would follow the nonpartisan campaign model crafted by Governor Warren.[10] Brown's strategy was to capture the political center while appealing to traditional Democratic groups, including the AFL, which had its own history of bipartisanship. The AFL California Federation of Labor endorsed Brown against their archenemy, Knowland, but they did not embrace the entire Democratic ticket. The AFL endorsed Republican Governor Goodwin Knight (along with the Democrat Claire Engle) in the race for U.S. Senate, backed the Republican candidate for state treasurer, and stayed neutral for the office of secretary of state (where Henry López was the candidate).[11]

This semblance of bipartisanship on the part of the AFL enabled the group to paint Knowland as an extremist and exploit rivalries within the Republican ranks. At a time when Knowland was attacking the evils of organized labor, the AFL arranged for Governor Knight and Vice President Richard Nixon to attend a Los Angeles Central Labor Council luncheon in early March. Accompanied by local officials and aides to national labor leaders George Meany and Walter Reuther, Nixon and Knight praised labor's role in society, including their contribution to reducing discrimination on the job. The scene—which the AFL's *Los Angeles Citizen* underscored with headlines such as " Vice-President Nixon Praises American Unions"—illuminated the tensions within the Republican Party. Nixon was, after all, a GOP anti-communist, pro-small business centrist as well as a representative of President Eisenhower. The luncheon thus sent a powerful message that Knowland's attacks on unions did not represent a Republican Party position and the reverberations of this event affected GOP party activists as well as helped labor solidify support among its Republican members. Furthermore, Nixon and Knight's stated opposition to job discrimination, following upon the statement in Los Angeles the previous month by U.S. Labor Secretary John Mitchell, helped place the struggle for a state FEPC in a more bipartisan and moderate political environment.[12]

For his part, Brown courted Mexicans throughout primary season. Early in the year he attended CSO's national board meeting in Fresno—a first for a gubernatorial candidate, and a powerful statement that Brown viewed the organization as central to reaching Mexican American voters.[13] Then in March, Brown addressed the Third Annual Awards Banquet of the Council on Mexican-American Affairs at the Statler Hotel in Los Angeles. Prior to the June 1958 primary, Brown also purchased time on Spanish language radio in voter-rich Southern California. He also appeared at least once on stage with López, at a rally at the Carpenters union hall in San Diego. Brown likewise expected to benefit from heavy Latino turnout expected in Los Angeles due to the enthusiasm for Roybal's candidacy and opposition to Proposition B to approve the contract with the Dodger baseball team for a stadium on land taken by eminent domain in Chávez Ravine.[14]

The statewide Democratic candidates all won their respective primaries, including Henry López in his campaign for secretary of state, although the Latino community lost in its opposition to Dodger Stadium.[15] A close examination of the results showed that despite the party's growing strength and CDC's ability to minimize intra-party primary fights, California voters continued to demonstrate a level of nonpartisanship that augured well for general election success. Brown, who used the primary to paint Knowland as out of the mainstream, ran up large numbers—out polling his GOP rival by 600,000 votes in a combined total of both the Democratic and Republican primary ballots. By contrast, López proved to be the weakest member of the slate, coming in some 300,000 votes behind Frank Jordan, the incumbent secretary of state. This was due to Jordan's winning almost a quarter of Democratic primary voters and López's decision not to cross-file in the GOP primary.[16]

In Los Angeles, Roybal came in first in a field of four candidates, providing a boost as he headed into a November runoff in nonpartisan county supervisor race against his colleague, City Councilman Debs. The challenge for Roybal, the most liberal of the candidates, was to pick up the votes of those who had voted for one of the two more conservative candidates. The race boiled down to two competing liberal coalitions. Roybal's political base continued to be progressive voters, minorities that placed a premium on fair employment, renters, and industrial unions, including the garment, steel, auto, and rubber workers that had members in the district. The campaign benefited from the support of the popular outgoing incumbent, John Anson Ford, whose outlook, like other key allies, was shaped by President Roosevelt and the New Deal. By contrast, Debs benefited from the support of a post-war coalition that emphasized progress based on economic growth, and enthusiastically backed the building of freeways (like those that cut up Boyle Heights) and large projects such as Dodger Stadium (that displaced low-income Mexican Americans in Chávez Ravine). This pro-building coalition benefited from the financial largess of developers and votes from union members tied to the Building Trades Council and the AFL Central Labor Council.[17]

The candidates and the initiative-related campaigns used the Labor Day weekend to kickoff the fall election activity, and to begin reaching out to an electorate that was more politicized than in previous years. The union-based coalition against Proposition 18, the so-called Right-to-Work initiative, enjoyed the greatest resources (exceeding the total money spent to promote both Brown and Knowland) and delivered the most urgent message. Organized labor had worked since January to educate its members about the threat posed by the initiative. This represented a formidable political base because about half of the state's families had a union member. The campaign also sought support from minority groups and the religious community, beginning with those affiliated with the California Committee for Fair Employment Practices. On a partisan level, the campaign portrayed the struggle as between Democrats and mainstream Republicans who were pitted against ultraconservative Republicans. These intertwined themes of protecting the economic health of the community, moral righteousness, and opposing extremism were delivered at the work site and in the neighborhoods. This was possible because organized labor built and operated the most extensive field campaign in the state's history, with union members and their allies walking door-to-door talking to voters at a previously unknown level in the large media-driven state. The campaign also invested more than half of its $2.5 million war chest in billboards, radio, and television commercials.[18]

In Los Angeles, the Catholic Labor Institute's annual Labor Day Mass and Breakfast attracted hundreds of unionists, including CSO members, as well as Catholic politicians such as Pat Brown and Edward Roybal. Bishop Alden Bell presided, giving the anti-Proposition 18 message a clerical blessing even though neither Cardinal Francis McIntyre nor the California bishops took a formal position. Monsignor George Higgins, the American bishops' representative on labor concerns issued an anti-Right-to-Work statement that was distributed in California, as did supportive Protestant and Jewish leaders. This helped inject a moral component to the struggle that had become a life or death struggle for organized labor in California.[19]

Henry López, Democratic candidate for secretary of state, campaigns in San Diego in August 1958 by offering voters a cool glass of lemonade. The son of a farm worker, López graduated from Harvard Law School and became the second well known Latino in the state at the time.
        (San Diego Union-Tribune Collection, San Diego Historical Society)

To rally the civil rights community, the labor movement brought in A. Philip Randolph, "father of the FEPC," to keynote a two-day Labor Conference on Human Rights at the Statler Hotel in Los Angeles in early October. The CSO, the NAACP, and the JLC cosponsored the conference with the Central Labor Council. Speakers included Councilman Roybal, State CSO President Tony Ríos, and Butchers Local 563 President J.J.Rodríguez. The labor-minority coalition reaffirmed labor's commitment to pushing for the enactment of fair employment legislation and stressed the stake minority voters had in preserving collective bargaining in the state. A strong labor movement contributed to raising wages and insuring equal treatment on the job; union resources were also central to the ongoing campaign for a state and local FEPC and the promotion of CSO's bill for Non-Citizen Old Age Pensions. According to Tony Ríos, the implication from the conference was clear: labor, with its future on the line and in need of a massive voter turnout by minority voters, was committing itself to going all out to ensure the passage of the state FEPC should the Democrats win the election.[20]

The labor and minority activists took the campaign to their respective neighborhoods. On Los Angeles' Eastside, the historic heart of CSO's operation, labor formed the Eastside Committee of the Committee to Save Our State. James Cruz chaired the group. He served as a business agent for the AFL Brick and Clay Workers, and was a member of the Los Angeles Democratic Central Committee and CSO's Labor Advisory Committee. The Committee to Save Our State kicked off its election outreach with a Saturday afternoon car caravan that snaked through the working class neighborhoods of Boyle Heights and Lincoln Heights, raising awareness of the election, and stopping at major shopping centers to distribute information to voters. Three days, later the group sponsored a rally at the Carpenters Hall at Brooklyn and Soto Streets. Activists and elected officials organized yet another rally a few days later to inaugurate a new headquarters on Brooklyn Avenue, which served as the dispatching center for the massive precinct walking operation against Proposition 18 and for the Democratic Party ticket. Congressman Chet Holifield, Assemblyman Edward Elliott, and City Councilman Edward

James Cruz of the AFL Brick and Clay Workers (second from left) coordinated No on Proposition 18 activities in Boyle Heights. He is joined in front of the Brooklyn Avenue campaign headquarters by Dave Fishman of the Painters Union (on left) and Sigmund Arywitz of the International Ladies Garment Workers' Union (on right).

(Urban Archives Center, California State University, Northridge)

Roybal all pledged to help defeat the initiative. "This threat to organized labor and the economic security of our community must be defeated at all cost if we are to maintain our democratic way of life," intoned Chet Holifield.[21]

Latinos were also well represented in the statewide efforts. An advertisement underscoring the breadth of the coalition included CSO activest Héctor Abeytia and attorney Gilbert D. López from the Fresno area. As the election approached, the campaign published a large ad in *La Opinión* that underscored the widespread opposition to the initiative in Los Angeles. In addition to the expected list of labor and CSO leaders, the ad touted opposition from candidates López and Roybal and from businessmen and professionals such as GI Forum leaders John Aragón, Raúl Morín, Frank Pax; religious leaders such as Rev. Rafael Ortiz; and prominent individuals like Dr. Francisco Bravo.[22]

Brown made a similar commitment to the Latino community. The gubernatorial candidate pledged himself to support a fair employment law, as is "now in effect in fourteen states." Moreover, he pledged to initiate "within thirty days of becoming governor" a meeting of "leaders in business, in labor, in government and in all aspects of our lives" to find solutions to challenges in the "field of human relations." The Democratic candidate stressed the state's diversity, recognizing the presence of "more than a million persons of Mexican descent in the state."[23]

Brown employed a number of techniques to reach Latino voters as part of a larger effort to turnout minorities, labor, and liberals. Under the auspices of "Community Groups for Pat Brown," the governor opened a headquarters at Fourth and Soto Streets in Boyle Heights, reinforcing the existing labor and Democratic outreach efforts in the now overwhelmingly Mexican American neighborhood. Labor leader and former CSO president J.J. Rodríguez served as a co-chair; while the group included attorney Philip Newman, theater owner Frank Fouce, and engineer Alexander Zambrano. The ethnic-oriented campaign made the evening television news and volunteers knocked on countless doors.[24] The Brown campaign had a similar effect in Northern California, even though there were fewer minority voters. For example, Louis Flores, a Korean War veteran, participated in the Brown and López campaigns while earning a degree in electrical engineering at the University of California, Berkeley. The campaign served to familiarize Flores and the other activists with each other. Along with the efforts to mobilize mostly liberal minority voters, Brown also sought out the political center. *La Opinión*, for example, publicized the formation of a "Republicans for Brown" group that no doubt helped reach moderate Latinos as well as Anglos.[25]

López, like other "down ticket" candidates, lacked sufficient funding to run a media or mail driven campaign, and relied instead on news coverage and grassroots campaigning among Latinos, labor, and Democrats. And unlike politically seasoned Brown, who had started his career as a Republican, López and most of the rest of the ticket did not have the capacity or inclination to reach across the partisan divide. López did have a few celebrity supporters. Actor Anthony Quinn served as the candidate's honorary campaign chair and former President Harry Truman campaigned with López and the other party nominees. The AFL California Labor Federation, which had stayed neutral in the primary, endorsed him. Moreover, the López campaign—like Roybal's before it—helped energize the growing number of Latino voters throughout the state. Many of these voters had been registered to vote by one of CSO's twenty chapters in California.[26]

CSO used the election to register new voters in places like Oxnard, an agricultural community south of Santa Barbara. There the organization established a new chapter in partnership with the CIO United Packinghouse Workers, who wanted to unionize the local workers.[27] "See, when you register, your name goes down on a list of Colonia voters [as those who live in the Mexican neighborhood were known] at the courthouse. The longer that list is, the more pressure we will be able to put on the politicians to get what we need in the Colonia," explained César Chávez, now CSO executive director. Registering to vote would empower the community. It was made easier by the presence on the ballot of two Mexican Americans: Henry López, candidate for secretary of state, and Port Hueneme Mayor Leo J. Ramírez, who was running for the Oxnard Harbor district board.[28]

The heart of the Latino campaigning remained in Los Angeles, where Latinos constituted a large voter block, where Roybal sought to motivate his historic coalition and to win over voters to whom he and Debs were unknowns. Roybal's campaign emphasized Supervisor Ford's support and the candidate's high ethical standards; his brochure alluded to the fact that in the wrong hands the job could lead to "selfishness and corruption."[29] Roybal likewise associated himself with the massive effort against Proposition 18, a position his opponent shared, which was reflected in the split loyalty of the AFL and CIO unions.

The saliency of religion and class increased when the Brown's opponents and the proponents of Proposition 18 attacked organized labor as corrupt and communist influenced and vilified the Democratic Party nominee for being subservient to the Pope. Ironically, the anti-labor attacks focused on UAW president Walter Reuther, who had helped drive the communists out of the CIO. The religious attack played on old fears. The flyer compared California to Spain, and asked: "Could Roman Catholic Brown, if elected Governor, be loyal to the state of California and the Vatican at the same time? . . . The Roman Catholic Church says No!"[30]

The November 1958 campaign concluded for Henry López and Edward Roybal in a grand open-air rally at the corner of Brooklyn and Breed Streets in Boyle Heights, the birthplace of modern Latino politics. Billed as a celebration of the "the East Side's Favorite Sons," the get-out-the-vote rally also stressed opposition to Proposition 18 and support for the larger Democratic ticket.[31] Grace Montañez Davis, the early Lincoln Heights CSO leader who oversaw the Roybal headquarters in her part of the city for the run-off, stated that she was "very optimistic, we felt like we had a good chance . . . [and] we worked hard to get people out. There was just an incredible amount of response in terms of volunteers."[32]

On Election Day, the voters trounced Proposition 18 and gave Brown a million-vote margin as part of an historic Democratic landslide unimaginable just a few years earlier. Post-election analysis of the returns demonstrated that Mexican Americans (along with unionists, Jews, and African Americans) voted overwhelmingly against Proposition 18. Moreover, the bitter battle over the role of unions in society extenuated the class divisions among the electorate; an astonishing 79 percent of working class voters backed Brown, far ahead of the 59 percent he won among the middle class. Given the disproportionate number of Latinos in blue-collar jobs, and the overwhelming opposition to Proposition 18 and strong support for Roybal and López, it is likely that a record number of Spanish-surnamed voters went to the poll. CSO President Tony Ríos estimated that support for Brown reached ninety percent. The overlapping labor, CDC, and candidate-oriented campaigns in 1958 succeeded in reassembling the liberal-labor-minority coalition formed by Roosevelt in the 1930s.[33]

So complete was the routing that Democrats took control of the governor's office and the state legislature for the first time in the century. The popular governor, Goodwin Knight, lost his race for the U.S. Senate, a victim of voter cynicism over the Republican candidates' switching offices and Knowland's attacks on organized labor. The results for the two Latino candidates was much less clear: under the banner head, "VICTORIA DEMOCRATA," *La Opinión* noted that incomplete election results made it impossible to determine if Henry López or Edward Roybal had won or lost their respective races.[34]

On election night López and Roybal trailed ever so narrowly with additional absentee ballot yet uncounted. The election officials ordered a recount of the hand-calculated results. On Thursday, two days after the election, the Los Angeles County Registrar of Voters announced that Roybal had won by 393 votes—139,800 to 139,407. "Complete L.A. Vote Returns: 10,000-VOTE ERROR; ROYBAL UPSETS DEBS," proclaimed a banner headline in the evening's *Los Angeles Herald-Examiner*. That evening's *Mirror's* banner headline stated: "DEBS TRAILING ROYBAL BUT STILL THINKS HE WILL WIN." The two papers ran front-page photos of a delighted Roybal kissing his wife, Lucille.[35] Then something happened. That night the County Registrar discovered boxes of previously uncounted votes. These newly located ballots gave Debs a 12,000-vote margin. Friday morning's *La Opinión* captured the conflicting results. The paper ran a large photo of a jubilant Roybal, surrounded by supporters, holding a sign, "Roybal Has Won." But the headline told a different story: "DEBS DEFEATS ROYBAL IN NEW RECOUNT."[36] Friday morning Roybal supporters protested the results, complaining about election irregularities. That evening, the *Herald-Examiner* ran a front-page cartoon showing Debs and Roybal on a seesaw, with the wooden plank balanced over a ballot box. It indicated that Debs was now up and Roybal down. The caption explained that the "Vote Tally in Third District Race is So Mixed Up That a Special Election May Be Called."[37] But no new election was called. The results of the fourth recount stood. Roybal's campaign manager Roger Johnson, many Latinos, and a number of journalists believed that the election was stolen but lacked proof. A disheartened Roybal accepted the official results.[38]

During the four days the Roybal saga occupied the front pages of the municipal papers, county officials around the state also conducted a recount in the race for secretary of state. On Saturday, the day after announcing Roybal's defeat, *La Opinión* reported that López was behind by only 10,000 votes in the recounting.[39] The optimism did not last. The final tabulation showed that López missed becoming the first Latino statewide elected official in modern California by fewer than 50,000 votes of five million cast—losing by one-tenth of one percent. The defeat was particularly painful because López was the only statewide Democrat to lose in the party's greatest sweep in the Twentieth Century, although another liberal partisan, Alan Cranston, also came close to losing, securing the post of State Controller by a mere 31,000 votes. In contrast to the razor thin margins by these two liberal candidates who did not hold elected office, Attorney General Pat Brown won by a million votes by running against a rightwing Republican as a nonpartisan Democrat supporting "responsible liberalism."[40]

Analyzing the secretary of state's race—which had eluded Democrats since 1891, even when they were winning other statewide offices—is challenging because in such a close contest any number of factors could have made the critical difference. In this "down ballot" race where name identification is important, López ran against an incumbent, Frank C. Jordan, whose father, also Frank C. Jordan, had served in that office. Second, López was not exposed to Republican voters in the June primary because he failed to cross-file, as had the other statewide Democratic candidates. Third, López's campaign was poorly financed. Fourth, López was the only Democratic candidate to face a minor party candidate— who received roughly 130,000 votes, more than the margin of difference between López's winning and losing, and thus probably played the role of a "spoiler." Fifth, there may have been a racial bias on the part of some voters. The deciding factor, however, was that López was the lone Democrat to start the November election behind and never caught up, although he reduced his negative vote margin from 300,000 in the June primary to 50,000 in November election. For his part, López, as a contemplative former candidate, attributed his narrow loss to Jordan's superior name identification and the presence of the third party candidate.[41]

In the final analysis, Governor Brown bore some responsibility for the Latino electoral setbacks. He forced Roybal off the Democratic ticket. The Los Angeles councilman would have likely won the race for lieutenant governor, given his name identification from the 1954 campaign and his coalition of supporters. While the issue of Catholicism did emerge in Brown's election it proved far from decisive. Further, Brown is also culpable for not promoting the Democratic ticket that he ostensibly headed.[42] While Brown courted Spanish-speaking voters more than any gubernatorial candidate since Culbert Olson, he avoided helping López garner Anglo support. Barrister Herman Sillas stated, "Pat Brown refused to share a platform with Hank López." This was due to "anti-Mexican bias" among the general public and a political calculation relative to the limited number of Latino votes "as a percentage of the total."[43] Democratic Party operative Don Bradley drew a different lesson. He believed that the Democrats lost the office because they nominated a little known attorney instead of a popular Los Angeles County Supervisor.[44] A prominent journalist postulated that López had lost the majority of politically moderate swing voters who were "Democrats-in-name-only."[45]

Regardless of explanation, the twin defeats of Roybal and López provided a disturbing setback to the Mexican American political movement since the formation of CSO a decade earlier. Still, there was much to celebrate. Soon after the election Roybal welcomed hundreds of activists from thirty-two CSO chapters in California and Arizona to Los Angeles' Alexandria Hotel to recognize the organization's phenomenal growth and to honor Saul Alinsky and Fred Ross for their commitment to Latino self-empowerment. Father William Barry gave the invocation and Laborers Local 300 president Mike Quevedo served as the master of ceremonies. Roybal and María Durán provided testimonials and the children from the Friendship Day Camp provided multicultural songs. Texas State Senator Henry B. González keynoted the banquet. A rising star in the Lone Star State, he symbolized Latino political progress and his presence indicates the degree to which CSO was extending its political ties throughout the Southwest.[46]

Upon assuming office in January 1959, Governor Brown and organized labor kept their commitment to make the enactment of fair employment a top priority. The Governor stated in his inaugural address that "Discrimination in employment is a stain upon California" and urged the enactment of the Fair Employment Practices Act by the legislature.[47] Inside the Capitol, Jesse Unruh, the Texas-born assemblyman who had run Brown's campaign in Southern California, shepherded the bill through the lower house. Governor Brown used his influence in the state senate. External pressure for the long sought measure came from the California Committee for Fair Employment Practices, and its constituent groups, particularly the AFL and CIO unions that enjoyed enormous influence given the lopsided defeat of Proposition 18 and their support of the new Democratic legislative majority. The FEPC's chief lobbyist, Bill Becker, emphasized the importance of the liberal-labor coalition in passing the landmark civil rights bill in a legislature with only two African Americans and no Latino or Asian members. Brown signed the measure, which was particularly memorable because it was his first bill.[48]

The enactment of fair employment legislation served as the culmination of a long struggle for job equality that featured Eduardo Quevedo and Edward Roybal, and engaged CSO's Tony Ríos, Herman Gallegos, and Margaret Cruz. Still, it was not seen as a Latino victory per se. It was a labor-liberal-minority coalition achievement where African Americans were the most visible group in the lobbying campaign. Not only was discrimination against African Americans seen by many as more severe than against Latinos, according to the bill's lobbyist, but the NAACP—unlike CSO—made the issue their top legislative priority, and C.L. Dellums chaired the California Committee For Fair Employment. This reality, and the governor's need to reward key supporters, became apparent in the selection of the new five-member Fair Employment Practices Commission charged with enforcing the new anti-discrimination law. Former Los Angeles Supervisor John Anson Ford was tapped to chair the board. Widely respected, the Roybal campaign chair and No on Proposition 18 co-chair was believed to be the best person to implement the controversial law. Brown also named California Committee for Fair Employment chair, C.L. Dellums, representing labor and the NAACP, to the board along with Carmen Warshaw, a Jewish businesswoman, civil rights supporter, and Brown's key

Southern California fundraiser (and Hope Mendoza Schechter's "sister."). The two remaining slots went to Anglos at the discretion of the Senate and Assembly leaders who provided the votes to ensure the bill's passage. Latinos enjoyed access to a majority of the board, but this was not the same as having one of their own on the board; as an interim step, CSO successfully pushed for a Spanish-speaking staff person to facilitate complaint investigations.[49]

The issue of appointments hit a raw nerve among the middle class Mexican Americans because Brown appeared oblivious to the pain in the community over the losses suffered by Edward Roybal and Henry López—or the pride for the extraordinary Latino voter mobilization. Brown failed to offer an administrative post to López, Roybal, or other well-qualified individuals. (Roybal, who wished to direct the state Welfare Department, became despondent, according to Hope Mendoza Schechter, openly wondering if he had a political future beyond the city council.) Nor did Brown appoint a significant number of Latinos to board and commission seats. By contrast, Controller Alan Cranston, who had relatively few patronage positions, named Henry López as a tax appraiser; and when he resigned shortly thereafter, Cranston filled the post with GI Forum activist Alexander Zambrano. Viewed collectively, often symbolic appointments resonated with the larger community but were most important for members of the emerging middle class. However, working class Latinos—through groups like CSO—focused foremost on issues, and appointments related to achieving a specific goal.[50]

CSO's top priorities were the adoption of a minimum wage for agricultural workers and the passage of the bill to provide Old Age Pensions for Non-Citizens. Bruce Allen, a San Jose area Republican and Edward Elliot, an East Los Angeles Democrat, jointly introduced the pension bill as AB 1.[51] The bill soon ran into trouble because it was not part of Brown's "package" of social service reforms and the chair of the policy committee charged with reviewing the bill in the Assembly refused to hear it. In an unusual parliamentary move that underscored the depth of support CSO (with the help of labor) enjoyed among its legislative allies, bill backers voted 54 to 19 to withdraw it from committee over the chairman's objections. The bill then went to the fiscal committee where its fate rested in the hands of Ways & Means Chairman Jesse Unruh, who was not a friend of CSO. In addition, it still faced objections from Brown. CSO lobbyist, Dolores Huerta, a Stockton schoolteacher, sought to negotiate with William Kolblentz on the Governor's staff. He told her "the Governor was not opposed to the measure in principle," according to Huerta, but it was "too expensive."[52]

Still, the pressure on the governor and other legislators continued to build as CSO brought to bear—directly and indirectly—the power of its coalition partners. This led to the formation of the Committee for Extension of Old Age Assistance to Non-Citizens. Monsignor Thomas J. O'Dwyer served as chairman, with CSO's Tony Ríos the vice-chairman. Max Mont, from the Jewish Labor Committee served as the secretary. The committee prepared a "Fact Sheet" for legislators and lined up additional supporters. These included: the County Supervisors Association of California, Los Angeles County Board of Supervisors, Catholic Welfare Agencies of Los Angeles, Catholic Welfare Agencies of San Francisco, Los Angeles Federation of Jewish Welfare Agencies, California Federation of Labor, and the California CIO Council.[53]

To these organizational allies, CSO added the weight of local elected officials in Los Angeles, home to Assemblyman Unruh and the largest delegation in the state capitol. At Roybal's urging, the Los Angeles City Council unanimously endorsed the bill. Roybal then sent copies of the resolution to Governor Brown and legislators representing Los Angeles, to which he received numerous pledges of support. "I will work hard for this passage of this bill," pledged Assemblyman William Munnell, from Boyle Heights.[54] "You can count on my support," added Assemblyman Tom Bane in the San Fernando Valley.[55]

CSO and its allies went to extraordinary lengths to enact the bill. According to CSO, the bill's authors tried other tactics. "Senator [Stanley] Arnold (D) [from rural northern California] had a bill SB 1069 that AB 1 was amended into," according to a CSO press release. "Again that bill passed the Assembly despite the Administration's opposition again voiced by Assemblyman Jesse Unruh." It now appeared that a majority of lawmakers would approve the bill. However, on the final day of the legislative session, it was referred to the Senate Rules Committee.[56]

Despite the frustration of losing a bill in a Democratic-controlled legislature, CSO took time to acknowledge its allies and to further educate its members on the importance of votes and coalitions. It had gotten this far because its annual voter registration drives had added Latinos to the rolls in legislative districts throughout the state. While coming up short, CSO's legislative allies had exhibited an unusual willingness to play hardball to achieve the group's top priority. CSO praised Bill Becker of the California Committee for Fair Employment Practices, Max Mont of the Jewish Labor Committee, and Monsignor O'Dwyer of the Catholic Church.[57]

The Brown administration was more helpful in advancing CSO's other priority—raising wages for farm workers. It aided the César Chávez-led effort in Oxnard, where CSO was seeking to force the growers to follow the law and hire "locals" before Mexican Nationals or "braceros." CSO National President Tony Ríos used its influence within the administration (Brown named an ILGWU staffer, Sigmund Arywitz, as the Labor Commissioner) to get Sacramento employment officials to disrupt the cozy relationship between their local field staff and the growers.[58] At about the same time, the Industrial Welfare Commission appointed two CSO leaders, Dolores Huerta of Stockton and Héctor Abeytia of Sanger to a wage board charged with raising the minimum wage for women and children in agriculture. Ernesto Galarza was named as an alternate. They were the first Latinos ever to serve on the industry-dominated board. John Henning, a former AFL official who had been part of CSO's 1957 panel on farm labor, made the recommendations as the director of the Department of Industrial Relations. [59]

In spite of Brown's cooperation with CSO on raising farm labor wages, the state's middle class Latino political leadership remained in a foul mood. They felt frustration over the dearth of Latino specific appointments and legislation that was only magnified by the perception that Roybal was cheated out of a seat on the board of supervisors and López's near miss at secretary of state.[60]

The growing tension came to boiling point at the March 1959 convention of the California Democratic Council at the El Rancho Motel in Fresno. "I called a meeting of all the Hispanic delegates and talked to them about organizing a political organization," stated Roybal. "We came to the conclusion that the Democratic Party in fact did not fully support [Henry López]. Not the Democratic Party, but Governor Brown and those on the ticket, did not fully support him."[61] The caucus, made up of some the most partisan and establishment-oriented Mexican American Democrats, decided that the best way to ensure their ethnic group's participation in politics was to form an organization *independent* of both political parties. Roybal appointed an Organizing Committee with himself as the chair and social worker Juan Acevedo as secretary.[62]

The Organizing Committee got a boost soon afterwards when Governor Brown appointed Acevedo to the California Youth Authority. This was a full time job that included perks such as secretarial services, a state car, and use of a state airplane. Born in Mexico, Acevedo received his citizenship for service in World War II, earned a Masters in Social Work from the UCLA and had worked in both Los Angeles and Riverside. He had also served on previous advisory boards, including the Governor's Youth Council Committee. According to Acevedo, Brown privately instructed him to use the position to organize Latinos throughout the state for the benefit of the Democratic Party. Acevedo communicated with those in the Roybal and López networks and with Mexican Americans serving on local city councils. He also collected the names of individuals interested in becoming more active politically. Reflecting on the importance of this appointment, Acevedo said "it was not until I was appointed to the Youth Authority Board, by Governor Brown in 1959, that people had access to [the necessary resources]" to organize politically on a statewide basis.[63]

Juan Acevedo was not Governor Brown's last Latino appointment. In early January 1960, he elevated Carlos Terán, Presiding Judge of the East Los Angeles Municipal Court, to the Superior Court. This represented an historic first since Molina and Terán had both served on the lower court bench. Three hundred attended the swearing-in and 600 attended a banquet honoring Terán on February 25, 1959. Brown's speech at the banquet underscored Terán's role in the history making appointment.[64]

The day after the triumphant Terán extravaganza and almost a year after the special caucus at the California Democratic Council convention, Councilman Roybal sent out an invitation for a planning meeting "to discuss the feasibility of a state-wide Latin-American

Coordination Committee" at the Hacienda Motel in Fresno.[65] The planning meeting attracted thirty-eight people who drew up recommendations for an organization name, outlined its general aims and organizational structure, which would be very similar to that of CDC, with local clubs, a regional structure, and statewide officers. The most heated discussion revolved around a name, which went to the generation's self-identity. The body decided upon the Mexican-American Political Association (MAPA). This represented an agreement to be openly political, to proudly use the word Mexican in their own communities and among Anglos, and to hyphenate Mexican with American in recognition of their U.S. citizenship. The group decided to return to Fresno in larger numbers the following month to launch the new group.[66]

Sandwiched between the two MAPA organizational gatherings was the Seventh Annual CSO Convention, which also met in Fresno. The 250 Mexican American activists represented nearly 10,000 members spread out through twenty-eight chapters in California and several in Arizona. The nonpartisan but politically muscular group celebrated their collective thirteen-year achievements—helping 40,000 Latinos obtain their citizenship, registering 227,000 to vote, and providing the political environment that had led to the election or appointment of some 100 Spanish-speakers to public office. CSO also welcomed Monsignor John O'Grady from the Washington, D.C.-based National Catholic Welfare Council, established priorities for 1961, and elected new leaders—with steel worker Tony Ríos from Los Angeles handing over the national presidency to social worker Herman Gallegos of San Jose.[67]

The selection of Fresno as the site for both the annual CSO convention and the founding of MAPA spoke volumes about its centrality in the auto-oriented state. Fresno, the largest city in the Central Valley, also boasted impressive gains since World War II for Latinos in both education and jobs where a majority now worked outside of agriculture. But Fresno also had a small but steady stream of new arrivals. One in five Latinos were born in Mexico. The new arrivals tended to move into the entry level housing left vacant by Mexican Americans moving into more middle class areas.[68] It was among the upwardly mobile that MAPA drew activists even as the largest block of Spanish-speaking voters remained in the old neighborhoods.

MAPA's Founding Convention of April 22-24, 1960 attracted 134 people from all over the state. The inchoate group, smaller than that which attended the CSO convention, was comprised largely of men in their thirties and forties. One participant, Frank López, the former labor radical who served as a Congreso officer in 1939, like Roybal, was shaped by the New Deal. Most of the others came of age politically in the 1940s or 1950s, and reflected a post-war frame of reference. They were for the most part white-collar professionals, blue-collar labor union officials, and small businessmen who also served as leaders of Democratic clubs and cultural organizations, including groups such as CSO, GI Forum, Council on Mexican-American Affairs, and Mexican Chamber of Commerce. While MAPA was far more secular than CSO, there was at least one church group represented—the San Francisco-based Catholic Guadalupe Society. Viewed numerically, the new organization was strongest in East Los Angeles; however, the delegates present also reflected the movement to the suburbs and organizations in small towns and cities, from Stockton to Santa Paula to Colton. Only nineteen women participated; some were active along with their husbands, like Lucille Roybal, and Beatrice Casillas, the state chair of the GI Forum Auxiliary. Others represented fraternal societies or political groups, such as Candy Veliz of the Club San Felipe in San Jose or Felicia Huereque of the Spanish American Voters in South San Gabriel.[69]

The general session began with introductory statements by Edward Roybal and Henry López. Roybal spoke on the "New perspective in the creation of a state-wide, non-partisan organization for the social, economic, cultural and civil betterment of Mexican-Americans and all other Spanish-speaking Americans, through political action." López focused on the mechanics of building an organization.[70] The delegates followed the general recommendation of the planning committee, with a passionate discussion around the name of the organization. "There had been *too much* evasion, there were too many people evading the use of the word Mexican, as though there was sometthing shameful about it," mused Henry López. "The [Latin American] guys from San Francisco thought that they were being left out," emphasized López, "but we said, 'Listen, we love you, we want you, but for our special psychologi-

THE MEXICAN-AMERICAN POLITICAL ASSOCIATION   183

cal reason we have got to confirm this as Mexican American.'"[71]

The group elected Councilman Roybal as president by acclamation and easily settled on other statewide and regional officers. In contrast to the early CSO, which drew female and male leaders from the garment and steel unions, MAPA's officers were all men with advanced degrees or small business owners. Henry López from Los Angeles, Louis García from San Francisco, and Héctor Moreno from San Jose were attorneys. Julius F. Castelan from Daly City was an engineer and Juan Acevedo was a social worker. Andrew Barrigán was the lobbyist for the California Federation of Teachers in Sacramento. Augustine Flores ran a furniture store in Riverside.[72] For a number of reasons, the group put forth self-made leaders, according to the GI Forum's George Sotelo, then an operating engineer who participated in MAPA's founding. These included a collective pride in their professional achievement, a belief they had the skills to run a statewide volunteer-driven organization, and the reality that their jobs provided the financial means and flexibility to attend daytime meetings.[73]

Not withstanding its differences from CSO in terms of funding and its members' class and gender, MAPA built upon the foundations of CSO, a point made by Herman Gallegos.[74] Operationally, CSO and MAPA played complementary roles. Put simply, CSO members were more likely to be working class and engaged in the fundamentals of building political power, starting with voter registration and citizenship classes. This represented a rare achievement at a time when most politically influential groups grew out of the middle class.[75] By contrast MAPA members followed the CDC model and were likely to be middle class. In effect they sought to utilize the growing block of Latino voters to elect Latinos and supportive non-Latinos candidates to public office. Members of this new middle class were also well positioned to participate in government conferences. Councilman Roybal and Judge Terán participated in the Eisenhower-sponsored White House Conference on Children and Youth.[76]

Looking back, former Supervisor John Anson Ford called the developments in the Latino community "spectacular" and noted that Latino advances had outpaced that of African Americans.[77] From an organizational vantage point, MAPA was the evolutionary product and beneficiary of earlier organizations. El Congreso and the Federation of Spanish-American Voters under Eduardo Quevedo had provided the first models of broad-based coalition politics and a high level of ethnic influence in local, state, and federal governments. CSO was singularly important in electing Roybal and formalizing the coalition with segments of organized labor, Jews, and the Catholic Church. It was chiefly responsible for leadership training and the ever expanding statewide voter base that had propelled Latino politics, including the growing number of local elected officials, through the fifties. At the same time, the California Democratic Council had provided a door through which Latinos could enter the state Democratic Party, and helped Roybal in 1954 and López in 1958 to secure their respective party nominations.[78] Likewise, the California Committee for Fair Employment provided a vehicle to work with a wide range of groups to advance civil rights objectives. MAPA provided a voice to the Mexican American middle class' desire to elevate their own to office, and to influence policies with the Democratic and Republican parties—even as Roybal, ever the coalition builder, declared its mission also incorporated the needs of "all other Spanish-speaking Americans."[79] Eager to open new doors of opportunity for themselves and for the larger community, MAPA and the network of activists within the more established groups—CSO, GI Forum, and LULAC—soon focused their attention on national politics.

CHAPTER 9

VIVA KENNEDY

AND

THE STRUGGLE FOR REPRESENTATION

The increased level of civic engagement, self-organization, and expanding voter base in California and other states during the 1950s
created the necessary conditions for Latinos to emerge as a national political force in the 1960s. However, a candidate was needed to inspire Latinos nationally as had Franklin D. Roosevelt in
the 1930s and 1940s. The ideal candidate would reach out to the
Latino community with the enthusiasm of Henry A. Wallace in
1948 but be grounded in institutions to which Latinos belonged: the
Democratic Party, the Catholic Church, the AFL-CIO, and veterans
groups. Other factors creating a particularly good opportunity for
ethnic empowerment were the narrow partisan division within the
nation and the lack of an incumbent in the 1960 presidential election. In a close election a relatively small number of voters could
tip the balance nationally by making the difference in a number of
key states.[1] One Californian, Carlos McCormick, sought to realize
this potential by leveraging his access to both a presidential campaign and the Latino community.

James Carlos McCormick was born in the Southern California
community of Santa Barbara. His Irish American father drove a
truck for a lumber company and his Mexican American mother
was a housewife. McCormick's memories were grounded in the
New Deal, but his experiences revolved around the 1950s Mexican
American civil rights era. Like others of this period he was an
idealist tempered by pragmatism. He attended the University of
Arizona, where he met and married Mercy Estrada, the daughter of
Ralph Estrada. Estrada was a prominent attorney and the Supreme
President of the Alianza fraternal society who had served with
Councilman Edward Roybal and CSO's Tony Ríos on the board of
the American Council of Spanish Speaking Organizations. Estrada
incorporated his son-in-law into the family's political affairs.[2]

Soon thereafter, Ralph Estrada arranged through U.S. Senator Carl Hayden (D-Arizona) for McCormick to receive a patronage job in the nation's capitol. The young man worked days as a security guard and attended night classes at George Washington University Law School. McCormick initially endeared himself to U.S. Senator John F. Kennedy by volunteering to translate Kennedy's press releases into Spanish. He served as Kennedy's representative to the GI Forum's 1959 convention in Los Angeles and encouraged Kennedy to join the organization, which he did in early 1960.[3] Kennedy was receptive to McCormick's help because it was free and, according to senior Kennedy advisor Clark Clifford, because the senator was becoming aware of Latino groups in the Southwest.[4]

In the spring of 1960, McCormick's role changed dramatically when he visited Arizona as part of the Kennedy entourage. This upset Senator Hayden, a supporter of Senate Majority Leader Lyndon B. Johnson who also sought the presidency, and he responded by firing McCormick from his patronage post. Columnist Charles Bartlett picked up the story. "This catapulted me into a position beyond my importance," said McCormick.[5] Kennedy responded to the now public attack on his volunteer by hiring the young Latino as a member of his relatively small staff.

During all of this, McCormick found time to start the Washington, D.C. chapter of the rapidly expanding American GI Forum. Though not a veteran, McCormick recognized the Forum's national reach. Soon the Forum appointed him as chair of its National Legislative Committee. "He had the most contacts, so we asked him to show us how the national political system works," recalled Dr. Héctor García.[6] McCormick strengthened his ties to CSO through his mother, who joined the new chapter in Santa Barbara. She took McCormick to a CSO meeting and introduced him to executive director César Chávez on one of his visits home.[7]

Senator Kennedy received his party's nomination in early July 1960 at the Democratic National Convention in Los Angeles. In his acceptance speech he stressed that "we stand today on the edge of a New Frontier," including "unconquered pockets of ignorance and prejudice, unanswered questions of poverty and surplus."[8] Following the convention, Carlos McCormick joined Kennedy and his top advisers at Hyannis Port, the family's summer home on Cape Cod, to plan their strategy. Kennedy decided to focus on the big states that held most of the electoral votes needed to win. Kennedy's inner circle talked about the "problems and possibilities in organizing the Spanish-speaking" and gave McCormick the task of organizing a Latino outreach program called Viva Kennedy.[9]

Carlos McCormick rented space for Viva Kennedy at 1512 K Street, in Washington, D.C., and gave himself the title of national executive director. He obtained the assistance of Arthur Valdez, who was loaned to the campaign by Congressman Joseph M. Montoya of New Mexico. McCormick facilitated the appointment of Dr. Héctor García as vice chair of the Democratic National Committee's Foreign Nationalities Branch. These initial moves strengthened Viva Kennedy's operational ties to the Congressional Latinos, the GI Forum, and the Democratic Party. McCormick also secured from the larger Kennedy campaign a commitment for three Latino-oriented candidate events.[10]

McCormick worked with the leading Latinos to construct a national organization capable of registering Latinos to vote, delivering a pro-Kennedy message, and then turning out the vote on election day. This started with a formal structure, led by two honorary co-chairs, Senator Dennis Chávez and Representative Joseph M. Montoya. Co-Chairs were then named from a number of states.[11] The elected officials provided credibility and the network of ethnic organizations provided volunteers and community ties. "These organizations—the GI Forum, LULAC, MAPA, and so forth, which had their own infighting and jockeying for positions—they all fell in under the banner of Viva Kennedy," according to Lorenzo Tapia, aide to Senator Chávez.[12]

Reaching Latinos was made easier, according to Viva Kennedy organizers, because of the candidate's personal characteristics, background, and the larger social context of his candidacy. "Here was an attractive war hero, who was macho, wealthy, and had a big family and an attractive wife," stated Carlos McCormick. "He's a Catholic like us, who's running for president and sees our problems and is concerned."[13] Frank Zaragoza, the president of the Minneapolis LULAC Council and a leader within the Operating Engineers Union, echoed this sentiment, saying Latinos "looked positively to Kennedy being Catholic, pro-worker, part of a big family."[14] He was seen as a Democrat and a "liberal Catholic" said attorney E.J. Salcines of Tampa, Florida.[15]

Believing that the election would be close, McCormick sought to identify areas with unregistered Latinos who, with the proper motivation, would register and then go to the polls to vote for Kennedy. In California, McCormick turned to CSO and its thirty chapters, which had a history of successful voter registration. Using money from the California Labor Federation, CSO hired twenty organizers and undertook the most extensive drive in its history. The CSO registered 140,000 Mexican Americans, bringing the statewide total to 440,000—or six percent of the all registered voters. McCormick believed that this was enough to determine the race if the other parts of the campaign came together as planned.[16]

The Kennedy campaign told *Time Magazine* about the successful registration drive in California. The reporter mistakenly gave the credit to Viva Kennedy, prompting a number of calls from CSO to the national Kennedy headquarters. Robert F. Kennedy, the candidate's brother and campaign manager, called CSO President Herman Gallegos and apologized for the misstatement.[17] To make amends, he invited Gallegos to talk to Senator Kennedy on his next trip to San Francisco. "I remember going to the hotel suite, the presidential suite, at the Sheraton Palace with Ralph Vega and several others," stated Gallegos. Kennedy said, "You guys did a hell of a job, and when I'm elected president, I want you all to come see me so we can talk about how to work with problems you are concerned with."[18]

Councilman Roybal was the chair of Viva Kennedy in California and attorney Henry López served as the state coordinator. Both men had statewide followings and were close to the California Democratic Council. This was important because Kennedy badly needed to pull in these former Stevenson partisans. Teacher and Unruh loyalist Ralph Poblano served as secretary. Attorney Philip Newman served as field director in Southern California. Newman's family had been close to Pat Brown since the forties. Other individuals oversaw finances, public relations, and constituency outreach to women, veterans, labor, social clubs, and students.[19] "In a sense, the MAPA people became the Viva Kennedy Clubs. We just called on them and said, 'How about being a Viva Kennedy Club for the campaign?'" recalls Henry López. He also mobilized his personal network. "You naturally go to people that you knew and I had a list from my [1958] campaign, so I could quickly spot Chicanos all over the state."[20] Personal and political networks integrated with existing organizations to form Viva Kennedy. Of the two oldest groups, the GI Forum easily folded into the campaign in California but also worked with their national organization. LULAC was likewise part of Viva Kennedy but was not as socially or politically integrated in California as in other states.

Nixon did not want to cede the growing Latino vote that Eisenhower and Knight had courted with some success. Republicans opened a "Solidaridad Latino-Americana Nixon" office in East Los Angeles. The Viva Kennedy newsletter ridiculed the operation, illuminating the overlay on partisanship and self-identity: "Those of us who are actually part of the Mexican American community of our county and who are not ashamed of it [and do not use] Latin-American or Spanish-American or any other diluted or camouflaged term."[21] Even outside the heavily Democratic Eastside, Nixon made little headway in the community despite forming a few "Arriba Nixon" clubs.[22]

One reason may have been the attacks on Kennedy for being Catholic. Protestant clergy claimed that a Catholic was unfit to be president because he would take orders from the Pope. This sent a powerful message to Latinos: it did not matter how rich and powerful you might become in America, if you were a Catholic you remained vulnerable. "Every time that he got put down for being a Catholic this made points with the Mexicans who are all Catholics," stated CSO's César Chávez. "[Latinos] looked at him as sort of a minority kind of person."[23]

Then, at the urging of Carlos McCormick, Kennedy used some of his most valuable airtime to speak about the plight of Latinos.[24] In his opening statement in the first-ever televised presidential debate held on September 26, 1960, Kennedy said:

> I am not satisfied until every American enjoys his full constitutional rights. If a Negro baby is born, and this is true also of Puerto Ricans and Mexicans in some of our cities, he has about half as much chance to get through high school as a white baby. He has one-third as much chance to get through college as a white student. He has about a third as much chance to be a professional man, and about half as much

chance to own a house. He has about four times as much chance that he'll be out of work in his lifetime as the white baby. I think we can do better. I don't want the talents of any American to go to waste.[25]

Kennedy's statement was electrifying and anticipated a shift in American politics because up to that point neither Latinos nor African Americans had ever decided a presidential election.

The campaign organized a two-day National Conference on Constitutional Rights on October 12-13 in New York City, attended by Viva Kennedy officers. Senator Kennedy and campaign manager Robert Kennedy carved time out of a hectic schedule to meet privately with the Latino leaders at the Waldorf Astoria Hotel. Present were California attorney Henry López, Arizona attorney Ralph Estrada, Texans Dr. Héctor García and State Senator Henry B. González, and New York Assemblymen José Ramos-López and Felipe N. Torres.[26] After the meeting, Senator and Mrs. Kennedy addressed Puerto Ricans at a rally in Spanish Harlem, where Mrs. Kennedy's spoke in Spanish.[27] She also taped the first ever Spanish-language presidential television commercial.[28]

Viva Kennedy used Kennedy family members as some of its most popular surrogates. Edward Kennedy did an event in San Diego County at the La Mesa home of educator Armando Rodríquez, the co-chair of the San Diego Viva Kennedy. Born in Mexico, but raised in Barrio Logan, Rodríguez won his citizenship in World War II and went to college on the GI Bill, and became a teacher. Like others in his generation, he had immersed himself in CSO, CDC, GI Forum, and MAPA, as well as the San Diego County Democratic Central Committee, which he chaired. Rodríguez said that the younger Kennedy stole the hearts of the overflow crowd when he sang "Jalisco" in his Boston accented Spanish, backed-up by a Mariachi band.[29]

In addition to the members of the candidate's clan, Viva Kennedy utilized prominent Latinos to speak on the candidate's behalf. One of the most popular was legendary Senator Dennis Chávez who had first come to Los Angeles two decades earlier to campaign for Roosevelt. The frail but determined seventy-two-year-old icon spent five days in early October barnstorming the state for the national ticket. The Viva Kennedy Club of Sacramento sponsored a rally and tamale buffet at the Catholic Newman Center. The next

U.S. Senator Dennis Chávez addresses a MAPA-sponsored rally for John F. Kennedy in Fresno. The aging senator barnstormed the state for Viva Kennedy.   *(Kenneth C. Burt)*

day Chávez traveled to Fresno for a reception at a local hotel under the aegis of the Viva Kennedy Clubs and MAPA. The 150-person crowd included people from the small agricultural towns of Delano, Hanford, Huron, Visalia, Madera, and Selma. "Jack Kennedy has more humanity in his little finger than Nixon does in his whole body," stated Chávez, who emphasized voting. "You may complain about police brutality and discrimination and things generally, but if you do not vote you'll deserve what you get." Chávez then went to vote-rich Los Angeles where he held a news conference and addressed a series of Mexican American events. From Los Angeles, Chávez went to Santa Ana, San Bernardino, and San Diego.[30]

One week before the election, Senator Kennedy made a final two-day swing through California. Two hundred thousand people turned out for Kennedy in Los Angeles, matching the turnout for Nixon a few days earlier.[31] On the trip, Kennedy signaled the importance of Mexican American voters by lunching on Olvera Street and by choosing the East Los Angeles Junior College Stadium as the site for his main speech. In a blending of traditional and modern campaign forms, the candidate paid to have the rally carried live on television, allowing voters at home to hear his message and to share in the excitement of his visit.[32]

A judicial election also animated Mexican American voters in Los Angeles. Governor Brown, after winning kudos for elevating

Carlos Terán to the Superior Court, angered the political activists by taking the advice of the local assemblyman and appointing a non-Latino, Howard Walshok, to replace him on the East Los Angeles Municipal Court. "I'll never forget when we went to Governor Brown and we asked Governor Brown to appoint Leo Sánchez. Governor Brown said, 'If the Mexican community wants a judge, let them elect him,'" recalled Joseph Sánchez, a young grocery store manager.[33] The GI Forum responded by recruiting Leopoldo Sánchez, a thirty-three-year-old war veteran interested in politics, to run against the appointed incumbent. Councilman Roybal, the GI Forum and the newly organized MAPA embraced the Sánchez campaign, as did Republican businessmen like Manuel Vega. The intense desire to elect a Latino judge was matched only by the desire to teach the governor a lesson. "There were hard feelings on the part of every one of my campaigners and we tried to have that feeling rub off onto the people we spoke with," recalled Leopoldo Sánchez.[34]

In the final week before the election, Mexican Americans in Los Angeles and across the state focused in a way not seen since the

Mexican Americans rallied to elect Leopoldo Sánchez to the East Los Angeles Municipal Court in 1960. (l to r) Edward Ramírez, Lucille Roybal, Edward Roybal, Manuel Vega, Leopoldo Sánchez, and Gloria Sánchez at a fundraising dinner.   *(Kenneth C. Burt)*

1949 Roybal campaign. Volunteers talked to voters over the phone and at their front doors. Jacqueline Kennedy underscored the importance of the vote by telephoning a number of Spanish-speaking voters. Surrogates traversed the state, addressing rallies in an effort to drive turnout even higher: Senator Edward Kennedy spoke in Santa Barbara, and El Paso Mayor Raymond Telles in Fresno.[35]

On Election Day Latinos in California went to the polls in large numbers; the high interest in the election drove overall turnout in the state above 80 percent for the first time since Truman's come from behind victory in 1948. A Republican backlash against the large number of first time Mexican American voters did produce several incidents of voter harassment reminiscent of the voter challenges experienced in San Jose in 1952. But for the most part the election proved to be an exhilarating experience.[36]

Kennedy and Nixon both went to bed on election night not knowing the outcome of the election. By morning it became apparent that Kennedy had won the presidency by the narrowest margin in history. Kennedy won the popular vote by less than 115,000 out of some 70 million votes. To the campaign's surprise, Kennedy lost California. McCormick stated that an additional half-day of the candidate's time would have put the senator over the top. Mexican American leaders in Los Angeles were ecstatic with the outcome in the contested judicial election as Leopoldo Sánchez ousted the appointed incumbent by a comfortable margin. For his part, the governor privately acknowledged his "mistake," according to his aide Frank Cullen.[37]

Mexican Americans accounted for the margin of victory in Texas and New Mexico, and helped in Illinois. Kennedy won Texas by 50,000 votes. Mexican Americans there gave him 91 percent backing, providing a 200,000-vote edge. In New Mexico, where Kennedy won by only 2,000 votes, his 70 percent among Mexican Americans provided a 20,000-vote edge. In Chicago where Mayor Richard Daley was an honorary Viva Kennedy Club member, he told Carlos McCormick that Mexican American voters contributed to his ability to carry the state of Illinois for Kennedy.[38]

Another way to look at the data is to compare the Latino vote with that of other groups. Kennedy received 85 percent of the Mexican American vote. This was higher than support from

African Americans (75 percent), Jews (82 percent), Slavs (82 percent), Italians (75 percent), and even the Irish (75 percent). New York Puerto Ricans, by contrast, had backed Kennedy with 77 percent support. One explanation of why Kennedy did better among Latinos than fellow Irishmen is that his campaign made a special appeal to the working class for support and this resonated more with Latinos than with the more established Irish Americans.[39]

John F. Kennedy thus served as the midwife to the birth of national Latino politics. "The Kennedys were learning, they wanted to know more about Hispanics," stated Carlos McCormick, the California native whose entrepreneurial skills in creating and overseeing Viva Kennedy catapulted Latinos to national prominence earlier than might have otherwise been the case.[40] The campaign also established a new national Latino political network, strengthened local organizations, and personally affected thousands of individuals, particularly in the four places where Kennedy spoke to large Latino audiences—New York City, Tampa, San Antonio, and East Los Angeles. Most importantly for California's Mexican Americans, the presidential campaign brought new recognition to the group even as it dramatically expanded the number of Latino voters and provided leadership opportunities to hundreds of activists. As a result, the community—who would begin to speak politically through the Roybal-led Mexican-American Political Association—was determined to achieve a new level of influence at all levels of government.

MAPA focused its attention on Washington, D.C. as Roybal and the other Viva Kennedy leaders looked to President Kennedy to reward the ethnic community with several major appointments. The Latino leadership sought the naming of the first Latino U.S. ambassador, the first federal judge, and the first high-ranking department administrator. It was an expectation that administration officials shared. The process of obtaining a federal post, however, often proved elusive. The multiple challenges are illustrated by the experiences of the three highest-profile California Latinos who sought a top-level job in the administration: Edward Roybal, Henry López, and Carlos Terán.

As a result of the efforts of Kennedy aide Carlos McCormick, who was working as the President's Latino liaison out of the

Democratic National Committee, and Senator Dennis Chávez, the Kennedy administration agreed that the post of Deputy Secretary of State for Inter-American Affairs should go to a Spanish-speaking person. This set off a spirited behind-the-scenes discussion over who would get the sub-cabinet position. Councilman Roybal was one of three major contenders. California U.S. Senator Claire Engle supported him as did State Controller Alan Cranston.[41] Senator Dennis Chávez, GI Forum founder Dr. Héctor García, and Carlos McCormick, the three most influential Mexican Americans with the Kennedy administration, all preferred University of New Mexico Professor Vicente Ximenes, a past national chairman of the GI Forum.[42]

President Kennedy gave Secretary of State Dean Rusk and Undersecretary of State Chester Bowles the right to make the appointment. They selected neither Roybal nor Ximenes, opting instead for a man with diplomatic experience: Arturo Morales-Carrión. A Cuban born, and Texas and New York educated professor, Morales-Carrión served as Secretary of State for Puerto Rico since 1953. He was the U.S. Commissioner for the Caribbean Commission, a member of the U.S. National Commission for UNESCO, and an Alternative U.S. Delegate at the Tenth Inter-American Conference.[43]

The appointment of Morales-Carrión was an important first for Latinos, but nevertheless it was seen as a setback for McCormick and for Mexican Americans in the Southwest. It reflected the reality that while the White House and members of Congress used their influence to create a consensus behind the selection of the first Latino to a sub-cabinet post, the actual selection was up to the State Department.[44]

During this process, McCormick was also busy trying to line up support for the appointment of the first U.S. ambassador of Latino heritage. He believed Henry López of California best fit the profile of what the Kennedy administration was seeking. The Harvard-educated attorney was a national key figure in Viva Kennedy and the Democratic Party's nominee for statewide office in California two years earlier. Further, he was from a large state with a high concentration of Mexican Americans—one that the president hoped to carry in 1964.[45]

McCormick went to work promoting Henry López in the State Department, on Capitol Hill, and within the White House. He thought he had succeeded in this effort when Undersecretary of State Chester Bowles selected López to be the first Ambassador of Mexican American heritage. López got a glowing recommendation from California's senior senator, Claire Engle, who told the White House that López was "probably the smartest Mexican American in California."[46] However, because Engle was not viewed as a major power in California, the Kennedy administration extended to Governor Brown and Assemblyman Jesse Unruh, whom they saw as critical to the president's western power base, the right to veto appointments. Both men had declined to assist López in 1958, when he secured the Democratic Party nomination for secretary of state with the backing of the California Democratic Council but not the party professionals. "Hank wasn't part of the so-called group," said Assemblyman Tom Rees, an ally of Unruh, whom he recalled as "a reward and punishment guy" intent on expanding his own power.[47] Unruh's principal competitor for control of the liberal movement was California Democratic Council, of which López was a recognized leader. So Unruh "torpedoed" the appointment, according to McCormick. "They said Hank was almost disbarred, which was a bold-faced lie."[48] Unruh thus blocked the López appointment and, with it, dashed the hopes of the state's Viva Kennedy movement.

With Henry López dead politically, the administration sought to appoint yet another Californian to an ambassadorial post. This time it zeroed in on Judge Carlos Terán. Unlike the Roybal and López names that had been put forward by the Viva Kennedy network, Terán was suggested by Governor Brown. Kennedy had met the fellow World War II veteran during his presidential campaign. Moreover, Unruh had no objections because Terán had aided Judge Walshok over Leopoldo Sánchez in their recent election. The White House notified Terán that he was under consideration and the story appeared in Los Angeles papers.[49]

The appointment of Carlos Terán, despite its historic importance, did not sit well with key activists. The Los Angeles chapter of the GI Forum notified its national leadership that Terán's appointment was problematic because he "did not back up Leopoldo Sánchez."[50] "Los Angeles is up in arms" at the idea of Terán's appointment, the

Southern California Forum leaders told Dr. Héctor García. Activists who had collected signatures on behalf of Terán's judicial appointment were now writing letters to President Kennedy and Governor Brown seeking to block his further advance. They asked their national leadership to back their high stakes power play.[51] The once-likely appointment never occurred.

The Kennedy administration, intent on naming the first Latino ambassador, and feeling the frustration of unmet expectations by Latino activists, selected El Paso Mayor Raymond Telles to be the U.S. Ambassador to Costa Rica. The Kennedy administration then turned to appointing the first Mexican American to the federal bench. The post went to a Lone Star Latino because the open seat was in South Texas. As a result, of the three top federal appointments, two ended up going to a Mexican American from Texas, and the third to Cuban-born Puerto Rican from the East Coast.

California Latinos received their most important appointment in the person of Carlos McCormick who became the Special Assistant to the Deputy Secretary of State for Inter-American Affairs in the State Department. He formally reported to Arturo Morales-Carrión, but also continued to serve as the president's liaison to Latinos. McCormick's appointment did not satisfy the California leadership's thirst for representation because, despite his strong roots in California, they saw McCormick as being from Arizona, due to his marriage into Ralph Estrada's family.[52]

Kennedy then appointed another Californian to a significant post but this too failed to satisfy most activists. The administration named Héctor Godínez as postmaster in Santa Ana in Orange County. Godínez, the son of a gardener, developed his leadership skills on the battlefield of World War II as a tank commander for General George C. Patton, coming home and rising to the national presidency of LULAC, where he came to Kennedy's attention. According to a longtime colleague, the word on the street was that Godínez "went from a letter carrier one day to being the postmaster the next because he helped to bring in the Hispanic vote for John Kennedy."[53] Despite the post's importance (Tampa, Florida, was the only other city to get a Latino postmaster), the appointment did not satisfy those around Roybal because it was not seen as a national position. Furthermore, LULAC was outside the dominant MAPA network that spearheaded Viva Kennedy in the state.

Two of Kennedy's policy initiatives—Alliance for Progress and the Peace Corps—did provide additional employment opportunities for Latino activists. The Alliance for Progress echoed Roosevelt's Good Neighbor Policy in its effort to assist in the economic development of Latin American nations while the Peace Corps was designed to export U.S. idealism and skills to developing nations. Among those benefiting from these appointments were two early CSO activists who subsequently became involved in partisan politics: Ralph Guzmán and Henrietta Villaescusa. Guzmán accepted an administrative post in the Peace Corps in Venezuela and Villaescusa assumed an administrative position with the State Department in Washington, D.C.[54]

Parallel to the efforts of these middle class Mexican Americans to secure appointments with the Kennedy administration, the

Henrietta Villaescusa and Congressman George Brown, a Roybal ally. The first woman CSO president worked for Brown in the district office and then moved to Washington, D.C. to help administer the Alliance for Progress.
(Kenneth C. Burt)

Community Service Organization—having won recognition for registering 140,000 new voters—focused their attention on Governor Brown and the state legislature. CSO set its sights on securing a long-sought piece of their domestic agenda: state legislation to provide financial support for elderly Mexicans who had lived in the state for twenty-five years but lacked citizenship papers. Much had changed since 1947 when the need for such financial support emerged as an issue during CSO's house meetings. CSO had pushed the idea in successive legislative sessions and each time the issue gained additional strength. The organization saw an opportunity for a legislative breakthrough due to Governor Brown's upcoming re-election and Kennedy's desire to be supportive.

This latest drive began three weeks after the November 1960 election when Councilman Roybal and CSO's Tony Ríos met with a dozen other civil rights leaders under the aegis of the California Committee for Fair Housing Practices. The group agreed to support "the CSO proposal to make possible Old Age Assistance to Aliens."[55] Those in the room included Assemblyman Augustus Hawkins, Thomas Pitts from the California Labor Federation, and Joseph Wyatt, leader of the California Democratic Council.[56]

Assemblyman Phillip Burton of San Francisco introduced the measure, Assembly Bill 5, along with fourteen co-authors. They reflected a range of organizational relationships, and included Vernon Kilpatrick who had introduced the first bill in 1953. Co-sponsors from the Central Valley reflected CSO's growth in that region. Assemblyman James Mills, a CDC liberal who won his election in 1960 because of the mobilization of Latino voters in San Diego for Kennedy, made this his first bill.[57]

"We did a big campaign," said CSO lobbyist Dolores Huerta. CSO generated thousands of letters, and delegations lobbied their legislators in the State Capitol.[58] Such efforts by CSO were reinforced and magnified by the larger civil rights coalition. Bill Becker and Max Mont of the garment union-headed Jewish Labor Committee delivered Labor, Jews, and other minority groups. Monsignor Thomas O'Dwyer rallied religious leaders. All tapped into their long-established relationships with legislators.[59]

Still, the measure faced multiple obstacles. The least problematic was Governor Brown who was sympathetic but was concerned about the bill's fiscal impact. The greater problems came from Assemblyman Jesse Unruh, then in the process of putting together the votes to become the Speaker, and Senate Social Welfare Committee Chair James Cobey, who represented Madera and Merced Counties in the Central Valley.

Burton began to alleviate Governor Brown's concern and to clear legislative hurdles by locating federal money to cover almost half of the $5 million additional costs anticipated in the first year, a prospect no doubt enabled by a political alliance with the Kennedy administration. At the same time, he held out a carrot to Los Angeles and other counties seeking financial relief by noting that individuals covered by state pensions would no longer apply for General Assistance for which the counties paid 100 percent. Burton also emphasized the modest nature of the bill, claiming that it would add only 8,000 seniors to the rolls. The Brown administration, confident that federal money would come and concerned with its own reelection the following year, adopted the bill as part of its "welfare reform" package and budgeted for the added expense.[60]

Soon thereafter, AB 5 passed the Unruh-controlled Assembly Ways and Means Committee, and sailed through the full Assembly.[61] CSO focused its attention on Senator James Cobey, of Merced, within whose committee the Non-Citizen Old Age Pension bill now rested. "We went to barber shops, grocery stores, and door-to-door to get people to sign letters," recalled Dolores Huerta. In classic Alinsky-style organizing, CSO also increased the creative tension by ratcheting up the lawmaker's discomfort. Some of the seniors "had four or five children in World War II, but they didn't speak English," Huerta recalled. "I dropped them off at Cobey's office. They sat there and held the pictures of their children in the service, some of whom had died for their country. They were told only to say, 'Pass AB 5.'" Burton also got Cobey's attention. He "held up all of his bills" in the Assembly Committee, recalls Huerta. She noted that "this broke the log-jam." The full Senate then passed the measure 28 to 1.[62]

On July 14, 1961, Governor Brown signed the bill before an audience of 200 CSO members from thirty chapters who had carpooled to the State Capitol in Sacramento. In applying his signature, Pat Brown stated that "Simple justice is done, at last." He added that it was a "significant part of the New Frontier," thereby linking his action and the successful CSO efforts to the Kennedy administration.[63]

CSO explained the victory to its members in terms of Latino self-organization, voter registration, and coalition politics. "In 1961, with 400,000 votes behind them and support from many other groups, the Bill was passed and signed," according to CSO. "Passage of the Bill was a dramatic exposition of the growth of CSO and its registered voters, for the pensions went to a group of people who, no matter how thankful they would be, would never be able to show their gratitude come next election day, for they were non-citizens."[64] The Legislature that passed the bill, moreover, did not include a single Mexican American.

The bill's legislative odyssey also illustrated the power of leadership. Dolores Huerta, Tony Ríos, and Bill Becker all agreed that the bill would never have passed without the extraordinary efforts of Assemblyman Phillip Burton.[65] But it also would never have happened without the support of Governor Brown and the Kennedy administration who agreed to share the added costs for the pensions. In retrospect, CSO's insistence on getting credit for registering 140,000 new voters in 1960 may have helped motivate individual legislators, the civil rights coalition, and state and federal officials. The Kennedy administration helped give an important policy victory to California Mexican Americans frustrated by a lack of federal appointments.

The old age bill was only a part of CSO's aggressive legislative agenda that included new efforts to curtail police abuse of minorities and the negative impact of urban redevelopment, such as the practice of razing low-income neighborhoods that left former residents without affordable housing. Nor was the pension bill the only legislative victory. Legislative chair Dolores Huerta was particularly proud of successful bills to stop local registrars from seeking to limit voter registration and to prohibit private parties from challenging the rights of Latinos to cast their ballot. SB 121 by Senator Albert Rodda of Sacramento "permits door to door registration anywhere within the county, and requires appointment of deputies," according the CSO's 1961 Legislative Report. AB 2292 by Assemblyman Burton states that "County Clerks cannot discriminate in appointment of deputy registrars because of race, color, national origin or creed." Huerta stressed that these bills were necessary because "CSO's voter registration efforts have consistently met opposition in county after county in securing appointment of deputy registrars and obtaining permission for door to door registration." She also hailed the passage of AB 370, by Assemblyman Robert Crown of Oakland. The measure prevented "challenges at the polls [and thereby] removed the constant intimidation on election day."[66] Governor Brown stressed his signing of this legislation earlier in the year at the LULAC convention in Anaheim.[67]

Governor Brown built on the goodwill established by his support of the Non-Citizen Old Age bill and other progressive legislation. He served as the Grand Marshall for the 1961 September 16th parade in East Los Angeles and then returned to the City of Commerce for luncheon in his honor with 150 prominent Mexican Americans. Councilman Roybal introduced the governor by noting that he had made more appointments of Latinos than his two predecessors combined and had recently signed the CSO-sponsored bill for Non-Citizen Old Age Pensions, themes Brown reinforced in his prepared remarks. Governor Brown stressed his appointment of Arthur Alarcón as legal advisor and Daniel Luevano, an early CSO activist, as chief deputy director of the Department of Finance. He also acknowledged the growing Latino vote. "Let us work together to prove that democracy works—as you did last year—when your impressive record of voter registration brought you national recognition," stated Brown.[68]

Mexican Americans were on a roll in California because at the same time CSO achieved its historic legislative victory, activists in Los Angeles won national recognition for helping to elect a new mayor. The incumbent, Norris Poulson, was a conservative Republican. His core support came from the business community, the Republican Party, and the *Los Angeles Times*, but over time the mayor had developed a working relationship with the Los Angeles County Federation of Labor. His opponent in the race, Samuel Yorty, was a maverick with populist views. For his campaign, Yorty focused on three groups alienated from City Hall: Anglos in the San Fernando Valley, African Americans in South Central, and Latinos on the Eastside.[69]

Latinos were receptive to Yorty. There was strong anti-incumbent feeling among voters and activists that was rooted in Mayor Poulson's use of eminent domain to displace low-income, Spanish-speaking residents in Chávez Ravine in order to build Dodger Stadium. In addition, the community leaders were looking for a candidate to support as a way of increasing their influence in the city. Yorty promised to integrate Mexican Americans into city government at an unprecedented level. Many key activists responded with enthusiasm. Eduardo Quevedo became the general chairman and Dr. Francisco Bravo the honorary chair of the Spanish-Speaking Committee to Elect Sam Yorty Mayor. Judge Leopoldo Sánchez, Laborers Local 300 leader Mike Quevedo, and Mexican American Opportunity Foundation founder Dionicio Morales also joined in. GI Forum leader Raúl Morín organized much of the door-to-door campaign.[70]

Yorty bested the incumbent in the runoff election by some 15,000 votes in a city with more than a million registered. Latinos made a critical difference, giving Yorty 58.3 percent support.[71] Mayor Poulson explained his defeat, saying, "In the districts where I won, there was a light turnout but in the Negro and Mexican districts the turnout was larger."[72] The victory was particularly sweet because *Newsweek* magazine gave Latinos credit for Yorty's win.[73] Sweeter still, Mayor Yorty quickly rewarded Latinos for their critical support. Yorty placed Dr. Francisco Bravo on the important Police Commission. He put Professor Julian Nava on the Civil Service Commission. More important still, Yorty placed civil servant Richard Tafoya on his personal staff where he functioned as the first deputy mayor of Mexican American heritage.[74]

On the heels of the Yorty, Kennedy and Sánchez victories, Latino activists focused on securing state and federal seats in 1962. The Democratically-controlled legislature drew seats using data from the 1960 Census with the idea of maximizing their partisan advantage. This was particularly important to the Kennedy White House that was counting on California, with its eight new congressional seats, to compensate for expected party losses in Northeast states with declining populations. This led the party leaders to reject the appeal of Roybal and other Latino leaders to create majority Latino seats for Congress and the state assembly.[75] Still, the legislature created new political opportunities for Latinos, as well as African Americans and Jews.

Roybal made the best of the situation, recognizing that he could get elected to Congress if he followed the model successfully employed thirteen years earlier to win the city council seat: build a multiracial, working class coalition. Roybal set his sights on a new Democratic leaning district with a Republican incumbent, Gordon McDonough. The district started in Boyle Heights and moved westward across downtown to Hollywood. Roybal's primary opponents included William Fitzgerald, a professor at Loyola University, who had the backing of Assemblyman Unruh. However, his toughest possible opponent, Judge William Rosenthal, agreed not to run, making it possible for Roybal to reassemble his important Latino-Jewish alliance. Roybal gained an advantage over his adversaries by utilizing his council post to polish his foreign policy credentials. Roybal represented Mayor Yorty at the four hundredth anniversary of Madrid, witnessed the "Berlin crisis," and visited the Holy Father in Rome.[76]

Despite Roybal's good chances, Mexican American activists were frustrated with having to fight a proxy war with Assemblyman Unruh. Their anger was intensified by the fact that Unruh was viewed as Kennedy's main person in the state. Latinos believed that their loyalty to the president should mean that his other allies should not seek to block their upward mobility. While Unruh did not check with the White House on which candidates to support, the split within the Democratic coalition was severe enough that Carlos McCormick flew to California in an effort to mitigate the damage. In a meeting with the MAPA board of directors, McCormick reiterated the White House's commitment to Mexican Americans. He likewise made it clear to Democratic Party leaders that the president would be pleased to see California send a Latino to Congress.[77] McCormick's political trip to California was possible because he had left the State Department to return to the Democratic National Committee as the assistant to the chairman.[78]

Roybal's campaign overlaid ethnicity, ideology, and competing power centers. He received the endorsement of State Controller Alan Cranston and the California Democratic Council, which brought in precinct walkers from Pasadena and Beverly Hills, according to CDC coordinator Keith Seegmiller. The Los Angeles County Federation of Labor, normally an Unruh ally, also chose to back Roybal, with whom it shared a thirteen-year relationship. Former Governor Culbert Olson, who helped launch Latino politics in California, served as the campaign's honorary chair. Roybal's liberal politics, years of relationships, and city council membership enabled him to win his party's nomination for Congress in a district with a minority of Latino voters.[79]

Shortly after the California primary, MAPA met at its third annual convention in San Francisco. There was much to celebrate. Roybal had won his primary along with three other Mexican Americans running for seats in the State Assembly. Moreover, Governor Brown showered Mexican Americans with appointments. Still, many remained angry with Unruh and the Latino leaders wanted more full time positions within the Brown administration. In this tense atmosphere, an off-hand remark set off a firestorm. "You people have got to understand, you've got to be patient," stated Lieutenant Governor Glenn Anderson at the MAPA convention. "You can't expect the children of a people that in the previous generation were for the most part fruit pickers to now be considered for all the top jobs in the State of California." The delegates booed Anderson off the stage and MAPA demanded a meeting with Governor Brown.[80]

Ironically, earlier in 1962, Brown made history by naming Arthur Alarcón as his chief-of-staff. But the Democratic governor failed to win praise for his top Latino appointee from the political activists because Alarcón was not one of them. The son of a union baker, he rejected his immigrant father's "far left ideas." He registered as a Republican while at UCLA before joining the Army and then becoming a Los Angeles Deputy District Attorney. Moreover, he had not utilized the Latino network to get his post. "My ethnic background, I would say, had if not nothing, then almost nothing to do with my [initial] appointment" as clemency secretary, according to Alarcón. "I had the respect . . . of police chiefs and sheriffs."[81] As the head of the 100-person staff, he worked behind the scenes to advance Brown's agenda. He did not see himself as responsible for advancing the goals of the organized Mexican American community.[82]

Brown acquiesced to the meeting demanded by MAPA. The governor had Anderson there to personally apologize. The two tried to repair the political damage created by the impolitic but well-meaning Anderson, who had long championed civil rights legislation and had co-sponsored the bill outlawing Latino school segregation. "We tried to emphasize," according to MAPA's Bert Corona, that "it wasn't a question of raising the issue on a personal basis, but we were more insistent than ever that this administration respond more positively to the issues that we felt were important." Governor Brown promised to be more responsive.[83]

Later that summer, MAPA endorsed Governor Brown's 1962 reelection against the Republican candidate, former Vice President Richard Nixon.[8] MAPA's support for Brown was good news for Kennedy, who was closely watching the California race. With Carlos McCormick's guidance the Democratic National Committee published a brochure, "Our Goal is Progress." The pamphlet emphasized the number of Latino appointments and the policy gains made during the past two years, and appealed for support of Democratic candidates.[84]

Roybal's fall 1962 campaign against McDonough emphasized his support for Kennedy and his domestic agenda. The Kennedy administration aided Roybal and many other Democratic congressional candidates by inviting them to the White House to receive a series of policy briefings and to have their photos taken with the president. Roybal used this photo throughout the campaign where he spoke to a myriad of groups and benefited from hundreds of volunteers who walked door to door on his behalf. This volunteer effort was reinforced by no less than three cabinet members who campaigned for Roybal in the district. In reaching out, the councilman did not forget his base among Latino voters; Eduardo Quevedo volunteered, as did activists associated with CSO, MAPA, and the earlier Roybal campaigns. Roybal gained visibility by riding in the Mexican Independence Day Parade. Governor Pat Brown and Richard Nixon also participated in the parade, an indication that both parties were courting the growing number of Latino voters.[85]

The desired highlight of the fall campaign—a personal visit to the congressional district by President Kennedy planned for

October 27—never happened due to the Cuban missile crises. The White House, however, did issue a letter endorsing Roybal that he used in a mailer.[86] Roybal's liberal coalition was augmented by the Democratic Party's get-out-the-vote drive designed to bring out voters for Governor Brown and paid for in part by Kennedy.[87] As a result, voter turnout increased and Roybal was elected to Congress with an impressive 56 percent of the vote and voters returned Governor Brown to office. Democrats now controlled a majority in the state legislature and in the state's congressional delegation.[88]

In winning a diverse district without a majority of Mexican American voters, Roybal demonstrated anew his appeal as a co-alition builder. Yet he was still very much an ethnic symbol with a statewide Latino constituency. This was underscored shortly after his election to Congress when he spoke at a banquet for two hundred activists gathered for the CSO national executive board meeting at Hanford, in California's agriculturally rich Central Valley. The growth of local Latino political power was exemplified by the participation of the local mayor, state legislator, and three Latino civic leaders: Hanford City Councilman John L. Carrillo, Planning Commissioner Jerome Salazar, and Beautification Commissioner Gilbert Padilla.[89]

These gains at the federal and local level were matched by the election of two Mexican Americans to the state legislature for the first time in modern history. Like Roybal, both served in World War II and were affiliated with MAPA and the GI Forum and gained experience and built a political base by serving on a city council. Teacher and Santa Fe Springs Mayor John Moreno won in a largely Democratic and heavily Latino district that included East Los Angeles. Businessman and La Puente City Councilman Philip Soto represented the developing suburbs in southeastern Los Angeles County, an area he estimated to be maybe ten percent Latino. Soto recalled that when he and his wife Nell moved to the suburbs "we were looked on not so much as Hispanics but just as part of larger, homogeneous group" who had left behind an urban life for suburban homes, barbecues, and Little League games.[90]

Soto's successful grassroots campaign utilized volunteers and raised only $3,500 against a large field of eight Anglo competitors. Soto credits his victory to having established some name identifi-

Assemblyman John Moreno
(California History Section,
California State Library)

Assemblyman Philip Soto
(California History Section,
California State Library)

cation as a local elected official, and the utilization of non-political social networks, along with support from largely Democratic Mexican Americans. This allowed him to win with 26 percent of the primary vote. He went on to win the general against an Anglo Republican with 56 percent of the vote in a "swing district," in large part because Governor Pat Brown beat Richard Nixon. Latinos were also starting to be placed in staff positions. For example, Congressman George Brown, whose East Los Angeles district bordered Roybal's, hired Grace Montañez Davis and Henrietta Villaescusa, products of the Lincoln Heights CSO.[91]

There was, however, little time to rest on their achievements in Latino Los Angeles because Roybal's move to Congress would create a vacancy within the important Los Angeles City Council. Roybal sought to increase the chances that a Mexican American would replace him. He addressed a large gathering of activists at a MAPA-led meeting at the Alexandria Hotel. He laid out the political dynamics, including the need for Latino unity. "Many of you are under the false impression that the Mexican-American lives in the greater majority in this district," said Roybal. "In the last 10 years the Mexican-American population has been less than the Negro community!"[92] Roybal sought another meeting to decide upon a sole community representative; he could also use the opportunity to talk with Black leaders to see if there was a Latino candidate whom they could support. For Roybal, the lesson from his 1949 election was clear: that in a cosmopolitan district where Latinos were a minority of the voters, they must unite behind a single candidate who also has the ability to work with other groups. Unfortunately, the political lesson from 1949 was not clear to a majority of those present at the Alexandria Hotel, who endorsed three different Latinos, thus ensuring a divided electorate.[93]

The problem was further complicated by the fact that the strongest candidate, Richard Tafoya, Roybal's cousin, was a polarizing figure. The majority of the city council and key liberals strongly opposed his patron, Mayor Yorty. Yorty had also angered the African American community by not following through on his promise to fire Chief of Police William Parker. Moreover, Tafoya was not seen as liberal enough for the progressive district. Meanwhile, absent an effort to find a Latino candidate agreeable to Black voters, a consensus developed among African Americans for Gilbert Lindsay, an aide to Supervisor Kenneth Hahn and a former janitor and CIO activist. Lindsay's supporters did not wait for the special election; instead they got allies on the city council to push through his interim appointment. Lindsay immediately reached out to the Latino community by hiring one of the candidates, Félix Ontiveros, to serve as his chief deputy, thus increasing the odds that he would win the upcoming election.[94]

In the runoff, Roybal and other Eastside activists endorsed Tafoya. These endorsements appear to have solidified the Latino support for Tafoya. But, in retrospect, the candidate emphasized the limited number of Spanish-speaking voters in the district due to the building of freeways, urban renewal, and a general movement to the suburbs. "Mexican Americans went into Pico Rivera, Whittier, and Montebello. The Jewish population, which was very liberal and which could have voted for a Mexican, moved out," said Tafoya. "Who moved in? Mexicans from Mexico, primarily, who didn't vote."[95]

The anger within the Los Angeles Latino community over Tafoya's defeat only intensified because Lindsay's 1963 election coincided with the election of two other African Americans, Tom Bradley and Billy Mills. There were three Blacks, one Jew, and eleven Anglos on the city council. A sense of shock and depression set in among Latino activists who never really believed they could lose the city council seat that for so long symbolized the community's political empowerment. For his part, Tafoya would follow other middle class Latinos out of Los Angeles; he would go on to serve as the Mayor of Montebello. Almost ignored by the Los Angeles-based activists was the fact that Latinos were achieving new firsts around the state; for example, John Sotelo won a city council seat in Riverside in April 1963.[96]

The loss of the Los Angeles City Council seat and the unmet expectations for federal appointments colored the perspective of California Latinos even as the Kennedy administration continued to court the Latino community. In 1963, President Kennedy invited Congressmen Edward Roybal of California, Henry B. González of Texas, and Joseph M. Montoya of New Mexico to the White House to talk about Latino concerns.[97] Roybal reported on the meeting in his address to the November 1963 MAPA Convention that followed upon the heels of Vice President Johnson's second visit to Los Angeles. Shortly thereafter, on November 22, 1963, Kennedy was assassinated in Dallas. The night before President and Mrs. Kennedy had been feted at the LULAC national convention; it was part of a White House Latino outreach that included a previous trip to Florida and a planned visit to California. But now Kennedy was dead. For his part, Roybal moved rapidly to help ensure the canonization of Kennedy and to associate himself with the martyred president. Like politicians and citizens across the nation, he sought to rename local institutions. Only Roybal took it one step further. He flew Attorney General Robert Kennedy to Los Angeles. There, Roybal accompanied Kennedy to a meeting of the Los Angeles Park and Recreation Commission to advocate the naming of a playground after his late brother.[98]

The Kennedy years in California were marked by historic advances, most notably the election of John Moreno and Philip Soto to the state legislature, and Edward Roybal to Congress. All three

President John F. Kennedy and Congressman Edward R. Roybal at the White House in early 1963. Roybal met with the president along with Henry B. González from Texas, and Joseph M. Montoya of New Mexico.

(Dr. Hector P. Garcia Papers, Special Collections & Archives Texas A&M University-Corpus Christi, Bell Library)

victories had built on earlier Latino political activity and Franklin Roosevelt's GI Bill that allowed Moreno to graduate from college and for Soto to learn a trade and then start a business. While Roybal, Moreno, and Soto participated in MAPA, at the local level in many communities such as Hanford in the Central Valley, CSO continued to be the dominant force in registering voters and lining up appointments to boards and commissions that provided a civic voice. Latinos working across organizational divides helped elect Los Angeles Mayor Samuel Yorty. Moreover, CSO as a statewide organization succeeded in getting the legislature, with the assistance of the Brown and Kennedy administrations, to provide Old Age Pensions for Non-Citizens, and to approve legislation eliminating the harassment of Latino voters. CSO and MAPA also participated in the Emergency Committee to Aid Farm Workers, the labor-based lobbying group that helped persuade President Kennedy to end the bracero program (about which more will be written in the following chapter). Talented individuals outside the MAPA-CSO-GI Forum axis assumed important roles, including Postmaster Héctor Godínez in Santa Ana, the former LULAC president, and Governor Brown's chief-of-staff, Arthur Alarcón. Despite such progress there were bitter disappointments, most notably the failure of Roybal and Henry López to obtain a position in the Kennedy administration, and the subsequent loss of the Los Angeles City Council seat held by Roybal when he moved to Congress. Taken as a whole, California Latinos saw more political advancement in 1960 to 1963 than in any previous three-year period. Success, however, only increased their expectations.

CHAPTER 10

VIVA JOHNSON, GOVERNOR BROWN, AND THE BIRTH OF THE UNITED FARM WORKERS

If the search for increased Mexican American representation in government characterized the early sixties, the years that followed increasingly focused on policy issues, most notably the struggle to overcome poverty and racial injustice, and to organize farm workers. President Lyndon B. Johnson used his State of the Union address in January 1964 to declare an "unconditional war on poverty," relating his own experiences with Mexican American children as a school teacher in Texas. Johnson demonstrated that Kennedy's unfulfilled agenda included a focus on Mexico and Mexican Americans, particularly in California, where Johnson had been sensitized to the concerns of community leaders on two visits the previous year as vice president. On February 21, 1964, President Johnson met Mexican President Adolfo López Mateos in Los Angeles. The historic event marked the first time that the presidents of the two neighboring nations had ever met in California. The Mexican president conducted a triumphant motorcade through East Los Angeles. Governor Brown, who had recently traveled to Mexico City to open up the state's first foreign trade mission, joined him at Lincoln Park. The two presidents then attended an evening fiesta at the Los Angeles Sports Arena.[1]

The Mexican government-sponsored fiesta honored President Johnson and celebrated the friendship between the two nations. López Mateos told the crowd that they had "the spirit of Mexico in your blood and flesh" but are now part of "another great county." Johnson followed López Mateos to the rostrum and likewise praised the Mexican American community. He stated "there is in this arena this afternoon the spirit of Hidalgo and Jefferson, and Juárez and Roosevelt."[2] The Sports Arena, the site of President Kennedy's 1960 nomination, was transformed into a celebration of Mexican American heritage and, according to community leader Dionicio Morales, a thinly veiled political rally that served as the unofficial kickoff for Johnson's 1964 election campaign in the Latino community.[3]

For Johnson, a master at interpersonal relations and the power of symbols, the highly successful rally was the culmination of a growing relationship with California Latinos that began in his final months as vice president. In the role as chair of the President's Committee on Equal Employment Opportunity, Johnson was only the second sitting vice president to come to Los Angeles to meet with Latino leaders—and the first since Henry Wallace in 1942. Johnson gave Congressman Edward Roybal and Judge Leopoldo Sánchez the honor of meeting him at the airport, and then riding together to the Statler Hilton Hotel, where he addressed one thousand Mexican Americans on the issues of education and employment. The luncheon committee included prominent individuals and organizations, including MAPA, CSO, GI Forum, Mexican Chamber of Commerce, Mexican-American Lawyers, and the Council on Mexican-American Affairs.[4] After his public address, Johnson invited twenty community leaders to his hotel suite. GI Forum leaders requested the Veterans Administration provide a job to disabled Congressional Medal of Honor recipient Rodolfo Hernández, of Fowler, a small town outside Fresno. The veteran leaders had learned that Hernández, who had a metal plate in his head, was homeless and unable to keep a job. Within two weeks, the Veterans Administration hired Hernández. It was a classic Johnson move, using the power of the federal government to aid someone genuinely in need and in the process to strengthen a political relationship.[5]

There were limits to the effectiveness of his personal touch, however. On November 14, 1963, only days before Kennedy's death, Vice President Johnson visited to Los Angeles again, this time to keynote a regional Equal Employment Opportunity Conference. Johnson sought to use his visit to respond to mounting criticism among Mexican American leaders, including publicized jabs at the administration by Congressman Roybal the previous week at the state MAPA convention.[6] On this trip Johnson had Congressmen Roybal and George Brown, along with U.S. Senator Claire Engle, travel with him to Los Angeles on Air Force Two. At the airport, the elected officials were met by a delegation of Mexican American leaders. Much of the good will soon dissipated due to the structure of the fair employment conference, which had a greater focus on African Americans than Latinos. The experience served to imprint on Johnson's mind the need to focus greater attention on Mexican Americans generally, and in California specifically, which he did within weeks of becoming president, starting with the rally in the Sports Arena.[7]

President Johnson recognized the high priority that California Latinos placed on receiving federal appointments and the simmering frustration on the part of community leaders that the top slots under Kennedy went to either Mexican Americans from Texans or other Latinos on the East Coast. The president moved quickly to rectify the situation. He named Daniel M. Luevano as the Undersecretary of the Army. World War II veteran, former CSO activist and attorney, he was Governor Pat Brown's Chief Deputy Finance Director. Luevano also had close ties to Congressman Roybal and California Assembly Speaker Jesse Unruh, whom he had aided as a consultant to the Assembly Ways and Means Committee.[8] According to Raúl Yzaguirre in the Washington, D.C. office of the GI Forum, the appointment made Luevano the highest-ranking Latino in the federal government.[9] Johnson also appointed two politically active businesswomen: he selected Frances Flores of Riverside, the national head of the GI Forum Auxiliary, for the Defense Advisory Council of Women in the Services and Hope Mendoza Schechter, of Sherman Oaks, the former CSO leader, for the National Advisory Council of the Peace Corps. In his first year of office, Johnson appointed eighty-three Latinos, more than President Kennedy had done in almost three years.[10]

Johnson also increased the number of Latinos attending the summer 1964 Democratic Convention, tripling the number coming from California. They reflected the growing geographic diversity. Only Roybal lived in the city of Los Angeles; the other three lived in the suburbs. Assemblyman Philip Soto hailed from La Puente, Henry Lacayo lived in Inglewood, and Alexander Zambrano resided in Downey. In another display of growing geographic clout, John Lozano lived in Orange County and Armando Rodríguez in San Diego County.[11] In terms of identity, all were seen as representative of the dominant Mexican American community, even though

Lacayo was part Nicaraguan and Roybal had Spanish roots in New Mexico. These delegates won their seats by helping to defeat a rival and more conservative slate headed by Los Angeles Mayor Samuel Yorty, which included a similar proportion of Spanish-speaking individuals.[12]

At the Democratic National Convention, Armando Rodríguez participated in the All American Council breakfast chaired by New York Mayor Robert F. Wagner. The council, with roots in Roosevelt's New Deal Democratic coalition, provided a collective voice for the representatives of the various foreign language communities, helping them bond with each other and with the party. "We realized that we were minorities that ended up being a majority," said Rodríguez, as the event included Italians, Slavs, and Poles as well as Mexican Americans, Latins, Hispanos, and Puerto Ricans. The convention also caused him to see himself as "more than a San Diegan, or a Californian."[13]

For the fall campaign against Senator Barry Goldwater of Arizona, the Johnson-Humphrey ticket turned to Latinos. When Carlos McCormick declined the opportunity to organize the Viva Johnson campaign, the White House turned to Professor Vicente Ximenes, a past national president of the GI Forum who was serving the administration in Ecuador.[14] Viva Johnson placed a great deal of focus on California because of its size and the narrowness of the 1960 contest between Nixon and Kennedy. The campaign selected Congressman Roybal to co-chair the state operation along with Assemblyman Philip Soto. Los Angeles labor and CSO leader J.J. Rodríguez, Teamster lobbyist Richard Amador, and Boyle Heights pharmacist and GI Forum activist Edward Ramírez were named as the campaign coordinators. Unruh also hired Amador, a product of the Stockton CSO, to run the operation out of the Los Angeles headquarters.[15] Attorneys Louis García and Louis Negrete headed the group in Northern California, and Gilbert López served as the chair in the Central Valley. The campaign also hired full-time Latino organizers, including Fresno-based Héctor Abeytia. MAPA, with thirty-six chapters in the state, announced its endorsement soon after Labor Day.[16]

MAPA was reaching for power under the new leadership of President Eduardo Quevedo and Vice President Bert Corona. The reemergence of these "movement Democrats," who had worked together in El Congreso in 1939, reflected the changing political dynamics in the state and nation, and within the Mexican American community. Corona, the former labor leftist, was now a business-man selling furniture in the San Francisco Bay Area. Two others from the forties filled out the leadership: attorney Manuel Ruiz, Quevedo's ally during the World War II years, was elected as Legal Counsel; journalist Ignacio López, the former federal Fair Employment Practices Commission staffer under Roosevelt, was named as the Southern California Director.[17]

Johnson and Humphrey both campaigned in Los Angeles during the final weekend before the November 1964 election. Congressman Roybal rode with the president and introduced Governor Brown who welcomed Johnson at a rally of 35,000 on the steps of City Hall. Congressman Roybal then joined vice presidential candi-date Hubert Humphrey for a rally at the East Los Angeles College Stadium where Governor Brown and Assemblyman Soto shared the stage.[18] Johnson went on to win in a national landslide. Among Mexican Americans, he received ninety percent support. This rep-resented a five-point increase over that provided Kennedy.[19]

Following the presidential election, MAPA sought a meeting with Governor Brown. The subject was agricultural workers. As a gesture of friendship, Brown invited thirty MAPA leaders to the Governor's Mansion for lunch on January 14, 1965. MAPA Vice President Bert Corona arranged for leaders from local MAPA chap-ters to attend, including Alfonso Gonzales, a former CSO member and Sacramento's first Mexican American attorney. He also invit-ed along representatives from other Mexican American organiza-tions, as part of efforts to unite the various statewide groups around a shared set of goals.[20] A year earlier, Governor Brown used the MAPA Convention to announce that he would oppose any further extension of the bracero program in California.[21] However, the at-mosphere became tense when a week before the meeting, MAPA President Eduardo Quevedo, Los Angeles CSO President Tony Ríos, and National GI Forum President Augustine Flores openly criticized the administration. "The farm labor drive now being con-ducted by the California Department of Employment is a smoke-screen," they stated in a press release. "It has been laid down at the

11[22] hour to cover its failure to prepare an effective and orderly shift from bracero to domestic manpower."[22]

At their meeting the Mexican American leaders expressed concern that Governor Brown had requested an exemption from the U.S. Department of Labor from implementing the law in California that ended the bracero program. The delegation also pressed the governor to appoint a person from within their organizational ranks to his personal staff. Brown readily agreed and said this person would work on the special problems of farm labor. A number of names were immediately suggested, including Ernesto Galarza (with the National Farm Labor Union in the forties) and Héctor Abeytia (a former organizer with the Agricultural Workers Organizing Committee). It was at the suggestion of Galarza, in 1963, that MAPA President Julius Castelan appointed a farm labor committee.[23] Now, according to Abeytia, Galarza deferred to him, saying that Abeytia "had urban and political experience and he is also a very rural guy."[24]

MAPA's agenda was advanced, ironically, by Brown's decision to replace Arthur Alarcón, his chief of staff, with Bill Becker, his civil rights advisor, in dealing with Latinos. Brown placed the Republican Alarcón on the Los Angeles County Superior Court. "Becker was an old labor man with a different view and approach to the Chicano community in the state," recalled Corona. Becker was, like Corona, a man of the liberal-left; he had organized farm workers with Galarza before becoming the lobbyist for fair employment. "He was very supportive and very understanding of our position that we wanted to build an independent political organization," stated Corona.[25]

Abeytia quickly came to an understanding with Becker that he would have access to the governor and complete latitude in performing his job, which he defined as "build[ing] a coalition to stop the bracero program." Abeytia remained concerned with the Economic Development Department (EDD), however. He told Becker: "I want to know if my efforts are going to be scuttled because the [EDD run] Farm Labor Offices are in bed with the growers." Becker responded by asking: "What do you suggest?" After consulting with Quevedo and Corona, it was decided that one of the first moves was to involve John Henning, who was now Undersecretary of Labor in the Johnson administration.[26]

Henning named four Mexican Americans as U.S. Department of Labor Farm Labor Consultants: Quevedo and Corona from MAPA, James Delgadillo from the GI Forum, and Albert Piñón from CSO. The four men were instructed to work with Abeytia in the governor's office. This was a major development because these volunteer leaders of the Mexican-American Unity Council would now receive federal paychecks and the political benefits of representing the Johnson administration. Abeytia also met with EDD Director Albert Tieburg, a lifelong civil servant who agreed to give him, according to Abeytia, "thirty-nine temporarily unassigned positions with undercover cars and no state license plates."[27] U.S. Secretary of Labor Willard Wirtz helped out by touring California farm areas and asking growers such embarrassing questions as, "Where's the toilets?"[28]

A crisis developed in May of 1965 when strawberry growers claimed "that the local people preferred welfare checks to earning a wage" and that they faced economic ruin unless braceros were immediately brought in to harvest the crops. Abeytia came up with an idea: Why not demonstrate to the growers and, more importantly, to the public and the politicians that domestic labor was indeed interested in working? Abeytia responded to a prearranged "demand" by MAPA. "So I called EDD and I called the growers, and I said, 'Bert Corona and these guys say they can get us all the [domestic] farm labor we want to pick those strawberries,'" said Abeytia. "There's no sense in Senator [George] Murphy dancing out there in the fields, saying that the crops are rotting."[29]

Héctor Abeytia set up a meeting in Sacramento on May 9, 1965. The parties agreed to meet the following day in San Jose to devise the details of the plan whereby EDD and the growers would split the costs of recruiting domestic laborers. Due to the efforts of Albert Piñón and Ernest Abeytia and other local leaders and their allies in the Brown and Johnson administrations, the growers had more than enough domestic field workers to pick the strawberry crop. Luis G. Juárez used his new column in the *San Jose Mercury News*, "Mexican-American Notes," to praise the recruitment program, and to highlight the $1.7 million federal Office of Economic Opportunity grant to fund nine regional offices, starting in the Gilroy, a small agricultural town south of San Jose.[30] To make matters worse for the growers, Governor Brown announced his plans to help the workers "take advantage of the president's anti-poverty program." This would include an increase in the minimum hourly wage and "housing, day care centers, health programs, compensatory education, sanitation, training programs, migrant service centers and rest stops for traveling workers."[31]

The growers expressed their frustration. "No doubt you've heard that the Mexican-American Political Association could dig up between 8,000 and 10,000 workers to save the strawberries and asparagus," announced the *California Farmer*, the organ of the California Farm Bureau, with more than a little satire. "Governor Brown has been made aware of the increasing political activity of the Mexican-American Community and has appointed Hector Abeytia of Fresno as the Governor's consultant on farm labor and Mexican-American problems." According to the growers, EDD could be renamed "the new state Mexican-American Department of Employment."[32]

The delegates to the MAPA convention in July 1965 were surprised to learn that the growers were not the only ones angry at MAPA's influence within the Brown and Johnson administrations. Dolores Huerta and about ten farm workers were picketing them. Huerta was a familiar face to many delegates who knew her from CSO days. She was at the convention as the co-founder with César Chávez of the independent National Farm Worker Association (NFWA). The NFWA had formed in 1962 after CSO refused to go along with Chávez's proposal to shift the mission of the civic organization towards farm labor organizing. During the last three years the NFWA had sought to organize members but, unlike other AFL-CIO unions in the fields, had not conducted strikes or sought contracts. MAPA leaders invited Huerta to address the convention. She said: "If you are helping the growers, you are not helping the farm workers . . . . You're just replacing the bracero program with a domestic slave labor program." Congressman Roybal, who was engaged in the national struggle to end the bracero program, defended MAPA's role. Looking back, MAPA's Robert Gonzales believes that the conflict was essentially a jurisdictional question over which group would drive the farm worker agenda.[33]

In contrast to the National Farm Worker Association's desire that MAPA stay out of the farm worker issue, the Agricultural Workers Organizing Committee (AWOC) approached Abeytia in the governor's office for help. The AFL-CIO union's strike in Stockton was going to be expanded to Delano where César Chávez's NFWA forces were based. AWOC's Al Green asked Abeytia to feel out Chávez to see if he would support the expanding strike. The leaders of the Mexican-American Unity Council set up a meeting with Chávez, who did not attend due to illness. Instead, he sent Huerta who stated that the farm workers did not need any help from "middle class sellouts." Following the meeting, Eduardo Quevedo and a couple of others went by Chávez's home to pay their respects, only to be thrown out. Chávez, the reluctant labor leader, also refused to meet with a labor delegation that included Roy Reuther, the brother of United Auto Workers president Walter Reuther.[34]

MAPA leaders Quevedo, Corona, and Abeytia, as well as other representatives from the Mexican-American Unity Council were in Delano on September 8, 1965 to demonstrate their support for AWOC's strike, which was strongest among Filipinos, but included some Latino and Anglo members. Anthony L. Ramos, secretary of the California Council of Carpenters, was among the labor leaders present.[35]

A week into the AWOC strike, on September 15, the NFWA held a mass meeting. The Chávez-led group was unprepared to strike but circumstances made it impossible to avoid. Chávez quoted Pope Leo XIII in urging the workers to walk off the job.[36] MAPA leaders Quevedo and Corona stayed in Delano for two weeks in order to provide assistance. This included Corona contacting old friends within the International Longshoremen and Warehousemen's Union at the Ports of Sacramento and Stockton to obtain bags of beans and rice for the strikers. For his part, Abeytia resigned from his job in the governor's office and stayed for sixteen weeks. He used his contacts in Sacramento to ensure that the state did not provide strikebreakers as it had done in previous labor-management conflicts.[37]

Despite such initial assistance, the strikers remained vulnerable. If this strike followed the course of previous agricultural battles going back to the 1930s, the growers would defeat their striking workers by either starving them into submission or using the power of law enforcement and the courts to crush the strike. In rural California the growers had all the power. The geographic isolation from the state's major population and media centers meant that few even knew about the strike, let alone the violence employed by growers and their law enforcement allies. The rigid power relationship presented a classic David v. Goliath situation.

Chávez knew he needed help from outside the region if his union was to survive. "Towards the end of [September 1965], César asked MAPA, asked me and I transmitted that request, that we support the farm workers in meetings with the governor, in meetings with state officials, and to get political support for them," said Corona. In response, the MAPA leadership met with Governor Brown. "The Governor was very, very distant about our requests. He said he was a next door neighbor of DiGiorgio [one of the struck growers, who also had a home in San Francisco], and that he was good friends of Einar Mohn who was with the Western Conference of Teamsters [who also claimed jurisdiction over field workers], and he had sympathies for César and the farm workers," stated Corona. "He had to think of these things in terms of relationships, statewide considerations, and the overall position of the Governor's posture in terms of being the leader for all of the State of California."[38]

The strikers were getting a more sympathetic response in the cities, especially from organized labor, the liberal-left and middle class Mexican Americans. In the best tradition of the social gospel, the National Council of Churches-affiliated Migrant Ministry rushed to help. Rev. Chris Hartmire, the ministry's head, assigned the Rev. James Drake to the strike and he soon became Chávez's administrative assistant. Hartmire was deep into the agricultural politics as a member of the Los Angeles-based anti-bracero coalition, Emergency Committee to Aid Farm Workers, which included Roybal and Ríos.[39] The strikers also received the backing of college students, some of whom like Jessica Govea (the daughter of a Tulare CSO leader) and Marshall Ganz (the son of a Bakersfield teacher and rabbi) would dedicate years to the union movement.[40]

While Chávez realized he needed assistance, his earlier refusal to meet with the United Auto Workers' Roy Reuther and Paul Schrade led the auto union to seek a more formal understanding.

The union invited Chávez to discuss possible UAW backing for the strike, symbolically holding the meeting near the Los Angeles airport at the office of Local 887 president Henry Lacayo. Chávez asked, "Would Walter Reuther come to Delano?" Lacayo recalled. "Yes, we can get him." The farm worker leader, who knew Lacayo from CSO days, agreed to accept UAW assistance, in the process forming a partnership with the nation's most dynamic and politically connected union.[41]

United Auto Worker Local 887 president Henry Lacayo, César Chávez, and UAW president Walter Reuther in Delano in December 1965. The UAW brought media attention and political and financial support to the striking farm workers. Lacayo, as the head of the largest local union in the state, was a powerful political figure. (Courtesty of Henry L. Lacayo)

Word spread in Los Angeles that UAW President Walter Reuther was planning to go to Delano after the AFL-CIO Convention in San Francisco, according to Ralph Arriola, a machinist at Poly Industries, one of several parts factories under UAW contract in the San Fernando Valley.[42] In Delano, Reuther marched with NFWA's César Chávez and AWOC's Larry Itliong and a mass of strikers and their urban supporters. Reuther also marked the 100th day of the strike by launching a national boycott of Delano grapes. They also sought to convince strikebreakers to leave the fields. "I went in there as part of the entourage," remembers the Spanish-speaking Lacayo, "and I even got on the megaphones and talked to the strikers."[43]

Reuther's visit came on the heels of the AFL-CIO's decision to pass a UAW-authored resolution supporting the strike and both AWOC and the independent, Chávez-led NFWA. These two actions helped change the course of the strike. First, Reuther and the striking farm workers made the national evening television news for the first time. Second, Reuther pledged to financially support the strike on a monthly basis, ensuring the strikers would eat. And third, according to UAW Regional Director Paul Schrade, the UAW president sent a powerful signal to other unions that Chávez, despite a refusal to affiliate with the AFL-CIO, should be supported.[44]

Organized labor and middle class Mexican Americans also joined together to support the strikers in Los Angeles. The Mexican-American Emergency Aid Committee To Aid Farmworkers sponsored a rally at the United Rubber Workers Hall in December 1965. Speakers at the rally included Assemblyman Philip Soto, Judge Leopoldo Sánchez, and organizer and academic Ernesto Galarza. Entertainer and former Tonight Show host Steve Allen provided a celebrity appeal and Hollywood glamour.[45]

In Sacramento, the Brown administration took innovative steps to better serve Spanish-speaking Californians. The state promoted the utilization of bilingual state employees in dealing with the public for the first time. This was important because while most Latinos were bilingual, some elderly members of the immigrant generation as well as newer arrivals were not. Brown also moved to shore up his support among the middle class political activists in Los Angeles by elevating Judge Sánchez to the Superior Court. Going into a reelection campaign, the governor then underscored the importance of Mexican Americans by keynoting a testimonial dinner for Sánchez.[46]

To Brown's dismay the farm worker issue only increased in its saliency. In early 1966, U.S. Senator Harrison Williams (D-New Jersey), the chair of the Subcommittee on Migratory Labor, decided to take the committee on a fact-finding mission to California's Central Valley. Senator George Murphy (R-California) was expected to attend the hearings as an advocate for grower interests. It was unclear if any other member of the subcommittee would attend. Here again the United Auto Workers intervened by encouraging subcommittee member Senator Robert F. Kennedy to attend. Kennedy advisor Peter Edelman remembers getting the call from top Reuther aide Jack Conway. "You know we've been very involved with the strikers, and Senator Williams of New Jersey's holding hearings out there and Bob [Kennedy's] on the committee," Conway told Edelman. He paused and then added, "we think it would be good if [Kennedy] went, Walter Reuther and I."[47]

In March of 1966, Senators Williams, Kennedy, and Murphy came to California. In Visalia, the committee heard MAPA's Bert Corona, CSO's Albert Piñón, and the GI Forum's Don Campos express support for the farm workers. After the hearing, the Latino leaders accompanied Kennedy to the airport, during which time they also discussed the concerns of urban Latinos. Senator Kennedy said, "Anything I can do for MAPA and CSO I want to do," according to Corona.[48]

The following day the hearings moved to Delano where the presence of three U.S. Senators raised tensions in the already polarized community. In the local high school gym, packed with farm workers, California's Catholic Bishops announced their support for the right of agricultural workers to unionize. This was a huge development. For the faithful, God's servants on earth now blessed their struggle. The bishop's announcement was also a positive development within political circles and further insolated the union from rightwing attacks that it was somehow subversive.

An even more dramatic moment followed. Senator Kennedy asked Sheriff Leroy Galyen why he had arrested a large group of strikers. The sheriff responded that it was done to protect the workers, because another group of men had told him: "If you don't get them out of here, we're going to cut their hearts out." Bewildered by the response, Senator Kennedy continued to probe. "So you came and you arrested forty-four people because somebody else was going to come and attack them?" "Yes," the sheriff responded. An angry Kennedy suggested that the sheriff use the upcoming break in the hearing to read the Constitution of the United States.[49]

After the hearing, Senator Kennedy visited Chávez at the strike headquarters. Kennedy had a new cause. According to Edelman, "something had touched a nerve in him and he was going to help."[50]

Chávez also felt this. "By the time the hearing ended Senator Kennedy was like a thousand percent behind us, endorsing our efforts." This had a dramatic effect inside and outside of the union. Chávez recalls hearing farm workers say: "Senator Kennedy says that the union's a good thing" and "I believe it now."[51]

Shortly after the hearings, Chávez announced that the union would undertake a 250-mile religious procession from Delano to the State Capitol in Sacramento to publicize their concerns. Assemblyman Philip Soto joined the march. They walked behind the symbols of their faith, heritage, and citizenship. A banner bearing Our Lady of Guadalupe joined the flags of Mexico and the United States. Henry Santiestevan, the pioneering Latino journalist now working for the UAW, oversaw the press relations.[52]

On Easter Sunday, the marchers were joined by 10,000 supporters at the State Capitol in the largest demonstration since the Great Depression. Latinos carried signs representing the MAPA and CSO, and the GI Forum assisted with security. Much of the crowd reflected support by labor, liberal, and religious groups, as well as college students. In his address, Chávez acknowledged their importance. The union leader also focused attention on who was not there: Governor Brown. He had chosen to spend the day with singer Frank Sinatra and his family in Palm Springs. The experience became a powerful metaphor. On this the holiest day for Christians, when the long oppressed farm workers were rising like Jesus from the tomb, Brown was with his rich and powerful friends. The governor's decision further strained relations with groups within the Democratic Party, who were supporting the farm workers' struggle.[53]

Despite the frustration with Governor Brown, the UFW and MAPA retained access to the administration. One of the most important developments was the creation of the California Rural Legal Assistance (CRLA), which held its first board meeting in Los Angeles, on May 14, 1966. CRLA was created to provide legal services for the rural poor and immediately set about establishing ten field offices around the state. It represented a collaboration between Mexican Americans, white liberals, private foundations, Governor Brown's Legal Advisor, and the federal Office of Economic Opportunity.[54] Former Brown staffer Héctor Abeytia was named as the executive director of an experimental statewide job training program. Los Angeles engineer Frank X. Pax (an unsuccessful assembly candidate) chaired the board, which included representatives from CSO, GI Forum, and MAPA.[55] Brown also addressed MAPA and the League of United Latin American Citizens events in a search for support for a third term as governor leading up to the June 1966 primary election.[56]

Brown won the June 1966 Democratic primary with a bare majority. Rival Samuel Yorty, the Mayor of Los Angeles, received 39 percent of the vote, including a quarter of the Latino ballots. Los Angeles physician and Pan American National Bank founder Francisco Bravo organized the pro-Yorty campaign within the Latino community.[57] It built upon a positive relationship between Latinos and the mayor that emerged from his 1961 election, and was nurtured by a record number of appointments, and support for Richard Tafoya's city council campaign in 1963. Others may have cast a protest vote against Brown because, according to San Francisco attorney Robert E. Gonzales, he would not meet with César Chávez.[58]

Two weeks after the primary election, Chávez's farm workers lost a disputed union representation election among DiGiorgio workers at Sierra Vista. "The day after that phony election, Dolores [Huerta] went to the Mexican American Political Association convention in Fresno to ask that they put pressure on Governor Brown to ask for new elections," stated César Chávez. "The Governor was running for reelection against Ronald Reagan, then, and he was in political trouble."[59]

Both Democratic and Republican candidates were focused on the 1966 MAPA Endorsing Convention, with its 350 delegates representing sixty-two local chapters. Ronald Reagan's Saturday morning appearance did not occur as planned. Instead of a personal appearance, Reagan addressed the delegates via a telephone hookup and refused to answer any questions. This upset many of the delegates. Yet Reagan's limited participation still represented a first for a Republican candidate for governor.[60]

Governor Brown addressed the delegates on Sunday. He reviewed the tremendous public policy advances made in the state over the last eight years. He stressed the record number of appointments to state posts, which included putting 1940s activists Richard Ibañez and Philip Newman on the bench. On the issue of the farm workers, Brown stated that "we have done much more for the farm laborer in California than any other state with the exception of Hawaii." California farm workers enjoyed "a minimum wage of $1.30 an hour for women and minors." Brown stated that in contrast to Reagan, who said he had "no sympathy" for the strikers, "I support the farm worker in his demand for the right to form labor unions."[61]

The MAPA Executive Board split three ways on how to handle the governor's campaign. One group wanted to endorse Brown with reservations. A second group wanted to teach the governor a lesson by not endorsing him at all. A third group thought a compromise could be worked out. Adding to the dynamic was the presence of National Farm Worker Association Vice President Dolores Huerta. Throughout the convention, she was busy lobbying the delegates not to endorse Brown until he openly supported the farm workers' struggle. When, on Sunday afternoon, the time came to make an endorsement, the group's leadership had still not reached a consensus.

With Héctor Abeytia, Bert Corona, Herman Gallegos, and Dolores Huerta negotiating with Lieutenant Governor Glenn Anderson and Undersecretary of Labor John Henning, a compromise was proposed. MAPA would endorse Governor Brown if he promised to nullify the questionable union representational election at the DiGiorgio ranch where the Teamsters had beaten the NFWA. Further, the governor must meet with the MAPA leadership the following day to discuss implementing this commitment. While the convention delayed the endorsement vote, Anderson located the governor. Forty minutes later, Brown, talking over the phone to the negotiating committee, agreed to the compromise. Hinting at what had been discussed, Gallegos told the convention delegates that he had just talked to the governor and "Brown favors a 'full investigation' of the election involving the DiGiorgio workers before DiGiorgio signs a labor contract with the Teamsters." MAPA then voted overwhelmingly to endorse Brown's reelection.[62]

The next day, on Monday, June 27, 1966 Governor Brown met with the MAPA leadership in his office in Sacramento for almost two hours. MAPA brought César Chávez, whom Brown had avoid-

Governor Pat Brown, accompanied by special assistant Héctor Abeytia and NFWA president César Chávez, talks to the press after brokering a deal to rerun a controversial union election at DiGiorgio.   (Kenneth C. Burt)

ed since the start of the strike. Brown reacted to Chávez's presence by saying, "this meeting is about two months overdue." After the meeting, Governor Brown, flanked by Abeytia and Chávez, announced that he would appoint "a person of national prominence" to investigate the disputed election.[63]

Ronald W. Haughton, a highly respected labor consultant from Wayne State University in Detroit, promptly recommended a new election, a decision to which both DiGiorgio and the Teamsters felt obligated to agree. The newly merged United Farm Workers Organizing Committee, AFL-CIO, went on to defeat the Teamsters. This election victory came at a critical time for the union and went a long way to establish that the majority of farm workers supported the Chávez-led organization.[64] About the same time, from his office in Washington, D.C., Californian Henry Santiestevan edited a special issue of the AFL-CIO Industrial Union Department magazine, *IUE Agenda,* with the headline, "Viva La Causa! The Rising Expectations of the Mexican Americans." It was the first national union publication to focus on rural and urban Latinos.[65]

In early August 1966, Latino leaders held a press conference in Los Angeles to announce the formation of a "Viva Brown" committee. Congressman Roybal spoke as the honorary chair. He stated, "the Mexican-American community feels the ultra-conservative philosophy as expressed by Mr. Reagan is against the best interests of our people." Assemblyman Philip Soto, MAPA President Eduardo Quevedo, and labor leaders Henry Lacayo and J.J. Rodríguez joined Roybal at the press conference along with Dr. Miguel Montes from the State Board of Education, Fred Silva from GI Forum, and Joseph Pacheco from LULAC. They then met with two hundred Latino leaders to "formulate plans . . . to penetrate areas of Mexican-American community."[66]

Brown thus brought liberal Mexican American activists back into the fold, but he faced obstacles on both his left and right flanks as he sought to reassemble the Democratic majority coalition. A segment of the Anglo liberal-left, particularly the leftwing of CDC and the emerging New Left, were openly hostile. They organized a Statewide Conference on Power and Politics at the East Los Angeles College for Saturday, October 1, 1966, one month before the general election. Organizers invited MAPA President Bert Corona to be a keynote speaker. He declined after it became increasingly clear that the conference appeared to be less about creating a long-term progressive majority than bashing Brown. Brown supporters reacted by organizing a counter conference at the Hollywood Palladium. Their special guests were César Chávez and Senator Edward Kennedy. The night before the dueling conferences, 300 United Farm Workers Organizing Committee members met in Delano and voted to back Brown. The announcement was made simultaneously next morning in Delano and at the Los Angeles conference.[67]

The decision by Chávez and the farm workers to embrace Governor Brown and the electoral process was profound. The union recognized that the governor could make a big difference in a labor conflict with the absence of either a state or federal law. The decision to embrace Brown also represented the payment of the political debt the union owed him for orchestrating the nullification of the DiGiorgio election.

Yet the event that engaged the largest number of Latino activists that Saturday was not in an auditorium or a ballroom but on the streets of East Los Angeles. Ronald Reagan campaigned among Latino voters on a walking tour of the busy Latino business district on Whittier Boulevard, ending at his campaign headquarters. Reagan was surrounded by placard waving supporters with signs reading "Ya Basta! Vote Ronald Reagan." The red and black posters featured a Reagan photo and sponsorship by "Mexican American Democrats for Reagan," an explicit appeal for cross-over voting, a technique used successfully by Eisenhower and Warren. Anti-Reagan activists waved their own "Viva Pat Brown" signs.[68]

Reagan was the first conservative Republican to campaign among Latinos, but he had reason for optimism due to the significant number who had voted for Yorty. Reagan's campaign manager, Stewart Spencer, had met with Dr. Bravo after the primary elec-

Ya Basta poster sponsored by Mexican American Democrats for Reagan.
(Kenneth C. Burt)

tion at the suggestion of Mayor Yorty. It was Bravo who came up
with the slogan, "Ya Basta" (We've had enough), which the Reagan
campaign used in repeated visits to the Mexican American community in Southern California. The phrase captured a collection of
grievances from the lack of Latino elected officials, to the unmet
social needs, to the perception that Governor Brown (and President
Johnson) favored African Americans. Moreover, the Republicans
targeted Mexican Americans most likely to be supportive. These
were white-collar employees and small business owners.[69]

Fighting for his political life, Governor Brown addressed Latino
audiences in Northern and Southern California.[70] The campaign
also brought in Senator Robert F. Kennedy to speak on his behalf.
Mexican Americans treated Kennedy like a rock star at the Jesuit-
run University of San Francisco. Eduardo Quevedo, Bert Corona,
and Herman Gallegos shared the stage with Kennedy.[71] Robert

*U.S. Senator Robert Kennedy campaigned for Governor Brown's reelection
in 1966. Here Kennedy is being introduced at a Latino rally at the Jesuit-
run University of San Francisco by Herman Gallegos, the CSO president
turned Ford Foundation consultant. To Kennedy's right is Eduardo Quevedo
and Bert Corona.* *(Kenneth C. Burt)*

Kennedy also appeared with Governor Brown, Congressman Roybal, and César Chávez at East Los Angeles Junior College. Chávez told the urban crowd that Brown had helped the union and "if Reagan would be elected I don't know if our union could survive." Kennedy then traveled to Oxnard and Fresno.[72]

The heightened role of Mexican Americans in the liberal Democratic Party coalition was captured during the final days of the 1966 campaign. On November 3, Governor Brown joined five hundred supporters at the Hollywood Palladium in a salute to Mexican American labor leaders. The guest of honor at the MAPA-sponsored banquet was United Auto Workers president Walter Reuther. John Henning represented President Johnson. The brainchild of Bert Corona and Henry Lacayo, the event highlighted MAPA and showcased the community's political ties to the President of the United States, the Governor of the State of California, and to the nation's largest union.[73]

For his part, Ronald Reagan used the campaign's final days to stump the state along with the other Republicans running for statewide office. He sought not a personal victory but a wholesale change in the ideological direction of state government. Reagan often appeared at these events with Mariachi bands and used the slogan, "Ya Basta," to end his speeches. This demonstrated the candidate's comfort with Latinos and the campaign's belief that a significant number of Latinos, like other pieces of the old New Deal coalition, would vote for him.[74]

On Election Day, Governor Brown suffered a humiliating defeat. Ronald Reagan, the actor turned "citizen politician," defeated the two-term incumbent by more than a million votes in a state where Democrats outnumbered Republicans. In so doing, Reagan repeated the earlier victories of Earl Warren and Goodwin Knight, who also won by garnering substantial support from Democratic voters. And like his GOP predecessors, he courted and won a significant number of Latino voters. The Reagan supporters came largely from three sources: longtime Republicans (active since the Eisenhower and Warren years), disenchanted Mexican American Democrats (who voted for Yorty in the primary), and more newly arrived Cuban Americans (who fled Castro's communism). To his credit, Governor Reagan remembered his Latino supporters. He appointed more Latinos to boards and commissions, and to administrative jobs, than any of his Republican predecessors.[75]

Reagan named Armando Delgado as a special representative to the Latino community. *San Jose Mercury* columnist Luis G. Juárez praised Delgado's appointment, stating that this was the first administration "to create a direct line" between the governor and Latinos. He also praised the appointment of local educator Mark Guerra to the Fair Employment Practices Commission.[76] From Southern California, Reagan named Dr. Tirso del Junco, a Cuban American, to the Board of Medical Examiners, and Julio Gonzales, the longtime Los Angeles Police Department community relation officer, to replace Juan Acevedo on the California Youth Authority.[77] Such appointments broadened the number of Latinos in state service but they also "caused political friction" within the community, according to Ralph Guzmán, because they were "politically atypical with the heavily Democratic Mexican American community."[78] Conflicts also arose over public policy as Reagan sought to eliminate funding for the California Rural Legal Assistance and to bring back braceros to undercut striking farm workers.

Campaigns revolve around candidates and the effectiveness of campaign strategies and tactics. But they also reflect larger social trends. For California Democrats, the political terrain was changing faster than they could understand. The 1964 Johnson campaign two years earlier proved to be the highpoint for modern liberalism, with the president winning a landslide and garnering 90 percent of Latino support. The pendulum swung far to the other side in just two years, with Brown losing by a landslide and Latino support dropping to roughly 75 percent. Two points are particularly salient in understanding this political development.

First, the perspectives of Latino voters were shaped by the larger political context. Brown—and liberalism—had become identified with student demonstrations in Berkeley, African American rioting in Watts, and the farm workers strike in Delano. Unrelated in their specifics they helped define the political environment in different ways to different people. While participants saw them as part of new movements towards greater equality, politically moderate swing voters saw them as evidence of the unraveling of the established social order. The Democrats most likely to vote for

Reagan (later labeled "Reagan Democrats") shared this perspective; many had recently entered the middle class and felt threatened by the turmoil. Some were blue-collar union members who
decided not to vote on pocket book issues, instead to make political judgments based on issues like race and crime. The Mexican
Americans in this group came largely from the developing suburbs
in the Southeast areas of Los Angeles County, small cities represented by Assemblyman Philip Soto, for whose ex-urban residents
Little League had replaced young gangs and who feared old urban
issues entering their new communities.[79]

For traditional Mexican Americans—who worked hard, went to
church, and focused on family life—there was a parallel shift in
their thinking. Some were offended by middle class college students who, instead of appreciating their privileged status, spent
their time protesting the still popular Vietnam War or adopted a
Hippie lifestyle that they could not understand. There was also
growing resentment towards the Democratic elected officials' response to African American protests. Some were angry that the
government seemed to reward often-violent demonstrations with
additional financial aid; others perceived the Democrats in office to
be favoring African Americans over Mexican Americans in the War
on Poverty (which will be discussed more in the next chapter). A lot
had changed and voters expressed their anxiety at the ballot box.[80]

A second consideration was the limited ability of Mexican
American leaders to advocate a particular candidate. In this, there
was little change between 1964 and 1966, but there is a marked
contrast with the period between the late forties and early sixties
when CSO chapters (often strengthened by outside funding) systematically registered voters and ran get-out-the-vote campaigns.
Despite the best efforts of the volunteer-driven Mexican American
activists, there was a widespread absence of a year-round organization capable of mobilizing voters at the neighborhood level. In its
absence, campaigns targeted urban neighborhoods with large numbers of Latinos who needed encouragement to get to the polls. This
had a declining effectiveness as turnout actually dropped in urban
sections of Los Angeles from 1964 to 1966. Moreover, these in-
ner-city residents represented a declining percentage of the Latino
vote. An increasing number of middle class voters lived in the sub-

urbs. For them, the Democrats' traditional class-based issues had a declining appeal. Moreover, neither the organization nor the technology existed to reach out to Latinos living in largely Anglo communities. In other words, the traditional liberal Latino leadership lacked the organization to deliver the vote (particularly the urban vote) at the very time that the increasingly diverse community was open to supporting Republican candidates who reached out to them with larger themes they found appealing.

Liberal Latino leaders were also becoming more radical at the very time voters' were expressing a more conservative outlook. They could not fathom Mexican Americans voting for Reagan or the fact that every Democratic Mexican American legislative candidate lost at the polls. The most painful defeat was that of Assemblyman Philip Soto, one of five Democratic legislators defeated in the Reagan landslide. His district boundaries had been modified to conform to the California Supreme Court's "one person, one vote" requirement and was near the epicenter of the revolt by Reagan Democrats against their party. Soto was vulnerable to the seismic shift in public opinion, he said, because he represented a "swing district" where the results at the top of the ticket affected candidates farther down on the ballot. To his credit, Soto ran way ahead of Governor Brown but it was not enough to retain the seat.

The impact of Soto's defeat was magnified by three other factors. First, Anglo legislators continued to use the power incumbency to represent overwhelmingly Latino areas, including Boyle Heights, where Roybal started his political career two decades earlier. Second, Assemblyman John Moreno had lost his reelection in 1964 after only one term. Third, Latinos failed to win a newly created state senate seat in East Los Angeles in 1966. Taken together, these facts seemed to point to some form of institutional discrimination or subordination of Latinos within the political arena. A closer examination points to other factors, including the absence of Latino unity.

In the Boyle Height-based assembly seat, Latino activists had repeatedly failed to put together a race-based coalition in the overwhelmingly Latino district. They had trouble because the labor movement and other interest groups continued to reward the incumbent for backing their issues. So, too, did many Latino voters. However, with an incumbent aging, the seat would most likely open up in two years. This would create an ideal opportunity to elect a representative in the heart of Latino Los Angeles. Whether this would occur, however, was questionable based on two other election results.

Two years earlier, Assemblyman John Moreno was defeated in the 1964 primary in a "safe" Democratic seat. How did this happen? Moreno got arrested for drunk driving. Many Latino activists believed his behavior hurt the larger community. "John Moreno is one of the handful of elected officials of Mexican extraction. As such, his responsibilities transcend those of his district and, in many ways, he was the image of Mexican Americans," wrote *The Eagles*. The Latino paper stressed that Moreno had "let down" some "1,500,000 Mexican-Americans in California."[81] On the urging of MAPA President Eduardo Quevedo and others, Dionicio Morales entered the primary against Moreno and earned the endorsements of Pico Rivera Councilman Frank Terrazas, Santa Fe Councilman Ernest Flores, and the Los Angeles County Federation of Labor. Morales, moreover, had twice met with President Johnson and boosted a resumé that included employment with the federal government, the Catholic Church, and the Amalgamated Clothing Workers. As a consequence of the spirited contest between the incumbent, Moreno, and the challenger, Morales, a third candidate, Jack Fenton, entered the race. The Italian American won the largely Latino seat with a plurality of the vote in the primary.[82]

The disappointment in the state assembly races in 1966 should have been counterbalanced by an historic breakthrough—the election of the first Mexican American to the state senate. As a result of a California Supreme Court ruling, the seats in the upper house were redrawn to reflect population and not county boundaries. This increased Los Angeles' share of senate seats from one to eleven, including one in the heavily Latino Eastside. Unfortunately, in the euphoria over the new seat, community leaders forgot one of the most fundamental lessons from 1964 Moreno-Morales debacle (and Roybal's victory in 1949): victory is best achieved by uniting behind a single Latino candidate. As a result, Assemblyman George Danielson was able to narrowly defeat Richard Calderón, a social worker-turned-school teacher endorsed by Roybal, and a host of other candidates in a crowded primary. By contrast the more cohesive African America and Jewish communities in Los Angeles each won their first senate seat.[83]

In backing Danielson (with whom they had a relationship), organized labor missed the opportunity to form a Latino-labor alliance. According to the UAW's Henry Lacayo, the real problem was that Roybal did not develop young leaders. Roybal should have introduced promising Latinos to a range of political figures, allowing them time establish relationships and to learn about policy concerns. Instead, when Roybal did endorse, he did so near the election when groups within the Democratic Party—and for that matter, the Latino community—had already committed themselves to a particular candidate. Roybal was uniquely positioned to develop a "farm club," to use the baseball metaphor, because organizations like MAPA lacked the ability to clear the field of multiple Latino candidates, to mobilize Latino voters, and to form partnerships with groups like organized labor headed by non-Latinos.[84]

The importance of coalitions within the Latino community and with other groups was applied—with some external pressure—in the spring 1967 campaign for a seat on the Los Angeles School Board. A number of competing factions had their own candidate, each wanting to be the first Mexican American school board member. The lack of Latino unity was particularly problematic because voters elected board members on an at-large basis. A coalition of liberals, Jews, Blacks, and unionists wanted to defeat a conservative incumbent, Charles Reed Smoot, to create a liberal majority. They offered to back a Mexican American against him if the community could agree upon a candidate. In response, dozens of groups came together under the aegis of the Congress of Mexican-American Unity, finally settling on Dr. Julian Nava.[85]

Nava had a compelling story that resonated with Latinos, liberals, and labor. A product of CSO, he grew up in the barrio, worked in an auto plant, and then earned a doctorate at Harvard University. He involved himself in the community and helped found the American Federation of Teachers at California State Northridge. The campaign leadership reflected his broad political support. African American City Councilman Tom Bradley, Jewish AFL-CIO head Sigmund Arywitz, and Judge Leopoldo Sánchez served as campaign co-chairs. Hollywood celebrities Steve Allen and Gregory Peck lent their names. Nava also picked up critical support from Episcopalian, Lutheran, Methodist, and Presbyterian leaders, as well as former governor Pat Brown, Alan Cranston, and Speaker Jesse Unruh. Mayor Samuel Yorty also provided assistance and backing by Senator Robert Kennedy added glamour to the candidate and his coalition.[86]

Nava assembled important building blocks for a successful coalition and vigorously made the case for why he was qualified and should replace the conservative incumbent. The San Fernando resident recalled "University lecturing, in addition to the CSO experience, had prepared me very well to speak to all groups across town." He was aided by the incumbent's offensive statement that Latinos' poor academic performance was due to their being "lazy." Nava forced the incumbent into a runoff where he defeated him. In so doing, Nava became the first Mexican American elected to the Los Angeles School Board. The Nava coalition in 1967 was strikingly similar to the Roybal's in 1949 and 1962; it demonstrated anew that voters would support a Latino candidate with a compelling story and a well-funded, organized campaign.[87]

Coalitions grew around causes as well as candidates. In retrospect, the unionization of farm workers in the sixties owes a great deal to the organization of Mexican Americans in the forties and fifties and to relationships on the liberal-left. César Chávez and Dolores Huerta were tutored on the social gospel by labor priests and, like many of their top lieutenants, trained by CSO. So, too, the conditions that made organizing more likely to succeed in the sixties was due, in large measure, to the end of the bracero program. This was the life mission of Ernesto Galarza, who published research material and pushed the issue with successive presidential administrations and key allies such as the AFL-CIO and the Catholic Church until legislation was passed under President Kennedy. Galarza was also the one who convinced CSO and then MAPA to make the issue a top priority. The Mexican American community used a great deal of its political capital to administratively raise wages and then to support the strikers. It is not an accident that Governor Brown chose the 1964 MAPA convention to announce his opposition to an extension of the bracero program in the state. And it was at MAPA's request that Brown hired Abeytia to oppose the bracero program. Even if some of his activities irritated the Chávez union, Abeytia's coordinated actions with the state and federal officials, including U.S. Secretary of Labor Willard Wirtz and Undersecretary John Henning, clearly signaled to the growers that the political tide was shifting, leaving them to complain about the state's "Mexican-American Department of Employment." Old relationships also played a part in the early boycott, including individuals from the labor movement and the faith community, and the use of MAPA's 1966 convention as the backdrop for the deal to have Governor Brown investigate the union's defeat in the representational election at DiGiorgio. Finally, Chávez recognized the importance of political engagement early on, announcing the farm workers' support for Brown's reelection in 1966 while sharing a stage with Senator Edward Kennedy. For MAPA and other urban Mexican Americans, the strike and boycott were not the only concern; Johnson's War on Poverty and the conflict in Vietnam would assume a growing amount of attention as community leaders—and a younger generation of Chicano activists—interacted with the Johnson administration.

CHAPTER 11

PRESIDENT JOHNSON, VIETNAM, AND THE POLITICS OF RACE

For President Lyndon Johnson and Latinos in California, 1964 was a year of high hopes, good will and historic breakthroughs as the president sought to recognize the community and the Latino political leadership sought ever-larger roles on the national stage. Latinos took great pleasure in having a president from the Southwest, especially one who focused on California's Mexican Americans through the appointment process and who selected Los Angeles for his February 1964 meeting with Mexican President Adolfo López Mateos. Johnson had ensured that Latinos played a significant role in the campaign and the community voted a record 90 percent support for the president. Johnson acknowledged a special relationship with Latinos in California and the nation by hosting a special victory party at his Texas ranch. Los Angeles pharmacist Edward Ramírez recalls flying from Los Angeles to Dallas with other Viva Johnson leaders. Met at the airport, Johnson staffers put them into a limousine for the ride to the president's ranch where President and Mrs. Johnson and Mexican President and Mrs. Gustavo Díaz Ordaz met them. Johnson had once again used the president of Mexico to reinforce his relationship with Mexican Americans. But Johnson, ever the master of symbols, had one more surprise for his guests. A hush fell over the crowd as a military helicopter approached and then touched down. Uniformed officers rolled out the red carpet and the honor guard in full regalia stood at attention. From the plane emerged a triumphant Undersecretary of the Air Force, Daniel Luevano. He was a symbol of ethnic pride, particularly for the veterans present and for Los Angeles Latinos.[1]

In the November 1964 election, Latinos in California also worked with African Americans to advance a larger civil rights agenda, organizing Mexican-American Californians Against Proposition 14. The voter referendum was designed to repeal the

Rumford Fair Housing Act passed the previous year by the same labor-based coalition that successfully lobbied for the 1959 fair employment act. The issue was placed on the ballot after the realtors collected enough signatures to hold a referendum on the issue. Roybal and Soto served as honorary co-chairs of Mexican-American Californians Against Proposition 14. Juan Acevedo, Tony Ríos, and Herman Sillas served as co-chairs. The fair housing coalition also included the three largest groups with Latino members: the Democratic Party, AFL-CIO, and the Catholic Church. MAPA President Eduardo Quevedo praised the church in his address to a Latino issues conference called by five dioceses in Northern California. The voters repealed the law but the court ultimately decided that voters did not have the right to deny equality before the law.[2]

Then, in an unpublicized act of solidarity, four MAPA leaders joined the Reverend Martin Luther King, Jr. on the march in Selma, Alabama. During that event, Alabama State Troopers attacked the non-violent protesters and the Ku Klux Klan murdered a white minister. Roybal and sixty members of Congress responded by demanding that the president act to protect the right of African Americans to vote. Roybal joined fellow Congressmen James Roosevelt and John Conyers from Detroit to lead 5,000 racially mixed marchers through downtown Los Angeles. The racist violence helped convince President Johnson and Congress of the need to enact the 1965 Voting Rights Act.[3]

But Latinos grew angry when anti-poverty programs all but ignored the reality that there were more poor Mexican Americans than poor Blacks in California. On April 24, 1965, the MAPA Executive Board had passed a resolution stating "with one or two singular exceptions the vast number of Poverty Councils in the various cities and counties do not up to this moment have significant representation of Mexican Americans." MAPA declared its intention "to fight and stop any and all anti-poverty proposals that have been worked up and submitted by the various cities and counties without the fullest participation of Mexican Americans in this planning and policy making."[4]

Within this radicalizing environment, Congressman Roybal and CSO, MAPA, and GI Forum leaders, along with other prominent individuals, came together with their counterparts from around the nation in June 1965 at the Mayflower Hotel, in Washington, D.C. for a Great Society Conference under the aegis of the Democratic National Committee. U.S. Senator Joseph M. Montoya, newly elected to fill the seat left empty by the death of Dennis Chávez, was present along with Vice President Hubert Humphrey and many cabinet and department officials. President Johnson hosted the group that evening at the White House.[5]

President Johnson sought to tie Latino leaders to the administration at the same time his staff sought to identify and recruit Mexican Americans for a growing range of political and civil service positions. In the months leading up to the Great Society conference, Roybal sent the names of "qualified Spanish-speaking individuals" to federal agency heads. The pace quickened after the conference.[6] The federal government also funded a variety of social programs sponsored by Latino groups such as CSO, GI Forum, and LULAC. This allowed the Community Services

Latino leaders at the White House. Pictured (l to r) GI Forum founder Dr. Héctor P. García, President Johnson, and Forum president Augustine Flores. Over García's shoulder is MAPA president Eduardo Quevedo.

(Dr. Hector Garcia Papers, Texas A&M University-Corpus Christi, Bell Library)

*Undersecretary of the Army Daniel Luevano arrives at a base. The former
CSO activist was the highest-ranking Latino in the federal government.*
(Courtesy of Daniel M. Luevano)

Organization to hire project staff, including Rosie Vásquez, a
young Latina trained by Father John V. Coffield in the Young
Catholic Workers, who become a mainstay in the organization in
Los Angeles for the next 30 years.[7]

Yet many believed that Johnson was doing too little for Mexican
Americans, particularly in contrast to his commitment to African
Americans. A turning point in the state's Mexican American leadership's relationship with the federal government occurred in March
1966. The federal Equal Employment Opportunity Commission
(EEOC) invited fifty Mexican American leaders to a special regional meeting in Albuquerque. Their concern was that "there was
no program in EEOC that was directed at Mexican Americans," according to Armando Rodríguez, the San Diego-based activist working in Sacramento as a consultant to the California Department of
Education. "At this conference we expected to have input to create
the concept, because there was a series of meetings that we were
all involved [with] in Washington, D.C. under a fellow by the name
of David North at the White House."[8] However, when they arrived

the evening before the hearing was set to begin, Rodríguez learned that only one EEOC commissioner would be present. He pulled together the other delegates and they collectively decided to show their displeasure by walking out the next morning when the hearing opened. Rodríguez, the first Latino high school principal in San Diego and a delegate to the 1964 Democratic National Convention, was an unlikely protest leader. But he felt that the moment had come to make a statement. He later acknowledged, "It wasn't an easy thing to do."[9]

Armando Rodríguez with Governor Pat Brown in 1965. The former CSO leader served as the first Latino education consultant with the Department of Education, and was an unlikely protest leader against the Johnson administration. *(Courtesy of Armando Rodríquez)*

The next day the fifty delegates walked out of the hearing with the support of the major Mexican American organizations. The delegates demanded a meeting with President Johnson, the appointment of a Mexican American EEOC Commissioner, and the participation of Mexican Americans in the upcoming White House Civil Rights Conference that had been designed to address the needs of African Americans.[10] (Johnson had appointed the first Spanish-speaking and Spanish-surnamed commissioner, Aileen C. Hernández, a CSO activist and a former Los Angeles ILGWU organizer. However, she turned out to be a light-skinned African American married to a Latino.[11]) Congressman Roybal and MAPA Vice President Bert Corona expressed their solidarity after the event; Corona saw it as the "beginning of a new militancy."[12]

A reporter asked President Johnson at a White House press conference about the growing frustrations. Johnson stated that Mexican Americans "are entitled to more consideration in Government employment" and "have been discriminated against in housing, in education, in jobs." Asked if Mexican Americans would be welcome at the upcoming White House Civil Rights Conference, the President sidestepped the question and stated that his "door is always open" to Mexican Americans. "I am very anxious to exchange views with them. If they are ready for a conference, I will be ready for one."[13] Soon thereafter six Mexican American leaders, including MAPA's Eduardo Quevedo and Bert Corona, and the GI Forum's Augustine Flores, dined with President Johnson and his domestic policy advisor Joseph Califano at the White House.[14]

Despite access to the president and top administration officials, 1966 turned into 1967, and Mexican Americans still did not have a commitment from the White House to sponsor a conference to address their concerns. This occurred in large measure because of indecision on the part of President Johnson himself. In an effort to push the president to act, Congressman Roybal and MAPA leadership employed a number of tactics. The first involved emissaries. In February 1967, former CSO president Herman Gallegos and Notre Dame sociologist Julian Samora met with Johnson aide Harry McPherson over breakfast in Washington, D.C. The two consulted for the Ford Foundation and served as Johnson appointees on the federal Commission on Rural Poverty.[15]

The Mexican American leaders also reached out to political allies in an effort to underscore the urgency of the situation. The Los Angeles County Board of Supervisors passed a resolution urging Johnson to call the conference. More importantly to the White House, the California Democratic Congressional Delegation approved a similar resolution. The message was unambiguous. An internal White House memorandum stressed that Congressmen Roybal and George Brown "are increasingly concerned about themselves, and incidentally the President."[16]

At the same time, MAPA sought to expand its base within the community in the hopes of increasing its influence and to prevent the grassroots anger at Johnson from being turned against it. This led to the Mexican American Legislative Conference at Sacramento Junior College on March 17-18, 1967. MAPA, GI Forum, CSO, LULAC, and the Association of Mexican American Educators (AMAE) co-sponsored the event with the Catholic Council for the Spanish Speaking and the United Farm Workers Organizing Committee. Some 700 activists attended. Ernesto Galarza keynoted the conference. In his address, Bert Corona stated that the conference goal was to press for proposed legislation, including a bill creating bilingual education.[17]

Mexican American leaders enjoy a private meal with President Johnson and domestic policy adviser Joseph Califano in the White House. MAPA president Eduardo Quevedo is second from right.   (Lyndon B. Johnson Library)

MAPA President Bert Corona launched an assault on federal agencies that he believed were not adequately serving the community. On May 3, 1967, Corona attacked the U.S. Civil Rights Commission at its meeting in San Francisco. Corona also charged the Post Office with racist hiring practices. MAPA then set up pickets in a number of cities, including Riverside where protesters greeted customers outside the Main Post Office. "We want jobs, not poverty handout! We want equal opportunity to the good things of America, not just the opportunity to die in Vietnam," stated their handbill.[18]

Corona was using the power of protest to nudge government officials into action. He was also using the direct action as a way of building a cadre of activists deployable in the forthcoming presidential race. But to have a national impact the California-based leader understood that he must patch together a network of Latino activists and organizations among Latinos in other states, including key primary states. In relatively short order MAPA organized affiliates in Arizona, Indiana, Illinois, Texas, and Washington, as well as Washington, D.C. In many cases this involved formalizing relationships with people Corona had known for decades in the liberal-left or trade union movement.[19]

After a long delay President Johnson was ready to act. He swore-in Vicente T. Ximenes to be on the Equal Employment Opportunities Commission on June 9, 1967 at an elaborate ceremony in the White House. With Congressman Roybal and other dignitaries present, the president then signed an executive order creating a Cabinet Level Inter-Agency Committee on Mexican-American Affairs. Having done so, he swore-in Ximenes as its director.[20] Johnson privately told Ximenes to hold his meetings next to the president's office and to periodically mention the president's interest in his work as a way to encourage cooperation by the cabinet members.[21] It was a masterful stroke according to Raúl Yzaguirre, who stressed that Johnson managed to give the impression that the entire government would now be focused on Mexican American concerns.[22]

MAPA's Bert Corona joined in praising Johnson. In a highly laudatory telegram, he said Latinos were "rejoicing for your most timely appointment of one of the finest human beings from the Mexican American community." He then thanked the president for his "steadfast support of the highest aspirations and deepest desires of the Mexican-Americans and other Spanish-Speaking Americans."[23] Civil Service Commissioner John W. Macy, Jr. forwarded the message to Johnson, calling it "[t]he most significant piece of correspondence yet received." The administration also worked to rebuild old relationships, with "Dick Murphy, the Assistant Postmaster General for Personnel [meeting] with Corona after Ximenes' swearing-in."[24]

In addition to pushing a Mexican American agenda in Washington, D.C, Ximenes also took to the road to sell Latinos on the president's goals and to listen to concerns in the field. In July 1967 Ximenes represented Johnson at the annual MAPA convention, where Congressman Roybal and César Chávez also spoke. Ximenes met privately with twenty-five California leaders in the Riverside Mission Inn room of CSO president Albert Piñón. The consensus was that there would not be a White House sponsored conference on Mexican American issues. Consequently, the Latino leaders decided to hold their own state conference and create "white papers" to be used when advocating for changes in federal laws and regulations.[25] Ximenes worked with the Democratic National Committee, as Carlos McCormick had done, to publish a brochure describing its work on behalf of "Mexican-Americans, Puerto Ricans and Hispanos."[26]

Two months later Vicente Ximenes announced the White House Conference on Mexican-American Affairs would be held on October 27 and 28, 1967 in El Paso, Texas. The leaders of CSO, MAPA, GI Forum, and LULAC were all offered prominent roles. Ximenes hired Polly Baca to serve as press spokesman for the inter-agency committee, making her the first high profile Latina in the nation's capitol.[27]

California Latino leaders responded to the planned White House conference by deciding to hold a pre-conference meeting at Camp Hess Kramer in Malibu on October 6, to prepare for the national confab. Congressman Roybal agreed to be the keynote speaker. Juan Acevedo, MAPA's founding secretary, whose own roots in Los Angeles Latino politics went back to the forties, continued to act as the point person between political activists, Roybal, and the White House.[28] Following a meeting in Senator Montoya's office in Washington, D.C., Roybal shared his private thoughts with

Acevedo, saying: "Ximenes is making all the plans and rules [for the White House Conference], so that whatever criticism arises can only be directed at him."[29] Acevedo continued to work with the pre-event committee chairs, including Héctor Abeytia, César Chávez, Bert Corona, and Albert Piñón. Speaking for the steering committee, Acevedo told the chairs that "[t]he most significant factor at this conference will be your position papers." He added that the event "has taken on an even greater significance with the pending El Paso hearings, and we would like to ensure that it reflects the best that California has to offer."[30]

César Chávez, who had previously supported the idea of the conference, wrote Ximenes, declining the request that he participate. "I think that your and the President's concern for *most* Mexican-Americans is commendable," said Chávez, but that "the administration is not ready to deal with specific problems affecting farmworkers."[31] Others not on the initial guest list sought to participate, including David Santiago at the Los Angeles-based Council of Puerto Rican Organizations, which was tied-in to the ethnically diverse LULAC. Roybal made the arrangement for him to participate.[32]

When the California Mexican American activists gathered in Malibu, some sought to focus on preparing for the White House conference while others expressed their skepticism. During the three-day meeting, two hundred representatives from CSO, GI Forum, LULAC, AMAE, and MAPA approved the drafted position papers, which were then sent to Ximenes at the White House.[33] The California group also voted to send a five-person delegation to El Paso. "We're going to make sure this is not another L.B.J. propaganda-type conference," MAPA President Bert Corona told the press.[34] There was additional tension within the community; some did not like the idea that Acevedo, a Roybal functionary, and Ximenes, Johnson's Mexican American advisor, vetted delegates.[35] In the midst of this tense and delicate situation, Roybal and twenty-nine other Congressmen announced their opposition to Johnson's bombing of North Vietnam. Thus Roybal aligned himself with the most liberal elements of his party.[36]

Roybal's opposition to Johnson's policy on Vietnam emboldened critics of the president's program directed towards Mexican Americans. A few days later, when the MAPA Executive Board met in San Diego to hear from its investigating team, it voted 58-5 to boycott the El Paso Conference.[37] It was a startling development. Moreover, it represented a political break with the Johnson White House with whom the other Mexican American organizations were working closely. Louis Flores of Napa recalled MAPA believing that the upcoming conference "was more show for Johnson than a sincere effort to develop Latino power."[38] This was significant because Flores, like others within the MAPA leadership, had links to the Johnson administration. He had worked with César Chávez and others to found the California Human Development Corporation, which started in 1967 with a federal job training grant. He and Robert Gonzales of San Francisco decided to accompany Corona to El Paso for the purpose of picketing the White House Conference.[39]

This decision seemed to contradict MAPA's mission to increase Latino influence within the political process; furthermore, it had little chance to have a negative impact on the event. Some two hundred community leaders from California were already planning to attend and fifteen of the most prominent had prepared issue papers. These presenters included public officials such Los Angeles School Board Member Julian Nava, academics like UCLA Professor Ralph Guzmán, and program operators such as Héctor Abeytia, now director of the Fresno-based Manpower Opportunities Project.[40] Other California Latinos, such as Daniel Luevano, Richard Amador and Armando Rodríguez, held federal posts that were tied to Vicente Ximenes at the White House.

President Johnson and the Cabinet Level Inter-Agency Committee on Mexican-American Affairs pulled out all the stops to create two very memorable days and for their effort achieved glowing headlines in Spanish-language papers such as *La Opinión* in Los Angeles. President Johnson introduced Mexican President Díaz Ordaz to a Joint session of Congress on October 27, 1967, where he spoke fondly of the U.S.-Mexican relationship. He then hosted a state dinner in Díaz Ordaz's honor at the White House, to which he invited a number of Mexican Americans.[41] Two thousand miles away, in Texas, Vice President Hubert Humphrey addressed one thousand civic leaders at the opening of the Cabinet Committee Hearings on Mexican-Americans Affairs.[42]

"The President requested results, not reports. We are here to discuss the future, not the past—the solutions, not the problems," intoned Humphrey. He said it was "already well known" that a Mexican American "earns less than half as much as other citizens of the Southwest, has almost double the unemployment rate, and obtains five years less schooling." He spoke with pride of the "excellent and proven Federal programs designed to support grassroots initiatives in the Southwest, including Head Start, the Neighborhood Youth Corps, Adult Basic Education Program, and the Migrant Opportunities Program." The vice president acknowledged Dr. Héctor García and Ambassador Raymond Telles and singled out César Chávez as "a man of unselfish dedication and personal courage who has aroused the conscience of this nation."[43]

The conference participants divided into six subject groups where a cabinet member or other top official led the discussion in conjunction with a prominent Mexican American. Secretary of Agriculture Orville Freeman and GI Forum National Chairman Louis Téllez led the discussion on agriculture. Housing & Urban Development Secretary Robert Weaver and CSO President Albert Piñón from San Jose led the discussion on urban issues. These groups discussed topics based on the presentations of prepared papers by Latino experts in their respective field.[44]

The second day of the El Paso Conference was filled with yet more symbolism, as Johnson arrived and combined words with deeds to underscore his commitment to working with the Mexican American leaders and to maintaining bi-national relations. Johnson and Díaz Ordaz both addressed the conference. The delegates then boarded chartered buses to the Mexican side of the border where three hundred thousand Mexicans witnessed the two presidents signing the Chamizal Treaty. The treaty gave back to Mexico land that had come into U.S. possession with the changing route of the Rio Grande. That evening, delegates and special guests, such as actor Ricardo Montalbán, joined Johnson and Díaz Ordaz for a private celebration.[45]

Most participants believed that the White House Conference on Mexican-American Affairs was a huge success and the GI Forum's historian concluded that the conference "played an important role in convincing policymakers in Washington that more needed to be done."[46] It also proved to be a joyous opportunity for Latinos to celebrate their Mexican culture and to discuss public policy with the top leaders in the federal government. This led to an invaluable networking opportunity for program leaders such Dionicio Morales, who presented a paper on "Equal Opportunity in Training." At one of the receptions he asked President Johnson for some job training funds. This led to the Los Angeles-based Mexican American Opportunity Foundation being awarded a two million dollar contract which was extended to $3 million, making it, according to Morales, the largest contract ever provided a Latino run program.[47]

This support for a pioneering California anti-poverty program was followed up by visits to the state from top-level federal administrators. U.S. Civil Service Commission chair John W. Macy arrived in mid-November 1967 where he visited the East Los Angeles State Service Center. Ximenes arrived two weeks later. Community leaders and anti-poverty program administrators joined him for breakfast and he then toured two federally funded anti-poverty programs.[48] Officials in Washington also reached out to local program leaders and Johnson ordered a survey of "health, housing employment, education and language problems faced by Spanish-speaking citizens" by the Bureau of Labor Statistics and the Census Bureau.[49]

The alternative Raza Unida Conference in El Paso started out at the Hotel Paso del Norte, with the rooms paid for by Ford Foundation consultant Herman Gallegos, using funds from the United Auto Workers and Protestant churches. In a symbolic move, the group soon moved to the Sacred Heart Catholic Church in the barrio. Corona led the rump group along with radical firebrands such as Rodolfo "Corky" Gonzales from New Mexico. Most of those present were young and the event has been viewed by some observers as central to the developing if yet unnamed Chicano movement. It was also a precursor to the formation of the La Raza Unida Party in 1970. Yet despite the articulated enmity towards Johnson and other established political leaders, this conference emerged with critical support from the California-based progressive wing of the Mexican American community and their allies in other states. Corona, Gallegos, Galarza, and others played a role; Ernesto Galarza spoke at both conferences.[50]

The La Raza Conference participants expressed their desire for greater self-determination in different ways. The most immediate outgrowth was formation of the Southwest Council of La Raza, with the UAW's Henry Santiestevan as founding director. The Council consisted of state and local groups stitched together by MAPA but that continued to operate under their own banners. Herman Gallegos and Julian Samora had penned the theoretical underpinnings for the group the previous year in *La Raza: Forgotten Americans*. They recognized that the existing Mexican American organizations "have been able to maintain operations over a period of years without outside support" but were limited in their ability to meet the demands of the community due to insufficient funding. They sought to create a Latino-led umbrella organization with a capacity to raise outside funding in order to meet the growing needs of the community. To illustrate this model, they cited two California-based efforts.

> The organizing talents of Fred Ross and Saul Alinsky, plus contributions from the Industrial Areas Foundation, helped create the CSO in California during the 1950s. This example illustrates how the aspirations of a group can be effectively aided with outside support. Similarly, the massive voter registration of the CSO and the 'spontaneous' 'Viva Kennedy' movement in 1960 helped move the Spanish-speaking people into the spotlight of American politics.[51]

Gallegos and Samora naturally turned for organizational development to the Ford Foundation, for whom they were consultants. They also worked with other leaders, such as Corona, Ernesto Galarza, and Henry Santiestevan who, as United Auto Worker president Walter Reuther's top Latino staffer, also played an important role in securing Ford Foundation assistance.[52]

Looking back, the tumultuous years after the Watts Riots and the start of the farm workers strike in Delano produced a number of historical breakthroughs and positive developments that were not always appreciated at the time because of the revolution of rising expectations. The White House Conference on Mexican-American Affairs and the cabinet level committee did focus unprecedented attention on Latinos whom only a few years earlier were rarely if ever thought about in the nation's corridors of power. A host of new programs were started to improve educational and economic conditions. In addition, numerous Latinos were appointed to high-level positions within the federal government. Other precedents were also set. Where Kennedy invited the three Mexican American members of Congress to the Oval Office, Johnson entertained the leaders of the four largest organizations at the White House. While appointed late in Johnson's term, the prominent role of Vicente Ximenes built on and expanded the earlier role of Carlos McCormick as the Latino liaison—a position maintained by subsequent presidents. Johnson had built on the early, tentative steps taken by his predecessor, and boldly, if awkwardly and inconsistently, involved local Mexican Americans in the formation of national public policy and increased the role of Latinos in the federal government.

The ultimate assessment of the success or failure of the White House Conference Mexican-American Affairs was largely predictable: those who participated in it generally provided accolades; those who protested outside were more likely to render a critical assessment. Professor Julian Nava saw it as "very historic."[53] For some, like Dionicio Morales, the reward was immediate and measurable because his Los Angeles-based job training program received a huge boost in funds. So, too, Congress' passage of the nation's first bilingual education bill could be linked to the El Paso Conference and the overall efforts of Johnson's Interagency Committee. Other changes would take more time. Most policy proposals needed to be translated into actual programs with full-time staff, thus it took time for agency and department heads to institutionalize affirmative action. Because of this, the most profound gains and thus the full impact of the White House Conference—would not occur immediately. They would require a second Johnson term, which appeared to be a near certainty.

But even as Johnson pushed policies favored by Latinos he encountered growing opposition from conservatives in Congress and from members of his own liberal alliance. This included a backlash from big city mayors. It was "inevitable," according to Daniel Luevano, first western director of the Office of Economic Opportunity (OEO), because by giving minorities control over federally-funded but locally-controlled programs, President Johnson was creating alternative power centers that would at times be in conflict with local elected officials. OEO thus "overreached itself politically," according to Luevano. Still, the programs, including the California Rural Legal Assistance, were important because they "opened the doors" for Latinos to participate in the community's economic uplift and provided a new tool in dealing with rural communities dominated by growers. The political challenge for the White House was that the mayors and the minorities were both central to the Democratic party coalition.[54]

The future was uncertain in terms of politics. MAPA's attack on President Johnson and the White House's Mexican-American Conference was a high-risk gamble. It had already resulted in MAPA not being invited to participate with other national groups in the post-conference process of refining the president's Latino agenda to be pursued by the federal agencies and where necessary, taken to Congress for enabling legislation or program funding. San Diego educator Armando Rodríguez, who led the Albuquerque walkout and then became President Johnson's point person on bilingual education, declared: "You don't break with the White House unless you have more power than the White House."[55] Others were not so sure.

This much is evident. MAPA made a profound decision in voting to boycott the White House Conference that strained its relationship with President Johnson and with the other Latino organizations. Was the decision well thought out or was it made in the heat of the moment? Who made the decision? What were the operating assumptions? The decision deviated from past practice in at least two ways. First, Corona and Quevedo consciously used the 1964 Johnson campaign to build MAPA and to develop relationships that resulted in access to top federal officials. Second, Corona and Quevedo recognized the inherent weakness in MAPA, CSO, GI Forum, LULAC, and UWFOC pursing separate agendas and worked tirelessly to bring the disparate groups together first in the Mexican-American Unity Council and then in issue conferences at Sacramento that included religious and labor representatives. By boycotting the White House Conference MAPA was going it alone at a time when the importance of the White House as a liberal power center had increased with the election of Governor Reagan.

MAPA's decision, which seemed to run counter to its mission of developing influence within the political arena, was made at a special meeting of the board of directors and not by the larger organization meeting in convention. In talking to key participants at the meeting, it is evident that MAPA operated under the assumption that liberals had a lock on the presidency and the Democratic Congress was permanent. The central issue was how to effectuate change. This was part of an ongoing discussion that included the decision to picket federal Post Offices. The administration validated the tactic in the minds of the activists by hiring additional Mexican American employees. Thus, in October 1967, MAPA debated the best way to advance Latino interests—was it by attending the conference to help shape policy development or was it picking the event to pressure the administration to adopt new policies? Some of those present believed in a variation of the "good cop, bad cop" routine where one group works inside the corridor of power while another ratchets up pressure for a favorable deal by making demands from outside in the streets. But what is exceptional is that MAPA, built around the effective use of the ballot box, would adopt the picket sign and allow the seemingly "nonpolitical" groups like CSO, GI Forum, and LULAC to work with the White House to help forge new understandings with the president of the United States. In seeking to pressure the White House to move more rapidly, MAPA appeared oblivious to the larger social trends evident in the 1966 election where voters elected more conservatives to Congress (reducing Johnson's flexibility) and a quarter of California Latinos abandoned the liberal alliance to help elect Governor Ronald Reagan.

MAPA's decision, which contrasted sharply with that of CSO, GI Forum and LULAC, may also have reflected changes inside the organization and its growing relationship to new and more radical organizations on college campuses and within the African American community. Corona's purposeful recruitment of student radicals to infuse new energy into the organization meant that MAPA had experienced a generational shift earlier than the other organizations. Moreover, the larger environment in California (unlike Texas, the headquarters for GI Forum and LULAC) was likewise shaped by the growing strength of the New Left, which condemned liberalism for not eradicating poverty, racism, and war.[56] MAPA's evolving strategies and tactics also reflected a change in leadership. MAPA had emerged as a national political player with Eduardo Quevedo and Bert Corona partnering with Congressman Edward Roybal and others. Quevedo and Corona had known each other since El Congreso where they shared a progressive vision, but were on the opposite side of the liberal-left divide in 1939. With Quevedo's premature death in 1967, Corona assumed the reigns of MAPA and appears to have suffered from not having the pragmatic wisdom of his old friend. This is important because Corona, the brilliant organizer, could also be an ideologue. As a Los Angeles longshoremen's union leader Corona had followed an earlier "movement" out of the Democratic Party in 1948, only to return later as a suit-wearing, liberal businessman active in CSO and the California Democratic Council.

Seen from a national perspective, Corona and other Californians were less "loyal" to individual politicians, according to Raúl Yzaguirre, the Texas farm worker and GI Forum activist who became the third and longest serving head of the National Council of La Raza. For those outside of California, it was unconceivable to break with an incumbent with whom they had a long relationship and who had delivered more for Mexican Americans than all his predecessors combined—even if you did not get everything you wanted.[57] Whether MAPA and its allies in other states would remain isolated politically or would regain their influence depended, in part, on the larger political developments in the state and nation.

CHAPTER 12

ROBERT KENNEDY, HUMPHREY, AND THE 1968 PRESIDENTIAL ELECTION

For Latinos, who had grown to ten percent of the California population, 1968 began with President Lyndon B. Johnson demonstrating his commitment to the community. He started the New Year by signing the nation's first bilingual education bill. Formally an amendment to the Elementary and Secondary Education Act, authored by Congressman Edward Roybal, it fulfilled one of the dreams expressed by the 1939 Congreso. Weeks later, the Johnson administration forced Governor Ronald Reagan to back down from his efforts to strip federal funding for the California Rural Legal Assistance. The federal government also moved to block Reagan's efforts to import braceros by forming a committee to investigate the issue that would include César Chávez and Bert Corona.[1] In taking these bold actions, the president demonstrated his support for Mexican Americans and his eagerness to implement the policy "solutions" articulated at the October 1967 White House Conference in El Paso. To further underscore the administration's commitment, Vicente Ximenes, director of the Inter-Agency Committee on Mexican-American Affairs, arranged for the secretaries of Agriculture, Labor, Housing and Urban Development, and Health, Education and Welfare, and the director of the Office of Economic Opportunity to sign-off on the conference report. This was another first. Never before had the federal government's top administrators committed themselves to implement a pro-Latino program, let alone one drafted by the community leaders themselves.[2]

Even in California, where the Mexican-American Political Association (MAPA) and the United Farm Workers Organizing Committee (UFWOC) were openly critical of Johnson, the president enjoyed widespread support. Congressman Roybal agreed to serve on a pro-Johnson "unity slate" for the 1968 Democratic National Convention, as did two prominent labor leaders: Los

Angeles County Federation of Labor president J.J. Rodríguez and United Auto Workers (UAW) Local 887 president Henry Lacayo.[3] At the same time, several prominent Latinos agreed to support Johnson's lone opponent, Senator Eugene McCarthy, who was running a campaign based on opposition to the U.S. involvement in Vietnam. These included Rudolfo Acuña, a young faculty member at Pierce Junior College in Los Angeles' San Fernando Valley, Dr. Ernesto Galarza, and early Los Angeles CIO and El Congreso leader Frank S. López.[4]

Corona, Chávez, and other key Latinos in the state remained non-aligned, hoping that Senator Robert Kennedy might enter the race. Unsure about Kennedy's intentions, Bert Corona sent MAPA's Sacramento lobbyist, Jack Ortega, to meet with McCarthy's national campaign officials. When asked what McCarthy would do for Mexican Americans, Richard Goodwin, a former aide to President Kennedy who was now working for McCarthy, offered to let Ortega head "Mexican Americans for McCarthy," but failed to articulate policy positions to advance Latino interests.[5] That was

Senator Robert Kennedy, pictured between Helen and César Chávez, joined the farm labor leader for the Mass ending his fast for non-violent social change.   *(Walter P. Reuther Library, Wayne State University)*

significant since McCarthy co-sponsored an anti-bracero bill with George McGovern in 1960 and Goodwin helped shape the Alliance for Progress.[6]

Most California activists in 1968 were not focused on legislative or presidential politics, but rather on César Chávez's fast for non-violent social change. During the fast, several thousand high school students in Los Angeles walked out of classes with under the banner of the United Mexican American Students (UMAS). Congressman Roybal immediately flew to Los Angeles to meet with the students along with School Board Member Julian Nava. Roybal expressed his support for "constructive educational objectives of the majority of student protestors."[7] But the student walkout, "the first major mass protest explicitly against racism undertaken by Mexican Americans," according to activist Carlos Muñoz, signaled a radicalization taking place among the young.[8]

On Sunday, March 10, in Delano, César Chávez broke his fast at an ecumenical service with Senator Kennedy at his side and surrounded by ten thousand supporters. Kennedy also took the time to meet with Los Angeles high school students who were receiving aid from American Federation of Teachers Local 1021, MAPA, and parent groups.[9] As he departed, remembered Dolores Huerta, farm workers started yelling, "Kennedy for President. Kennedy for President."[10] This led Kennedy to address the workers from the top of the automobile in which he was riding. As he traveled to the airport Kennedy told Chávez aide Rev. James Drake: "I think I'm going to run."[11]

His running for president in 1968 ran counter to the expectations of political insiders. Democratic party leaders fully expected Johnson to be reelected in 1968, and Kennedy was widely seen as a leading candidate in 1972. Moreover, it was late in the nominating process and Kennedy had done nothing to prepare for a national campaign. However, events were challenging the standard political calculations. Kennedy viscerally felt the growing discontent among students opposed to the Vietnam War, and of Latinos, African Americans, and poor whites unable to fully participate in America's unprecedented prosperity. Yet it was the reaction to events half way around the world that produced the most dramatic results. Communist North Vietnam's 1968 Tet Offensive shook American confidence in the inevitability of U.S. victory in Vietnam—and in

President Johnson. Senator McCarthy's long-shot campaign against Johnson received unanticipated support in the New Hampshire primary, the first in the nation, in March 1968. Four days after the New Hampshire primary, Senator Robert F. Kennedy declared his candidacy for the presidency of the United States.[12]

The Kennedy campaign moved rapidly to lock up the two largest states, California and New York. With delegates from these two mega states secured, Kennedy then intended to woo the party bosses and union leaders who controlled delegations in the large industrial states. To achieve this, however, he needed to demonstrate he could be elected by competing, with little preparation, in every remaining primary: Indiana on May 7, Nebraska on May 14, Oregon on May 28, and California on June 4.

The campaign scrambled to construct a national organization and to design television commercials for immediate airing in the battleground states. Television allowed Kennedy to bypass party leaders to communicate directly with the voters. Most of the commercials, like network shows at the time, were in black and white, and designed to appeal to middle class Anglos. Kennedy allocated an unprecedented one million dollars for TV in the four states. Three-quarters would go to California where ads would run for seven weeks in the state's ten media markets.[13] The campaign would utilize the fifty-one Spanish radio stations in California to reach voters in the major markets, as well as the small, geographically isolated Latino communities.[14]

Latinos were part of the Kennedy campaign from the earliest days. The farm workers were an obvious ally, so were urban Latinos. "Bert Corona, who is with MAPA, is hooked up with Chávez's organization," noted Kennedy operative Dave Hackett, following a meeting with Richard Boone, director of the UAW's Citizens Crusade Against Poverty. The meeting served to link the campaign with the UAW's network of activist-oriented organizations.[15] The UAW had helped establish The East Los Angeles Community Union, or TELACU, and Kennedy had authored the national legislation creating community development corporations, as part of his innovative efforts to use private enterprise in the war on poverty.[16]

Kennedy's national campaign brought on board two talented Mexican Americans, Californian Henry Santiestevan and Polly Baca, who was most recently the press person for Vicente Ximenes at the White House. Kennedy appointed the fifty-two-year-old Santiestevan as the national chairman of Viva Kennedy and the twenty-seven-year-old Baca as the deputy. The daughter of a farm worker in Colorado, Baca had gotten her first job in Washington, D.C. thanks to Carlos McCormick, and then had worked in New York for a labor union with a large Puerto Rican membership. Corona was named national coordinator and would assist the campaign from his base in California.[17]

Henry Santiestevan.
Senator Robert Kennedy tapped
the Washington, D.C.-based
Californian to organize the 1968
Viva Kennedy campaign.
The founding director of
the Southwest Council of La Raza
enjoyed strong ties to national labor
and liberal leaders as well as
to CSO, MAPA, and the UFW.
(Stina Santiestevan)

In California, the Kennedy forces focused on compiling a list of delegates, 174 people who could provide material assistance to ensure the success of the campaign and who would represent the senator at the Democratic National Convention should he carry the state's winner take all primary. Assembly Speaker Jesse Unruh, as the head of the Kennedy campaign in California, effectively reached out to legislators and party leaders. He relied heavily on the UAW's Paul Schrade, who worked with MAPA President Bert Corona, to place a record number of Latinos on the slate. The delegation included Corona, longtime Los Angeles activists Ralph Guzmán and Hope Mendoza Schechter (a first for Mexican American women), San Jose businessman Earnest F. Abeytia, Reedley College Physics Professor Albert E. Molina, and San Bernardino County Supervisor Rubén S. Ayala.[18]

Schrade called Chávez on Kennedy's behest and the two had a heart-to-heart discussion. "I told him about my problems with Walter

[Reuther]," who was loath to oppose an incumbent whose help he needed to ensure a good contract with the auto makers. Chávez replied, "I'm going to have a problem with [AFL-CIO president] George Meany and that means a lot of money." Meany was close to President Johnson and a major underwriter of the farm workers' union. Despite such challenges, the two leaders decided to "go for it," according to Schrade. Chávez agreed to be a Kennedy delegate.[19] Chávez formalized the United Farm Workers Organizing Committee's decision to endorse Kennedy that night at a quickly called membership meeting attended by eight hundred. According to Dolores Huerta, "It wasn't a hard decision to make because Bobby had been with us from the very beginning."[20]

Senator Kennedy embarked on his first tour of California on March 24, 1968. In voter-rich Los Angeles, he began with a motorcade and a rally at Olvera Street, the birthplace for Latino Los Angeles and the site of El Congreso's party in 1939. "Two weeks ago, I came to California to pay homage to one of the great living Americans: César Chávez," Kennedy told the adoring crowd.[21] Now the campaign needed to put together an organization, and to register as many potential supporters as possible in the two and a half weeks remaining before the April 11 voter registration deadline.

MAPA and the United Farm Workers used their organizations to register new voters throughout the Central Valley, running the most intense campaign since the CSO voter registration drive for John F. Kennedy in 1960. Chávez made his first public appearance since ending his twenty-five-day fast at a voter registration rally at the Merced County Fairgrounds.[22]

The two organizations also focused on the urban centers, particularly East Los Angeles, where MAPA had a large membership and the farm workers maintained a powerful boycott apparatus. "You Can Vote, BUT Are You REGISTERED?" shouted a mimeographed flyer jointly produced by the two organizations. The flyer had a picture of Kennedy flanked by a striking farm worker. The senator was quoted as saying: "We must direct our nation's resources to end the crisis in the cities and poverty in farm communities. To do this we must have peace in Vietnam." Corona was quoted as saying: "Mexican Americans must use the vote to gain power and representation."[23]

Farm worker organizer Fred Ross oversaw the Los Angeles drive, working some of the same neighborhoods where he had registered voters for CSO twenty years earlier. For its part, CSO registered "more than 10,000" according to CSO's Rosie Vásquez.[24] The result of the drive in Los Angeles and other cities was the rapid registration of 100,000 new voters in California, eligible to vote along with the roughly half million registered over the previous twenty years.[25] The Kennedy campaign estimated that there were now 700,000 Latino voters in the state.[26]

President Johnson then changed the political calculus in California and the nation on March 30 when he went on national television and announced that he would not seek reelection. The president's political operation moved to support Vice President Humphrey, who decided not to contest the California primary, although Johnson's "unity slate" would remain on the ballot. The *Los Angeles Times'* poll gave Kennedy 32 percent, McCarthy, 24 percent, and Humphrey 6 percent in the state. Despite his popularity, the problem for Kennedy was that his support was concentrated among those least likely to vote—young people and minorities, particularly Mexican Americans.[27]

MAPA was intent on playing a national role for Kennedy, starting with the Indiana primary. It would be the first contest between Kennedy and McCarthy and a stand-in for Vice President Humphrey, Indiana Governor Roger Branigin. Believing that in a close race Indiana's 20,000-member-strong-Latino community could make a difference, MAPA President Bert Corona dispatched MAPA organizers Jack Ortega and Chris Carlos to Indiana, with the approval of Senator Edward Kennedy, who was assisting his brother in the campaign. Ortega arrived in Indiana on April 10 and quickly opened a "Latinos for Kennedy" headquarters and began to put together a campaign in the Mexican American and Puerto Rican neighborhoods. This included coordinating the efforts of the year-old local MAPA chapters and students sent in to assist from Chicago, where the farm workers had a grape boycott committee. Ortega also worked with Santiestevan in Washington, D.C. to develop Spanish language campaign material. Kennedy's labor outreach workers included Los Angeles UAW staffer Henry C. González who had been sent to work with the Indiana UAW.[28]

Ortega rapidly immersed himself in local politics and learned first-hand the power of machine politics. "Ortega reports that talk of vote-buying for Governor Branigin is rife in Lake County, and that agents of the Johnson-Humphrey Administration are directing this activity," according to internal Kennedy campaign documents. "Cris Aldrete, Special Assistant to DNC Chairman [John] Bailey (in charge of Mexican Americans and Spanish-speaking Affairs), is reportedly to be the key to this activity, and the word is that jobs in local poverty programs are being offered to Mexican Americans who will swear by Branigin."[29]

Despite such efforts by the White House, the Viva Kennedy efforts were taking shape. With less than a week to go before the election, Senator Robert Kennedy spoke to 7,000 enthusiastic Latinos at a rally sponsored by Viva Kennedy at the Washington High School gymnasium in East Chicago. Special guests included Puerto Rican community leader Juan Santiago and MAPA President Bert Corona. The campaign also ran ads on Chicago's WTAQ's Spanish-language programs and *El Puertoriqueño* and the *Latino Times*, published a message of support for Kennedy from César Chávez.[30]

On Election Day, Indiana Latinos went to the polls in record numbers, helping Kennedy achieve an upset victory.[31] The MAPA and UAW organizers returned to California to find the campaign floundering and with McCarthy ahead in the polls. Kennedy needed Mexican Americans, his most loyal constituency, more than ever. The national campaign directed resources into Viva Kennedy. Jack Ortega assumed control of the Fresno-based Central Valley campaign, which included agricultural workers and young professionals such as attorney Armando O. Rodríguez. Herman Gallegos oversaw the Northern California campaign out of San Francisco.[32]

Henry Santiestevan and Polly Baca flew to California— Santiestevan for the duration of the campaign. The two convened a seventeen-person meeting of the campaign's top Latino leadership on Sunday, May 12 at the Stardust Motel in Delano. A week earlier, the farm town, already rocked by the agricultural strike, experienced a high school student walkout. The campaign summit included key figures from MAPA, the UFWOC, and United Mexican American Students. "Henry's role emerged from the meetings and discussions on Sunday and Monday as one not only of a top-level contact in the Kennedy operation, but also a mediator between various Mexican American groups in California," wrote Baca. "Henry's previous friendships with each of these organizations should assist in ironing out any difficulties that might arise."[33]

Santiestevan pieced together the largest grassroots organization ever in the Los Angeles Latino community. He worked with talented and younger community leaders such as Manuel Aragón, director of the Economic and Youth Opportunities Agency, as well as elder statesmen such as Tony Ríos from CSO. He also worked closely with UAW officials who had ties into the Latino community through TELACU, run by union staffer Esteban Torres, and a series of bilingual Community Centers that the union operated to assist people seeking employment and social services. The campaign also integrated the UFWOC's Los Angeles boycott apparatus into the presidential campaign. Santiestevan likewise navigated between conflicting interests. He approved tacit support for Richard Calderón, running for the state senate against George Danielson, who had edged him out by five hundred votes in the previous primary.[34]

For its part, the Kennedy campaign was unusually effective because it reached into every Mexican American community in the state and incorporated ethnic leaders in a myriad of roles. In Oakland, the campaign sponsored a Kennedy Coffee honoring Jean Kennedy Smith at the Edgewater Inn. Close to twenty percent of the "hostesses" were Latinas. In neighboring Contra Costa County, MAPA State Secretary Jayne Ruiz, a moderate Republican, organized the local Viva Kennedy operation out of her Pittsburg home.[35] In the wine producing counties of Napa and Solano, MAPA's Louis Flores organized a Community Endorsement meeting at the fairgrounds and then marshaled enthusiasm into the campaign.[36] Four hundred miles to the south, in Oxnard, MAPA President Vincent Godina, who had led the local picketing of the United States Post Office, set up a headquarters on the city's main street and organized block captains to go door-to-door throughout the *Colonia*.[37] In Delano, politics fused with economics as Chávez learned that the growers were cynically aiding McCarthy.[38]

At each site, the campaign used tailored literature. The Kennedy campaign produced a Spanish language leaflet with a photo of the senator sharing bread with Chávez at the end of his fast, and with quotes from the farm labor leader and MAPA's Bert Corona.[39] Viva Kennedy published a bilingual eight-page tabloid that explained the candidate's record, and urged readers to "report to the nearest headquarters" from a list of seventy-eight (fifty-four organized by MAPA and twenty-three by the UFW). Campesinos Para Kennedy locations included Woodland and Yuba City, cities in rural Northern California. One whole page of the tabloid was used to explain the physical voting process in step-by-step detail.[40]

The largest block of potential Mexican American voters, however, were in Los Angeles County where more than a fourth of Kennedy's sixty-five headquarters operated under the auspices of Viva Kennedy. The heart of the campaign was on the Eastside. "There were a lot of people who worked on that," recalls the UAW's Henry C. González. "I'm talking about blood and sweat, and night and day."[41] For its part, the UAW pulled hundreds of autoworkers out of the factories to campaign full-time for Kennedy in the final weeks of the campaign. They were joined by some 250 farm workers from Delano, housed in local Catholic facilities, and volunteers recruited through Spanish-language radio ads that promised "long hours, little sleep, low pay and a chance to help elect the next President of the United States."[42]

Then, with only five days to go until the California primary, McCarthy beat Kennedy in Oregon, a state with few poor or minority voters. (Chávez had made one foray into the state to speak at a small farm worker rally.[43]) This shattered the myth of invincibility that surrounded Kennedy and placed California, a pillar of the Kennedy strategy, in doubt. Kennedy told reporters that the campaign might not continue if he lost here.

Kennedy responded to the loss in Oregon by ratcheting up his already extensive California campaign—and by taking a huge gamble. He agreed to debate the lesser-known McCarthy. Despite the debate's potentially critical impact, there was little time to prepare as Kennedy was in the midst of an emotional and physically draining final four-day tour of California. "People were just responding like you can't believe. This guy just drew them by the droves," stated UAW activist Ralph Arriola, who took a leave from his job to run a Kennedy headquarters in San Fernando.[44] The largest Latino events were a May 29 rally at the East Los Angeles Community

College and a motorcade through East Los Angeles. Latinos also joined other supporters for a citywide rally at the Los Angeles Coliseum that featured Latina movie star Raquel Welch. Kennedy then barnstormed through heavily Latino towns in the Central Valley, stopping in Fresno, Madera, Merced, Turlock, Modesto, Stockton, and Lodi.[45]

The following day, Saturday, June 1, Kennedy was in the San Francisco studio of KGO TV to debate McCarthy on ABC News' "Issues and Answers, A Special Report." Pundits called the debate a draw. Kennedy demonstrated a far better understanding of California's multicultural mosaic, specifically referencing Mexican Americans. Senator McCarthy, by contrast, often sounded like much of the rest of the national policy elite who viewed urban issues through a black and white prism, although in his closing comments the Minnesota senator did stress his commitment to farm workers.[46]

In the final days, the Kennedy campaign used César Chávez, a hero to the liberal-left, to woo San Francisco Bay Area voters, particularly students at Merritt Community College in Oakland and the University of California, Berkeley, a McCarthy stronghold. When critics shouted, "Where was Kennedy when we were in New Hampshire?" the farm labor leader replied, "He was with me in Delano."[47] Chávez also traveled to Southern California, mixing Kennedy campaign time with a new assault on the growers and their allies in the state and federal government. At a press conference at the Los Angeles County Federation of Labor, he announced an expanded national boycott in response to a "conspiracy" between the growers, Governor Reagan, and the federal Immigration and Naturalization Service. Under Reagan, California had decertified that strikes were in progress, the first step to bringing in foreign nationals or other strikebreakers.[48]

Senator Robert Kennedy spent the day before the election barnstorming through San Francisco neighborhoods. MAPA leader Margaret Cruz, placed on the State Medical Quality Board by Governor Brown, was one of twenty volunteers with the candidate, handing out literature. This included a street corner rally at 24th and Mission in the heart of the city's Latino district, with its large number of voters from Central America and Mexico.[49]

Senator Kennedy started Election Day by having breakfast

with Mexican American student leaders at Lucy's El Adobe in Hollywood, owned by Lucy and Frank Casado, an early MAPA officer.[50] At the breakfast, college student Phillip Castruita pounded his fist on the table while making a point, causing coffee to spill on the senator. Kennedy stopped the young man from apologizing, saying: "never ever stop fighting for what you believe."[51] The students then joined tens of thousands of Mexican Americans walking door-to-door throughout the state. The message was simple: today is the day that César Chávez needs you to vote for Bobby Kennedy. For many with a picture of the martyred President John F. Kennedy next to the Holy Father in their home, and who had followed the Senator's career, no reminder was necessary. Voting for Kennedy had reached a religious level: A Holy Day of Obligation. He was *their* senator. And Latinos would stand by him.

When the votes were counted, the outpouring of Latino supporters in urban and rural areas had made the difference, allowing Kennedy to beat McCarthy by less than 150,000 votes. Kennedy won as many as fourteen of every fifteen votes in some precincts in predominantly Latino areas that also experienced higher than usual voter registration levels and turnout at the polls. In one precinct in Long Beach, south of Los Angeles, for example, turnout jumped four-fold over the previous primary election, going from 58 to 201, with Kennedy winning 187 of those votes.[52]

Kennedy remained secluded in his room at the Ambassador Hotel, waiting until he was sure that he could declare victory. Around midnight he came down to thank his supporters. Dolores Huerta accompanied him, an exhausted César Chávez having already gone home to sleep. "When Bobby came, and was going to give his speech, I was walking with him, I was giving him this report," recalled Huerta. "He said, 'I hear that in some precincts we got 90 percent of the vote out.' I told him that 'in some precincts, we got 99 percent.' It was unheard of. Ninety-nine percent of the people who were registered actually voted," stated Huerta. "He gave me this big old hug."[53]

Despite the late hour, more than two thousand people remained packed inside the hotel ballroom, a rainbow of partisans united in excitement and anticipation. Latino business people, autoworkers, and farm workers from the Central Valley—all put their lives on hold as the campaign became a cause, with a larger than life candidate on whom they projected their hopes and aspirations for a newer and better world. It was a night to remember. A surge of joy went through the assembled crowd as Kennedy addressed a national television audience. He started by thanking key supporters, beginning with those who had turned out the Mexican American vote. Kennedy now had the momentum; the campaign would quickly shift its energy and organization towards the upcoming primary in the senator's home state of New York. For many activists like Hope Mendoza Schechter, the Democratic Party nomination seemed achievable. Then something unexpected happened. Palestinian militant Sirhan Sirhan, angry at Kennedy's support for the State of Israel, assassinated the candidate as he walked through the kitchen on his way to a planned press conference. News of the tragic event quickly followed the shots that were heard in the ballroom full of stunned and then weeping supporters.

Nowhere was the pain felt more than among California Latinos. The following day César Chávez, Bert Corona, Dolores Huerta, and Henry Santiestevan issued a joint statement: "We want Senator [Edward] Kennedy to know and the nation to know that from our sadness arises increased determination to realize the dignity and social justice, self-determination and fulfillment of expectations he fought to help us to achieve."[54]

California Latinos lost the chance to elect a president with whom they shared a visceral connection and around whom they could organize a national pan-Latino coalition. Also shattered was the farm workers' dream of having a president who would aid their organizing drives. For many older activists, the loss of Senator Kennedy only increased the pain still felt over the death of President Kennedy. For young radicals, part of the emerging Chicano movement, who did not share such a strong identity with Presidents Roosevelt and Kennedy, the senator represented the last chance for the two-party political system. Said César Chávez, whose movement bridged the generations, "A vacuum was created when he died."[55]

The vacuum within the Latino community was exacerbated by the polarization among voters, with the Democrats moving further left and Republicans moving further right. The 1966 governor's race had witnessed the rise of Ronald Reagan and the New Right.

This trend continued in 1968. Max Rafferty, the ultra-conservative Superintendent of Public Education, defeated U.S. Senator Thomas Kuchel, a pro-civil rights moderate with ties to Mexican Americans in the Republican primary. In the Democratic Party, California voters were the first to reject the Johnson-Humphrey administration.

The 1968 California primary helped transform the popular political perception of Latinos. "Up to the race with Robert Kennedy in California, Democrats did not think that Latinos were a political force—but a group that you gave lip service to," stated Louis Flores, who organized pro-Kennedy forces in the Napa wine country. "The Kennedy campaign forced the Democrats to come to terms with Latinos as a political force."[56] Mexican Americans were well positioned to get credit for their role in the California primary because of the candidate's narrow win and their overwhelming support for Kennedy. The media's interest in Latino voters was also magnified because of the emergence of César Chávez as a Mexican American folk hero and Senator Robert Kennedy's tragic death. Ultimately, it was the journalists, in their first draft of history, who gave Mexican Americans credit for Kennedy's narrow win in California's presidential primary.[57]

Just as the Kennedy campaign reintroduced the image of Mexican Americans as important politically, so too the election rectified the nagging absence of a Latino in the California state legislature. The breakthrough came in the Boyle Heights-based assembly district where the incumbent retired, but it was a close call. A multitude of candidates, representing various factions within the Mexican American community, filed for the seat—as did a single Anglo candidate. It initially looked as if the 1966 debacle in the heavily Latino senate district was about to repeat itself. Recognizing that the seat could be lost despite overwhelming Latino registration, Congressman Roybal intervened, backing his administrative assistant, Alex García. "Roybal called me and asked me to help," said UAW Local 887 president Henry Lacayo. The union agreed, putting money and people in the race. This allowed García to edge out the Anglo candidate despite multiple Latino candidacies dividing the Spanish-speaking vote.[58]

MAPA delegates representing seventy-seven chapters met in mid-June. It started out as just another annual meeting, with addresses slated by César Chávez and Democratic U.S. Senate candidate Alan Cranston. But the Kennedy assassination, combined with a generational shift within the organization, completely changed the dynamic. A number of the new chapters had formed to organize support for Kennedy; while others came together the year before to promote the picketing of the Post Office and other activities outside the group's ballot box orientation. As a result, the delegates were younger, less likely to wear suits and dresses, and more radical. They voted to move the convention from the Ramada Inn in the Los Angeles suburb of Pico Rivera to El Rancho High School to be closer to "the people." It was a precursor to other changes within the organization's position on issues and leadership.

For the first time, MAPA voted to oppose the Vietnam War. Sentiment had been building for such a move for a couple of years, particularly from young Chicanos, but MAPA president Bert Corona preferred to hold back on criticizing the war in Southeast Asia with the hopes of gaining concessions from President Johnson for the War on Poverty in California. All that had changed. MAPA had broken with Johnson and Humphrey and then backed Kennedy. According to Robert Gonzales, Kennedy's opposition to Vietnam provided the tipping point in overcoming the resistance from moderates and World War II and Korea veterans within the group.[59]

The decision that was to have the greatest long-term consequences, however, was the change in MAPA leadership. The successful team of Eduardo Quevedo and Bert Corona had come to an end with Quevedo's death shortly after their dinner meeting with President Johnson in the White House. Now it was time for Corona to rotate out of office. Corona backed Abe Tapia, a thirty-one-year-old mail carrier in Oakland and a leftist firebrand with limited political experience. According to a contemporary report, Tápia told the delegates that "he was poor and not well-educated, and this gave him a closer tie to the community."[60] The older delegates overwhelmingly supported MAPA Legal Counsel Manuel Ruiz, a mainstay in Latino organizations since the 1930s. "It was 'old school' versus Abe and new radicals," said Robert Gonzales.[61] Tapia narrowly edged out Ruiz. A philosophical Louis Flores emphasized that "times had changed" and so had "what people were looking for" in a MAPA president.[62]

MAPA decided not to endorse in the presidential race based on the notion that the two parties had not selected their candidates, although it was clear to most observers that Vice President Hubert Humphrey would face off against former Vice President Richard Nixon. With Republicans eager to recapture the White House, Nixon spent the summer building unity within his party. By contrast the Democrats continued to battle over a nomination that was, for all practical purposes, already secured. The date of the convention, in late August, meant that Humphrey would have little time to pull the fractured party together after formally securing the nomination.

Humphrey sought to use the summer months to emerge from Johnson's shadow and to define himself. To demonstrate an affinity with the Latino community, Humphrey assumed national leadership on the issue of bilingual education. "I urge that the Senate act to restore the cuts made in the House," announced Humphrey. "I shall further urge that, if necessary, the Administration seek a supplemental appropriation for this program."[63] He also completed a new book, *Beyond Civil Rights: A New Day of Equality*. In it he

Vice President Hubert Humphrey and UAW Local 887 President Henry Lacayo. The Los Angeles labor leader was one of Humphrey's most important allies in California.   (Photo courtesy of Henry Lacayo)

stated, "where 'anti-discrimination' laws alone are not enough, 'affirmative action' must take account of race."[64]

The campaign likewise looked for a venue for Vice President Humphrey to address a national Latino audience, settling on the GI Forum's 20th annual convention. It was held in Corpus Christi, Texas, over the weekend of August 9-11, just two weeks prior to the 1968 Democratic National Convention. Humphrey delivered a clarion call for justice. He reached out to supporters of Robert Kennedy and to members of other organizations, singling out "LULAC, the Community Services Organization, and others, like MAPA, a political force out in California." He talked poignantly of his meeting with César Chávez on his recent trip through California. But he spent most of his time focused on issues.[65]

Humphrey spoke of his own effort to get Congress to fund bilingual education and the importance of making the federal government a "model employer." He talked about the need to "giv(e) the poor a greater voice in the planning and the implementation of local community action programs" and his "tie-breaking vote, as President of the Senate, when an attempt was made to revive the Bracero Program." He endorsed the right of farm workers to be covered by the protections of the National Labor Relations Act. Humphrey also implied his support for the grape boycott. He said: "I do not believe that any person can really enjoy their meal if they know that the food they are eating—and you really pay plenty for—has been prepared, produced and processed under conditions that are less than fair labor standards."[66]

Humphrey indicated that he would go beyond the Kennedy and Johnson administrations in advancing Latino interests. The life long civil rights and labor liberal made a heart felt pitch for continued civic engagement. "We do not need to take to the streets. We need to take to the ballot box," intoned Humphrey. "[T]he Spanish-surnamed peoples, the Mexican Americans, can set an example for all minorities—an example of peaceful, effective, active political action." He also recognized the tenor of the times. Humphrey stated, "there is ferment in America today not because we're not doing anything. We're restless and we're anxious, and at times we are frustrated because we have been able to do some things and we want to do much more."[67]

The accolades in Corpus Christi were replaced by brickbats in Chicago at the Democratic Convention. Due to President Johnson's decision not to run again and talk of violence, hundreds of thousands of peaceful protesters stayed home. Instead, thousands of mostly Anglo men, many of whom rejected electoral politics, and saw a role for revolutionary violence, descended on the Windy City. At the same time many of the delegates elected on Kennedy and McCarthy slates were determined to fight his nomination and to push a minority plank on the Vietnam War despite Humphrey's inevitable nomination. Confident of victory and seeking to build a bridge to the liberal anti-war activists, Humphrey formally released his delegates and "called for free elections in South Vietnam in which every group could participate," including the communists.[68] Yet the compromise inside the convention drew much less attention than the conflict outside where television crews filmed the street violence between far left radicals and the police. It was an unmitigated disaster, according to Henry Lacayo, the lone California Latino invited to Humphrey's suite during the convention. Hope Mendoza Schechter, a Kennedy delegate concerned about winning in November, concurred, singling out Tom Hayden, a leader in the Student for a Democratic Society (SDS), for disrupting the convention.[69]

Even before Chicago, Nixon reached out to middle class Mexican Americans. The Republican campaign designed a "Southwest Strategy" to build on the gains Republicans made in 1966 among Latinos for Governor Reagan.[70] In July, the Nixon campaign paid for a half-hour of television time in California billed as "Nixon Answers," where the candidates answered questions on Mexican American concerns, among other issues.[71]

In reaching out to middle class and socially conservative Mexican Americans, Nixon, like Reagan before him, did not hesitate to attack the more radical elements or even reformers such as César Chávez. "The California grape boycott has become a national issue; across the continent, Labor Day parades carried signs that read 'Boycott California grapes.' And Hubert Humphrey has gone on record publicly endorsing this form of illegal economic pressure," stated Nixon, on September 5 in San Francisco. "To maintain consistency in support of the rule of law, Mr. Humphrey should immediately withdraw his endorsement of the illegal boycott."[72] The

United Farm Workers Organizing Committee responded to Nixon's attack on the boycott but refused to endorse Humphrey. The union appreciated Humphrey initiating a meeting with the union, and his pro-boycott statement at the GI Forum Convention but according to Dolores Huerta the heightened interest in their cause seemed politically motivated.[73]

With the farm workers refusing to back Humphrey, MAPA held its National Endorsing Convention in Fresno's Hacienda Motor Hotel in early September 1968. The debate over presidential aspirants was spirited as both Humphrey and Nixon employed pro-civil rights surrogates to make their case. Assemblyman William Bagley represented Nixon. Congressman Phillip Burton spoke for Humphrey. "We must put somebody in the White House who is concerned with the same social problems we are interested in," stated Burton. "It's either Nixon or Humphrey—that's it—and I cast my lot on the side of Hubert Humphrey."[74] The angry delegates did not share Burton's pragmatism. In the balloting, Humphrey received thirty-two votes, Nixon three, and "no endorsement" 120.[75] According to MAPA General Counsel Robert Gonzales, the decision to snub Humphrey reflected the reality that the pragmatic center within the organization had not yet established a niche within his national campaign. Humphrey's top Latino supporters were "old guard" leaders from Texas and New Mexico.[76]

For Humphrey, the decision by MAPA to sit out the presidential election and the UFWOC's lack of interest in the campaign represented a disaster because Mexican Americans represented the most animated piece of California's Democratic mosaic. The lack of engagement by the state's two most important Latino political forces was symbolic of a larger problem for Humphrey in the state. The California Democratic Council, the umbrella organization for Democratic club volunteers, voted to support a McCarthy write-in campaign.[77]

Throughout the month of September, the Humphrey campaign in California and other states seemed like a death train. The campaign was out of money and at each stop he was met by as many anti-war demonstrators as campaign supporters. "Dumping the Hump was the visceral need," recalled Students for a Democratic Society leader Todd Gitlin, who remembered that the student radicals were consumed by moral righteousness and oblivious to the consequences of aiding Nixon.[78] Still worse, due to the lack of funds, there were no Humphrey television commercials, little literature, and almost no work to rally the party's core constituency groups.

Emblematic of the crisis within the Humphrey campaign was the candidate's September 25 trip to Los Angeles. The *Washington Post* contrasted Humphrey's appearance before largely white audiences to his campaign's belief that their only chance in California depends on "mobilizing those least likely to vote, the state's substantial Negro and Mexican American population. This technique is credited with Robert F. Kennedy's victory here last June." Humphrey did make an unscheduled stop at Lucy's El Adobe where he met with U.S. Senate candidate Alan Cranston and proprietor Lucy Casado.[79]

But the trip to Los Angeles turned out to be a pivotal moment. Humphrey told a radio interviewer: "The President has not made me his slave, and I am not his humble servant." The campaign proceeded to purchase half an hour on NBC TV, its first media buy of the campaign, for Humphrey to tell the nation that, "As President, I would be willing to stop the bombing of North Vietnam as an acceptable risk for peace." The statement was electric. Within moments of the speech, the phones began ring in the Humphrey headquarters. People wanted to help by donating their time and money.[80]

That same day, in Washington, D.C., U.S. Senator Joseph M. Montoya joined San Francisco Mayor Joseph L. Alioto in announcing the support for Humphrey of "21 nationality organizations." Alioto, the Italian American chair of the party's nationality division and a product of the Catholic Worker movement, had won his mayoral election with support of MAPA and the Centro Social Obrero, a Mission District-based unit of the Laborers Local 261 that served Central and South American workers. Alioto went on to appoint David J. Sánchez as the first Latino on the San Francisco Board of Education. He would soon appoint MAPA's Robert Gonzales as the first Latino member of the Board of Supervisors.[81] While Latinos supported this larger ethnic outreach effort, for the first time in history the Democratic Party created an autonomous outreach program approximating the organization directed at the larger African American population.[82]

Senator Montoya and Congressmen González and Roybal co-chaired the Arriba Humphrey (Up with Humphrey) campaign. Almost immediately, however, internal dissention beset the outreach effort. The co-chairs were the highest-ranking elected officials, but they were also Johnson loyalists. This did not sit well with the more anti-establishment activists. The *Albuquerque Journal* reported that these Kennedy Latinos saw Montoya and González "as hopelessly Old Guard and out of touch with the new movement springing up among Mexican Americans." Furthermore, the Kennedy Latinos were not suffering from political isolation. They remained organized under the auspices of the Ford Foundation-funded Southwest Council of La Raza.[83]

As serendipity would have it, Mexican Americans associated with the Kennedy campaign were meeting in Minneapolis' Dykman Hotel, on October 5-6, as part of a larger gathering of the New Democratic Coalition. The Latino leaders from Arizona, California, New Mexico, Texas, and Minnesota demanded to meet with Humphrey to obtain a "clarification" on a number of his domestic policy issues, including the farm workers' grape strike. Twin Cities labor leader Frank Zaragoza recalls the animated debate as "a pretty heated discussion . . . a power play in national politics." The candidate agreed to meet representatives of the Kennedy Latinos the following Friday at New York City's Waldorf Astoria Hotel. The delegation included MAPA's Abe Tapia and Bert Corona.[84]

In the interim, Cris Aldrete met with former Kennedy campaign officials Henry Santiestevan and Polly Baca in Washington, D.C. in search of a creative compromise. The solution was to form a parallel organization complimentary to Arriba Humphrey. Viva Humphrey would incorporate the Viva Kennedy people into the campaign without alienating Mexican American leaders already supporting Humphrey. One of the first moves was to bring Santiestevan into the campaign as national coordinator for Viva Humphrey. Another step was to begin to close the gap between the two groups at the top levels by naming Montoya, González, and Roybal as co-chairs of Viva Humphrey.[85]

The Humphrey campaign also touched bases with the farm workers. Working through AFL-CIO Director of Organizing William Kircher, who was living in Delano, the campaign learned that the

Let Us REMEMBER...

NUESTROS MÁRTIRES

MAPA and the UFW jointly produced this Hubert Humphrey for president brochure in 1968 that featured the martyred Kennedys on the cover and Senator and Mrs. Edward Kennedy on its back panel.   (Kenneth C. Burt)

UFWOC was ready to take action and "that Cesar Chavez will work for us no matter what Abe Tapia (MAPA) does."[86] Dolores Huerta said later that the union feared Nixon and appreciated Humphrey's increased attentiveness, for which she credited "pressure from the AFL-CIO."[87] For his part, Bert Corona submitted to the Humphrey campaign "a memo of points on which the VP should be knowledgeable."[88]

At the Waldorf Astoria, where John F. Kennedy had entertained his Latino leadership eight years earlier, Humphrey sealed the deal with the five Mexican American leaders. The 1968 Viva Kennedy leaders "pledged themselves to do everything within their means" to help elect Humphrey. In return, Humphrey agreed to a four-point program: 1) Mexican American participation in high government decision making; 2) policies to help develop Mexican American communities; 3) full support of Chávez and his efforts to organize farm workers, and 4) to end discrimination against Mexican Americans in government employment.[89]

Mexican Americans were soon on the move to support Humphrey in California. The UFWOC and MAPA leaders jointly produced a bilingual brochure, "Let Us Remember . . . Nuestros Martires," that pictured the martyred John and Robert Kennedy on the cover and Senator and Mrs. Edward Kennedy and Vice President and Mrs. Hubert Humphrey on the back. Inside was an appeal for Humphrey from Chávez and MAPA's Tápia.[90]

Soon, however, a firestorm developed within MAPA. Tapia neither asked the organization for authorization to negotiate with Humphrey nor had he sought to have MAPA's board of directors ratify the endorsement after the fact. As a result, some chapters refused to distribute the literature, according to chapter chair Ray Solis in Hayward.[91] "Abe's participation in the Humphrey campaign was viewed as a violation or a betrayal of the tenants of the constitution and purposes and principles of MAPA," conceded Bert Corona, because the delegates voted to remain neutral in the presidential contest.[92]

Still, the national momentum continued to build for Humphrey within the Latino community in California and throughout the nation. On October 17, Democratic National Chairman Lawrence F. O'Brien announced the appointment of the Viva Humphrey state chairs in the Midwest, Northwest, and Southwest. He added, "similar campaign efforts under the 'Viva Humphrey' banner are also moving forward among Puerto Ricans and Cubans in their population areas."[93] Some ten days later, with about two weeks before the election, the national campaign provided its first Latino-oriented campaign material. Half a million Viva Humphrey tabloids, fifty thousand buttons, and one hundred thousand bumper stickers were air expressed to local organizers.[94]

Having completed the Viva Humphrey material, Santiestevan headed to Los Angeles as he had done for Robert Kennedy. There he assumed control of the pro-Humphrey campaign in the Mexican American community. Congressman Roybal aided the campaign and the AFL-CIO was in the midst of its own mass mobilization for Humphrey. Striking farm workers imported from the Central Valley did the core of the door-to-door work in Los Angeles.[95]

The activity in the precincts was reinforced by the campaign's most precious resource—the candidate's time. Starting on October 22, Humphrey began a three-day tour of primarily Latino areas in Texas and California. A *Los Angeles Times* poll gave Nixon an eleven-point lead in California: 44 to 33, with Alabama Governor George Wallace at 7 percent.[96]

At an evening rally in East Los Angeles, Humphrey focused on the needs and interests of Mexican Americans. "There's a lot we have to do together. We know the issues—the injustices that have to be corrected . . . the wrongs that have to be righted." Humphrey stressed that "*It is* only right for *every* child to get a fair chance to develop his full potential from pre-school as far as his ability will carry him. *It is* only right for *every* man to be trained for a decent job—and then to have that job." The vice president then made his strongest statement yet in support of the farm workers whose plight had become of central importance to this urban barrio. "When I am President, I intend to see the farmworkers *get* this right [to collective bargaining]," stressed Humphrey, saying that "Mr. Nixon doesn't understand this . . . but it's about time he learned." He also announced a new public-private partnership to "train 17 hundred people right here in East Los Angeles . . . in El Monte and Lincoln Heights—in plastics, in electronics and other industries." The candidate provided a sense of urgency. "California may very decide who is President for the next four years. I will stand with you every day of my Presidency—just as I always have. I ask you to stand with me now."[97]

California looked as if it might decide the election. With Humphrey only a point or two away from catching Nixon in his home state, both the Democratic and Republican party candidates returned to Los Angeles for their final day of campaigning. Humphrey and his running mate, Senator Edmund Muskie, rode in a motorcade through the Los Angeles garment district, accompanied by Congressman Roybal, Speaker Unruh, and Alan Cranston.[98] Nixon rallied his faithful in the suburbs. The mobilization continued into Election Day, with both candidates using phoners and walkers to turn out their vote. The farm worker-drive mobilization was extensive, but not as universal as it had been for Kennedy. But would it be enough?

The election was so close that Vice President Humphrey and former Vice President Nixon—like Nixon and Kennedy in 1960—went to bed not knowing whether they had won or lost. The race ultimately turned on California and Texas, the two large states with sizable Latino populations that went for Humphrey by 90 percent, numbers not seen since the Johnson landslide in 1964. Humphrey won in Texas due to an all-out mobilization of Mexican Americans and a temporary unity of the major Anglo factions. In California, the Mexican American community turned out for Humphrey in huge numbers, but it was not enough to overcome the disunity among other sectors of the party, most notably leftist anti-war activists (who were a larger force in California than in Texas). Had Humphrey carried California, no candidate would have received an Electoral College majority and the next president would have been selected by the Democratic-controlled U.S. House of Representatives.[99]

President Nixon quickly reached out to Latinos as had Governor Reagan. The president replaced the liberal GI Forum's Texas and New Mexico-based axis in Washington, D.C. with more conservative Mexican Americans from California. Nixon named Martín Castillo to chair the Cabinet Level Inter-Agency Committee on Mexican-American Affairs, which Congress renamed the Cabinet Committee on Opportunities for Spanish-Speaking People in 1969, adopting the more inclusive term used by El Congreso. Nixon appointed Henry Quevedo to serve as Cabinet Committee's executive director. The son of Eduardo Quevedo, the pioneering California Latino political leader, Henry Quevedo earned his Republican credentials as an unsuccessful candidate for the state assembly from Los Angeles. In accepting the post he fulfilled the bipartisan vision articulated in the founding of MAPA. The response to these appointments varied, however, but largely reflected the reactions two years earlier to Governor Reagan's victory and subsequent appointments of Latinos. The new officials elated Republicans and those wishing to see Californians in ever more prominent roles. They befuddled some partisan Democrats could not fathom Mexican Americans working for Nixon. Still others believed Latinos would benefit from the increased attention being lavished on the community by the two major political parties.[100]

For California Democrats, 1968 is remembered as a year of tragedy due to the assassination of Senator Kennedy and the subsequent election of President Nixon. In Humphrey's defeat, liberal Latinos lost the opportunity to work with a man who in his congressional career was the leading advocate for civil rights and organized labor. Humphrey's early embrace of affirmative action put him ahead of those advocates who had continued to focus on anti-discrimination laws. Because of Humphrey's defeat, few recall that 1968 represented high water mark for Latino participation in Democratic party politics.

The Sleeping Giant, the phrase coined by Roybal in 1957, was awake. Latinos had registered and turned out in record numbers. Support in the primary for Kennedy was nearly universal and Humphrey tied Johnson's record 90 percent backing at the polls. Latino support for Humphrey was actually more impressive than it had been for Johnson because it occurred in an election where the Democratic nominee enjoyed much lower support from the general public. While Latino voters provided near total support for Kennedy and Humphrey, each candidate enjoyed a different but overlapping base of support. Kennedy's core backing came from MAPA, UFW, UAW, and the United Mexican American Students (UMAS). Humphrey's key supporters included the GI Forum, AFL-CIO, Great Society non-profits, Congressman Roybal and, for the all-important final push, the United Farm Workers. Henry Santiestevan, pioneering Los Angeles journalist, UAW operative and the founding director of the Southwest Council of La Raza, served as the architect of both Viva Kennedy and Viva Humphrey in 1968, and oversaw operations in his native city.

The decade between 1958 and 1968 proved to be the high mark for Mexican American support for Democratic candidates. The convergence of the 1958 Pat Brown, Henry López, and No on Proposition 18 campaigns realigned California Latinos with the Democratic Party after a flirtation with Eisenhower, Warren, and Knight. The scope of civic engagement expanded in the 1960 and 1964 presidential elections before declining in 1966, a year in which Latino turnout dropped and a quarter of those voting cast a ballot for Republican Ronald Reagan. In 1968, Mexican American Democrats came home, but there were new troubles on the left as exemplified by MAPA's decision to sit out the race despite a clear contrast between candidates. The 1966 and 1968 elections illuminated the end of the near consensus Latino support for Democrats as well as the unraveling of the New Deal Democratic majority coalition, despite pundits' efforts to attribute the results to any number of election specific factors.

For Democrats, the mid-to-late-sixties represented the beginning of a two-front war (not seen since 1948), with attacks on liberalism coming increasingly from the left as well as the right. Professor Rodolfo Acuña exemplifies this trend. Once a Eugene McCarthy delegate candidate to the Democratic National Convention, he refused to vote for Humphrey because "I was disillusioned with the Democratic Party" over the issue of Vietnam.[101] This anti-Democratic Party position, increasingly popular with the new generation of Chicano intellectuals, had a profound consequence for Latino participation in electoral politics and the prism through which students viewed their parents' political engagement. Instead of groups like United Mexican American Students (UMAS) continuing to channel students into Democratic Party campaigns, and benefiting from established political networks and the new political paradigm that Mexican Americans were critical to winning in California, many young people opted out of electoral politics. Others challenged the legitimacy of parents' allegiance to the party of Roosevelt and Kennedy and the thirty-year struggle to acquire a civic voice in the political area. Even as these idealist youths explored radical alternatives, such as the La Raza Unida Party, a growing number of pragmatic and increasingly conservative members of the growing middle class started to move into the Republican Party. Nixon and Reagan facilitated this movement by appointing Latinos to prominent government positions, at once demonstrating a new level of GOP inclusiveness while helping to create a cadre of activists and officials able to help contest for Latino votes in future elections.

Despite the fact that Latinos remained underrepresented at all levels of government, much progress had been achieved. The dynamic period between 1938 and 1968 witnessed the systematic effort by Latinos to participate in the decision making process with the twin goals of crafting more Latino friendly public policy and electing Latinos to office. To this end, Latinos created a series of politically oriented organizations, established a number of non-profits, won the placement of Latinos in appointed and elected posts, and successfully lobbied for a number of bills. Legislative victories include the outlawing of school segregation and poll site challenges to a voter's literacy, and the creation of Non-Citizen Old Age Pensions and bilingual education. The foundation for this long-term political power, a growing voter base, was limited by the relative size of the Latino community and by the rate of naturalization and voter registration. The dramatic upward trajectory of Latino power, especially in California, was captured by the two elections that bookend this period. The Mexican American community was a footnote in the 1938 California gubernatorial election but a key player in the 1968 presidential election, helping Senator Robert Kennedy win the California Democratic primary and nearly enabling Hubert Humphrey to beat Richard Nixon in his home state and thus secure the presidency. This reinforced the belief that Latinos were "learning to make use of the most effective channel open to democracy's cultural minorities—the ballot," as the *Daily News* noted after Roybal's 1949 election. Latinos also achieved the liberal paper's hope that this civic engagement would lead to "bridge-building" between Latinos and other groups.[102]

CHAPTER 13

REPUBLICANS, CHICANOS, AND LATINO POLITICAL MACHINES

For California Latinos, 1968 represented a major turning point. Hubert Humphrey had won the backing of nine out of ten Latino voters, despite efforts by Richard Nixon and the Republican Party to woo Mexican Americans and the handful of people who sat out the election to protest U.S. involvement in Vietnam. Beginning in 1969, an assault on liberalism and the traditional Latino attachment to the Democratic Party came from the right and left. With an eye towards his reelection, President Nixon sought to gain the support of Mexican Americans in the Southwest. Based on the elections in 1960, (where Nixon had lost by the slimmest of margins,) and 1968, (where he narrowly won,) the White House believed that a change of six percent of the Mexican American vote would lead to victory in California, as well as Texas, New Mexico and Illinois. In the 1966 campaign, Governor Reagan had demonstrated that a Republican candidate could achieve this goal, and much more, by courting both small businessmen and blue-collar workers. Nixon used the power of his incumbency to exploit growing societal divisions by emphasizing a shared commitment to traditional values of family, faith, and military service. He reached out to Latinos through the renamed Cabinet Committee on Opportunities for Spanish-Speaking People, headed by Californian Martín Castillo.

Nixon also created new opportunities. He started by appointing Hilary Sandoval as director of the Small Business Administration, making her the highest-ranking Latina government official in history, and demonstrating recognition of the developing women's movement. Nixon then established the Office of Minority Business Enterprise, in the hope that Latino business owners would support him as they had the Eisenhower-Nixon administration. Nixon appointed two longtime Los Angeles community leaders whose public service dated to the late 1930s: attorney Manuel Ruiz and Dr. Reynaldo Carreón. Ruiz became a member of the U.S. Civil Rights Commission, and Carreón served on an advisory committee to Volunteers in Service to America (VISTA), started in 1965 as a domestic Peace Corps. Nixon also worked to nullify the traditional Democratic bias of groups like LULAC and GI Forum, which were dependent on discretionary federal funding to run their social programs.[1]

At the same time that the president pursued the growing middle class Latinos, he and the Republican Party benefited politically from—and encouraged—elements within the developing Chicano movement to disrupt the historic relationship between the community and the Democratic Party. Young Chicanos attacked the assumptions of Mexican American community leaders (just as black power militants decried the non-violent tactics and integrationist goals of Rev. Martin Luther King, Jr.). They criticized their parents' generation for being insufficiently militant and argued that people of Mexican heritage represented a racial versus an ethnic minority by emphasizing the preponderance of Indian blood. Young women sought to redefine the role of Latinas within the home, community, and society; many adopted Dolores Huerta—mother and farm worker strike leader—as a heroine. Some "nationalists" argued for Mexico's retaking of the Southwest. On campus, the United Mexican American Students (UMAS), which had participated in the 1968 Kennedy campaign, was transformed into the statewide El Movimiento Estudiantil Chicano de Aztlán (MEChA). Others, such as those in the Los Angeles-based Centers for Autonomous Social Action (CASA), adopted a Marxist analysis that assumed that Chicanos were all part of one large working class.

Nationalist and class-oriented Chicano leaders criticized the Democratic Party for being insufficiently supportive of Latino concerns and for being aligned with corporations and militarism. While such an analysis would have been shared by communists and other leftists during the New Deal, Chicano leftists differed from their earlier counterparts in that they did not seek to form labor-minority coalitions or to work within the Democratic Party to alter government policy. Instead they railed against "the system," opting to work in community based organizations or supporting candidates associated with La Raza Unida Party. For many, protests replaced the ballot as the favored method of seeking social change and altering government policy. Third party activist Richard A. Santillan contended, "The Mexican-American tried to work in the two-party system, but the system failed him."[2] Fellow La Raza Unida organizer Carlos Muñoz stated that "[Mexican Americans] perceived US society as democratic: all Mexican Americans had to do was to vote and elect their own to political office." But, he emphasized, if this were true there would be more Latino elected officials.[3]

Ironically, the person most often put forward to personify the Chicano movement, César Chávez, rejected this separatist impulse and remained a progressive force within the Democratic Party. This led to tension between prominent Latino leaders, and between radicals and institutions within the larger society. For example, young Chicanos accused the Catholic Church of being racist and disrupted the 1969 Christmas Eve Mass conducted by Cardinal Francis McIntyre in Los Angeles. This physical confrontation obscured the more nuanced relationship between the institutional church and the faithful. This was, after all, the same archdiocese that sponsored CSO, appointed Father Mark Day as the UFW's spiritual advisor in 1968, and spent millions for church schools, hospitals, and social services in Latino communities.[4]

In contrast to those who sought to disrupt church services, César Chávez and other pragmatic progressives encouraged the church (and organized labor, which was also under attack by some Chicano activists) to more fully address Latino concerns and to increase the role of Latinos within the respective organizations. These reform efforts led to the appointment of Mexican American bishops and the formation of the Campaign for Human Development to underwrite social action projects, including community organizing.[5] For its part, the national AFL-CIO formed the Labor Council for Latin American Advancement (LCLAA); early CSO president and butcher J.J. Rodríguez served as a founding member, along with Los Angeles auto worker Henry González and rubber worker Albert Hernández. The politically connected Hernández served as a field representative for the Los Angeles County Federation of Labor and as president of the still functioning Catholic Labor Institute.[6]

In San Francisco, the Mission Coalition Organization (MCO) represented some four hundred business, labor, religious, political, and community organizations that collectively spoke for the Latino community with roots in Mexico as well as in Central and South America. MCO interacted with local, state, and federal officials, pushed for funding and appointments to city boards and commissions, and helped select the board for the government-funded non-profit, Mission Model Neighborhood Corporation. Politically influential leaders included Roger Cárdenas, vice president of Local 2 of the hotel workers, who served as MCO's Labor Vice President, and Abel González, president of the Centro Social Obrero, who served as one of Mayor Joseph Alioto's appointees to the Mission Corporation.[7]

On some issues, the radicalized youth received help from their elders, particularly those with roots in the progressive movements. The Congress of Mexican American Unity, headed by United Auto Worker Esteban Torres, was among the earliest supporters of the National Chicano Moratorium in East Los Angeles on August 29, 1970. The Latino anti-war demonstration attracted upwards of 30,000 people and incorporated political organizations, as well as rival gangs, who focused their energy on protesting the twin evils of war and racism. Police overreaction to the demonstration led to the tragic police shooting of Rubén Salazar, a popular *Los Angeles Times* columnist and news director for KMEX. Henry Nava, CSO's second president, joined his son at the protest, as did Tony Ríos. Congressman Edward Roybal became a national advocate for U.S. withdrawal from Vietnam. César Chávez and the UFW assumed an increasingly visible role in the anti-war movement as the Nixon administration bought boycotted grapes for the troops in Southeast Asia. And in a dramatic switch, the California GI Forum came out against the Vietnam War in 1970.[8]

The relatively small number of Latinos in elected office remained an unresolved issue that concerned activists of varied political backgrounds. Demand by younger activists for symbolically powerful campaigns overwhelmed the older activists who had previously labored to assemble the majority coalitions. This tension played itself out in the 1970 elections as the leftist-led MAPA endorsed four Latinos for statewide office: Ricardo Romo for governor, Cecilia Pedroza for lieutenant governor, Herman Sillas for controller, and Julian Nava for superintendent of public instruction. The twenty-nine-year-old Romo was running on the Peace and Freedom Party ticket, the ideological heir to the old Independent Progressive Party. Sillas and Nava, on the other hand, were liberals who declined to join a third party but whose candidacies represented a symbolic statement that reflected the larger nationalistic impulse present among the activists. These campaigns contrasted sharply to the earlier statewide campaigns of Edward Roybal and Henry López who secured their respective party endorsements by building a coalition. The symbolic candidacies represented a coming together of those who wished to send a protest message to the Democratic Party and those who wished to withdraw from it.[9] For the general election, MAPA reaffirmed its support of Peace and Freedom candidate Romo over Republican Governor Ronald Reagan and Democratic Assembly Speaker Jesse Unruh.[10] After the election where Romo received a nominal vote total, *San Jose Mercury* columnist Luis G. Juárez criticized the activists' growing ethnocentricity, stating that it "had never been a popular stand to take even in a predominately Mexican-American or other minority area."[11]

The conflict between liberal coalition builders and radical separatists became bitter in a special election for an open state assembly seat in Los Angeles in 1971 that assumed national attention. Latinos comprised almost a fifth of the voters in the multiethnic district left vacant by David Roberti's move to the state senate. Democrats assembled a coalition to ensure the election of a twenty-nine-year-old Chicano Democrat, Richard Alatorre, who served as an aide to Assembly Majority Leader Walter Karabian. The plan was to elect Alatorre to the multicultural district and then to add Latinos to the district as part of the 1972 reapportionment process being overseen by Assemblyman Henry Waxman. Karabian oversaw the Alatorre campaign, and he brought in Senator Edmund Muskie, the Democrats' 1968 vice presidential candidate and then the leading presidential contender in 1972, to campaign for Alatorre. Heated opposition to Alatorre emerged from La Raza Unida Party, comprised mostly of MEChA activists and other young radicals but also assisted by Bert Corona, who had left the two-party political system, and was then organizing Centers for Autonomous Social

Action. In this effort to pull Latino voters away from the Democratic Party, the radicals received secret funding from the Nixon campaign. Moreover, Donald Segretti and a special group within the Nixon administration, known as the "Plumbers Unit," infiltrated the Alatorre campaign in an effort to sabotage it from within. The La Raza Unida candidate, Raúl Ruiz, garnered eight percent of the vote in the runoff, which was enough to throw the election to the Anglo Republican, John Brophy. As a consequence, La Raza Unida kept a Chicano Democrat out of the state assembly and denied a seat to the UFW champion.[12] The results drew a strong partisan response. La Raza Unida partisans celebrated the results while the Assembly Elections and Reapportionment chair, Henry Waxman, stated: "The reason (Alatorre) lost was a cynical alliance of neo-segregationist in the Chicano community with the Republican Party."[13]

By the 1972 election, the UFW was the strongest Latino political force in California and a potent symbol adopted by liberals across the nation (and by many Chicanos, with the notable exception of the La Raza Unida Party). The union recognized the centrality of civic life to its survival. This is because grower-friendly legislators "introduced legislation in California and other states outlawing boycotts and strikes at harvest time, and setting up election procedures geared to letting a very few people determine whether they wanted a union," recalled Chávez.[14] The UFW adopted a dual strategy, remaining a presence in the streets while expanding its relationships within the corridors of power. For example, supporters in San Diego demonstrated against the Republican Party's decision (later reversed) to hold its convention there.[15]

The union's ascendancy within the Democratic Party was symbolized by the selection of Vice President Dolores Huerta as the co-chair of the California delegation to the Democratic National Convention. The convention nominated George McGovern, a liberal opposed to the Vietnam War. Moreover, this was also the first national convention to use quotas to ensure adequate representation for women and historically underrepresented minority groups. The party even raised money to help low-income delegates attend the convention, according to Hope Mendoza Schechter.[16] At the 1972 convention in Miami, Senator Edward Kennedy brought down the house by addressing the delegates as "Fellow lettuce boycotters."[17]

The UFW needed the support of voters and longtime allies in the AFL-CIO and Catholic Church to defeat grower initiatives. The most stunning UFW victory occurred in November 1972 when California voters defeated Proposition 22, to eviscerate the union's rights and undermine existing contracts. Chávez and the UFW won in large measure because the "good government" secretary of state, Jerry Brown, the son of former governor Pat Brown, claimed that the proponents misrepresented the issue to get it on the ballot. The UFW's victory was particularly impressive because California voters, including about a quarter of Latinos, supported President Nixon's reelection.[18]

Nixon initially believed (based on running against a more centrist opponent) that the 1972 election might be much closer than the forty-nine-state landslide it turned out to be. In preparation for a close vote where Latinos might determine the election, Nixon sought to win at least a third of the national Latino vote. He would achieve this by courting the most conservative one-fifth of the Mexican American community based on values and ideology, and then use his executive power to win over moderates by delivering more in terms of major appointment and program funding than had either Kennedy or Johnson. At the same time, the administration would support La Raza Unida Party.[19]

The first part of this strategy rested on high profile appointments. Nixon reached into California for three major appointments. Henry M. Ramírez, whom the president knew from his hometown of Whittier, replaced Martín Castillo as chair of Cabinet Committee on Opportunities for Spanish-Speaking People. He appointed Phillip V. Sánchez, a former Fresno congressional candidate, as the Director of Office of Economic Opportunity, which controlled funds for the anti-poverty programs. The next appointment also broke a second gender barrier as the president named Los Angeles businesswoman Romana A. Bañuelos Treasurer of the United States. This made her the first to serve in a presidential cabinet. It also meant that her signature would appear on new dollar bills, bringing pride to activists of both parties. The appointment likewise extended Nixon's reach into Latino Los Angeles because the tortilla manufacturer was closely associated with Dr. Francisco Bravo and the Pan American National Bank.[20]

President Richard Nixon with Treasurer Romana Bañuelos at the White House in 1971. The Los Angeles businesswoman was the first Latino to serve in a presidential cabinet and further stood out as a Latina Republican. (National Archives and Records Administration)

The Nixon administration then decided to use federal resources for political purposes even as it sought to cut money for anti-poverty programs and to shift responsibility for allocating funds to the states under its New Federalism. To identify sources of federal funds and to extract maximum political benefits it established the "Brown Mafia," which later formalized its name as "Spanish-speaking Constituent Group Task Force". The group included Henry M. Ramírez from the Cabinet Committee and Alex Armendáriz from the president's reelection committee. Armendáriz's role was similar to that of Carlos McCormick and Vicente Ximenes, when they worked at the Democratic National Committee, except the Nixon operative exercised vastly greater powers. Armendáriz had to sign off on any federal grant to a Latino group. Nixon thus funded pro-Nixon groups and anti-Democratic groups. The administration also used the power of purse and appointments to get groups established by Democratic activists, who had been rewarded for participation in the 1964 Viva Johnson campaign, to either sit out the election or to support him. Nixon succeeded in getting Judge Alfred J.

Hernández, the former president of LULAC, to serve as the head of Spanish-Speaking American Democrats for the President.

Latinos within the Nixon campaign did help achieve a new relationship between the presidential campaign and the community. Unlike previous Democratic efforts, where Latinos asked for funds to use campaigning, Nixon Latinos raised money for the larger campaign, setting up the National Hispanic Finance Committee (NHFC). Under the direction of Californian Benjamin Fernández, the NHFC set up a national organization with operations in California and other states. The group held a testimonial dinner in Los Angeles that attracted upwards of 4,000 middle class Latinos. Nixon, who had previously given Fernández a $600,000 grant from the Small Business Administration, rewarded him after the election with an appointment as a special envoy to the inauguration of President Alfredo Stroesner of Paraguay.[21]

The increased ties between Mexican Americans, the Nixon administration, and the Republican Party upset many longtime activists. "This radical change from the traditionally Democratic affiliation was hard to accept, especially by the more liberal element of the Chicano community," noted *San Jose Mercury* columnist Luis G. Juárez, who urged the two parties to compete for the loyalty of Mexican American voters in the state.[22] Los Angeles journalist Tony Castro gave credit to Nixon's outreach efforts for the "remarkable transformation in the politics of Mexican-Americans from a predictable, homogeneous block into a fluid, ticket-splitting electorate that—much like the rest of America—has become disillusioned with politicians and parties."[23]

In California during the early seventies, voters elected a growing number of middle aged Mexican Americans and younger Chicanos to the state legislature. Each election reflected local conditions as well as statewide trends underway for some time. In 1970, Peter Chacón was elected to the assembly from San Diego. Born in Phoenix, Arizona, he served in World War II and, in 1946, relocated to San Diego where he became a teacher. In 1972, UFW Legislative Director Art Torres, the son of a unionized butcher, defeated former Assemblyman Philip Soto and others to win the Boyle Heights-based assembly district as Alex García moved up to fill the previously Anglo held state senate seat for East Los

Angeles. That same year, there were Latino breakthroughs in three assembly districts. Richard Alatorre won the urban Los Angeles seat on his second try; La Puente Councilman Joseph Montoya won a seat in suburban Los Angeles; and professor Ray Gonzales won an assembly seat in Bakersfield in the Central Valley. Two years later, in 1974, San Bernardino County Supervisor Rubén Ayala won a special election to the state senate. There were, of course, losses as well. The most disappointing defeat was in San Jose where grocery store owner Ernest Abeytia was a prototype of the Mexican American activist. Abeytia lost the primary election in 1970 by the slimmest of margins: 149 votes, due to another Latino serving as a spoiler.[24] Still, the number of victories for Latino candidates was significant. By working "within the system," building on decades of CSO-led voter registration drives, expanding Latino organizational development, and backing candidates who had often established themselves by holding a local office, Latinos won a record number of legislative seats. Importantly, for the first time, they were doing so in urban, suburban, and rural areas.[25] (In 1978, San Mateo County voters elected Marz García to the state senate, but the moderate Republican did not identify himself as Latino and made no attempt to recruit Latinos into the GOP.)

Despite the gains in the state legislature, California's overwhelmingly Democratic Latinos remained outside the highest levels of power in both Sacramento and Washington, D.C. during the administrations of Governor Reagan and President Nixon. It was not until the election of Governor Edmund G. "Jerry" Brown, Jr. in 1974 that the Mexican American activists returned to political influence in California, a position they shared with a number of younger Chicanos. During the campaign, the UFW used a sit-in at Brown's campaign headquarters to force the candidate to announce his support for their legislative agenda. This was possible because in the increasingly media-driven California, Chávez was a celebrity and the farm workers were a symbol that had become central to the identity of Latinos, liberals, labor, and the faith community. The union was also stronger than ever, having signed contracts representing 70,000 workers without the benefit of a collective bargaining law.[26]

MAPA endorsed Brown, who addressed the convention along with his opponent, Houston Flournoy, a first for a Republican gubernatorial candidate. MAPA also backed Mervyn Dymally for Lieutenant Governor and March Fong for Secretary of State (who respectively became the first African American and first Asian American statewide elected officials) and William Bagley, a liberal Republican, for controller.[27] Under the presidencies of attorney Armando O. Rodríguez of Fresno (who was elected to the Fresno Board of Supervisors in 1972) and businesswoman Margaret Cruz of San Francisco (the first woman to lead a national Latino organization), MAPA had sought to reengage in mainstream state politics. The re-linking of MAPA to mainstream politics involved both the endorsement of Democratic and Republican statewide candidates and the recognition of Latino

Congressman James Corman, U.S. Senator Alan Cranston, UAW leader Henry Lacayo, Congressman Edward Roybal, and Secretary of State and gubernatorial candidate Jerry Brown gather at the United Auto Workers convention. In the mid-1970s, old-line labor liberals exercised influence within the Democratic Party.   *(Courtesy of Henry Lacayo)*

elected officials. This included highlighting the top elected officials in the state at MAPA's 1973 convention. The convention luncheon featured four county supervisors and the dinner honored the Legislative Chicano Caucus. The effort to strengthen its relationship with Latino and non-Latino elected officials was necessary because MAPA had shrunk to only thirty chapters, less than half of its peak in 1968. This was largely due to Abe Tapia's radical leadership that included support for La Raza Unida Party.[28]

The emphasis on Latino elected officials also reflected their growing numbers in the dozen years since MAPA's founding convention. This time a survey found that more than 200 Spanish-surnamed individuals were serving in local posts, including twenty-one mayors in cities such as Morgan Hill and Winters in Northern California; Dinuba, Delano, and Parlier in the Central Valley; La Puente, Norwalk, and Montebello in Los Angeles County; and Carpenteria, Coachella, and Colton in greater Southern California. Only one mayor and sixteen of the officials were Latinas. Two of the mayors and nineteen of the officials, or nearly ten percent, were Republicans; none of the technically nonpartisan local officials identified themselves as part of a third party. The overwhelming majority of officials, like Latino voters generally, were Democrats.[29]

Democratic Governor Jerry Brown was non-traditional, part of the new generation with roots in the old. The son of former Governor Pat Brown, he had attended the seminary and marched with César Chávez. Where his father had been slow to embrace Latino aspirations, including symbolic appointments, the son would advance them to the point of being ahead of the political curve. Where his father had sought to balance the interests of the UFW, the Teamsters and the growers, Brown aligned his administration with *la causa*. Jerry Brown also nurtured a more personal link to the Mexican American generation. Estranged from his father, he was "adopted" by early MAPA leaders Frank and Lucy Casado and spent time at their El Adobe Restaurant in Hollywood, the site of Robert Kennedy's final breakfast and Humphrey's symbolic cup of coffee during the 1968 campaign. Brown appointed Lucy Casado to represent him at the Democratic Party's state conventions.[30]

Governor Brown recognized the longing of the Mexican American community for positions of responsibility; moreover, there were still "firsts" to achieve and a ready pool of talented women and men to fill these positions. Brown started with high-level appointments to state government. He named Mario Obledo to head the vast Health and Human Services Agency. Obledo was the first Latino to serve in a governor's cabinet and had oversight of a large number of departments. But Brown went beyond appointments. His administration adopted "goals and timetables" to guide hiring and promotional decisions so that departments reflect-

Cruz Reynoso was appointed to the California Supreme Court by Governor Jerry Brown. The politically active barrister was a mainstay in CSO and MAPA prior to serving Governor Pat Brown and then overseeing the California Rural Legal Assistance.   *(Kenneth C. Burt)*

ed the composition of the state. After the Brown won reelection with 81 percent of the Latino vote, he elevated Cruz Reynoso from the Court of Appeals to the Supreme Court. Reynoso was prototypical of his generation of Mexican American public servants—veteran, CSO and MAPA activist, assembly candidate and gubernatorial appointee of Pat Brown. Not surprisingly, his appointment drew attacks from some conservative judges and Attorney General George Deukmejian, one member of the three-person Commission on Judicial Appointments. Governor Brown called the attacks "an almost racist campaign. . .of orchestrated vilification."[31] Brown also appointed a number of Latinas, most notably Irene Tovar to the State Personnel Board, and Vilma Martínez to the University of California Board of Regents.[32]

In terms of public policy, Governor Jerry Brown's most important contribution to the Latino community concerned organized labor. Since before the founding of El Congreso in the late thirties, Latinos had tried to organize agriculture but had been stymied—until recently—by the power of agribusiness and the lack of collective bargaining rights granted to other workers by President Roosevelt. The United Farm Workers made collective bargaining legislation a top priority. In the months after Brown's inauguration, the union brought pressure to bear on the new governor, who helped craft the 1975 Agricultural Labor Relations Act with four co-authors, including Assemblyman Richard Alatorre. Brown then appointed a pro-UFW board majority. He also banned the short handled hoe as the result of the arduous effort by the California Rural Legal Assistance to document its responsibility for back injuries.[33]

Two years into the Brown administration, Democrats returned to the White House for the first time since President Johnson. MAPA endorsed Jimmy Carter over President Gerald Ford, and California Director of Motor Vehicles Director Herman Sillas served on the campaign's nineteen-member National Hispanic Advisory Committee.[34] In another first, Henry Lacayo served on Carter's transition team. Lacayo, the Los Angeles-based labor leader, had become the national political director for the United Auto Workers. In this capacity, he integrated Latinos into the National Leadership Conference on Civil Rights. "When I walked into a room I didn't represent Latinos, I represented a million auto workers," he recalled.[35] Lacayo was instrumental in placing Latinos from various countries of origin in federal jobs in government and politics. His sister, Carmen Lacayo, a former nun who worked at the campaign headquarters in Plains, Georgia, became the first Latina to hold the position as the First Vice Chair of the Democratic National Committee. She was, moreover, a Californian of Mexican and Nicaraguan descent.[36]

Carter selected yet another Californian with UAW ties. Esteban Torres, TELACU's first executive director, was then serving in the UAW's International Affairs Office. He wanted the post of Assistant Secretary of State for Inter-American Affairs. Carter offered Torres the post of United States representative at the United Nations Educational, Scientific, and Cultural Organization (UNESCO). Torres accepted the deal, according to Lacayo, after Carter agreed to give the position ambassadorial rank. A number of other people associated with TELACU, which had helped the Carter campaign through its nonprofit voter outreach program, won slots in the administration. This included Gloria Molina, an aide to Assemblyman Art Torres, who became the assistant director of personnel at the White House, and TELACU executive director David Lizarraga, who was placed on the National Commission on Neighborhoods. Under Lizarraga, TELACU became a political and economic force but veered far from its founding mission of organizing poor people.[37]

As part of his organizational outreach, President Carter invited MAPA President Margaret Cruz and two dozen organizational heads to the White House. For MAPA, it was nice to be welcomed once again in the White House.[38] However, much had changed in the decade since Johnson had invited the leaders of MAPA and three other groups to dine as the representatives of the Mexican American community. By the late 1970s there was a proliferation of organizations around the nation but few had the multi-state reach and the depth of community ties once enjoyed by the older Latino groups. Moreover, foundation-supported groups had started to replace the groups once backed by labor and church organizations; faith communities did seek a revival of sorts through the foundation-supported but parish-based Industrial Areas Foundation.[39]

The National Council of La Raza (NCLR) was the brightest star in this new constellation. With roots in the anti-Johnson protests in El Paso in 1967, the once regional Southwest Council of La Raza sought to represent Latinos coast to coast. The organization was on its way to becoming a major institution driven by a professional staff and underwritten with corporate and foundation support. According to founding director Henry Santiestevan, "without the Ford Foundation's commitment to a strategy of national and local institution-building, the Chicano movement would have withered away in many areas."[40]

To this end, the NCLR abandoned much of its original electoral orientation to adopt a non-partisan focus on advocacy and providing needed social programs—despite Congressman Henry B. González's early criticism that the Ford Foundation was financing "irresponsible" militants.[41] The group's evolution reflected the foundation's desire to become non-partisan (an issue that had shaped CSO's development) as well as a desire to work with Congress and presidents of both parties to help shape public policy.[42]

The group's first two heads, Santiestevan and Herman Gallegos, were Californians with ties to CSO; its third, and ultimately most influential executive director, Raúl Yzaguirre, was a former farm worker and Texas protégé of GI Forum Founder Dr. Héctor García. In a sense, the old Kennedy and Johnson supporters came together to create a new institution that incorporated elements of the Chicano movement and grew in influence over the next thirty-five years, with Yzaguirre retiring in 2004. Despite deciding to drop its progressive and explicitly political orientation, the National Council of La Raza came closest to the national pan-Latino organization dreamed about in the formation of the National Congress of the Mexican and Spanish-American Peoples of the United States in the late 1930s.[43]

In California, Mexican Americans sought to strengthen their collective voice by forming the Mexican-American National Organization (MANO) in the late 1970s. The group brought together members of the older groups—GI Forum, LULAC, MAPA, and the Association of Mexican American Educators—along with a number of newer groups, such as the Hispanic Women's Council and the Personnel Management Association of Aztlán. In the spring of 1979, MANO greeted President Carter on his arrival in Los Angeles with a full-page advertisement in the *Los Angeles Times*. The ad accused Carter of breaking his promises to the Latino community, and asked: "Why can't we have a Mexican-American

U.S. Ambassador to Mexico in order to improve relations?"[44] The following year, as Carter fought back a challenge from Senator Edward M. Kennedy for the Democratic presidential nomination, he named Professor Julian Nava, the CSO activist-turned-Los Angeles School Board member, as the first Mexican American ambassador to Mexico.[45] Carter also benefited politically from the efforts of the recently formed Hispanic American Democrats, whose pillars included TELACU's David Lizarraga.[46]

For many activists, Carter's actions were too little, too late. Moreover, in 1980, the special bond between California Latinos and the Kennedy family trumped any remaining loyalty to Carter as it had before to Johnson. In the 1980 California Democratic primary, the UFW and MAPA endorsed Senator Kennedy, as did state legislators Alatorre and Torres. For many now-aging activists, it was the grand finale in a long-running drama of American presidential politics that had started with Franklin Roosevelt. In 1960, President John Kennedy had selected a Californian, Carlos McCormick, to develop and lead Viva Kennedy. Robert Kennedy went far beyond his brother and identified himself with the cause of the farm workers while working with MAPA and other urban Latinos. For his part, Senator Edward Kennedy had assumed Robert Kennedy's passions while evoking the dream of Camelot, a time of idealism dashed by the murder of Martin Luther King, Vietnam, and Watergate.

The California primary campaign in 1980 was also a signal event for another reason: the UFW played a pivotal role not only in the Kennedy campaign but in a number of legislative races linked to the struggle for the assembly speakership. César Chávez and the UFW (along with former Governor Pat Brown) went all out to elect Howard Berman of Los Angeles in order to forcibly replace Speaker Leo McCarthy of San Francisco. McCarthy, an Irish Catholic labor liberal, had angered the UFW the previous year by appointing Assemblyman Floyd Mori, a pro-grower Democrat, to head a special legislative oversight committee investigating a strike in the vegetable industry. By contrast, Berman had co-authored the 1975 Agricultural Labor Relations Act.[47]

The Chávez-Berman alliance in 1980 reflected a shared animus with McCarthy. It also reflected a long-term connection between

Latino and Jewish political leaders. In the absence of a sizable number of volunteers in politics (the California Democratic Council, the AFL-CIO, and the Democratic Party no longer mobilized people), Berman's organization had pioneered new political techniques. Berman's political partner, Congressman Henry Waxman, likewise had ties to Latino Los Angeles. He supported Alatorre's election in 1971 and his uncle, Al Waxman, as editor of the *Eastside Journal,* had supported the Sleepy Lagoon Defense in the 1940s. Together, Berman and Waxman recruited and elected candidates based on an ability to raise money from liberals and then to spend it on computer generated mailers and slate cards to targeted voters.[48]

For the 1980 primary election, Berman and Chávez agreed to run Alameda County Supervisor Charles Santaña against Assemblyman Floyd Mori in a district located between Oakland and San Jose. For the UFW, it was payback time. The union's boycott apparatus went into high gear; farm workers walked precincts in the district's Latino areas and Chávez reconnected with voters he had recruited into CSO almost thirty years earlier in what was now Union City. This created a conflict for some other groups. According to Ray Solis, the Hayward MAPA chapter had played a major role in Santaña's initial election to city council but they also enjoyed a good relationship with Mori, whom they ultimately endorsed for reelection.[49]

Berman and Chávez formed a similar partnership in Los Angeles County. The two backed Monterey Park Mayor Matthew "Marty" Martínez against Assemblyman Jack Fenton, who had taken advantage of the earlier split in the Latino community to beat Assemblyman John Moreno in 1964. They also backed Louis Domínguez in a tight primary battle for the right to take on incumbent Gerald Felando in Long Beach.

On primary Election Day, the UFW helped defeat Mori and Fenton, the two Democratic incumbents, sending shock waves through the State Capitol. Martínez went on to win in the November 1980 election in a heavily-Democratic district, while Santaña lost to his Republican opponent, thereby missing out on the opportunity to be the first Latino state legislator from Northern California. Domínguez won the contested primary but lost to his Republican incumbent in November.[50]

The election established the UFW as a major political player, its influence strongest in the urban areas where the union enjoyed strong support among liberal and Latino voters, even if there were some conflicts with groups like MAPA. The union enjoyed a strategic legislative alliance with Berman, operated the most effective network of campaign organizers and volunteers, and—for the first time—controlled one of the largest political bank accounts. The UFW provided Santaña $30,000 in the primary and gave Domínguez a combined $45,000 for his two races, both very large sums at the time. The union also gave generously to pro-UFW Berman allies, including Tom Bates of Berkeley. The UFW's $286,750 in total expenditures placed it among the top ten donors to legislative and ballot measures in 1980.[51]

Having the support of a majority of the new Assembly Democratic Caucus, Assemblyman Howard Berman was set to become speaker and the UFW expected to use its close relationship to Berman and its vaunted organizational capacity to institutionalize its power in the state legislature. A former Chávez aide, Assemblyman Art Torres was set to become majority leader. These well-constructed plans were soon challenged. Instead of supporting the victorious Berman, Leo McCarthy decided to throw his support to Willie Brown and Brown convinced Alatorre to help make him the first African American speaker. Alatorre then convinced Torres to join him, giving Brown a majority in the Democratic Caucus. Brown likewise made a rare deal with the Republican Caucus to vote for him, negating the need to get any votes from Berman supporters in the formal vote in the full assembly. This outraged many Democrats and further worried the UFW, because the Republicans were strongly pro-grower. In the weeks leading up to the leadership vote, the UFW conducted a high profile, high stakes lobbying campaign in East Los Angeles. The union conducted a massive petition campaign and, according to the *Los Angeles Times'* Frank del Olmo, "Chávez also persuaded several prominent community leaders—businessmen, attorneys, educators, even priests— to talk to Torres and Alatorre." All to no avail.[52]

With Brown's victory, Assemblyman Alatorre secured his own status as the most influential Latino in the state legislature and, for a time, California politics.[53] Speaker Brown named Alatorre to chair the Reapportionment Committee to oversee the redrawing of the legislative boundaries following the 1980 Census. In this capacity, Alatorre helped Brown consolidate power and he represented Latino participation in the new ruling coalition. During the 1970s, the statewide Latino population had grown by 92 percent due to immigration and childbirth, from 2.37 million to 4.54 million. Latinos now constituted twenty percent of the state's population but held few legislative or congressional seats. Alatorre was limited in his ability to draw legislative districts favorable to Latinos because of the importance of votes and coalition politics. Congressman Phillip Burton helped achieve the most notable aspect of the redistricting process: the creation of a second Latino-dominated congressional seat in Los Angeles County, won by Carter appointee and UAW operative Esteban Torres, in the San Gabriel Valley. Mid-year, Assemblyman Martínez was elected to fill the seat of a retiring congressman, giving Los Angeles County Latinos a third seat.[54]

Martínez's election to Congress was part of an assembly plan to elevate Berman and friends to higher office, thus ensuring that they would not regroup and challenge Speaker Brown. The move expanded the number of UFW congressional allies. In the state legislature, the desire to protect remaining incumbents combined with the vested interests of other minority machines to reduce possibilities for new "Latino seats." Equally important was the reality that few Latinos were voting—and voters, not residents, decided elections. The low point was in Assemblywoman Gloria Molina's Boyle Heights-based district, where only seventeen percent of the population registered to vote. This small number of voters made it difficult for Latinos to compete in less homogeneous areas where the Latino proportion of the population should have made them a powerful force. Assembly Speaker Willie Brown summed it up with this comment: "They are fine people, but if they're not registered to vote they can't help you much."[55] MALDEF was outspoken in its criticism of the assembly proposal. The Senate plan likewise drew protests from MALDEF, but was praised by the UFW, Santa Ana City Councilman Al Serrato, and Paul Sepúlveda, a former head of MAPA in Orange County.[56]

Speaker Brown's comments about the dearth of Latino voters angered some activists in the months leading up to the 1982 election to succeed Governor Jerry Brown, whose strongly pro-Latino record contrasted sharply with the modest legislative gains under Willie Brown. Added to this frustration was the reality that Ronald Reagan won at least a fourth of the California Latino vote (and more nationally) in his victory over President Carter in 1980. Moreover, the Republicans had garnered very good press in their public support for more Latino-dominated legislative districts (even if their primary goal was to create more Republican seats). President Reagan sought to institutionalize Latinos in his party, forming the Republican National Hispanic Council in 1981, and appointing non-California Latinos to his cabinet. In California, a Cuban American, Dr. Tirso del Junco, became the chair of the Republican Party. Reagan also began to challenge the gains of the New Deal and the Great Society by seeking to roll back civil rights, attacking organized labor, and beginning the defunding of American cities.[57]

A number of individuals within MAPA sought to have Latinos serve as the "balance of power" between the two major parties. This involved getting the attention of Democrats by welcoming Republicans into MAPA, which enjoyed a mini revival under Presidents Eduardo Sandoval and Julio Calderón. The organizational revival was based on their ability to use the media, Governor Brown seeking the organization's input on appointments, and the bringing together of other Latino groups for quarterly meetings with the governor. MAPA's shift towards bipartisanship reflected their own increasingly moderate politics and a desire to remain influential in a state and nation moving further to the right politically.[58]

As part of the Republicans' pursuit of the increasingly bipartisan MAPA, President Reagan invited its president, Julio Calderón, to the White House for the signing of the twenty-five-year extension of the Voting Rights Act. Calderón welcomed the president's attention and that of Republican leaders in the state legislature. A former member of the La Raza Unida Party, Calderón rose through MAPA's leadership ranks as a Democrat, but then decided to re-register as a Republican. He sought to leverage his willingness to switch parties to encourage further GOP outreach and appointments, which dovetailed with the national Republican strategy of courting Latinos. Calderón also advanced the idea of having the Republican legislative leadership support (and fund) Hispanic candidacies for the state legislature, starting in Riverside County.[59]

A strong movement developed within MAPA to have the organization endorse Governor Brown in his 1982 U.S. Senate campaign against San Diego Mayor Pete Wilson and to support Republican State Senator George Deukmejian for governor against Los Angeles Mayor Tom Bradley. Ultimately, MAPA remained within the Democratic fold only after Bradley's campaign paid to bus delegates to the endorsing convention and engaged talented operatives such as Latina Ellie Peck, the daughter of a Sacramento cannery worker who served as an aide to former Speaker Leo McCarthy. It was an expensive triumph because MAPA's backing had more symbolic value in a media-driven campaign than any votes, volunteers, or money that accompanied it. The need for the Bradley campaign to spend money not to lose the endorsement speaks volumes of their frayed relationship. Bradley had been close to Roybal and CSO throughout the 1950s, and worked with MAPA during the early sixties. But Mexican Americans split their votes in his victorious 1973 mayoral campaign that was based primarily on a Black-Jewish coalition.[60] A number of Latino activists felt Bradley never fully incorporated them into his ruling coalition despite appointing as deputy mayors, Grace Montañez Davis, who had started in the Lincoln Heights CSO, and Manuel Aragón, who helped Santiestevan coordinate Viva Kennedy in Los Angeles, and who enjoyed strong MAPA roots. This lack of Latino involvement was due in part to the reality that most Latinos at the time lived outside the Los Angeles city limits. It also did not help that Mario Obledo ran against Bradley in the 1982 primary, where he received five percent of the vote. The previous year the *Los Angeles Times*' Frank del Olmo had written: "Deukmejian [and other Republicans] want Obledo to fall on his face so that Latino voters will turn against the Democrats in the general election."[61]

Bradley's campaign worked the established liberal networks within the African American, Latino, and Jewish communities while reaching Anglos through television ads that reminded voters that, as a former police officer, he was tough on crime. He also promised to bring jobs to the state. A group known as Viva Duke competed for the Latino vote. Deukmejian, of Armenian heritage, reached out to Latinos as fellow "ethnics," promising to incorporate Latinos within top levels of his administration. Members of Viva Duke also believed that Deukmejian would be freer to reward them with appointments because he would not owe anything to African Americans. It was clear that his Latino appointees would be moderate because as Attorney General, Deukmejian had voted against the confirmation of Justice Cruz Reynoso.[62]

There was a growing divide in the direction of the two most prominent Latino political organizations. MAPA felt pulled to the right by its largely middle class and increasingly third generation membership, some of whose members saw political volunteerism as a route to government jobs. By contrast, the UFW increasingly represented newly-arrived Mexicans (and non-voters) at the bottom of the socio-economic ladder, who were interested in maintaining the viability of the Agricultural Labor Relations Act. The UFW had developed a relationship with Mayor Bradley, who had endorsed its consumer boycotts. The UFW also feared Deukmejian because he was backed by growers. The Deukmejian strategy of courting middle class Mexican Americans while attacking the UFW replicated the 1966 Reagan and 1968 Nixon campaigns.[63]

On Election Day 1982, as much as one-third of Latino voters cast their ballot for the Republican, which was the margin of difference in the very close election. Governor Deukmejian kept his promises and became the first Republican governor to appoint Latinos to top posts, starting with his own staff. The governor appointed Gilbert Avila as a senior assistant. A young MAPA activist in the early 1960s and a former Democratic candidate for the state assembly, Avila went on to serve as the California Hispanic Coordinator for President Gerald Ford and as a special assistant to Attorney General Deukmejian. The governor appointed Andrés Méndez as director of Veterans Affairs, Mark Guerra as director of Fair Employment and Housing, and Chon Gutiérrez as assistant director of Finance. He named Kathy Calderón as deputy director of Boating and Waterways (and then Undersecretary of the Business, Transportation and Housing Agency). Democratic appointees agreed to reregister as Republicans. Assembly Minority Leader Robert Naylor said at the time, "Our future as a political party is in the hands of the Hispanics, due to their increasing percentage of the population."[64]

A law and order Republican, Governor Deukmejian helped lead a statewide campaign to remove Chief Justice Rose Bird from the Supreme Court because of her opposition to the death penalty, which voters overwhelmingly supported.[65] The issue of crime had become the Republicans' "wedge issue" of choice, ideal for their partisan use because it consolidated conservative support while dividing Democrats, including moderate and liberal Latinos. As it grew in strength, the anti-Bird campaign expanded its sights and voters ultimately removed Justice Cruz Reynoso and another justice, as well. Deukmejian replaced Reynoso with a Mexican American who shared his pro-death penalty stand, John A. Arguelles. Governor Pat Brown appointed the former Montebello City Councilman to the Municipal Court in 1963. He was subsequently elevated to the Superior Court by Ronald Reagan, and to the Court of Appeals by Deukmejian.[66] On the issue of agricultural unionization, Governor Deukmejian kept his promises to the growers. He appointed an anti-labor majority on the Agricultural Labor Relations Board, hired an anti-labor general counsel, David Stirling, and dismantled much of the board's enforcement machinery. This further emboldened the growers, who refused to negotiate with the UFW, despite its winning hundreds of union representational elections.[67]

Even before Deukmejian's election, the UFW had begun to think seriously about the consequences of Governor Brown's departure, and the rise of the two new legislative leaders, Senate Pro Tem David Roberti and Assembly Speaker Willie Brown. The UFW met with a number of allies, including Assemblyman Richard Alatorre and the United Auto Workers, according to Chávez aide Marc Grossman. The UFW asked: "How do you become a player in the legislature?" The political insiders recommend the union give "a lot [of money] to the leadership" and allow them to distribute the funds to individual legislators as they saw fit.[68]

The UFW adopted this strategy. It met separately with Roberti and Brown and agreed to support their leadership in return for a commitment to oppose amendments to the Agricultural Labor Relations Act. The legislative leaders also agreed to hire pro-UFW staff persons that would help ensure that bad bills died in the policy committees. The UFW donated $150,000 to Brown's campaign committee, and another $110,000 to Roberti's leadership fund. Soon thereafter, the new relationship was tested. In the 1982 election, Assemblyman Art Torres challenged Senator Alex García for his seat. The UFW decided to endorse García's reelection—donating a whopping $45,000 in direct contributions, busing in farm workers to walk precincts, and mobilizing the old boycott apparatus. Some speculated that his was a way to punish Torres for double-crossing Chávez in the speakership fight, but Grossman emphasized that the election "was Roberti's first test of leadership."[69] The union had a huge stake in his being able to maintain power in the state senate by helping Roberti defend a member of his caucus. García, the ex-Roybal aide, ultimately lost his seat to Torres, the former Chávez protégé, but the union demonstrated its loyalty and clout.[70]

During the fall campaign, the union also made a second donation to Speaker Brown, bringing its total to $250,000. It likewise contributed to a number of other Latino and non-Latino campaigns, including $10,000 to former anti-war radical Tom Hayden, who now headed up the most vibrant grassroots organization in the state, the Campaign for Economic Democracy (CED), that provided a route for anti-war activists to reenter the Democratic Party. He was running for a Santa Monica-based assembly seat. Under the guidance of Dolores Huerta, the UFW had partnered with CED to elect hundreds of progressive delegates to the 1982 California Democratic Party convention, where they formed a strategic alliance with the still formidable Howard Berman. The UFW thus played a nuanced game of power politics in a dynamic political environment where its influence in a generally conservative era was amplified by its bank account. The UFW finished the 1982 election year as the second largest political action committee in the state, behind only the California Medical Association.[71]

In the Assembly, Brown hired Chávez spokesman Marc Grossman. Grossman formally worked for the newly-created unit known as the Speaker's Office of Majority Services, which Brown used to ingratiate his caucus members to him and strengthen their positions in their respective districts. For example, this unit organized an Alatorre-sponsored community event where volunteers painted over graffiti. To maximize the political benefits, they arranged for the newspapers to cover the event and then sent copies of the resultant article, along with a letter from Alatorre, to district voters. At election time, Brown's staff transferred to his campaign payroll to work on targeted legislative races. A legislator's career—and the interests of a group such as the United Farm Workers—was thus protected in return for loyalty to Speaker Brown.[72]

This UFW alliance with the Democratic legislative leaders proved critical because a growing number of Latino voters and Californians (and Americans) generally were turning away from the union's liberal-left tradition and from the party of Roosevelt and Kennedy. In the 1984 election Ronald Reagan won in a landslide, winning nearly half of the national Latino vote. Reagan won the support of a sizable number of "ticket splitters" whom, in the California political tradition, voted for candidates of both parties. The size of Reagan's Latino support represented both a growth in Latino voters and a more permanent shift in allegiances. A Field Poll conducted the next year showed that in terms of self-identification, Latinos represented twelve percent of the California Democratic Party (the same as African Americans), but also seven percent of the Republican Party. The Republican's wooing of Latinos, started by Governors Warren and Knight, and then advanced again by Governors Reagan and Deukmejian, and by Presidents Eisenhower, Nixon and Reagan, had had an accumulative impact. This trend among Latino voters, moreover, was part of a larger political shift. The Field Poll showed that a plurality of state voters identified as Republican for the first time in modern history.[73] For groups like the UFW, the Democrats (with districts gerrymandered to maximize party strength) provided a lifeline in a hostile political environment.

With Republicans in control of the governor's office and the presidency, a number of Democratic political activists focused their attention on local politics.[74] Two elected to office in this period are representative of the upward mobility within the community. In Sacramento, Joe Serna was elected to the city council in 1981 and as mayor in 1992. The college government professor won in a district with relatively few Latinos based on his leadership skills and ability to assemble a coalition, including organized labor. His values and skills grew out of his early life as a farm worker in Lodi and his experiences with César Chávez and the UFW. As mayor, he hired the city's first Latino police chief, Arthuro Venegas, another former farm worker, who became a citizen after service in Vietnam.[75] About the same time, Ronald González, Jr., a teacher turned computer executive, was elected to the Sunnyvale City Council. He then moved to the Santa Clara Board of Supervisors— where he served with former MAPA official Blanca Alvarado—before being elected mayor of San Jose in 1992.[76] Serna and González made history as the first Latinos to be elected mayors of major cities in California, and both achieved these historic firsts by assembling—as had Roybal—a broad coalition that allowed them to win in a district without a Latino majority.[77]

Latino candidates in other cities had less success than Serna and González in building bridges to other groups to secure that first step on the political ladder. In the early 1980s, faced with the reality of perilously low voter participation, and with fewer ties to old allies, a number of Latino activists sought to change the rules of the game as the best way to gain advantage at the ballot box. Ultimately the most effective change was the creation of "majority minority" districts. This was achieved through a combination of federal intervention and legal action. At the urging of Congressman Roybal and others, Congress amended the federal 1965 Voting Rights Act in 1975 to include Latinos. The U.S. Justice Department's subsequent interpretation of this change had far-reaching consequences. The federal government had decided that all levels of government had the affirmative responsibility to create districts dominated by minorities even if it involved piecing together non-contiguous areas. Latino legal advocates pushed for district elections in cities, counties, and school districts to give Latinos representation where they were having trouble winning in an at-large system.[78]

The U.S. Department of Justice sued the City of Los Angeles for not creating a council district in which a Latino could be assured of winning. As a byproduct of an out-of-court settlement, Boyle Heights City Councilman Art Snyder resigned in 1985. Assemblyman Alatorre was elected to the post with the help of Speaker Brown. Alatorre thus became the first Latino on the city council since Roybal resigned to take his seat in Congress some twenty-three years earlier. On the council, Alatorre became an ally of Mayor Tom Bradley; but the percentage of Latinos serving on boards and commissions rose only from nine to sixteen percent from 1973 to 1991. Richard Alarcón broke another barrier and was elected to represent the eastern portion of the San Fernando Valley in 1993, giving Los Angeles Latinos a second city councilman on the Los Angeles City Council.[79]

In another instance, a federal appeals court made a landmark ruling in a 1989 case involving Watsonville, an agricultural town where Latinos constituted 48 percent of the population and 38 percent of the citizens. Despite a significant presence, between 1971 and 1985 nine Latinos had run and lost in racially polarized municipal elections. "Based on this decision, any county, school district, or special election district which conducts at-large elections may be in violation of the Voting Rights Act if there is a significant [Latino] population geographically concentrated and there is a history of unsuccessful Latino candidacies," according to voting rights attorney Joaquín G. Avila. Raised in Compton, California, Avila graduated from Yale University and Harvard Law before becoming the president and general counsel of MALDEF, and then going into private

A proud Congressman Edward Roybal with Assemblywoman Gloria Molina (and husband Ronald González) at her swearing-in as the first Latino on the Los Angeles County Board of Supervisors in 1991.

(Courtesy of Gloria Molina)

practice. The Watsonville case had statewide importance because at the time there were "at least 137 cities in California having a Spanish Origin population of 10 percent or more that [held] at-large elections and [had] no Latino representation."[80] Over the next few years, Avila worked with local government bodies throughout the state to draw or redraw district lines.[81]

The biggest change was to occur within the Los Angeles County Board of Supervisors, which then had a conservative Anglo majority. In 1988, MALDEF, the ACLU of Southern California, and the U.S. Department of Justice sued, claiming that the board had purposely drawn the lines to prevent the election of a Latino. After extensive maneuvering, the board created a largely Latino district. Assemblywoman Gloria Molina, who had started out as a youthful volunteer for Robert Kennedy, had become the first Latina on the Los Angeles City Council by defeating Larry González, who was backed by Alatorre, Torres, and Speaker Brown.[82] Now head of her own political machine, she won a bruising three-way fight with Art Torres and Republican Joan Flores by splitting the middle class areas and doing well among the poor in Boyle Heights. In victory, Molina became the first Latina on the Los Angeles Board of Supervisors. At her swearing-in, Molina opined that she should not have been the first Spanish-speaking supervisor: "This victory should have been celebrated 30 years ago. That is why I want to dedicate this victory to Congressman Ed Roybal. They stole the election from him 30 years ago."[83]

Changes in the Voting Rights Act had a similarly dramatic impact on the state legislative races following the 1990 census, despite an acknowledged undercount of minorities. This was due to a second decade of unprecedented growth in the Latino population. Latinos now comprised 37.8 percent of Los Angeles County and more than a quarter of the state. When Republican Governor Pete Wilson and the Democratic-controlled Legislature failed to agree on a reapportionment plan, the issue went to the State Supreme Court. The Court—using the new interpretation of the Voting Rights Act—exaggerated the effects of the demographic changes by reducing the number of politically moderate, mixed suburban-urban districts in favor of Democratic-oriented, urban, majority-minority districts, and Republican-oriented, Anglo-dominated suburban districts.

Race-based reapportionment thus served to reduce the lag-time between demographic change and political representation by radically
changing the districts on the incumbents. The effort to create Latino
districts resulted in a fourth Latino seat in Congress and the addition of legislative seats in the Eastern and Southeastern portions of
Los Angeles County. Among those who would win a congressional seat was Assemblywoman Lucille Roybal-Allard who took her
father's seat. In so doing, she became the first Latina of Mexican
heritage to be elected to Congress. Another victorious Latina with
ties to the past was Nell Soto. She won a seat in the state legislature
where her husband, Philip Soto, had served from 1963 to 1967. The
1990 statewide reapportionment also produced the first large number of Latino legislators outside of Los Angeles.[84]

Congressman Edward Roybal's retirement in 1992 was part of a
larger generational turnover, but it held special significance because
he had come to personify the upward trajectory of California Latino
politics. A transplant from New Mexico, Roybal grew up in the Great
Depression, identified with the downtrodden, and became active in
politics in the context of the liberal-left and the New Deal. Roybal
had achieved standing in the Latino community as the first Latino
member of the Los Angeles City Council and as the first member
of Congress from California in modern times. He was also the first
major party nominee for statewide office and the founding president
of CSO and MAPA. In these capacities, he sought to elect Mexican
Americans to office and to enact public policy that was beneficial to
Latinos and to working families generally. In his legislative agenda
and as a candidate, Roybal was both a Latino advocate and a coalition builder. He worked particularly closely with organized labor and
the Jewish community, groups of people that he had known in Boyle
Heights since the 1930s. The Boyle Heights experience also accounts for his progressive politics. This was manifested by his greater comfort in working with Chicano movement leaders and his early
opposition to continued U.S. participation in Vietnam. In these actions, he stood apart from many of his Latino colleagues in Congress.
Roybal's major shortcoming was the limited use of his network of
supporters to help elect other women and men to public office.

Roybal, to his credit, created two very important support systems, the Congressional Hispanic Caucus (CHC) and the National

Association of Latino Elected and Appointed Officials (NALEO). Moreover, as a member of Congress, he used his good offices to support a network of groups that grew out of the Great Society. These include the National Council of La Raza (NCLR) and the Mexican American Legal Defense and Education Fund (MALDEF).[85] The Roybal-MAPA axis also helped secure funding for a number of organizations that continue to provide a more economic focus. These include California Rural Legal Assistance (CRLA) and the California Human Development Corporation (CHDC), as well as a number of urban groups. Under the leadership of co-founder Arabella Martínez, the Oakland-based Unity Council completed the $100 million Fruitvale Transit Village. It is a "mixed-use project in Oakland that features affordable housing, retail shops, a health clinic, a senior center, landscaped open space, parking, and the city's largest library—all immediately adjacent to the Fruitvale BART station."[86] The Los Angeles-based TELECU has undertaken numerous economic development projects in Los Angeles.[87] The Mexican American Opportunity Foundation (MAOF), led by founder Dionicio Morales, the former garment union organizer, is a huge presence in Southern California. So, too, is the CHARO Development Corporation, founded by former Teamster lobbyist Richard Amador, that has done a lot to promote small business. Likewise, the Center for Employment Training (CET) has grown from a small program run by CSO stalwarts out of Our Lady of Guadalupe Church in San Jose to a national enterprise operating in thirty-one centers in eleven states and the District of Columbia.[88]

Two years after Roybal's retirement from Congress in November 1994, Latinos achieved a historical breakthrough. For the first time, Latinos outnumbered African Americans in the state legislature. The new members included Liz Figueroa, elected to the assembly from a district that included parts of Santa Clara and Alameda Counties, for which Charles Santaña had competed a decade earlier. As a Latina born in San Francisco to parents from El Salvador, Figueroa broadened the legislative representation in terms of gender, ethnic heritage, and geography.[89]

Assemblyman Richard Polanco from Los Angeles served as the leader of the Chicano/Latino Caucus. An Alatorre ally and former TELACU official, backed by the UFW in his first unsuccessful assembly campaign in 1982 and then elected in 1986, he did more than anyone else to elect Latinos to the state legislature. Working with political consultant Richie Ross, a former UFW staffer, Polanco recognized that there was a basic organizational void in the Latino community with the political decline of CSO, MAPA, CDC, AFL-CIO, and the end of the Campaign for Economic Democracy. Even the UFW was not the force they had once been as declining membership led to a dramatic reduction in precinct walkers and political donations.

The UFW was also going through a generational change. The death of César Chávez in 1993 left a void in leadership; moreover, Dolores Huerta left to pursue other interests, including the formation of the Dolores Huerta Foundation, to train community activists. The best known Mexican American activist, Chávez had contributed much to motivate Latinos to register and to vote, first with CSO and then with the UFW. Like Roybal, Chávez demonstrated a gift in forming Latino, liberal, labor, and religious coalitions. This inclusiveness extended to the use of language. In his 1984 address to the Commonwealth Club, Chávez used the terms Mexican American, Chicano, and Hispanic. While the ultimate goal of the union leader was the empowerment of farm workers, he recognized that the UFW was also a social movement and that citizenship and voting—by farm workers and their urban supporters—were central to achieving power and overcoming exploitation. Chávez was posthumously awarded the Presidential Medal of Freedom, making him only the second Mexican American so honored. (The first was GI Forum Founder Dr. Héctor P. García; Cruz Reynoso subsequently received the nation's highest civilian award.) Arturo Rodríguez, Chávez's son-in-law, with a Masters in Social Work, assumed the presidency of the United Farm Workers.[90]

An astute tactician and strategist, Polanco quickly solidified his seat that included African American strongholds in Pasadena and then turned his attention to expanding Latino power in the state legislature. He soon recognized the role of money in Speaker Brown's operation. The opportunity to elect more Latinos rested, as Polanco saw it, in raising large sums of money from business and then using it to run consultant-driven and mail-oriented election campaigns for targeted seats. As the caucus grew in size its influence grew exponentially.[91] This Latino-business alliance produced generally moderate public policy and focused on existing voters. Moreover, the press recognized the growing divide between more affluent Latinos and the working class immigrants. *Sacramento Bee* columnist Dan Walters put it succinctly: "Anglo voters and middle-to-upper income Asians and Hispanics are identifying more strongly with the Republican Party. And while they may be outnumbered in the general population, they are the most likely to be politically active—to register and vote."[92]

Walters' observations reflected polling after the 1986 and 1990 elections. In 1986, Latinos provided a record forty-five percent of their support for Deukmejian's reelection. This likely indicated approval for the attention that Deukmejian and President Reagan were showering on Latinos, as well as the lack of a compelling Democratic candidate. Likewise, a resonance in the Latino community for social conservatism that emphasized family values, fighting crime, and support for small business greatly contributed to this support. So powerful was this trend that in 1990 Latinos gave Republican Pete Wilson, the mayor of San Diego, forty-five percent of their votes. It appeared that almost half of the Latino vote was readily available to the Republican Party.[93]

Obviously, Latino politics in California was in flux. The generation of political pioneers—represented by César Chávez, Dolores Huerta, Henry Lacayo, Mario Obledo, and Cruz Reynoso—achieved career-high levels of influence in the Brown and Carter administrations in the middle and late 1970s. But these were the exception to the partisan shifts where Republicans won all other gubernatorial and presidential elections during the fifteen years between 1969 and 1984. The emergence of Hispanic Republicans correlated to the rise of moderate Latino Democrats and the general decline of progressive Democrats. Both the left and the right had succeeded in weakening the Democratic Party's hold on the community, but the Republican Party was proving to be the long-term winner.

In the general absence of grassroots social movements, liberal Latinos utilized the court system or formed alliances with Democratic legislative leaders. While these moves produced tactical victories in an increasingly hostile political environment, the failure to invest resources in naturalization and citizenship classes, voter registration, and get-out-the-vote drives served to depress Latino working class participation in politics. It also failed to incorporate potential new voters among the millions of immigrants and their children who arrived in the state from Mexico and Central America during the seventies and eighties. In the short run, the absence of voter registration drives and citizenship classes served the purpose of Latino and Anglo incumbent legislators who did not want large blocks of new voters in their districts. Thus, the general appeal to more moderate and more established voters coincided with positive effects of business funding many Latino campaigns. In the long run, however, the dearth of new voters would have a disastrous effect, leaving the immigrant community vulnerable to attack.

CHAPTER 14

PROPOSITION 187
AND
THE REBIRTH OF
LABOR-BASED COALITIONS

By the early 1990s, California was politically bifurcated. Republicans controlled the governor's office, while the state legislature remained in Democratic hands. To some degree, this dichotomy was due to the fact that GOP leaning districts produced a larger number of voters for statewide elections; it also reflected the skill of Republican gubernatorial candidates to use issues such as crime in appealing to conservative Democrats and independents. However, with California in recession and suffering through an alarmingly high rate of unemployment, the millions of Spanish-speaking and often undocumented immigrants in the state were emerging as a focus of voter frustration. Groups like the Community Service Organization had spent considerable effort to naturalize immigrants and to involve them in civic life in the 1950s and early 1960s, and had even won for long-term non-citizens the right to obtain old age benefits. But for the past two decades, the dominant civil rights groups had fought to prevent discrimination against immigrants but failed to systematically promote citizenship and voter registration within the increasingly diverse Latino community. This left the mostly post-1965 immigrants from Mexico and Central and South America with little voice in the civic arena. Those Latinos who did vote increasingly favored greater restrictions on immigrants entering the United States.[1]

A Field Poll in 1993 showed that illegal immigration was a "very serious" issue to three of every four voters. "Right now, this issue is equal to Proposition 13 in term of its volatility among voters," said Assembly Speaker Willie Brown, referring to the voter revolt in 1978 that had lowered property taxes. Recognizing voter frustration, Senator Richard Polanco announced, "The Latino caucus believes we need to take a tough stance on illegal immigration." Suggestions included stronger enforcement of laws preventing the hiring of undocumented workers, increased penalties for immigrant smugglers, and the deportation of those who commit felonies. Assemblyman Louis Caldera, from Boyle Heights, expressed the concerns of his constituents. "They say things like, 'I'm an immigrant myself, but we've got to do something. We're getting overcrowded, the quality of life is deteriorating and there are fewer jobs." By contrast, Assemblyman Cruz Bustamante recognized the need for immigrants—legal and illegal—in agriculture. "In the area I represent, the Central Valley, we could not conduct [farm] business without the immigrants," said Bustamante. "Those [farm workers] do not come from the welfare rolls, as some people think they should. They do not come from our colleges. And they don't come from the cities."[2]

Despite the anxiety over immigration, Democrats began the 1994 election cycle encouraged by their party's chances to retake key statewide offices due to the unpopularity of Governor Pete Wilson. The Democrats nominated State Treasurer Kathleen Brown, daughter of former governor Pat Brown and sister of former governor Jerry Brown. Primary voters also nominated State Senator Art Torres to be the party's nominee for Insurance Commissioner. The former UFW legislative director was the first Latino to win his party's statewide nod since Henry López in 1958. As the longest-serving Latino lawmaker in the state legislature, Torres was both a skilled legislator and mentor to a diverse range of younger women and men in the state capitol.

When the Republicans fell behind eighteen points in the polls, Governor Wilson and the California Republican Party decided to use immigrants as scapegoats for the state's economic malaise. Wilson spent $2 million to air television commercials supporting Proposition 187 to deny undocumented immigrants access to public education and health care. The advertisements showed Mexicans illegally crossing the border while an announcer intoned, "They just keep coming."

The loudest voices in defense of the immigrant community came from Los Angeles Cardinal Roger Mahony and a number of AFL-CIO unions. Proposition 187 opponents, however, were far from unified. They essentially split into two distinct camps. One group developed a message of fairness that they thought would appeal to the politically important moderate voters. The second group articulated a pro-immigrant message and acknowledged that the initiative would very likely pass. They sought to use the proposed law to mobilize millions of Latinos, including those ineligible to vote. This strategy was more effective than the call to moderates. Prior to the election, 100,000 Latinos marched in Los Angeles, many carrying Mexican flags, causing support for the initiative among Anglos to increase. Meanwhile, Latino opposition intensified due to news coverage on Spanish language television. On Election Day, a majority of Latinos voted against the Proposition 187, as did Asian Americans and Jewish voters.[3]

Nonetheless, Proposition 187 passed by a landslide, winning 59 percent of the vote. Governor Wilson, who had laid claim to the issue, beat Kathleen Brown, whose campaign ran out of money for television commercials a week before voting. Wilson and Proposition 187 helped propel a Republican tidal wave that resulted in the GOP taking control of the state assembly and nearly winning a majority in the state senate. Art Torres lost his campaign to become the first statewide elected Latino official in modern times. Democrats also lost control of Congress for the first time since 1946 when Harry Truman was president. Interestingly, neither Proposition 187 nor the presence of Art Torres on the ballot substantially increased Latino turnout. Latinos constituted only eight percent of the statewide electorate. "The sleeping giant was in a coma on November 8," said a frustrated Art Torres. Reflecting on the election, Torres attributed his defeat to the collapse of the Brown campaign, which reduced the number of Democratic voters who went to the polls. Some Latino activists and elected officials maintained a sense of optimism amidst despair over the successful exploitation of the immigration issue by the Republican Party. So, too, did the Latino community's institutional allies. "We lost the battle, but we need to win the war," said Father Pedro Villarroya, who headed up the Los Angeles Archdiocese's Latino ministry. "We need to vote."[4]

The Republican Party continued its anti-Latino drumbeat into 1995 and 1996, cementing Proposition 187 in the collective memory, even though it was appealed in the courts and eventually overturned. Furthermore, with the November 1994 Republican takeover of Congress, House Speaker Newt Gingrich adopted the anti-immigrant agenda: "House GOP Charts California Agenda," read one headline in the *Los Angeles Times*.[5] Congress proceeded to deny benefits to undocumented and legal non-citizens alike. President Bill Clinton signed the bill, but he also made it easier to become a citizen by cutting the time it took the federal government to process applications from two years to six months. Fearing more attacks on immigrants and wishing to obtain the power of the vote, an unprecedented number of Latinos completed the naturalization process and registered to vote.[6] Moreover, the California Democratic Party sent a powerful signal that Latinos were welcome in the party of Roosevelt and Kennedy by electing former Senator Art Torres as their party chair. He remains in the post a decade later.[7]

Having successfully tapped into resentment against the undocumented, the state and national Republican parties decided to further exploit Anglo frustration by targeting affirmative action in the 1996 elections. In California, the Republican Party embraced Proposition 209, known as the California Civil Rights Initiative. The voter initiative would end affirmative action while retaining the state's anti-discrimination laws, including the 1959 Fair Employment Practices Act. MALDEF officials and other civil rights advocates believed this would reduce minority opportunities for college entrance and employment. Proponents argued that affirmative action led to racial quotas and less qualified applicants. This ideological debate was shaped by events in Washington, D.C., where conservative Republicans, led by Speaker Gingrich exercised disproportionate impact over federal policy. President Clinton sought to preserve some affirmative action programs by adopting a "mend it, don't end it" strategy. Early polling showed that 71 percent, including a majority of Latinos, supported Proposition 209. Divisions developed between activists and the Democratic Party, and between women's groups and minority advocates. Several key activists who were products of the 1960s sought to use the initiative to organize the African American, Asian, and Latino communities. Among Latinos, this meant building on the political momentum achieved in the losing campaign against Proposition 187.[8]

The 1996 presidential campaign of Republican U.S. Senator Bob Dole, which linked affirmative action to immigration issues, openly appealed to racial antagonisms. This was significant on two levels. First, Senator Dole was a mainstream Republican who had supported affirmative action since the era of President Richard Nixon. Nixon had expanded affirmative action programs into the construction industry. Dole shifted positions only after conservative Republicans took control of the House of Representatives. Washington, D.C.-based neoconservatives like Linda Chávez, a veteran of the Reagan White House, helped construct the intellectual basis for Dole's anti-affirmative action position. Second, Republicans saw the divisive issue of race as the best chance to carry the state and thereby drive President Clinton from the White House. Clinton generally avoided the issue, focusing instead on the need to expand education and employment opportunities. But Democrats did pay for some television ads that animated minority group opposition to Proposition 209.[9]

On Election Day 1996, 80 percent of California Latinos voted to reelect President Clinton, the best performance for any Democratic candidate in the state since Hubert Humphrey in 1968. The overwhelming Latino vote was likely due to the positive appeal of an attractive candidate and a negative reaction to the Republican Party's transparent and reoccurring effort to exploit racial antagonisms. The results also reflected a changing voter profile. A third of the Latino voters had become eligible to vote due to either naturalization or turning eighteen since the passage of Proposition 187 two years earlier.[10] There was also a corresponding decline among Anglo voters resulting from the downsizing of the aerospace industry and the relocation of many of these workers out of state. Consequently, Los Angeles County voted for Clinton in 1992 and 1996, allowing the Democrats to carry the state in a presidential election for the first time since 1964.[11] Moreover, Democratic Latinos exercised increasing political leadership at the municipal level, with Latinos serving as mayor in forty-two California cities.[12]

The debates over Propositions 187 and 209 provided a civics lesson for the immigrant communities of California, with the importance of voting reinforced yet again with the passage of Proposition 227, to outlaw bilingual education.[13] The external attacks on the working class immigrant community also produced new interest in the plight of immigrants by progressive non-Latinos, organized labor, the Catholic Church, and the Democratic Party. The time was

ripe for a reemergence of the aggressive activism of Latino coalition politics formally practiced so successfully by Roybal, CSO,
segments of organized labor, and the liberal-left. Many of the key
leaders in this effort were activists trained by Bert Corona, César
Chávez, and Dolores Huerta in the 1960s and 1970s.[14]

The most important new leader was Miguel Contreras. James
Wood, the executive secretary-treasurer of the Los Angeles County
Federation of Labor, hired the forty-one year-old Contreras as the
group's political director. This made him the first Latino to hold such
a post since Henry Santiestevan worked for the Los Angeles CIO
Council in the early 1950s.[15] Wood recognized the potential power
within the immigrant community and saw in Contreras the leadership skills to build on the CSO and UFW activist tradition. Born
into a farm worker family in Dinuba, south of Fresno, Contreras
first met César Chávez in 1968 when the labor leader came to town

*Dolores Huerta addresses a rally in opposition to Proposition 209, elimi-
nating affirmative action in higher education and state and local government. The Latina icon personified the linkage between CSO and the UFW,
and the current efforts to elect Latinos to office and to end the attacks on
immigrants.*   *(Courtesy of Dolores Huerta Foundation)*

to rally support for Robert Kennedy. After Kennedy's assassination, Contreras joined the UFW's Ranch Committee and in 1973 moved to Toronto, Canada, to organize the grape boycott. He learned to work with unionists, liberal activists, and students, as well as ministers, priests, and rabbis. Returning to California, Contreras became an organizer for the Hotel Employees and Restaurant Employees in San Francisco, getting his first job with the help of Local 2 Vice President Roger Cardenás. Contreras worked with some of the best organizers of the time, including César Chávez, Dolores Huerta, and Fred Ross. He also enjoyed ties to the dominant Latino power-broker, Richard Polanco, whom he met through the UFW. In mid-1995, at age fifty-one, Woods died of cancer, elevating Contreras to the top spot within the Los Angeles County Federation of Labor more than a decade earlier than anticipated. Contreras sought to use developments within the labor movement and the immigrant community to reshape state and local politics.[16]

Contreras started as the top labor official in Los Angeles at about the same time as the union movement elected fresh, more aggressive leadership at the state and national levels. Art Pulaski replaced the retiring John Henning as the head of the California Labor Federation. A machinist by trade, Pulaski came of age politically by working in progressive labor-community coalitions. He immediately set out to develop a strong member-to-member political program pioneered by the CIO in the 1930s but no longer utilized in any significant fashion.[17] The new AFL-CIO president, John Sweeney, was influenced by Catholic labor priests in New York the 1940s.[18] Sweeney's partner in the new labor movement was executive vice president Linda Chávez-Thompson (no relation to the neoconservative leader of the same name). The Texas native thus became the first Latina to help guide a labor movement that had changed greatly since the 1940s and even the 1960s in terms of industries and the size of the Latino workforce.[19]

The foundation for much of the old CIO in California was gone: auto, steel, rubber, and aerospace plants had closed, as had the canneries and furniture plants and many garment factories. These bastions of the old labor movement had been replaced by public employee unions that were given the right to collective bargaining by Governor Jerry Brown in the mid-1970s. As a result, by the 1990s the Service Employees International Union (SEIU) had replaced the United Auto Workers as the largest labor organization advocating for community coalitions.[20]

This new labor movement included a number of Latino leaders in Los Angeles. Eliseo Medina, a former UFW leader, was responsible for overseeing SEIU's growth in the region. Local Latino leaders included Gilbert Cedillo, general manager for SEIU Local 660, and Mike García, president of SEIU Local 1877. Latino educators included United Teachers Los Angeles (UTLA) president John Pérez.[21] María Elena Durazo and Christina Vázquez assumed the leadership of UNITE HERE, the merged union of hotel workers and garment workers. The United Farm Workers reestablished their grassroots political operation in Los Angeles. Within the building trades, Mike Quevedo, Jr., nephew of Eduardo Quevedo, led the Laborers Union in Southern California.

Even as Contreras tapped into the increasing number of Latino-led unions, he also consciously extended invitations to African American and Jewish labor leaders. He started an annual Martin Luther King Day breakfast and supported the renaissance of the Jewish Labor Committee, and likewise reached out to business and political figures in these communities. Contreras also succeeded in reviving labor's links to the faith community, progressive academics, and the liberal-left. At the same time, he reached out to journalists, notably Frank del Olmo at the *Los Angeles Times*, Harold Meyerson at the *LA Weekly*, to *La Opinión* and, last but not least, to Spanish language radio and television.

Contreras immediately began to look for political opportunities. The goal for organized labor was, as for Latino Los Angeles, to demonstrate that it was still relevant politically by moving beyond backroom deal making. This meant developing successful long-term strategies to mobilize its members to walk precincts and to get out the vote in ways that the labor movement had not been able to undertake effectively for years. Contreras found his opportunity in the 1996 state legislative elections. While the pervasive mindset appeared locked on low expectations, Contreras recognized that victory would produce a high level of rewards for the labor movement and working families. "Assembly Democrats are saying, we will win in the Salinas area . . . , we will win in Orange County . . . , but don't think we can win in Los Angeles," Contreras said afterwards. "We said, no, we are targeted and we are focused and we are working in conjunction with the national AFL-CIO. So we are going to put all the unions on the same page when it comes to politics in November 1996."[22] The new labor movement in Los Angeles focused on "kitchen table economics" and delivered the message by mail and by 3,500 union volunteers who walked door-to-door in these targeted districts.

At the same time, the Opportunity PAC—run by SEIU, California Teachers Association, California Federation of Teachers, California Faculty Association, and others—spent hundreds of thousands of dollars on these races that were under-funded because the Assembly Democrats were investing resources elsewhere. The California Labor Federation and State Senator Hilda Solis also provided an additional reason for newly-registered Latinos to cast their ballots. They sponsored Proposition 210 to raise the minimum wage that received the backing of Cardinal Roger Mahony. On Election Day 1996, the Assembly Democrats lost every one of their targeted races. By contrast, organized labor, under the aegis of the Los Angeles County Federation of Labor, helped three Democrats achieve upsets in the historically Republican suburbs of Glendale, Pasadena, and Cerritos. Among these new legislators was community college professor, Sally Morales Havice.

The new Democratic majority then set about selecting a new speaker of the assembly. Several legislators maneuvered to advance their election, including Cruz Bustamante of Fresno and Antonio Villaraigosa of Los Angeles. While Bustamante and Villaraigosa shared membership in MEChA while in college, they chose very different routes to the state assembly. A product of City Terrance and Boyle Heights, the young Villaraigosa joined MEChA at UCLA and worked with Bert Corona in CASA before graduating from the Peoples School of Law. Villaraigosa moved into the political mainstream by becoming the president of an American Federation of Government Employees local, then an organizer for United Teachers Los Angeles, and the president of the ACLU. Villaraigosa worked closely with Supervisor Gloria Molina, who had first appointed him to the Metropolitan Transportation Authority board. With Molina's help, Villaraigosa won his multicultural assembly seat in 1994 (the year before Miguel Contreras took over the labor council) by forming a progressive labor-community coalition to defeat Bill Maybie, Polanco's chief of staff.[23]

By contrast, Bustamante entered the state legislature as the anointed candidate of Latino Legislative Caucus chair Richard Polanco and Assembly Speaker Willie Brown. The son of a barber in Dinuba, Bustamante's family came to California from New Mexico. He became part of the political establishment as a field representative for State Assemblyman Bruce Bronson. Bustamante was the first beneficiary of voter-approved term limits, approved by voters as Proposition 140, which would start forcing out incumbents in 1998. When his boss resigned early to take another job, the Assembly Democrats rallied behind Bustamante. They raised the necessary funds, kept other candidates out of the race, and sent in their staff to walk precincts. In office, Bustamante courted agriculture and portrayed himself as a political moderate in tune with the Central Valley.

In the speakership fight, Latino Caucus chair Richard Polanco anointed Bustamante (over Villaraigosa), in part because he had a better chance to secure support from politically moderate legislators. The Latino Caucus united behind Bustamante and Polanco helped line up the necessary votes to defeat Minority Leader Richard Katz, the assembly's highest-ranking Democrat. Bustamante won— and thus became the first Latino Speaker of the State Assembly. Bustamante used his power to restore some programs used by immigrants that had been cut by Congress. The legislature did not, however, rescind the law passed in the previous session and signed by Governor Wilson requiring citizenship as a precondition to obtaining a driver's license.

The Los Angeles County Federation of Labor's new approach to politics was to link elections and policy. This meant campaigning on working class issues and then demanding that elected officials deliver for their constituents. The labor movement also organized around local issues. Just as CSO had used sidewalks as a rallying cry, so the labor movement stressed the need to build new schools and to repair old buildings to accommodate Latino students. In the spring 1997 municipal election, organized labor worked with the Latino community to pass Proposition BB, a massive $2.4 billion school bond in Los Angeles. The demographic reality was that Latinos comprised seventy percent of the students compared to fourteen percent of the electorate and voted in even smaller numbers; indeed, Latinos had comprised only eight to ten percent of the voters in previous elections.

The school construction bond, moreover, needed a two-thirds vote to pass. The United Teachers Los Angeles and other groups made a tremendous effort to use Latino self-interest in improving public schools to encourage citizenship and to increase voter registration and turnout at the polls. This included a major push for voter registration by Spanish language television stations and a grassroots effort in the San Fernando Valley by Valley Organized in Community Efforts (VOICE), an affiliate of the Industrial Areas Foundation. As a result, Latino turnout in the election reached an historic high—fifteen percent. The race also marked the first time that the number of Los Angeles Latino voters exceeded African Americans. Journalists recognized the election's significance. "I'm determined to fight for my rights," stated Augustina García, a Guatemalan immigrant living in Pacoima, told the *Daily News*. "I don't want to be anonymous anymore."[24] *Los Angeles Times* columnist Bill Boyarsky compared the election to the watershed races of Edward Roybal and Robert Kennedy and those "pulled into politics by César Chávez's farmworkers." He noted the Latino middle class' role in providing "political leaders for the new voters."[25] At the same time, the school bond achieved the necessary two-thirds support at the polls with the help of labor and business, and Anglo, African American, and Jewish voters.[26]

With Los Angeles labor having helped expand the number of Latino voters to pass the school bond and having previously demonstrated that they could deliver the winning margin between two self-selecting assembly candidates, Contreras then sought to prove that the new labor movement could elect one of its own. The opportunity presented itself in late 1997—only months after the Proposition BB victory—in a special election to replace Boyle Heights Assemblyman Louis Caldera, who President Clinton appointed Secretary of the Army. Boyle Heights was the birthplace of CSO and the historic center of progressive Latino politics. However, those days seemed long ago and in definite need of revival. Caldera's heir apparent was Eastside School Board Member Vickie Castro, a moderate Democrat focused on Latino concerns and protégé of Supervisor Gloria Molina. The Los Angeles County Federation of Labor endorsed former union official Gilbert Cedillo, a progressive coalition builder with ties to the Chicano movement and the old Mexican American and Jewish groups central to Boyle Heights in the 1940s. Most importantly, as the leader of the SEIU union representing county workers, he had played a pivotal role in saving the County General Hospital, where large numbers of uninsured Eastside residents obtained healthcare. He put thousands of protesters in the streets and had national union leaders pressure President Bill Clinton to provide a partial bailout.

SEIU leader Gilbert Cedillo addresses the Jewish Labor Committee. Behind him were María Elena Durazo and Miguel Contreras.

(Courtesy of Slobodian Dimitrov)

Cedillo, the crusading labor leader, started the campaign far behind Castro, the entrenched politician, who enjoyed a huge lead in the polls, ample financing, and a traditional résumé. Had Cedillo run a standard campaign he would have lost badly, as Roybal had against Christensen in 1947. He could win only if the campaign became a cause, with labor and its allies dramatically enlarging the number of voters. These goals were achieved by three separate but reinforcing efforts. Cedillo's campaign made the case that he would do a better job fighting for immigrants and working families. The Los Angeles County Federation of Labor stressed working class economics in its campaign to its members delivered through the mail, door to door, and over the phone by the efforts of a dozen full-time organizers who mobilized hundreds of unionists. Equally important, María Elena Durazo, as president of the Hotel Employees and Restaurant Employees (HERE) Local 11, and the elderly Bert Corona, as head of Hermandad Mexicana Nacional, organized a "new voter" program. It targeted those still angry at Pete Wilson over Proposition 187 and who benefited from keeping the county hospital open. One pro-Cedillo mailing included a button that read, "Cedillo Sí, Wilson No." For his part, Corona was able to help bring together the foreign-born community and the labor movement for Cedillo. He had mentored a number of young activists in CASA in the 1970s, including Cedillo and Durazo, and these labor leaders had made a name for themselves advocating for immigrants. This labor-immigrant alliance received help in the form of mailers in the final days of the election paid for by business interests prodded to act by Latino Caucus chair Senator Richard Polanco.[27]

This "new style" of campaigning was reminiscent of Roybal's initial win in 1949—when CSO brought thousands of new voters to the polls—and it worked. Voter turnout in the special election increased dramatically, providing the votes for an impressive Cedillo victory. The election results sent shockwaves through the political establishment. Politics in Latino Los Angeles had changed course again. In the succeeding years, the County Federation of Labor has become a machine, consciously constructing a Latino-labor alliance, as well as becoming a force in other ethnic and minority communities. This was due to its unique ability to deliver thousands of campaign volunteers at a time when activists are absent from many campaigns. It was also due to the ability of organized labor to target large sums of money, spent wisely with the aid of top-flight political consultants. The ability to exercise such influence was also, in part, the result of the sizable influx of Latinos into Los Angeles and the corresponding flight of Anglos and much of the traditional business elite. It reflected, too, labor's ever-present attempts to speak for working families and for immigrants beyond its own membership, such as passing a Living Wage Ordinance.[28]

The working class, Latino-friendly policy victories have been possible, in large part, because of labor's partnership with progressive regional foundations, academics, the clergy and community groups. The most important of these groups is the Los Angeles Alliance for a New Economy (LAANE). It drove both the Living Wage Ordinance and the strategic use of Community Redevelopment funds to uplift workers directly (through higher wages) and indirectly (by making it easier to unionize workers employed by city contractors). HERE Local 11 leveraged LAANE's research and labor's relationships in city hall to get employers at the Staples Center and at Los Angeles Airport to give up their fight against unionization. Viewed another way, the Los Angeles County Federation of Labor became the muscle and LAANE the brains of this new dynamic that was (and still is) funded in large measure by progressive foundations. The Living Wage movement also served to insert the issue of poverty into the public dialogue for the first time since the War on Poverty. Unlike the 1960s, when the focus was on the unemployed and pockets of poverty, the attention was on the working poor. Where there is enough union density, labor partnered with employers to create training programs to train workers and provide for upward mobility on the job.[29]

Support from the faith community flows naturally out of personal experiences, according to María Elena Durazo, president of HERE Local 11, for it is the parish priest that the migrant and the urban poor alike turn to in difficult times.[30] Today, bishops Gabino Zavala of Los Angeles and Richard García of Monterey often cite their own immigrant experience as they speak out for the newly arrived and the marginalized. It is a continuation of the tradition popularized by César Chávez, for whom a banner of Our Lady of

Guadalupe led every march, many of which incorporated members of the clergy. This labor-church relationship most often revolved around policy issues related to economic and social justice, just as it did in the 1940s when the Catholic Church backed CSO and the Catholic Labor Institute. In recent years, Cardinal Roger Mahony—who as Bishop of Stockton was one of Governor Jerry Brown's original appointees to the Agricultural Labor Relations Board—has offered Mass to striking janitors. He also welcomed labor and legislative leaders to the newly-constructed Cathedral of Our Lady of the Angels in 2003 for a Cinco de Mayo breakfast co-sponsored by the Los Angeles County Federation of Labor and the Latino Legislative Caucus. Cardinal Mahony addressed an immigration reform rally sponsored by labor that drew 20,000 people to the Los Angeles Sports Arena in 2001. Much of the audience came from religious congregations organized by the Industrial Areas Foundation. The IAF and LAANE worked with Catholic, Protestant, and Jewish leaders, many of whom are also present in Clergy and Laity United for Economic Justice (CLUE).

So, too, the Latino business community has once again assumed its earlier role as an advocate for ethnic interests. It is a tradition personalized by Eduardo Quevedo, a small businessman who served as the president of a number of Mexican American organizations from the 1930s to the 1960s. Members of the Los Angeles Mexican Chamber of Commerce also represented the community on civic boards in the 1940s. MAPA's founding of statewide offices in 1960 came almost entirely from the world of business and the professions. The difference today is that business-oriented leaders now come from large as well as small firms. These women and men are helping to elect candidates, providing leadership to a host of non-profits, including civil rights groups, think tanks, and economic development centers. People such as Anita Gabrielian (AT&T), Andrés Irlando (Verizon), Mónica Lozano (*La Opinión*), Frank Quevedo (Southern California Edison), and Peter Villegas (Washington Mutual) are playing influential roles in civic life in Southern California, and beyond. So, too, do ethnic chambers continue to play a broader role than their Anglo counterparts. "Hispanic chambers are different," emphasized Dennis King, executive director of the Hispanic Chamber of Commerce Silicon Valley. The result, according to King, is that the San Jose-based chamber works with the South Bay AFL-CIO Labor Council, and supported increasing the local minimum wage.[31]

Such policy is most often driven by politics. The changing of the formal political rules in California also contributed to the lessening of the power of Senator Polanco and other incumbent politicians and the rise of more immigrant and labor-oriented politicians. For the Latino community, policy changes and a growth in the number of Latino elected officials was not a foregone conclusion. Voter-approved term limits represented both a threat to existing Latino-held seats as well as the promise for Latinos to obtain Anglo-held seats.[32] This is because under the new rules, elected officials may serve only three two-year terms in the Assembly, and two four-year terms in the Senate. The City of Los Angeles followed by imposing term limits on their council members. These limits have led to a turnover in the ranks of once entrenched politicians. Up-and-coming elected officials still need to establish name identification and develop a fundraising base. Those in office continue to influence the election of their replacements. Still, there has been a fundamental shift in power away from politicians and towards the constituency groups—such as organized labor—who participate in this game of musical chairs.

The new Los Angeles-based labor-community alliance came into its own in Sacramento with the election of Assembly Speaker Antonio Villaraigosa, who followed Bustamante into the powerful post with the support of Richard Polanco. Villaraigosa's commitment to uplifting Latinos and other people in economic need (as opposed to targeting resources explicitly by race) is evidenced in his crowning legislative achievement, the Healthy Families program, which expanded health coverage to low income children without health insurance. When forced out of the legislature by term limits, Villaraigosa ran for Mayor of Los Angeles in 2001. Early polls gave him only four-percent support; it was a measure of how little television coverage state legislators receive in a region that focused on celebrity and criminality. The County Federation of Labor decided to go all out in their support and Villaraigosa sought to construct a coalition based on the Roybal model. The coalition carried Villaraigosa into the runoff with James Hahn. Hahn was the son of the former county supervisor who had built a legacy in the African American community, in part, by hiring and supporting Gilbert Lindsey against Richard Tafoya for Roybal's city council seat in 1963. Just days before the election, polls showed Villaraigosa and Hahn in a 47-47 tie. But in the end, Villaraigosa came up short. He was hurt by Hahn's television commercials that tied him to a convicted drug dealer. He also suffered from miniscule support by African Americans and disunity among Latinos, most notably Assemblyman Tony Cárdenas and City Councilman Alex Padilla's support for Hahn in the San Fernando Valley. However, Villaraigosa's near miss galvanized local activists and generated national attention. Two years later, Villaraigosa reentered the political arena; he defeated a sitting city councilman from Boyle Heights by increasing voter turnout twenty-five percent with the help of organized labor. Once again Villaraigosa had a platform.

The Los Angeles County Federation of Labor also extended its influence deep into the Los Angeles suburbs. This included electing two dynamic Latinas in the San Gabriel Valley. Labor helped State Senator Hilda Solis defeat Congressman Matthew Martínez. It drew national attention because he was the only congressional incumbent nationally to lose in the 2000 Democratic primary. Contreras used the Solis victory as a symbol of labor's rising expectations, and the need for politicians to become worker advocates. In contrast to Martínez, Solis was a dynamic leader. Solis used her own campaign funds to help finance a statewide initiative to raise the minimum wage. As chair of the Senate Labor Committee, she worked closely with representatives of many unions. Solis also frequently partnered with UFW co-founder Dolores Huerta to champion progressive causes. According to Contreras, his willingness to go after an incumbent member of Congress was influenced by his own role in the UFW's defeat of Assemblyman Mori in the 1980 primary election. Organized labor then helped elect Assemblywoman Gloria Romero to replace Solis in the State Senate. Romero had been a leftist in the 1960s and an ardent UFW supporter, as well as an early member of her professors' union. She started her electoral career as a trustee of the Los Angeles Community College District.[33]

Cedillo, Villaraigosa, Solis, and Romero were not the only ones to emerge from the ranks of the progressive labor-Latino alliance, which has scored its most dramatic success in Los Angeles. In 2002, Cedillo moved to the state senate, filling the seat occupied by the termed-out Richard Polanco. This opened up the Boyle Heights-based seat in the state assembly. The progressive candidate for the seat was Fabian Núñez. The twelfth child born to a maid and gardener in San Diego, the thirty-five-year-old Núñez had attended college and became a labor organizer. Núñez came to prominence in East Los Angeles fighting the passage of Proposition 187. Soon thereafter, he assumed the post of political director for the Los Angeles County Federation of Labor before becoming the director of governmental affairs for the Los Angeles Unified School District. The more moderate Latino candidate, Pedro Carrillo, served as an aide to Congresswoman Lucille Roybal-Allard. In many ways, the liberal Roybal-Allard represented a continuation of the later stages of her father's career, where he was more statesman than activist. California Chamber of Commerce-led business interests pumped vast resources into both Carrillo's formal campaign and a series of "independent expenditures." However, labor was determined to win. The Los Angeles County Federation of Labor and the Opportunity PAC spent some $500,000 on mailers, precinct walkers, and Spanish language television advertisements. Núñez's win represented a major victory for organized labor.

In his freshman year in the assembly, Núñez sought to become the Speaker. If he won, he would become the first person to serve a four-year term as speaker since the advent of term limits. Núñez faced off against two other Los Angeles Latinos—Dario Frommer, of Glendale, and Jenny Oropeza, of Long Beach. All three were beneficiaries of labor's largess but they represented different kinds of districts. Núñez came from a progressive Latino district while Frommer and Oropeza represented more moderate and largely non-Latino districts. The child of an ILGWU attorney, Frommer went to law school and then worked for Senator Art Torres, the California Democratic Party, and Governor Gray Davis, along with college teaching. Oropeza, a student government official at California State University, Long Beach, worked her way up the political ladder by serving on the Long Beach school board and city council. Oropeza sought to break the gender barrier. No woman of any background had ever been elected the speaker of the state assembly. Núñez

emerged victorious. He received invaluable assistance from Speaker
Emeritus Antonio Villaraigosa and Los Angeles County Federation
of Labor head Miguel Contreras. This represented a bold intervention into a process based almost entirely on relationships between
legislators.

While the power struggle between Latino legislators in
Sacramento was shaped by personality, gender, ideology and coalition building skills, Latino legislators were no longer exclusively
Democratic. Riverside County prosecutor Rod Pacheco won a five-
way Republican primary in 1996 with 43 percent. He easily won
the general election to become the first Latino Republican legislator. Two years later, in 1998, he was reelected without opposition
and joined by three other Latino Republicans: Abel Maldonado,
Robert "Bob" Pacheco, and Charlene (González) Zettel. All won
largely Anglo, Republican-leaning districts. The child of a farm
worker who went on to become a grower, Maldonado won a seat
on the Santa Maria City Council (San Luis Obispo County) at age
twenty-six. He won a four-way Republican assembly primary with
32 percent. In Southeast Los Angeles County, Robert Pacheco
won his four-person primary with 24 percent of the vote. Poway
School Board member Charlene Zettel, the first Latina Republican
in the state assembly, won her three-way primary with 34 percent. According to Republican election and redistricting expert T.
Anthony Quinn, the three won their primary elections because of
the "open primary" law that allowed voters to cast ballots in either party's primary. This resulted in Democrat registered Latinos
"crossing over" in the primary. In the case of Charlene Zettel, she
also received the help of a handful of unions. Rod Pacheco and
Zettel obtained leadership positions in the Republican Caucus but
all four found it a challenge to remain a moderate in the conservative GOP. Moreover, only Maldonado succeeded in moving up to
the state senate, although the conservative wing of the Republican
Party did block his effort to make history as the first Republican
statewide elected official. In 2007, Maldonado and Bonnie García,
a New York-born Puerto Rican teacher who represents the agriculturally rich Imperial County, are the only Latino Republicans in the
state legislature.[34] This decline may be attributed to the short exis-
tence of the open primary (which the court ruled unconstitutional)

and the surge of new post-Proposition 187 voters contributing to Democrats winning once Republican-leaning districts. "Between 1996 and 2000, Assembly Republicans lost 11 districts in large part because of Latinos," according to Quinn.[35]

One of the final barriers to Latino political empowerment in California was broken in 1998 when voters elected former Assembly Speaker Cruz Bustamante as Lieutenant Governor. Bustamante's election came in a year when voters elected Gray Davis as the fourth Democratic governor in the Twentieth Century. The 1998 campaign was similar to the 1958 gubernatorial campaign in many ways. Davis, like Pat Brown, positioned himself as a moderate liberal who was anti-crime and pro-civil rights; the two also enjoyed a surge in pro-labor voters due to an anti-labor proposition on the ballot. (Proposition 226, in 1998, would have effectively prevented unions from donating to political campaigns.) In winning a statewide of-fice, Bustamante thus achieved the longtime dream of community activists that eluded Edward Roybal, Henry López, and Art Torres. For his part, Governor Davis appointed businesswoman Margarita Contreras-Sweet as Secretary of Business and Transportation, mak-ing her the first Latina to hold a cabinet-level post. He also appoint-ed Carlos Moreno to the Supreme Court. Moreno was a product of working class Los Angeles and graduated from Yale University and Stanford Law School.[36] His appointment filled a void that ex-isted since the departure of Cruz Reynoso and John Arguelles. In the area of policy, Davis expanded funding for education and chil-dren's health insurance, and he signed Senator Cedillo's measure to allow undocumented immigrants to obtain drivers licenses. (The legislature repealed the law after Davis was recalled and Governor Arnold Schwarzenegger threatened to turn the issue into a divisive voter referendum). Davis also signed the first bill to strengthen the Agricultural Labor Relations Act and helped defeat Proposition 54, which would have prevented the collection of racial data, including information needed by doctors to find cures for diseases.

As 2005 approached, City Councilman Antonio Villaraigosa faced a question: should he challenge Mayor James Hahn or wait four years until the incumbent was termed out? The charismatic Villaraigosa started with a base distributed among Eastside Latinos, Westside Jews, and elements of the liberal-left, including a cohort of labor-backed elected officials representing Latinos, African Americans, and gays and lesbians. He also enjoyed a strong fundraising network (that included affluent Latinos) and believed that with Contreras' help the Los Angeles County Federation of Labor would remain neutral in the race. With this in mind, Villaraigosa decided to run for mayor of Los Angeles in 2005. He mobilized existing supporters and then won over many African American leaders (who had supported Hahn four years earlier) and other immigrant groups, such as Korean Americans. He won over the Tony Cárdenas-Alex Padilla organization (that opposed him last time) by intervening to keep Padilla as president of the Los Angeles City Council against a strong challenger. The endorsement of Senator John Kerry (for whom Villaraigosa served as national co-chair of his 2004 presidential campaign) reinforced the councilman's momentum and helped secure white votes in the San Fernando Valley, as did the endorsement of Republican Assemblyman Keith Richmond. The only setback for the challenger was losing the neutrality of the Los Angeles County Federation of Labor (due to SEIU's decision to

Cruz Bustamante became the first Latino Speaker of the Assembly and the first to win statewide office, serving two terms as lieutenant governor.
(Courtesy of Donna Binder)

Speaker Fabian Núñez and Mayor Antonio Villaraigosa tour the USC Medical Center. The two made improving health care and public education a priority, and emerged as prominant figures on the national political scene.   *(Courtesy of Fabian Núñez)*

vote as a block for Hahn). Still, little work followed the official labor endorsement and Villaraigosa received the bulk of labor money through the individual unions. The California Teachers Association and United Teachers Los Angeles were most generous. They spent three-quarters of a million dollars in television and radio ads as part of an independent expenditure. In the final days both the *Los Angeles Times* and the *Daily News* endorsed him. "Villaraigosa's drive, people skills and knack for coalition-building earned our endorsement in 2001," noted the *Times*, before concluding: "He is the best choice to lead Los Angeles [in 2005]"[37]

On Election Day, Villaraigosa decisively defeated Mayor Hahn, becoming the first Latino mayor since Cristobal Aguilar left office in 1872. The 59 to 41 percent margin represented a victory for his coalition strategy of reaching out to every group and every geographic region of the city. Latino elected officials, such as Assemblywoman Cindy Montañez, in San Fernando, partnered with hundreds of farm workers and hotel workers who helped turn out the Latino vote in the Northeast San Fernando Valley. The Villaraigosa campaign oversaw a parallel operation in East Los Angeles, the political birthplace of California Latino politics. These efforts to turnout the vote reinforced the desire by many Latinos to elect one of their own. For the first time, Latinos represented 25 percent of the total city electorate; an overwhelming 84 percent of which voted for Villaraigosa. He also enjoyed majority support from three important groups: Jewish voters, union members, and liberals. Among identified ethnic and racial groups, Villaraigosa won the support of 55 percent of the Jewish voters (17 percent of the total), 48 percent of African Americans (15 percent of the electorate), and 44 percent of the Asian voters (5 percent of the total). Celebrating the victory, the rainbow of multicultural Los Angeles and various faith traditions joined Villaraigosa on stage.[38]

The architect of modern Latino politics in Los Angeles, Miguel Contreras, was not present to appreciate the historic moment. Two weeks before Villaraigosa's triumphant election, which rebuilt the old Roybal coalition, Miguel Contreras died of a heart attack at age fifty-two. While the Los Angeles County Federation of Labor did not campaign for the eventual victor, Contreras, more than anyone else, had helped construct the foundation for victory by increasing Latino voter registration and by restitching together the pieces of progressive Los Angeles that provided the basis for Villaraigosa's campaign. Moreover, he did not discourage the teachers from endorsing Villaraigosa nor did he dampen enthusiasm within the UFW and UNITE HERE to conduct "nonpartisan" voter turnout efforts in heavily Latino areas. Beyond the mayoral election, Contreras led the movement that redefined the role of local government in helping to create a livable city for immigrants and working families. Contreras was central to the Democrats retaking control of the state assembly in 1996, which resulted in Cruz Bustamante's election as assembly speaker, and in the subsequent elections of Speakers Antonio Villaraigosa and Fabian Núñez. The ultimate coalition builder, Contreras helped elect Asian and African American legislators supportive of working class and Latino issues.[39]

Labor had helped to redefine California politics and to ensure a large Latino role in the term limited environment. A Field Institute study in 2000 captured both the dramatic increase in the number of Latino voters, since Pete Wilson helped pass Proposition 187 in 1994, and the untapped reservoir of potential voters. In 2000, there were 6,025,641 Latino adults in California. Seventy-five percent were citizens. Of these, 52 percent—or 2,350,000—were registered. More than a million, or 46 percent of the total voters, registered between 1994 and 2000. Two academics, Luis Ricardo Fraga and Richard Ramírez, summarized the data on new voters:

> Of these more recently registered voters, 50 percent are under the age of 30, 44 percent were born outside the United States, 42 percent reside in Los Angeles County, 38 percent had less than a high school education, and 34 percent had incomes less than $20,000 a year. Perhaps most significantly, 59 percent of these registered as Democrats, and only 18 percent registered as Republicans.[40]

In other words, roughly half of today's Latino voters registered to vote in the five years after Proposition 187. These new voters are overwhelmingly affiliated with the Democratic Party, in large measure because Republican Pete Wilson led the Proposition 187 campaign and because Latino Democrats in the state legislature are generally seen as responsive to the concerns of immigrant and working families.

These numbers reveal a genuine, far-reaching impact on California's political makeup. "In 2000, 60 percent of all registered Latinos are registered as Democrats and 22 percent as Republicans. This is in contrast to the overall California population: in 2000, 42 percent of the state's electorate was registered as Democrat and 39 percent as Republican."[41] Latinos thus account for the main reason why the Democrats remain the majority party in California. Latinos are also the largest block within the majority party. Prospects for Latino candidates would increase, however, if the two million currently eligible but unregistered voters chose to become part of the political process. There are two other groups of potential voters. The first are students who become eligible to vote at age eighteen. The second group is legal residents who were unable to pass the citizenship test after Proposition 187 due to limited English skills. These include former farm workers who, having reached the age of fifty-five, are eligible to take the citizenship test in Spanish, thanks to the CSO's amendment of the McCarran immigration reform bill more than fifty years earlier. The potential clearly exists for Latinos to comprise a third of the total electorate and half of the Democratic Party.

The growth in Latino voters contributed to yet another trend: the emergence of Latinas as appointed and elected officials. These developments followed the historic election of Gloria Molina as the first assemblywoman and then as a county supervisor in Los Angeles. Molina mentored other women, including Hilda Sólis. She also supported the election of Lucille Roybal-Allard, although as a legacy candidate Roybal-Allard benefited from her father's political connections. Assemblywoman Nicole Parra of Hanford also benefited politically from her own father, Kern County Supervisor Pete Parra, in a Central Valley seat stretching from Fresno to Bakersfield. Throughout the nineties and into the Twenty-first Century more and more women ran for office. Many, like Solis, Gloria Romero, and Jenny Oropeza, began their elected careers by serving as trustees for school or college districts. Others started out by serving on local city councils. In the June 2006 Democratic primary, Anna Caballero, the mayor of Salinas, competed with Ana Ventura Pheres, the former mayor of Watsonville. Both women started out as California Rural Legal Assistance attorneys and were the first Latina mayors in their respective cities. Caballero benefited by coming from the larger of the two cities and won the primary with the help of business interests.

While the total number of Latinas (and Latinos) in office has fluctuated due to term limits at the state and local level, there is no limit to the number of years a person can serve in Congress. And here the rate of Latina elected officials is most pronounced at the congressional level. Five of the seven members of Congress from California are Latinas: Grace Napolitano, Lucille Roybal-Allard, Linda Sánchez, Loretta Sánchez, and Hilda Solis. All represent the Los Angeles-Orange County area, along with Xavier Becerra from Los Angeles and Joe Baca from Riverside. This means that these five women are likely to remain as important and powerful politicians for years to come. Moreover, the total number of Latino held seats should increase in the coming years to include other regions. The ability of women to secure elected positions is likely to continue because throughout California there are women at every level throughout the "political pipeline"—from city council to the state legislature.

The dramatic growth in the number of Latino voters and elected officials is based on an expansion in the number of Spanish-surnamed voters and the ability to win in districts without a Latino majority. The means to mobilize the citizenry is possible because of the expanded methods of communication, the most important of which is the development of the Spanish language media that includes television, radio, and newspapers. These outlets interpret events through an ethnic lens, which has led to some advocacy journalism (particularly when the interests of the community are threatened). Equally important, these outlets place a higher premium on politics and policy than do most English language media. The chronicler of Latino life since the inception of El Congreso, *La Opinión* has dramatically expanded its daily circulation throughout Southern California. Numerous weekly papers fill an important communication role. The old *Eastside Sun* is now the flagship for a chain of Los Angeles weeklies, owned by Dolores Sánchez, early MAPA activist and daughter of a garment worker who backed Roybal in his 1949 city council campaign. In the Central Valley, the McClatchy Newspapers launched *Vida en el Valle*. Spanish television, which pioneered the development of public service programming with Eduardo Quevedo in the early 1960s, has become an important tool for candidates and an important information source for Latino voters. Univision's "Voz y Voto" (Voice and Vote) is now the most popular public service television program in the state.[42]

There are powerful parallels between the post-Proposition 187 era and the years following the Zoot Suit Riot. Both events traumatized the Latino community, particularly immigrants and their children. Both events led to a sustained effort by Latinos and their labor and religious allies that transformed politics for years to come. This included a dramatic new emphasis on naturalization, voter registration, and get-out-the-vote activities. The two events not only changed how Latinos viewed their role in society, but how others saw the growing Latino community. While some viewed Latinos with fear and suspicion, others have reached out to the community, particularly those on the liberal-left with roots in the New Deal and the late sixties. This is critical because just as much of CSO's organization was funded by the Industrial Areas Foundation, so today much of the effort to speak for immigrant workers comes from organized labor, the Catholic Church, and progressive foundations.[43]

The main difference between the two periods is the sheer size of the Latino community. Latinos are now the largest block among the state's diverse electorate in a leadership role within the state legislature. This newly achieved institutional power—and the adroit use of coalition politics—is exhibited in the selection of the five Democratic Assembly Speakers elected in a post-Proposition 187 and term limited environment. Three—Bustamante, Villaraigosa, and Núñez—are Latino, while the fourth, Herb Wesson, is African American, and the fifth, Robert Hertzberg, is Jewish. Speaker Hertzberg married Dr. Cynthia Telles, the daughter of President Kennedy's first Latino ambassador, and he established a name for himself in Los Angeles, in part, by raising money for Villaraigosa and other Latino candidates.

There are yet other parallels between these in the area of leadership. In the 1940s, Hispano transplants from New Mexico like Eduardo Quevedo and Edward Roybal provided invaluable guidance to Mexican immigrants and their children, just as in the 1990s many of those helping to empower Latino immigrants had ties to earlier Mexican American and Chicano movements. Relative to the election of Latinos to statewide office, the Art Torres campaign in 1994 and the Cruz Bustamante campaign in 1998 were based on coalitions and constructed with the goal of winning. In this, they had more in common with the Roybal and López campaigns in 1954 and 1958 than they did with the largely symbolic efforts in the 1970s and 1980s. There is yet another parallel between CSO and the Miguel Contreras-led Los Angeles County Federation of Labor. Both organizations utilized issues and candidates to motivate Latinos to register and to go to the polls to exercise their civic voice. They then used this increased voter participation to nudge elected officials to address their issues. There are many similarities between the Roybal and Villaraigosa coalitions in that they were based on Latino vote mobilization while forming alliances with other groups within the liberal-left, including organized labor and African American, Asian, and Jewish voters.

As the 2007 legislative session begins, the Latino Legislative Caucus remains both influential and diverse, with the ever-changing membership shaped by individuals' personal experiences and relationships, areas of policy interest, gender, ideology, and legislative district. Assemblyman Joe Coto, from San Jose, chairs the caucus and the vice chair is Senator Gilbert Cedillo from Los Angeles.

While the caucus formally acts when there is a consensus among its members, its members' influence is omnipresent because so many hold leadership and policy positions in their respective houses, beginning with Assembly Speaker Fabian Núñez, Assistant Majority Leader Kevin de León, Assembly Rules Committee chair Héctor de la Torre, and Senate Majority Leader Gloria Romero. In the Senate, Latinos chair seven committees. They are Ronald Calderón, Elections and Reapportionment; Denise Moreno Ducheny, Budget; Dean Florez, Government Organization; Abel Maldonado, Agriculture; Gloria Negrette McLeod, Local Government; Jenny Oropeza, Revenue and Taxation; and Gloria Romero, Public Safety. Latinos play an even larger role in the Assembly, chairing nine policy committees. Committee chairs include Juan Arámbula, Jobs and Economic Development; Anna Caballero, Local Government; Joe Coto, Insurance; Edward Hernández, Public Employees and Retirement; Pedro Nava, Transportation; Nicole Parra, Agriculture; Mary Salas, Veterans Affairs; Lori Saldaña, Housing and Community Development; and Alberto Torrico, Government Organization. Parra also chairs the Democratic Moderate Caucus, which serves as a counterbalance to the Progressive Caucus, formed by Cedillo and other legislators, many of whom have roots in the social movements. Finally, Speaker Núñez is expected to work closely with Governor Schwarzenegger. The governor, having won reelection with thirty-nine percent of the Latino vote, begins 2007 seeking to govern in a "post-partisan" manner that emulates much of the spirit of Earl Warren and Goodwin Knight.[44]

CONCLUSION:
LOOKING BACK
AND
LOOKING FORWARD

The genesis of the modern Latino political and civic voice in California emerged during the era of President Franklin Roosevelt's New Deal. The first Latino activists and elected officials left a legacy that has profoundly shaped modern politics in three distinct ways.

First, the axiom that voters and their votes count was the driving force behind early political organizing efforts in the community. This remains true today. Once Latinos register and vote, they participate in the political process in forceful numbers that must be reckoned with by candidates and officeholders who understand the dynamics of the newly registered and engaged voter. The challenge for liberal and progressive Latino candidates is the continuing demographic gap between voters and non-voters, despite the millions of post-Proposition 187 voters who have already shifted the composition of the electorate to form a solid Democratic majority in the state. A 2006 study by the Public Policy Institute examined the differences between the sixteen million adults who vote and the twelve million who do not exercise the franchise. Latinos comprise 14 percent of voters—and 63 percent of non-voters. The huge racial disparity also reflects a number of socio-economic factors. For example, 77 percent of voters are homeowners while 66 percent of non-voters rent. This has created a situation where voters are wealthier, better educated, and more opposed to paying taxes while non-voters need greater public services.[1] To move towards a greater balance between voters and non-voters will require Latino legislators, non-profit voter registration organizations, and the Democratic Party to place greater emphasis on registration (and citizenship for those unable to vote), and adopt policies that encourage non-voters and occasional voters to go to the polls. An influx of millions of new Latino voters will likely swell the rolls of the Democratic Party and lead to an increased number of Latino voters and candidates—with a stronger push for government services, such as education and healthcare, that provide a gateway into the middle class.

The second key for Latino political success is that while the number of Latino voters makes a difference, so do political alliances. Simply put, coalition building wins elections and furthers Latino interests on all levels—politically, socially, and economically. California Latinos played an important part in the progressive coalition that elected Governor Culbert Olson in 1938, and in return received a judicial appointment, several board and commission seats, and the veto of anti-immigrant legislation. The number of appointments and policy achievements have grown steadily with the size of the Latino electorate and the expanded of role of Latinos in state, nation, and local campaigns. The first major Latino political figure, Eduardo Quevedo, provided a link between the activists from the 1920s and the 1930s, and served as the nexus between the Latino and liberal political blocs because of his history in both communities. Likewise, Edward Roybal made his entry onto the Los Angeles City Council in 1949 by building on relationships with business and labor leaders, service on the Democratic Central Committee, and by organizing the Community Service Organization. Roybal and CSO likewise formed alliances with other groups, most notably segments of organized labor, the Jewish community, and the Catholic Church. Roybal and CSO also formed bonds with Japanese Americans and African Americans (some of whom, like Assemblyman Augustus Hawkins, had previously supported Quevedo for the state assembly). These relationships developed into the dominant labor-based liberal civil right coalition from the late-1940s to the mid-1960s. And in the early 1970s, liberal Democrats helped elect Richard Alatorre to a multicultural assembly seat in central Los Angeles. Even today, there is a direct correlation of pragmatic idealism that connects Quevedo and former Congressman Edward Roybal to Los Angeles Mayor Antonio Villaraigosa and Assembly Speaker Fabian Núñez. Each candidate recognized the importance of building coalition to further the Latino political and social experience. All four men came out of social movements and their candidacies represented a cause.

Roybal pioneered the multi-racial, working class coalition, which Villaraigosa would later adapt and utilize three generations later in Los Angeles.

The third successful principle of Latino politics is that once coalitions are in place, it is imperative to continually work within these important extended alliances that include unions, business, veterans, religious, and non-profit Latino advocacy groups. This is necessary regardless of the racial or ethnic composition of the electorate. Mayors Antonio Villaraigosa, Joe Serna, and Ronald González all won their respective races by reaching out to ethnically and racially diverse voter blocs while stressing unifying themes. By contrast, successful candidates in overwhelmingly Latino districts focus less on reaching out to non-Latino voter blocs, and work with constituency groups such as organized labor, that can mobilize their members and get-the-vote-out. At the same time, it is important to reach out to the business community and individual contributors (as well as labor) to fund campaigns.

As a result of the dramatic growth in the number of Latino voters and elected officials, Speaker Fabian Núñez and the Latino Legislative Caucus have greatly influenced the rules by which citizens elect their representatives. A case in point is the contentious issue of reapportionment. For decades, Latino advocates complained that the lines were drawn to make it harder to elect Spanish-surnamed individuals. Political activists overcame the challenge by building coalitions and then going to court to force majority minority districts. In recent years, "good government" advocates, newspaper editorial boards, and others have sought to take the power of redistricting away from the legislature. In 2006, Speaker Núñez spoke favorably about reform efforts but members of the Latino Caucus helped kill the bill. The motive was clear: after decades of having the reapportionment process used against them, the Latino-led legislature did not want to relinquish the ability to draw district lines that ensure the election of a heavily Latino Democratic majority after the 2010 census, and for years into the future. Only the possibility of extending term limits—and the careers of incumbent legislations—is likely to alter the fundamental political calculation.

NOTES

GUIDE TO NOTES

For a complete citation of Books listed in the Notes, see Select Bibliography.
Listed below is a list *Abbreviations* used to shorten the Notes and a separate list
of collections of Papers cited in the Notes.

Abbreviations

AQ	*American Quarterly*
BBM	*B'nai B'rith Messenger*
BC	*Belvedere Citizen*
CE	*California Eagle*
CF	*California Farmer*
CG	*Common Ground*
CHSQ	*California Historical Society Quarterly*
CJ	*California Journal*
CSAOHP	California State Archives Oral History Program
CSM	*Christian Science Monitor*
CNS	Community News Service
CSPO	California State Printing Office
CVKWB	California Viva Kennedy Weekly Bulletin
DN	[LA] *Daily News*
ELAG	*East Los Angeles Gazette*
ELAT	*East Los Angeles Tribune*
ESJ	*Eastside Journal*
ESS	*Eastside Sun*
FB	*Fresno Bee*
FNB	*Forum News Bulletin*
FOIA	Freedom of Information Act
IVP	*Imperial Valley Press*
JSDH	*The Journal of San Diego History*
LAC	*Los Angeles Citizen*
LAE	*Los Angeles Examiner*
LAEH&E	*LA Evening Herald & Examiner*
LAM	*Los Angeles Mirror*
LAS	*Los Angeles Star*
LAT	*Los Angeles Times*
LH	*Labor's Herald*
LO	*La Opinión*
MV	*Mexican Voice*
NR	*New Republic*
OHI	Oral History Interview

OHP, CGS	Oral History Program, Claremont Graduate School
OHP, UCLA	Oral History Program, UCLA
OPC	*Oxnard Press-Courier*
PHR	*Pacific Historical Review*
PW	*People's World*
ROHO, UCB	Regional Oral History Office, UC, Berkeley
SCQ	*Southern California Quarterly*
SB	*Sacramento Bee*
SFC	*San Francisco Chronicle*
SDU	*San Diego Union*
SJM	*San Jose Mercury*
SL	*Steel Labor,* Western edition
WP	*Washington Post*
WPQ	*Western Political Quarterly*
WUSA	*Working USA*

List of Papers Cited & Location of Depositories

Archives of Labor and Urban Affairs, Wayne State University (ALUA, WSU), Detroit

Archives and Library, International Longshore and Warehouse Union (A&L, ILWU), San Francisco

Brown, Edmund G. "Pat" Papers, Bancroft Library, University of California, Berkeley

Archives and Manuscripts, Catholic University of America (A&M, CUA), Washington, D.C.

California State Archives (CSA), Sacramento

California State Law Library (CSLL), Sacramento

California State Library (CSL), Sacramento

Civil Rights Congress Papers, Southern California Library for Social Studies and Research (CRCLA, SCLSSR), Los Angeles

Eisenhower, Dwight D. (DDE) Library, Abilene, Kansas

Ford, John Anson Papers, The Huntington Library, San Marino, California

Gallagher, Leo Papers, Southern California Library for Social Studies and Research, Los Angeles, Los Angeles

Galarza, Ernesto Papers, Special Collections, Stanford University

Garcia, Dr. Héctor P. Papers, Special Collections & Archives, Texas A&M-Corpus Christi

Hawkins, Augustus Papers, Special Collections, University of California, Los Angeles

Healey, Dorothy Papers, Special Collections, California State University, Long Beach

Humphrey, Hubert H. (HHH) Papers, Minnesota Historical Society (MHS), St. Paul

Knight, Goodwin Papers, California State Archives, Sacramento

Jewish Community Relations Committee (JCRC), Urban Archives Center, California State University, Northridge

Labor Archives & Research Center, San Francisco State University (LA&RC, SFSU)

Johnson, Lyndon B. (LBJ) Library, Austin, Texas

Los Angeles City Archives (LACiA)

Los Angeles County Archives (LACoA)

Los Angeles County Registrar of Voters (LACRV)

Los Angeles County Federation of Labor Papers, Urban Archives Center, California State University, Northridge

Mont, Max Mont Papers, Urban Archives Center, California State University, Northridge

National Archives (NA), Washington, D.C.

Nixon, Richard M. (RMN) Library, Yorba Linda, California

Olson, Culbert Papers, Bancroft Library, University of California, Berkeley

Quevedo, Eduardo Papers, Special Collections, Stanford University

Roosevelt, Franklin D. (FDR) Library, Hyde Park, New York

Ross, Fred Papers, Special Collections, Stanford University

Ross, Fred Sr. Papers, Archives of Labor and Urban Affairs, Wayne State University

Roybal, Edward Papers, Special Collections, California State University, Los Angeles

Roybal, Edward Papers, Special Collections, University of California, Los Angeles

Ruiz, Manuel Papers, Special Collections, Stanford University

Southern California Library for Social Studies and Research (SCLSSR), Los Angeles

Special Collections, University of California, Los Angeles

Truman, Harry S. (HST) Library, Independence, Missouri

United Farm Workers (UFW), Office of the President Papers, Archives of Labor and Urban Affairs, Wayne State University

United Steel Workers of America (USWA) Papers, Historical Collections & Labor Archives, Pennsylvania State University

Wallace, Henry A. Papers, Special Collections & Manuscripts, University of Iowa

Warren, Earl Papers, California State Archives, Sacramento

INTRODUCTION

1   Cover, "Latino Power: L.A.'s New Mayor—And How Hispanics Will Change America's Politics," *Newsweek*, May 30, 2005.

2   DeSipio, *Counting on the Latino Vote;* de la Garza, et al., *Barrio Ballots;* Pachon and DeSipio, *New Americans By Choice.*

3   See *Perspectives on Politics*, June 2006, American Political Science Assoc., at www.apsanet.org/section_682.cfm.

4   Acuña, *Occupied America* and *Anything But Mexican;* Camarillo, *Chicanos In California;* Chávez, *¡My People First! ¡Mi Raza Primero!;* García, *Chicanismo;* García, *Mexican American;* Gutiérrez, *Walls and Mirrors;* Gomez-Quiñones, *Chicano Politics;* Muñoz, *Youth, Identity, Power;* Pitti, *The Devil in Silicon Valley;* Sánchez, *Becoming Mexican American.*
     Books on Mexican Americans and Presidents John F. Kennedy and Lyndon B. Johnson tend to be Texas oriented, with a limited discussion of California-based personalities, organizations, and issues. See García, *Viva Kennedy;* Pycior, *LBJ & Mexican Americans.* More Californians are in de la Isla's *The Rise of Hispanic Political Power*, a pan-Latino examination of politics since 1968. Burt, *The History of the Mexican-American Political Association and Chicano Politics in California* is MAPA's only published history. Matt Garcia examines Fred Ross's pre-CSO organization of the Unity Leagues in *World of Its Own.* For other organizational histories, see Allsup, *The American G.I Forum;* Kaplowitz, *LULAC;* Márquez, *LULAC;* Ramos, *The American GI Forum.*

5   The use of electoral coalitions is part of the "incorporation model", see Browning, et al., *Protest Is Not Enough.*

6   García, *The Making of Mexican American Mayor*, p. 6.

7   For consistency, the text will use standard Spanish punctuation on surnames, while recognizing that some activists and elected officials chose not to do.

8   Lubell, *Future of American Politics* emphasizes ethnic "firsts." The importance of "firsts" is examined by F. J. Guerra in "Minority Electoral Representation Patterns During the Pat Brown Years," in Schiesl, ed., *Responsible Liberalism.*

9   Progressive reforms of the early 20th Century created non-partisan municipal government with civil service employment, allowed candidates to run in all parties' primary elections without a party designation, and instituted voter initiatives so voters could go "over the heads" of their elected representatives.

10   Hayes-Bautista, *La Nueva California*, pp. 16-20; Baldassare, *California in the New Millennium,* p. 3; *California Statistical Abstract* (Sacramento: State of California, 1970), p. 11; *California Statistical Abstract* (Sacramento: Department of Finance, State of California, 2001), p. 11; *Democracy At Work, The Official Report of the Democratic National Convention, 1948* (Philadelphia: Local Democratic Political Committee of Pennsylvania, 1948), p. 553.

11   This study falls within new Cold War historiography as in Cherny, et al., *American Labor and the Cold War;* Stromquist, ed., *Labor's Cold War.*

12   Vargas, *Labor Rights Are Civil Rights,* p. 284.

13   Guzman, *The Political Socialization*, p. 127.

14   Zieger, *The CIO: 1935-1955*, p. 375.

15   For more on labor priests, see Heineman, *A Catholic New Deal,* and Higgins, *Organized Labor and the Church.*

16   Louis DeSipio, "Latino Issue Agendas in 2004 and the Foundation of Inter-Group Alliances," Latinos & Jews: A Conference of Historical and Contemporary Connections, UC Irvine, Jan. 23, 2006.

CHAPTER 1
THE BIRTH OF CALIFORNIA LATINO POLITICS

1   "Dio Principio El Congreso H. Americano: Se inauguró solemnemente; habló el vice-gobernador; Y entre otros oradores, el delegado enviado por la CTM," *LO*, Apr. 29, 1939, p. 1; "Digest of Proceeding, First National Congress of the Mexican & Spanish American People of the United States," b. 13, f. 9, Galarza Papers; "U.S. Latins Open 3-Day Congress: Spanish Americans To Tackle Problems of Southwest Minority," *PW*, Apr. 28, 1939, p. 3; Misc. articles, Apr. 1939, b. 7, f. Olson Papers; Misc. articles, b. 21, f. Scrapbook, Quevedo Papers.

2   Letter, Olson to Quevedo, December 19, 1938, b. 1, f. 8, Quevedo Papers. See also "Eduardo Quevedo, A Biographical Presentation," March 8, 1964, b. 1, f. 3, Quevedo Papers; Jaime González Monroy interview, June 22, 1997; Frank López interview with Luis Arroyo, Sept. 1 & 15, 1978; Edward Quevedo (son) interview, Feb. 12, 1996; Camarillo, *Chicanos In California,* p. 61; García, *Memories of Chicano History*, pp. 124-125; García, *Mexican Americans*, pp. 155-158; Gómez-Quiñones, *Roots of Chicano Politics*, p. 384.

3   "Dio Principio El Congreso H. Americano," *LO*, Apr. 29, 1939, p. 1; "U.S. Latins Open 3-Day Congress," *PW*, Apr. 28, 1939, p. 3.

4   "Dio Principio El Congreso H. Americano," *LO*, Apr. 29, 1939, p. 1.

5   John Bright, "Las Mañanitas: A New Awakening for the Mexicans in the United States," *Black & White* 1:1 (June 1939): 14-15.

6   Brochure, "Progress with Patterson," Campaign Literature Files, 1938-1939, California Room, CSL.

7   "Dio Principio El Congreso H. Americano," *LO*, Apr. 29, 1939, p. 1; "U.S. Latins Open 3-Day Congress," *PW*, Apr. 28, 1939, p. 3.

8   "Dio Principio El Congreso H. Americano," *LO*, Apr. 29, 1939, p. 1; "U.S. Latins Open 3-Day Congress," *PW*, Apr. 28, 1939, p. 3; Wilson Carey McWilliams interview, February 9, 2001; McWilliams, *Education*.

9   "Digest of Proceeding, First National Congress," 13/9, Galarza Papers; "U.S. Latins Open 3-Day Congress," *PW*, Apr. 28, 1939, 3; "Southwest Congress Raises Minorities' Problems, Spurs Unity," *PW*, May 1, 1939, p. 3.

10 Denning, *The Cultural Front*, p. xiv.

11 "Digest of Proceedings, First National Congress," b. 13, f. 9, Galarza Papers; Zieger, *The CIO*; Gómez-Quiñones, *Roots of Chicano Politics,* p. 383, emphasized Communist Party efforts to organize Latinos.

12 Robert Lacy, *Ford: The Men and the Machine* (Boston: Little, Brown, 1986), pp. 218, 386.

13 David Nasaw, *The Chief: The Life of William Randolph Hearst* (Boston: Houghton Mifflin, 2000), pp. 474-477, 496-498, 508-511.

14 Kennedy, *Freedom From Fear*; Arthur M. Schlesinger, Jr., *The Politics of Upheaval* (Boston: Houghton Mifflin, 1960).

15 Burke, *Olson's New Deal for California*, pp. 1-35; Robert Gottlieb and Irene Wolt, *Thinking Big: The Story of the Los Angeles Times....* (New York: Putman's, 1977), p. 226; Greg Mitchell, *The Campaign of the Century* (New York: Random House, 1982).

16 "We would have nothing to do with the Democratic Party [in 1934], and so we were left on the outside, denouncing the [EPIC and Sinclair] movement," recalled Dorothy Healey, in Healey and Isserman, *California Red*, p. 57.

17 Vicki L. Ruiz, "Una Mujer sin Fronteras: Luisa Moreno and Latina Labor Activism," *PHR* 73:1 (Feb. 2004): 1-20; Carlos Larralde and Richard Griswold

del Castillo, "Luisa Moreno: A Hispanic Civil Rights Leader in San Diego," JSDH 41:4 (Fall 1995).

18 Burke, *Olson's New Deal for California*, p. 34.

19 "Digest of Proceedings, First National Congress," p. 2, b. 13, no. 9, Galarza Papers; "Dio Principio El Congreso H. Americano," *LO*, April 29, 1939, p. 1; "U.S. Latins Open 3-Day Congress," *PW*, April 28, 1939, p. 3; "U.S. Latins Map Defense of Democracy: Southwest Congress Raises Minorities' Problems; Spurs Unity," *PW*, May 1, 1939, p. 3.

20 Proceedings, Forth Annual Conference, American Committee for Protection of Foreign Born, p. 51, b. 1, f. 20, Olson Papers.

21 Resolution, Political Action, "Digest of Proceedings, First National Congress," b. 13, f. 9, Galarza Papers.

22 Letter, Henry Marquez and Sofia Quintana to John Anson Ford, Oct. 31, 1938, b. 75, f. B III 5 idd(4), Ford Papers; Invitación, b. 4, f. 16, Olson Papers; Statement of the Vote, August 30, 1938, CSA; Bynum and Jones, *Biscailuz* is a positive portrait of the Spanish-speaking sheriff while Escobar, *Race, Police, and the Making of a Political Dynasty* shows his negative role in relating to Latino youth.

23 Burke, *Olson's New Deal for California*, pp. 35-38; McWilliams, *California*, pp. 196-197; Starr, *Inventing The Dream*, pp. 235-282.

24 Burke, *Olson's New Deal for California*, pp. 31-32.

25 "Expert from 'The Hoot': A Sincere Movement in Realization," *MV*, July 1939, p. 13.

26 "AFL Stresses Removal of Color Bar in All Unions," *LAC*.Apr. 21, 1939, p. 3.

27 "Mexicans Assail L.A. Supervisor: Brand Relief Ban Threat 'Un-American Because It Is Inhuman,'" *PW*, Mar. 28, 1939, p. 3; "In Re Pan American Day, Apr. 14, 1939: Resolution of Endorsement," Board of Supervisors, Mar. 21, 1939, Minute Book No. 249, pp. 149-150, LACoA.

28 Board of Supervisors, March 21, 1939, Minute Book No. 249, LACoA, pp. 156-157.

29 "Mexicans Assail L.A. Supervisor: Brand Relief Ban Threat 'Un-American Because It Is Inhuman'," *PW*, Mar. 28, 1939, p. 3.

30 "Los Angeles, Sede del Congreso Mexicano," *LO*, Mar. 12, 1939, p. 3.

31 Frank López interview.

32 Josephina Barbaoa Fierro (de Bright) OHI 1982, LA&RC, SFSU; "Las Mañanitas," *Black & White* 1:1 (June 1939): 14-15; Patrick McGilligan and Paul Buhle, *Tender Comrades: A Backstory of the Blacklist* (New York: St. Martin's Press, 1997), pp. 128-154; Vicki L. Ruiz, "Una Mujer sin Fronteras."

33 Letter, Stanley Mosk to author, July 20, 2000.

34 "Candidate's Statement by Gilbert L. Olson" and "Democratic Platform," *The Democratic Leader*, Primary Election, 1938, California Room, CSL.

35 Description of AB 2839, in *California Legislature, Fifty-Third Session, 1939, Final Calendar of Legislative Business* (Sacramento: CSPO), p. 657. The aforementioned bills are AB 150 and AB 1835.

36 Augustus Hawkins interview, June 28, 1998, June 6, 1999; Chapter 643, Statutes of California, 1939, CSA.

37 SB 40, as amended, in Senate Bills, 1939, CSLL; *Journal of the Senate,* 53rd Sess., Legislature of the State of California, 1939, p. 1179; *Journal of the Assembly*, 53rd Sess., Legislature of the State of California, 1939, p. 3168-9; García, *Mexican Americans*, pp. 159-160; Gómez-Quiñones, *Roots of Chicano Politics,* p. 386.

38 "Oust Radicals From Cal Relief Jobs As Demos Bolt Olson: See Grand Jury Probe of State Offices, Depts," LAEH&E, Mar. 31, 1939, p. A-16.

39 James Gregory, *American Exodus: The Dust Bowl Migration and Okie Culture in California* (New York: Oxford University Press, 1989), p. 98.

40 Gov. Proclamation, MF2:4(13), CSA; Gov. Olson, Race Relations Day, Golden Gate International Exposition, San Francisco, July 8, 1939, b. 6, f. 2, Olson Papers.

41 *IVP*, May 23-May 31, 1939; "Imperial Fair Board Denies Meeting for Labor League," *SB*, May 25, 1939, p. 22; "Olson Move Opens Imperial Fair Site To Labor League," *SB*, May 27, 1939, p. 3; Program, LNPL, LA County: Labor Day Unity Picnic, L.A. Labor Papers.

42 Denning, *The Cultural Front*, pp. 261, 269; Weber, *Dark Sweat, White Gold*, pp. 180-199.

43 "Spanish Speaking People's Congress," *UCAPAWA News*, Oct. 1939, p. 16.

44 LaRue McCormick, OHI 1976, ROHO, UCB; b. 21, f. Scrapbook, Quevedo Papers; b. 2, f. 8 and 9, Gallagher Papers.

45 "Autopsy Surgeon Finds Body of Hanged Boy Unmarked: Committee Investigating Whittier School Tragedy Will Make Report to Governor," *LAT*, Nov. 10, 1939.

46 Letter, Gallagher to Olson, Nov. 21, 1939 with attached, "Report of Committee Appointed by Governor Culbert L. Olson to Inquire into the Cause of the Death of Benjamin Moreno at the Whittier State School," b. 2, f. 8, Gallagher Papers.

47 Letter, M. Stanley Mosk, Executive Secretary, Governor's Office, to Hon. Harry B. Riley, State Controller, et al., Oct. 19, 1939, Olson, Appointments, General, F3674:1493, Governor's Papers, Culbert Olson, CSA; Ad, "Hon. A. P. (Tony) Entenza Says," *California Jewish Voice*, May 2, 1935, p. 2.

48 "Spanish to Vote for Retirement Warrants," n.p., Oct. 28, 1939, b. 21, f. Scrapbook, Quevedo Papers.

49 Burke, *Olson's New Deal for California*, pp. 107-112; Starr, *Endangered Dreams*, pp. 197-222.

50 "Spanish Speaking People's Congress," *UCAPAWA News*, Oct. 1939, p. 16. The new name is reflected on the stationary in Letter, Fierro de Bright to Ford, Sept. 1, 1939, b. 75, f. B IV 5 idd (5), Ford Papers.

51 B. 13, f. 9, Galarza Papers; Sánchez, *Becoming Mexican American*, discusses the "shift in tone" of the resolutions but downplays its significance by stating there "more immediate concerns for the Latino delegates" (p. 245-246). He and most Chicano historians emphasize the ideological breadth within the coalition and date the group's decline to World War II related developments (p. 249).

52 Resolutions, "Digest of Proceedings, First National Congress," b. 13, f. 9, Galarza Papers.

53 Statement of Vote, CSA; Klehr, *The Heyday of American Communism*, pp. 270-273; Minutes, LA CIO Council, April 5, 1940, p. 1, L.A. Labor Papers. For Patterson quotes, see "Ellis Patterson Not Qualified For U.S. Senate," *LAC*, May 24, 1946, p. 1.

54 Letter, McWilliams to Olson, March 25, 1940, b. 1, f. 1, Olson Papers; Burke, *Olson's New Deal for California*, pp. 141-142; Majka and Majka, *Farm Workers, Agribusiness, and the State*, p. 121, b. 13, f. 9, Galarza Papers; Delegate lists in Statement of Vote, May 7, 1940, CSA.

55 DNC Papers, Misc. Papers 1932-1948, f. List of Delegates to Democratic Convention-1940, FDR Library; Statement of the Vote, May 7, 1940, CSA.

56 García, *Mexican Americans*, pp. 157-158.

57 Ibid., p. 125.

58 Email, Jaime González Monroy to author, April 23, 2002.

59 Henry and Stina Santiestevan interview; *Yearbook*, 1939, Occidental College. A similar frustration was expressed by progressive liberals. See Winter Scobie, *Center Stage: Helen Gahagan Douglas, A Life* (New Brunswick, N.J.: Rutgers University Press, 1995), pp. 105-110.

60 "Special Bulletin, Preparation for the Second Congress of Spanish Speaking People in California," b. 13, f. 9, Galarza Papers.

CHAPTER 2
EDUARDO QUEVEDO AND THE SEARCH FOR A WAR-TIME VOICE

1   A. de Hoyos, "The Down of Prosperity," n.d., n.p., b. 21, f. Scrapbook, Quevedo Papers.

2   Sandy Esters, questionnaire, Boyle Heights Project, 1991, Jewish Historical Society of Southern California.

3   Archie Green interview, Oct. 30, 2004.

4   Stanley Bunyan interview, July 6, 1996; Ralph Poblano interview, Oct. 17, 1994; Hope Mendoza Schechter interview, Sept. 3, 1994; Margarita Durán Méndez interview, Mar. 11, 1995; Tony Ríos interview, 1994-1997; Deborah Dash Moore, *To the Golden Cities*, p. 191; David P. Shuldiner, *Of Moses and Marx: Folk Ideology and Folk History in the Jewish Labor Movement* (Westport, Conn.: Bergin & Garvey, 1999), pp. 147-154; Max Vorspan and Lloyd P. Gartner, *History of the Jews of Los Angeles* (San Marino, Calif.: The Huntington Library, 1970), pp. 242-243.

5   "Eduardo Quevedo Speaks his Mind," *La Pressa de Hoy*, b. 21, f. Scrapbook, Quevedo Papers.

6   B. 21, f. Scrapbook, Quevedo Papers.

7   Candidate's Affidavit of Receipts & Expenses, 52nd Assembly District, Primary, 1940, and Statement of the Vote, 1940, CSA; "The Eastside Journal Recommends," *ESJ*, Aug. 22, 1940, p. 1; "Organized Labor's Official Ticket," *LAC*, Aug. 23, 1940, p. 1; b. 21, f. Scrapbook, Quevedo Papers.

8   Executive Appointments, Governor's Office (Olson), F3680-10, CSA.

9   Members of County Central Committee, Democratic Party, 1940, LACRV.

10 Program, Mass Meeting, Sept. 28, 1940, in HAW Speech, 9-28-40, Wallace Papers; Louis H. Bean, Frederick Mosteller, and Frederick Williams, "Nationalities and 1944," b. 41, f. Nationalities and 1944, Louis H. Bean Collection, FDR Library; Culver and Hyde, *American Dreamer*, pp. 247-251; William E. Leuchtenburg, *Franklin D. Roosevelt and the New Deal, 1932-1940* (New York: Harper & Row, 1963), p. 317; Allan M. Winkler, *Home Front U.S.A.: America During World War II*, 2nd ed. (Wheeling, IL: Harlan Davidson, 2000), p. 89.

11 Address by Governor Olson, Aug. 24, 1942, b. 5, f. 2, Olson Papers; Starr, *Endangered Dreams*, p. 211.

12 "Veterans, Mexican Voters Endorse Al Waxman for Council," *ESJ*, Mar. 20, 1941, 1; "Public Invited To Free Rallies," *ESJ*, March 27, 1941, p. 1.

13 Richard Ibañez interview, July 19, 1997; California Secretary of State, *Executive Records*, p. 287, F3689:9, CSA.

14 Augustus Hawkins interview; Letter, Olson to Quevedo, July 17, 1941, b. 1, f. 9, Quevedo Papers.

15 Armando M. Rodríguez interview, Apr. 6, 2003; California Secretary of State, Executive Records, F3680:9, p. 397, CSA; "Molina," *The Martindale-Hubbell Law Dictionary*, 1942, p. 70.

16 James Daugherty interview, Feb. 11, 1995.

17 Sánchez, *Becoming Mexican American*, p. 249. For civil rights activities of the Latino left, El Congreso, and the CIO Council, see Luis Leobardo Arroyo, "Chicano Participation in Organized Labor: The CIO in Los Angeles, 1938-50, An Extended Research Note, " *Aztlan* 6:2, pp. 280-284.

18 "We Do Our Share," *MV*, Summer 1941, p. 3.

19 Hope Mendoza Schechter interview; Sherna Berger Gluck, *Rosie The Riveter Revisited: Women, the War and Social Change* (New York: Meridian, 1987), p. 74.

20 Winkler, *Home Front U.S.A.*, p. 75.

21 "Discrimination—And Us," *MV*, Spring 1942; Sánchez, *Becoming Mexican American,* pp. 255-264.

22 Morin, *Among The Valiant*, pp. 24-25; Permanent Display and Memorial, U.S.S. Arizona Memorial, Honolulu, Hawaii.

23 "Condena El Prejuicio Racial Aqui," in Apr. 8, 1942, in b. 21, f. Scrapbook, Quevedo Papers.

24 Vicki L. Ruiz, "Una Mujer sin Fronteras: Luisa Moreno and Latina Labor Activism," *PHR* 73:1 (Feb. 2004): 14-16.

25 "E. Quevedo and F. Rubio Drafted as Candidates To Assembly Districts," *Aristo News*, May 30, 1942, b. 21, f. Scrapbook, Quevedo Papers.

26 B. 21, f. Scrapbook, Quevedo Papers.

27 Augustus Hawkins interview; b. 1, f. 3, Ruiz Papers; b. 1, f. 10, and b. 2, f. 3 & 5, and b. 21, f. Scrapbook, Quevedo Papers.

28 Bert Corona interview, Aug. 9, 2000.

29 B. 1, f. 10, Quevedo Papers.

30 Address by Governor Olson, August 24, 1942, b. 5, f. 2, Olson Papers.

31 "Mexico Cabinet Chief Arrives for Celebration: Secretary of Interior to Aid Independence Day Observance," *LAT*, Sept. 15, 1942, p. A-1.

32 Editorial, "Mexican Independence Day Significant," *LAT*, Sept. 15, 1942, p. 4.

33 "Leaders of Two Nations Join in Hailing Mexico's Freedom: Record Breaking Fete Here Featured by Military Parade," *LAT*, Sept. 17, 1942, p. 1; Photo essay, "Los Angeles Mexican Independence Day Celebrates Watch Parade," *LAT*, Sept. 17, 1942, p. D.

34 Francis J. Weber, *Century of Fulfillment: The Roman Catholic Church in Southern California, 1840-1947* (Mission Mills, Calif.: The Archival Center, 1990), pp. 481-496; Francis J. Weber, "Irish-Born Champion of the Mexican-Americans," CHSQ 49 (Sept. 1970): 233-249; "Mexican Labor Leading Topic at Los Angeles Conference: Need of Organization Stressed by Bishop Cantwell at C.C.I.P. Meeting," *NCWC Review*, May 1930, p. 18, NCWC, Social Action Dept, Catholic Conference on Industrial Relations, b. 35, f. Los Angeles, Mar. 1930, A&M, CUA.

35 HAW Speech, 9-16-42, Wallace Papers.

36 "Leaders of Two Nations Join in Hailing Mexico's Freedom: Record Breaking Fete Here Featured by Military Parade," *LAT*, Sept. 17, 1942, p. A-1.

37 Wallace's secretary alludes to the political overlay in a letter to Olson, b. 4, f. 3, Olson Papers.

38 John Morton Blum, ed., *The Price of Vision: the Diary of Henry Wallace, 1942-1946* (Boston: Houghton Mifflin, 1973), pp. 116-117.

39 B. 1, f. 10, Quevedo Papers.

40 Hill, *Dancing Bear*, p. 98.

41 Burke, *Olson's New Deal for California*, pp. 207-229; Carrillo, *The California I Love*; Harvey, *Earl Warren*, p. 37; Starr, *Embattled Dreams*, pp. 245-250, 263.

42 Jaime González Monroy interview.

43 LaRue McCormick Oral History, p. 69; Press telegram, Tom Cullen to People's World, October 22, [1942], b. 1, f. 1, Sleepy Lagoon Papers, Special Collections, UCLA; b. 21, f. S, Quevedo Papers; Denning, *The Cultural Front*, pp. 397-402.

44 Josephina Barbaoa Fierro [de Bright], taped interviewed, D. Obserwiser, July 1982, LA&RC, SFSU.

45 Letter, Philip M. Connelly to Abe Isserman, Mar. 8, 1943, and Letter, Philip M. Connelly to Alice Greenfield, May 6, 1944, b. 11, f. Sleepy Lagoon Case: Correspondence, 1942-1945, L.A. Labor Papers.

46 Alice Greenfield McGrath interview, Apr. 14, 1995; Carey McWilliams, Oral History Interview, Joel Gardner in 1978, pp. 149-150, OHP, UCLA; Vicki L. Ruiz, "Una Mujer sin Fronteras," p. 17; Sleepy Lagoon Papers, UCLA.

47 Alice Greenfield McGrath interview.

48 Ford, *Thirty Explosive Years in Los Angeles County*, p. 135; Gutiérrez, *Walls Mirrors,* pp. 124-125; Pagáa, *Murder at the Sleepy Lagoon*.

49 George P. Sotelo interview, Feb. 10, 1996.

50 Letter, Quevedo to Elmer Davis, n.d., b. 1, f. 11, Quevedo Papers.

51 Letter, Ford to Rockefeller, June 9, 1943, b. 75, f. B IV 5 i dd, Ford Papers.

52 "First Lady Traces Zoot Riots to Discrimination," *LAT*, June 17, 1943, p. A.

53 "Mrs. Roosevelt Challenged on Zoot Statement," *LAT*, June 18, 1943, p. A; Editorial, "Mrs. Roosevelt Blindly Stirs Race Discord," *LAT*, June 18, 1943, Part II, p. 4.

54 Jaime González Monroy interview.

55 Alan Cranston interview, Feb. 20, 1996.

56 Ibid.

57 Ibid. See also, Justin Hart, "Making Democracy Safe for the World: Race, Propaganda, and the Transformation of U.S. Foreign Policy During World War II," *PHR* 73:1 (Feb. 2004): 49-84.

58 "2 Civic Groups to Fight Nazi Propaganda: Far-Reaching Study of Youth Gang Wars Will Be Made; Units Organize Tomorrow," and photo caption, O'Dwyer File, Clippings, Special Collections, University of Southern California.

59 List of Groups Working on Latin-American Situation," b. 75, f. B IV 5 i dd (9), Ford Papers.

60 Carey McWilliams Oral History, pp. 158-159; Earl Warren, OHI, 1971, 1972, Amelia R. Fry for the ROHO, UCB, pp. 241, 244; Ed Cray, *Chief Justice: A Biography of Earl Warren* (New York: Simon & Schuster, 1997), p. 148; Starr, *Embattled Dreams,* p. 111.

61 "700 Hear Mexican Youth Problem Stressed at Meet," *SJM*, June 26, 1944.

62 "Spanish-Americans Ask Fair Play, Says Chavez," *LAT*, Oct. 19, 1944, p. 12.

63 Ibid; "El Jueves Sera El Homenaje A Dennis Chavez: Numerosos artistas de Hollywood estarán presentes," *LO*, Oct. 17, 1944, p. 1; b. 2, f. 3, Quevedo Papers.

64 B. 2, f. 3, Eduardo Quevedo Papers; Welcoming Committee for Senator Chavez," b. 75, f. B IV 5 i dd (10), Ford Papers.

65 Letter, Sheridan Downey to Oscar R. Fuss, July 8, 1942, b. 11, f. Sleepy Lagoon Case: Correspondence, 1942-1945, L.A. Labor Papers.

66 Letter, Matthew Torok, Federation of Language Groups, to Ruiz, Oct. 6, 1944, and Oct. 14, 1944, and text of Ruiz broadcast, in b. 16, f. 2, Ruiz Papers.

67 *DN, LO*, and *LAT*, October 17-21, 1944; b. 2, f. 3, Quevedo Papers.

68 "Chavez Hits Race, Religious Discrimination in America," *DN*, Oct. 20, 1944, p. 3.

69 [Quevedo,] "Spanish Americans," [n.d.,] b. 16, f. 2, Ruiz Papers.

70 Ibid.

71 Leaflet, "Don't Mess It Up Now, Buddy!" FEPC, Pamphlet File, SCLSSR.

72 B. 16, b. 3, Ruiz Papers; *Assembly Final History*, 1945 (Sacramento: State of Calif.), p. 401; *Assembly Journal* (Sacramento: State of Calif.), May 3, 1945, 2615.

73 "House Okehs Repeal of School Segregation Law," *SB*, Apr. 11, 1947, p. 4; "Separate Schools Bill I Given Approval," *SB*, June 4, 1947, p. 4; Governor's Office, MF3:1(43), CSA; Gonzalez, *Chicano Education in the Era of Segregation*, pp. 28, 147-155.

74 Dionicio Morales interview, July 29, 2003.

75 Brochure, "Elect Eduardo Quevedo for Councilman, 9th District," b. 2, f. 6, and b. 21, f. Scrapbook, Quevedo Papers.

76 *Fair Employment Practices Act: Hearings before a Subcommittee of the Committee on Education and Labor, United States Senate, on S. 101 and S. 459* (Washington, DC: GPO, 1945).

77 Saul E. Bronder, *Social Justice and Church Authority: The Public Life of Archbishop Robert E. Lucy* (Philadelphia: Temple University Press, 1982); Privett, *The U.S. Catholic Church and Its Hispanic Members*; NCWC/USCC, b. 90, f. Social Action: Spanish Speaking, 1944, and 1945, A&M, CUA.

78 Emanuel Muravchik interview, Sept. 29, 2002; Zane Meckler interview, Mar. 29 and Apr. 5, 1996; "Jewish labor Maps Campaign Against Bigotry," *LAT*, July 17, 1946, Part II, p.3; *LAC*, Sept.-Nov., 1946; Taft, *Labor Politics American Style*, pp. 177-178.

CHAPTER 3

EDWARD ROYBAL & THE BIRTH OF THE COMMUNITY SERVICES ORGANIZATION

1 Harvey, *Earl Warren*, p. 142.

2 Gayle B. Montgomery and James W. Johnson, *One Step From the White House: The Rise and Fall of Senator William Knowland* (Berkeley: University of California Press, 1998), pp. 52-63.

3 Philip Newman interview, June 22, 1997; *LO*, Sept.-Nov. 1946, part. "Hablo James Roosevelt En El Shrine," *LO*, Oct. 18, 1946, p.1; "Wallace Due Tomorrow," *LAEH&E*, Sept. 14, 1942, p. A-2.

4 Roger Johnson interview. Confirmed by Philip Newman interview; Edward Roybal interview, Nov. 2, 1981, and Mar. 10, 1995.

5 Edward Roybal interview; "Earl Robinson to Emcee Pan-American Festival," *CE*, Jan. 25, 1945, p. 12; Horwitt, *Let Them Call Me Rebel*, pp. 223-225; Members of County Central Committees, May 1944, LACRV; b. 2, f. 3, Quevedo Papers.

6	Roger Johnson interview; Philip Newman interview; Edward Roybal interview; Guzman, *The Political Socialization*, p. 170.

7	Roger Johnson interview.

8	Jaime González Monroy interview; Anthony Macías, "Bringing Music to the People: Race, Urban Culture, and Municipal Politics in Postwar Los Angeles," *AQ* 56:3 (Sept. 2004), p. 702.

9	Tony Ríos interview; "Anthony Ríos Dies; Built Latino Political Power," *LAT*, May 22, 1999, p. B1.

10	"Welcoming Committee for Senator Chavez," Oct. 11, 1944, b. 75, f. B IV 5 i dd (10), Ford Papers; Quevedo, "Candidate's Affidavit of Receipts and Expenditures for Primary Election," City Council, Apr. 3, 1945, b. 2, f. 3, and Seez-It-All, "Nothing Sacred," Aristo, [1945], b. 21, f. Scrapbook, Quevedo Papers; Waxman, "Column Left: Strictly Politics," *ESJ*, Feb. 2, 1947, p. 1; "Shalmo Defeat 'Is Main Issue' in Council Race," *PW*, Feb. 19, 1947, p. 3.

11	Letter, James H. Burford, Director of Political Action, to Sir and Brother, Jan. 12, 1947, with attached minutes, LA CIO PAC Committee, Dec. 19, 1946, b. D, f. CIO PAC-LA Council, L&A, ILWU.

12	"Christensen Changes Mind; Will Not Leave 'His People,'" *ESJ*, Jan. 1, 1947, p. 1; "Election Rally Set for Jan. 31," *PW*, Jan. 2, 1947, p. 3; "3 Labor Men Among 107 Los Angeles Candidates," *PW*, Feb. 17, 1947, p. 3; "Shalmo Defeat 'Is Main Issue' in Council Race," *PW*, Feb. 19, 1947, p. 3; "UAFL April Endorsements," *LAC*, Apr. 7, 1947, p. 1; "Campaign for Christensen Goes Into High Gear," *ESS*, March 14, 1947, p. 1; "United AFL Okays Five Progressives," *PW*, March 10, 1947, p. 3; "We Recommend These Candidates," *CE*, Mar. 27, 1947, p. 1; *PCAction*, June 1947, p. 3, Edward Mosk Clippings, Independent Progressive Party Papers, SCLSSR.

13	Letter, Dorothy Healey to author, Mar. 10, 1995.

14	Filmore Jaffe interview, Mar. 7, 1997; Hope Mendoza Schechter interview; *ESJ*, Mar. 1947; Members of Democratic County Central Committee, LACRV; "City Council Choices Made," *LAT*, Mar. 30, 1947, Part II, p. 2; 1946 Gubernatorial Campaign Files, Warren for Governor Committee, Warren Papers.

15	For Latino troop strength, see Department of Defense, *Hispanics in America's Defense* (Washington, DC: GPO, 1990). For a veteran's view, see "Private Citizens, First Class," in Morin, *Among The Valiant*, pp. 277-280.

16	Roger Johnson interview; Edward Roybal interview.

17	"Labor En Pro De Eduardo Roybal," and ad, "Deposite Su Voto Por Roybal, Candidato Mexicano," *El Pueblo*, Mar. 29, 1947, in author's collection; Stanley Bunyan interview; Roger Johnson interview; Filmore Jaffe interview; Philip Newman interview; Tony Ríos interview; Edward Roybal interview.

18	"Daily News Endorsements Made in City Council Elections on April 1," *DN*, Mar. 26, 1947, p. 1; "City Council Choices Made," *LAT*, Mar. 30, 1947, Part II, p. 2.

19	Tabulation of Returns, Council District 9, May 27, 1947, LACiA.

20	Tony Ríos interview.

21	CPO Ticket, Fiesta Dance, in author's files.

22	Roger Johnson interview; Fred Ross, unpublished ms., untitled, p. 29, b. 21, f. 8, Ross Papers.

23	Horwitt, *Let Them Call Me Rebel*, pp. 225-227; b. 8, f. 1, Ross Papers, Stanford. Quote from Ross, untitled ms., p. 7, b. 21, f. 9, Ross Papers.

24 Roger Johnson interview.

25 Horwitt, *Let Them Call Me Rebel*, pp. 225-227.

26 B. 8, f. 1, Ross Papers; Acuña, *Occupied America,* pp. 285-286; Garcia, *World of Its Own.*

27 Ross, untitled document, p. 3, b. 5, f. 12, Ross Papers.

28 Margarita Durán interview.

29 Tony Ríos interview.

30 Ruiz, *Cannery Women, Cannery Lives* and *From Out of the Shadows.*

31 Margarita Durán interview; Hope Mendoza Schechter interview.

32 Margaret Rose, "Gender and Civic Action in Mexican American Barrios in California: The Community Services Organization, 1947-1962," in Meyerowitz, ed., *Not June Cleaver*, pp. 177-200; Charlotte Negrete White, "Women in the Political Process: The Community Services Organization," paper at Claremont College, Dec. 5, 1994, provided to author by Margarita Durán Méndez.

33 Finks, *The Radical Vision of Saul Alinsky*, pp. 40-41; Fred Ross, unpublished ms., untitled, p. 15, b. 21, f. 8, Ross Papers. CPO was too close to CP (or Communist Party), according to Acuña, *Occupied America*, p. 286.

34 Tony Ríos interview.

35 Jaime González Monroy interview.

36 Horwitt, *Let Them Call Me Rebel.*

37 Jaime González Monroy interview; Henry Nava interview, Feb. 9, 1995; Tony Ríos interview; Edward Roybal interview; Margarita Durán Méndez interview.

38 B. 2, f. 1, Ross Papers; Richard Ibañez interview.

39 William Barry interview, Nov. 2, 1994; James Méndez interview; Tony Ríos interview.

40 William Barry interview; B. 2, f. 1, Ross Papers.

41 Scott Greer, "The Participation of Ethnic Minorities in the Labor Unions of Los Angeles County," Ph.D. diss., UCLA, 1952, pp. 146-150, 301-302.

42 Cass Alvin interview; William Barry interview; Abe Levy interview; James Méndez interview; Tony Ríos interview; Hope Mendoza Schechter interview.

43 Louis B. Perry and Richard S. Perry, *A History of the Los Angeles Labor Movement, 1911-1941* (Berkeley: University of California Press, 1963), p. 537.

44 Cass Alvin interview, May 6, June 27, 1995; Tony Ríos interview; Gomez-Quiñones, *Mexican American Labor,* p. 188.

45 Gomez-Quiñones, *Mexican American Labor*, p. 180. He and others have been critical of the union's commitment to Latinas. See John Laslett and Mary Tyler, *The ILGWU In Los Angeles, 1907-1988* (Inglewood, Calif.: Ten Star Press, 1989).

46 Abe Levy interview, May 31, 1996.

47 B. 2, f. 1, Ross Papers.

48 Hope Mendoza Schechter interview.

49 Konstantin Sparkuhl interview, May 31, 1997; Tony Ríos interview; Guzman, *The Political Socialization*, p. 140.

50 Henry Nava interview.

51 Hope Mendoza Schechter interview.

52 James Méndez interview.

53 Eliseo Carrillo interview, Aug. 4, 2001.

54 "Two Parades Mark Tribute on Labor Day," *LAT*, Sept. 2, 1947, p. 1; "Gigantic Labor Day Parade Hailed by Thousands in Downtown Area," *LAT*, Sept. 2, 1947, p. 3; "Public Welfare Duties of Labor Told by Priest," *LAT*, Sept. 2, 1947, Part II, p. 12.

55 Joseph Kearney interview, Jan. 23, 1995.

56 William Barry interview; Abe Levy interview; Tony Ríos interview.

57 William Barry interview.

58 Ralph Poblano Interview.

59 B. 2, f. 1, Ross Papers.

60 Henry Nava interview; Hope Mendoza Schechter interview.

61 Fred Ross, unpublished ms., untitled, pp. 24-28, b. 21, f. 8, Ross Papers.

62 Ibid.

63 Ibid.

64 Henry Nava interview.

65 Edward Roybal interview.

66 James Méndez interview; Henry Nava interview; Hope Mendoza Schechter interview; CSO, "Across The River," [p. 5], author's files; "X-Ray Used In Registration of Voters and Tests for TB," *DN*, Mar. 6, 1948, p. 2; Beatrice W. Griffith, "Viva Roybal—Viva America, *CG*, Autumn, 1949, p. 65.

67 Tony Ríos interview.

68 Margarita Durán Méndez interview.

69 Henry Nava interview.

70 Hope Mendoza Schechter interview.

71 "Spanish-Speaking Group Spurs Vote Registration," *LAT*, Mar. 15, 1948; "Latin Area Vote Increased," *DN*, Apr. 28, 1948; "Latin Vote Registration Doubled, Group Announces," *Belvedere Citizen*, Apr. 30, 1948, p. 1; Margaret Rose, "Gender and Civic Action in Mexican American Barrios in California," pp. 190-191.

72 Frank López interview; Jim Daugherty interview; Richard Ibañez Interview; Stanley Bunyan interview; Letter, Dorothy Healey to author, Mar. 10, 1995.

73 Tony Ríos interview.

74 Frank López interview; Chavez, Personal Information Sheet for Candidates' Committee of the LA CIO PAC, March 20, 1948, Candidates Endorsed by PAC, Mar.-Jul. 1948, L.A. Labor Papers; *Report on the Voting Record of the 80ᵗʰ Congress (first half) and the 1947 Session of the California Legislature* (Los Angeles: California Legislative Conference), b. 5, f. 16, CA CIO Council, SCLSSR; Minutes, NCPAC Office, January 28, 1946, b. 9, f. LA CIO Council-PAC, 1946-1949, L.A. Labor Papers; LA CIO Council Committees: PAC, Blank Petitions, etc., Oct.-Dec. 1948, L.A. Labor Papers; *ESJ*, Jan.-June, 1948; Statement of Vote, June 1946, and June 1948, CSA.

75 John Allard interview.

76 Richard Ibañez interview; "Justice For All," Elect Ibañez Judge, LA CIO Council Committees: PAC, 1948 State Primary Elections, L.A. Labor Papers; Palm card, "Ibanez for Superior Court Judge," author's files.

77 "CIO Charges Rump Bloc Endorses Anti-labor Men, *LH*, May 11, 1948, p. 2.

78 *LO,* May 1-10, 1948; "Henry Wallace Talks at Lincoln Stadium," *Lincoln Heights Bulletin-News*, May 13, 1948, p. 1; Zachary Karabell, *The Last Campaign: How Harry Truman Won the 1948 Election* (New York: Vintage, 2000), p. 124.

79 HAW Speech, May 16, 1948, Wallace Papers; "Candidate Makes Appeal to Mexican-Americans," *LAT*, May 17, 1948, p. 2.

80 Henry A. Wallace, "California and the New Party," *NR*, June 7, 1948, p. 12.

81 Edward Roybal interview

82 Marion Graff interview, Aug. 28, 2001.

83 Henry Nava interview; Hope Mendoza Schechter interview; Tony Ríos interview.

84 CSO, "Attention Voters, We Are 16,000 Strong," b. 15, f. Mexican Groups, 1948, JCRC Papers.

85 Editorial, "Process of Democracy," *DN*, June 9, 1948, p. 48.

86 Kenneth C. Burt, "Boyle Heights: Unsung Heroes," *ESS*, Sept. 20, 2001; "Program of the Industrial Areas Foundation-LA CSO," [1949], b. 5, f. 11, Ross Papers.

87 Memo, Miley to Ford, Sept. 16, 1948, b. 75, f. B 5 I dd (14), Ford Papers.

88 Ibid.

89 Telegram, Ben Shapiro, et al., to Fred Herzberg, b. 10, f. CSO-1948, JCRC Papers; Florence D. Mischel, ed., *Palimpsest: An Oral History of Seniel Lucien Ostrow* (Malibu, Calif.: Clef Press, 1985), pp. 68-69.

90 B. 10, f. CSO, 1948-1949, and b. 5, f. CSO-1949-1950, JCRC Papers; Memo, Miley to Ford, Sept. 29, 1948, b. 75, f. B 5 I dd (14), Ford Papers.

91 Memos, Mr. Miley to Mr. Ford, Sept. 16, 29, 1948, 1948, b. 75, f. B IV 5 i dd (14), Ford Papers; b. 10, f. CSO 1948, JCRC Papers; b. 4, f. 31, USWA Civil Rights Dept., and b. 7., f. 8, USA District 38, Civic Unity (1953), b. 7, f. 8, USWA Papers.

92 Henry Nava interview; Tony Ríos interview. FBI records on CSO obtained by the author under the Freedom of Information Act.

93 "Wallace Calls for Defeat of Downey," *PW*, May 19, 1948, p. 3; "S.F. Accords An Ovation to Wallace," *PW*, May 20, 1948, p. 3; Local 56 files, L&ILWU.

94 Sam Salazar interview, Jan. 10, 2006; "Wallace Blasts U.S. Policy as Step to War," *SDU*, May 20, 1948, p. 1.

95 Henry Santiestevan interview.

96 "Gay American Day Program Set For Today," *SJM*, May 16, 1948, p. 1.

97 Jaime González Monroy interview.

98 Statement of the Vote, CSA.

CHAPTER 4

ELECTING "ONE OF OUR OWN"

1 "Elect Henry Nava Head of Community Services Organization," *BC*, Feb. 4, 1949. The officers who guided CSO through its first year-and-a-half declined to run again, Ríos recalled, out of exhaustion and a desire to develop new leaders. This also enabled them to focus on Roybal's campaign.

2 Captioned photo, *SL*, Sept. 1949, p. 10.

3 Tony Ros interview; Roger Johnson interview; Edward Roybal interview; Lucille Roybal Allard interview, May 31, 1997.

4 Roger Johnson interview; James Méndez interview; Henry Nava interview; Tony Ríos interview; Edward Roybal interview; Hope Mendoza Schechter interview.

5 Paul Schrade interview, Jan. 31, 1997; James Méndez interview; Cass Alvin interview.

6   Letter, Joyce L. Kornbluh to author, Aug. 27, 1996.
7   Henry and Santiestevan interview.
8   James Méndez interview.
9   "Eduardo Quevedo, A Biographical Presentation," Mar. 8, 1964, b. 1, f. 3, Quevedo Papers.
10 Tony Ríos interview.
11 "City Council Favors Arms Aid to Israel," *Hollywood Citizen-News*, May 26, 1948, p. 6.
12 "Jewish, Mexican Americans Join in Celebration," *ESS*, Feb. 28, 1947.
13 Abe Levy interview.
14 Sam Margolis interview, Sept. 27, 1997.
15 Ed Buzin interview, Sept. 3, 1997.
16 Dave Fishman interview, Jan. 29, 1997.
17 Filmore Jaffe interview; Philip Newman interview; Tony Ríos interview.
18 Philip Newman interview.
19 Edward Roybal interview.
20 Quoted in Charlotte Negrete White, "Women in the Political Process: The Community Services Organization," paper at Claremont College, Dec. 5, 1994.
21 Leftists vied to define their relations with the Latino community. According to Ríos, the Trotskyite Socialist Workers Party aligned itself with Roybal prior to the Communist Party. For the SWP's perspective on CSO and Roybal, see *Internal Bulletin*, Los Angeles, Jan. 1949, pp. 4-6, Holt Labor Library, San Francisco; "Roybal Victory Shows L.A. Minorities' Power," *The Militant*, June 30, 1949.
22 Tony Ríos interview; "Edward Elliot Withdraws for Christensen," *ESS*, Mar. 4, 1949, p. 1; b. 2131, f. 49, 2-candidates, LACiA.
23 B. 2131, f.49, 2-candidates, LACiA; Statement of Vote, CSA.
24 "Edward Elliot Withdraws for Christensen" *ESS*, Mar. 4, 1949, p. 1; "Christensen Has Always Supported Labor in Council," *ESS*, March 25, 1949, p. 1; "Voter League OKs Candidates for April 5 Ballot," *LAC*, March 4, 1949, p. 1; *ESS*, 1947-1949; Information Sheet, Los Angeles Building and Construction Trades Council," n.d., b. 2, f. 29, Gallagher Papers.
25 Dorothy Healey claimed that the CP had told Christensen in 1947 that he should support a Mexican American in 1949, letter, Healey to author, Mar. 10, 1995.
26 "Hot Councilmanic Race Shaping Up in Ninth," *PW*, Jan. 12, 1949, p. 3.
27 John Allard interview; James Daugherty interview; Tony Ríos interview; Edward Roybal interview; letter, Dorothy Healey to author, Mar. 10, 1995.
28 "IPP Announces Support for Candidate," *ESS*, Mar. 18, 1949, p. 1.
29 Ismael Parra interview, Aug. 24,2001.
30 "L.A. Elections: CIO Council Supports Patterson, Bryant," *PW*, Mar. 21, 1949, p. 1.
31 Letter, John Allard to "Dear Sirs and Brothers," Mar. 19, 1949, 8/LA CIO Committees: PAC; blank petitions, 1949, L.A. Labor Papers, and b. G, f. LA CIO Council, L&A, ILWU.
32 "Roybal Wins City Council Race in L.A.," *LH*, June 14, 1949, p. 3.
33 Alan Bomser interview; Stan Bunyan interview; Dave Fishman interview; "City Elections," *The Craftsman*, Apr. 1949, p. 2, b. 2, f. 29, Gallagher Papers.
34 Letter, Dorothy Healey to author, Mar. 10, 1995.
35 Edward Roybal interview.

36 Roger Johnson interview; Tony Ríos interview; Edward Roybal; "Some lessons from the LA Councilmanic Elections," *PW*, May 9, 1949, p. 3.
37 Alice Greenfield McGrath interview.
38 "Christensen Endorsed By Labor League of Hollywood," *ESS*, Mar. 18, 1947, p. 1; "Hollywood Labor Group Backs Christensen," *Sentinel*, May 19, 1949, p. A4; "Voter League OKs Candidates For April 5 Polls," *LAC*, Mar. 4, 1949, p. 1.
39 Roy Brewer interview, Mar. 12, 1995; Stephen Vaughn, *Ronald Reagan In Hollywood: Movies and Politics* (New York: Cambridge University Press, 1994), p. 158.
40 Albert Johnson, Sr. interview, Dec. 31, 2000; "Form Group to Support Roybal," *ESJ*, Mar. 23, 1949, p. 11; "Candidates Qualifications Reviewed," *Sentinel*, Mar. 31, 1949, p. C7.
41 Gregory Payne and Scott Ratzan, *Tom Bradley: The Impossible Dream* (New York: PaperJacks, 1987), pp. 43-44.
42 "Form Group to Support Roybal," *ESJ*, Mar. 23, 1949, p. 11.
43 "Set Roybal Campaign Rally Here March 25," *ESJ*, Mar. 1949, p. 2.
44 Ad, "Let's Get Things Done," *ESJ*, Mar. 30, 1949, p. 10.
45 Connie Meza interview, Dec. 29, 2001.
46 Cass Alvin interview; Roger Johnson interview; Tony Ríos interview; Edward Roybal interview; Letter, Dorothy Healey to author, Mar. 10, 1995; Photo, *SL*, May 1949, p. 8; "Roybal Neighbors Assist Campaign," *ESJ*, Mar. 30, 1949, p. 9; Beatrice W. Griffith, "Viva Roybal—Viva America," *CG*, Autumn, 1949, p. 67.
47 "Daily News Choices," *DN*, Apr. 1, 1949, p. 2; "Few Voter Choices in Council Elections," *LAT*, Apr. 3, 1949, p. 1.
48 Tabulation of Returns, LACiA, with results in District 9 plotted on precinct map.
49 "Bowron To Speak At Euclid School," *ESJ*, May 25, 1949, p. 16; Fred Ross, unpublished ms., "Tony Ríos-Bloody Xmas," p. 17, b. 21, f. 9, Ross Papers.
50 "Some lessons from the LA Councilmanic Elections," *PW*, May 9, 1948, p. 3.
51 Rebecca Tuck interview, Sept. 27, 1997.
52 "Says Place to Protect Home, Liberty is in own Precinct," *DN*, May 24, 1949, Newspaper Clipping, 1949, Roybal Papers, CSULA.
53 de Graaf, el al., *Seeking El Dorado,* p. 329.
54 Tony Ríos interview; Henry Santiestevan interview; "Roybal Wins, 2-1, in L.A. Council Race," [CIO News], June 6, 1949; Roybal Newspaper Clippings, East Los Angeles Public Library.
55 "Roybal Campaigners Push 'Get Out The Vote, Activities," *PW*, May 31, 1949, p. 3; "Roybal Wins for L.A. Council," *PW*, June 2, 1949, p. 1.
56 Roger Johnson interview.
57 Minutes, JCRC, June 14, 1949, p. 2, in b. 10, f. CSO-1948-1949, JCRC Papers; "Roybal Wins, 2-1, in L.A. Council Race," [CIO News], June 6, 1949.
58 Roger Johnson interview; Tony Ríos interview; Minutes of the Staff Committee Meeting, July 5, 1949, b. 10, f. CSO, 1948-1949, JCRC Papers.
59 "Daily News Choices," *DN*, May 26, 1949, p. 2; "'Citizen' Endorsed Bowron For Mayor; Roybal For Council In 9th District," *BC*, May 27, 1949, p. 1.
60 Roger Johnson interview; Tony Ríos interview; "Roybal Race Highlights City Election," *LH*, May 17, 1949, p. 5; "Some lessons from the LA Councilmanic Elections," *PW*, May 9, 1949, p. 3.
61 Tony Ríos interview; Edward Roybal interview; Fred Ross, Jr. interview; Hope Mendoza Schechter interview.

62 "Tabulation of Returns, City Council District 9, City of Los Angeles, May 31, 1949," LACiA. See also Katherine Underwood, "Process and Politics: Multiracial Electoral Coalition Building and Representation in Los Angeles' Ninth District, 1949-1962," Ph.D. diss., UC, San Diego, 1992.

63 Tony Ríos Interview; CSO, "Highlights of the Past 20 Years," author's files; Minutes, JCRC, June 14, 1949, p. 2, in b. 10, f. CSO-1948-1949, JCRC Papers; Wilson, *The Amateur Democrat*, p. 286.

64 "Councilman Roybal Tells Local Group of CSO in His District," *LAS*, Oct. 27, 1949, Newspaper Clippings, 1949, Roybal Papers, CSULA; Beatrice W. Griffith, "Viva Roybal—Viva America," *CG*, Autumn, 1949, p. 67-68; Katherine Underwood, "Pioneering Minority Representation: Edward Roybal and the Los Angeles City Council, 1949-1962," *PHR* 66:3 (Aug. 1997): 408

65 "Councilman Starts Early Youth Probe," *DN*, n.d., Newspaper Clippings, Roybal Papers, CSULA; "Urge Community-Police Cooperation: Closer Ties Stressed to Avert Crime," *ESJ*, July 6, 1949, p. 1.

66 Chet Holifield, "Election of Roybal—Democracy at Work," *Cong. Rec.*, Aug. 9, 1949.

67 Ibid.

68 This theme was first postulated in Burt, "Latino Empowerment in Los Angeles: Postwar Dreams and Cold War Fears, 1958-1952," *Labor's Heritage* 8:1 (Summer 1996). Its interpretation differs from Margaret Rose's, "Gender and Civic Action in Mexican American Barrios in California: The Community Services Organization, 1947-1962," in Meyerowitz, ed., *Not June Cleaver,* pp. 177-200, that assumes the struggle of Latinas associated with the Communist Party influenced Mine-Mill were similar to that of Latinas in the Socialist Party influenced ILGWU.

69 "Roybal Takes Office," *CSO News*, July 6, 1949, p. 1, author's files.

CHAPTER 5
CIVIL RIGHTS AND COALITION POLITICS

1   Henry Nava interview.

2   Margaret Rose, "Gender and Civic Action in Mexican American Barrios in California: The Community Services Organization, 1947-1962," Meyerowitz, ed., *Not June Cleaver*, p. 179.

3   Max Mont, Weekly Report, August 7-12, 1949, author's files; b. 10, f. CEE 1948-1949, JCRC Papers.

4   Editorial, "Republicans Flunk Test," *DN*, Apr. 27, 1949, and "Warren Loses Inquiry on Racial Bans," *DN*, April 27, 1949, and "Fair Employment Practices Bill Loses in Committee," *DN*, May 12, 1949, in b. I-67, f. 3, JCRC Papers; Minutes, Program Planning Committee, June 13 and July 11, 1949, b. 5, f. 5, Ross Papers.

5   Healey and Isserman, *California Red*, pp. 112-113; Paul Jacobs, *Is Curly Jewish: A Political Self-Portrait Illuminating Three Turbulent Decades of Social Revolt, 1935-1965* (New York: Atheneum, 1965), pp. 184-188.

6   Editorial, "An FEP Ordinance," *BBM*, Sept. 2, 1949, p. 4; "Fight for FEP Ordinance in L.A., S.F. Gathers Steam," *PW*, Aug. 3, 1949, p. 3; Max Mont, Weekly Report, Aug.-Sept. 1949; Moore, *To the Golden Cities*, p. 222.

7   Don Parson, "'The Darling of the Town's Neo-Fascists': The Bombastic Political Career of Councilman Ed J. Davenport," *SCQ* 81:4 (Winter 1999): 467-505; "James Roosevelt Charged With 'Double-Crossing' His Party," *Merced Sun-Star*, Apr. 16,

1948; b. 10, f. CEE 1948-1949, JCRC Papers; Max Mont, Weekly Report, Aug. 7-19, 1949.

8   "City Council," *CE*, Aug. 11, 1949, p. 2.

9   "Grass Roots Support For FEPC," *CE*, Aug. 25, 1949, p. 18.

10 B. 10, f. CSO 1948-1949, JCRC Papers; [Ross] "Program of the Industrial Areas Foundation, Southern California Division," [1949,] b. 5, f. 11, Ross Papers. Quote from Minutes, Staff Committee, July 5, 1949, p. 2, b. 10, f. CSO.

11 B. 10, f. CSO 1948-1949, JCRC Papers; Minutes, CSO Program Planning Committee, Aug. 8, 1949, b. 5, f. 5, Ross Papers. One person stressed that the funds were necessary to ensure that Ross was present to help CSO "protect itself from being captured or exploited by Stalinists and Trotskyite elements," in memo, Bloom to Herzberg.

12 Edward Roybal interview; Tony Ríos interview; Horwitt, *Let Them Call Me Rebel*, p. 245; "Won't Sell to Mexicans, GI Developer Tells Roybal," *CE*, Sept. 8, 1949, p. 1; "Councilman Charges He was Victim of Minorities Ban," *DN*, Sept. 9, 1949, and "Roybal Refused Home Because of Race, Charges Real Estate Firms Here Are Discriminating," *ESS*, Sept. 7, 1949, Newspaper Clippings, 1949, Roybal Papers, CSULA.

13 Letter, Isaac Pacht, CEE, to Henry Nava, CSO, Aug. 18, 1949, with attachments, b. 5, f. 12, Ross Papers; "Write Your Council Representatives To Pass FEPC Resolution,"*BBM*, Sept. 2, 1949, p. 1; b. 10, f. CEE 1949-1950, JCRC Papers; Max Mont Weekly Reports, Aug. and Sept. 1949.

14 Letter, Fred Ross to Fred Herzberg, September 23, 1949, with attachment, b. 10, f. CSO 1948-1949, JCRC Papers; Fred Ross, Jr. interview; Tony Ríos interview.

15 Max Mont, Weekly Reports, Aug. and Sept. 1949; "Write Your Council Representatives To Pass FEPC Resolution," *BBM*, Sept. 2, 1949, p. 1.

16 "Big CIO Picnic," *The Beam*, USWA Local 2058, USWA Reel 855, James Thimmes Correspondence, Charles Smith, 1049, USWA Papers; Max Mont, Weekly Reports, Aug. and Sept. 1949.

17 Max Mont, Weekly Reports, Aug. and Sept. 1949.

18 Editorial, "The Council and FEPC," *LAT*, Sept. 23, 1949; Minutes, Greater LA CIO Council, October 4, 1949, b. 6, f. Local Industrial Council, Correspondence (1935-1955), Reel 1, Los Angeles, George Meany Center for Labor Studies.

19 Acuña, *A Community Under Siege*, pp. 29-30; Don Parson, "'The Darling of the Town's Neo-Fascists'"; Newspaper Clippings, 1949, Roybal Papers, CSULA.

20 Sam Ishikawa, "Report of the Pacific Southwest Regional Office," Japanese American Citizens League, Oct. 1, 1948-Dec. 15, 1949, attached to memo from Harry Honda to author, Jan. 4, 2001.

21 Hope Mendoza interview; Tony Ríos interview.

22 "CSO Speaks Up at Warren's Unemployment Conference," *CSO News*, Dec. 21, 1949, author's files; Max Mont, Weekly Report, Dec. 16, 1949; Letter, M. F. Small, A.A. to U.S. Senator Kuchel to Tom Bright, Dept. Sec., Gov. Office, Nov. 9, 1953, Race Relations, Knight Papers.

23 Ed Cray, *Chief Justice: A Biography of Earl Warren* (New York: Simon & Schuster, 1997), p. 140; Manuel Ruiz, "Biographical Sketch," Ruiz Papers.

24 Earl Warren Oral History, pp. 241, 244.

25 William Barry interview; Ralph Poblano interview; Hope Mendoza Schechter interview; Fred Ross, unpublished ms., "Tony Ríos-Bloody Xmas," b. 6, f. 7 & 16, b. 21, f. 9, Ross Papers.

26 Tony Ríos interview; Hope Mendoza Schechter interview; CSO, "Highlights of the Past 20 Years," author's files; Guzman, *The Political Socialization*, p. 141.

27 Hope Mendoza Schechter interview; Minutes, City Council, Apr. 18, 1950, Clerk's Office, City of San Fernando; Guzman, *The Political Socialization*, p. 141; Gómez-Quiñteros, *Chicano Politics*, pp. 54-55.

28 Tony Ríos interview; Photo, "Floral Homage," *LAE*, May 41, 1950, Newspaper Clipping, Roybal Papers, CSULA.

29 "19th District AFL Club Opens New Headquarters," *LAC*, June 2, 1950, 1; *Across The River*, [8-9], b. 4, f. 31, USWA Civil Rights Department, USA District 38, Civic Unity, USWA Papers; Flyer, "For A Democratic Government...", [1950], CFDG, author's files; "Local Community Services Organization Need Funds," *ESS*, Nov. 9, 1950, Newspaper Clippings, Roybal Papers, CSULA; Tony Ríos interview; María Durán Méndez interview; Hope Mendoza Schechter interview.

30 Hope Mendoza Schechter interview.

31 Ibid.; Flyer, "For A Democratic Government...", [1950], CFDG, author's files; Hill, *Dancing Bear*, p. 104; Rarick, *California Rising*, pp. 59-65; Janet Stevenson, *The Undiminished Man: A Political Biography of Robert Walker Kenny* (Novato, Calif.: Chandler & Sharp, 1980), pp. 146-147.

32 "Cops Came to Ask—They Got an Earful," *PW*, Mar. 22, 1950, attached to FBI report on CSO, August 17, 1950, obtained by author through the FOIA.

33 FBI Report on CSO, Aug. 17, 1950.

34 FBI File on CSO continues into the 1970s.

35 CSO, *Across The River*. Shanna Bernstein cites this phrase in her use of CSO as a case study to examine "the way civil rights groups looked to each other for strength and support as they struggled to establish their moderate stance and legitimacy in this conservative climate." Shanna Bernstein, "Building Bridges at Home in a Time of Global Conflict: Interracial Cooperation and the Fight for Civil Rights in Los Angeles, 1933-1954," Ph.D. diss, Stanford University, 2004, p. 221.

36 Daniel Luevano interview; Tony Ríos interview; Hope Mendoza Schechter interview; Daniel M. Luevano, OHI, 1988, OHP, UCLA, for the CSAOHP, pp. 74-81; CSO, "Highlights of the Past 20 Years," author's files.

37 "Spanish Vote Rallied in Los Angeles," *CSM*, May 29, 1950, Newspaper Clippings, Roybal Papers, CSULA.

38 "Cite Roybal for Valor in Office," *DN*, Nov. 6, 1950, and other items, including program, "Testimonial Dinner In Honor of Councilman Edward Roybal, Sunday, Nov. 5, 1950," in Newspaper Clippings, Roybal Papers; "500 Honor Roybal for Civil Rights Fight," *PW*, Nov. 7, 1950, p. 10.

39 Letter, Albert Lunceford, Greater Los Angles CIO Council, to Committee to Abolish Discrimination, CIO, Apr. 18, 1950, with attached, Resolution, Community Services Organization, adopted Apr. 4, 1950, b. 197, f. (Calif.) LAIUC, CIO Sec.-Tres., ALUA, WSU.

40 "Roybal Given Honors By Fortnight," *ESS*, Nov. 21, 1950, News Clippings, Roybal Papers, CSULA.

41 "Community Services Organization Doing Much to Clean Up City's Slum Areas," *DN*, Dec. 25, 1950, p. 2; "Acute Problems of L.A.'s Mexican American Residents Told," *DN*, Dec. 26, 1950, p. 3; "Bypassed 'Island' of L.A. Experience Awakening," *DN*, Dec. 27, 1950, p. 3; "Local Group Credited with Ending Racial Label in Enlistment," *DN*, Dec. 28, 1950, p. 3; "CSO Launches Slum Betterment Fund for 1951," *DN*, Dec. 29, 1950, p. 3; Editorial, "CSO Bridges

Gap for Minority Group," *DN*, Jan. 6, 1951, p. 28. These items and Holifield's earlier *Cong. Rec.* statement were reprinted in *Here Is Your Community Services Organization* [1951], USWA Civil Rights Dept., b. 4, f. 31, District 38-Civic Unity, USWA Papers.

42 Katherine Underwood, "Process and Politics: Multiracial Electoral Coalition Building and Representation in Los Angeles' Ninth District, 1949-1962," Ph.D. diss., UC, San Diego, 1992, p. 118; "Reaction Begins Its Drive Against Edward Roybal," *PW*, Feb. 19, 1951, p. 5.

43 *ESJ*, 1948 to 1952.

44 Stanley Bunyan interview.

45 "Here Are Candidates Endorsed in April 3 Primary—And Why They Deserve Support of Labor," *LAC*, Mar. 30, 1951, p. 1; *ESJ*, Feb.-Apr. 1951.

46 Tony Ríos interview; Henry Santiestevan interview; "USA Gives Heavy Vote In L.A. Clean-Up," *SL*, June 1949, p. 8.

47 Roger Johnson interview; Tony Ríos interview; Edward Roybal interview; campaign documents in author's files.

48 Acuña, *Occupied America,* p. 294; George J. Sanchez, "'What's Good for Boyle Heights Is Good for the Jews': Creating Multiracialism on the Eastside During the 1950s," *AQ* 56:3 (Sept. 2004): 643-645.

49 Newspaper Clippings, Roybal Papers, CSULA. For a contemporary left view of CSO, see Alfredo Montoya and Francisca Flores, *Toward Unity of the Mexican American People in the United States* (Los Angeles: National Association of Mexican-Americans: Oct. 14, 1950), Pamphlet Collection, SCLSSR.

50 "Reaction Begins Its Drive Against Edward Roybal," *PW*, Feb. 19, 1951, p. 5; FBI, Memo, Mar. 21, 1951, CSO FOIA FBI File.

51 "Thumping Success of 'Citizens' Big Dinner Assures Future Rallies," *ESS*, Mar. 1, 1953.

52 "Festival of Friendship . . . ," *ESS*, Newspaper Clippings, Roybal Papers, CSULA; Moore, *To the Golden Cities*, p. 207.

53 "Two more Roybal Hdqtr's Opened," *CNS*, Mar. 1, 1951, Newspaper Clippings, Roybal Papers, CSULA.

54 "Get Things Done in 51!" in author's files.

55 Sánchez, "'What's Good for Boyle Heights Is Good for the Jews'."

56 Brochure, Non-Partisan Committee to Re-Elect Ed Roybal, b. 9, f. LA CIO Council Committees: PAC Corres., Jan. 1951-Apr. 1951, L.A. Labor Papers.

57 Stanley Bunyan interview.

58 Clara Block interview, July 6, 1996.

59 Letter, Dear Neighbor from Sol Ruby, Wabash Area Committee To Re-Elect Councilman Ed Roybal, [1951], author's files.

60 "As the Daily News Sees Council Race," *DN*, Mar. 13, p. 28.

61 "Assemblymen Back Ed Roybal for Reelection," *LAC*, Mar. 23, 1951.

62 "The Contests for Council," *LAT*, Mar. 31, 1951.

63 "Father O'Dwyer Supports Edward R. Roybal for Re-election," *CNS*, Mar. 29, 1951, Newspaper Clippings, Roybal Papers, CSULA.

64 "Anti-Roybal Picture Irks Pat Brown," *DN*, n.d., Newspaper Clipping, Roybal Papers, CSULA.

65 "Republican Group to Elect Roybal Formed," *ESS*, Mar. 23, 1951, News Clippings, Roybal Papers, CSULA.

66 "League Analyzes Councilmanic Races," *L.A. Fire & Police Protective League*

News, Mar. 26, 1951, Newspaper Clippings, Roybal Papers, CSULA.

67　"Roybal Pre-Election Rally Tonight: 'Sun' Endorses Ed Roybal and Judge Ben Rosenthal," *ESS*, Mar. 29, 1951, p. 1; "You Are Invited!" *ESS*, March 29, 1951, p. 1; "Charles Lang, Nat Schneider Head Vets for Roybal," *ESS*, March 29, 1951, p. 1; "Roybal Rally Tonight," *CNS*, March 29, 1951, Roybal Papers, CSULA.

68　LACiA. See also Katherine Underwood, "Process and Politics," p. 125.

69　LACiA.

70　Guzman, *The Political Socialization of the Mexican American People*, p. 142.

71　Sánchez, "'What's Good for Boyle Heights Is Good for the Jews'."

72　Unlike the Communists, CSO members were neither deported nor subject to hearings by the California Legislature's Un-American Activities committees.

73　CSO, *Across the River*, [pp. 2-3].

74　John Thomas Berry, "Fair Employment in California: A Study of the Groups and Pressures Influencing Opinion on This Issue," Thesis, UC, Berkeley, 1951, pp. 55-56.

75　Assembly Interim Committee on Elections and Reapportionment, Transcript of Hearing, Dec. 15 and 16, 1960, in Los Angeles, pp. 237-238; Assembly Committee on Elections and Reapportionment, transcript of hearing, May 18, 1961 (Sacramento).

76　Platform of the Democratic Party of California, Adopted at Sacramento, Aug. 2, 1952, p. 10, b. 99, f. Speech Material, Hawkins Papers; T. Anthony Quinn, *Carving Up California: A History of Redistricting, 1951-1984* (Rose Institute of State and Local Government, Claremont McKenna College, n.d.), pp. 7-10.

77　Majka and Majka, *Farm Workers, Agribusiness, and the State*, p. 151.

CHAPTER 6

THE TONY RÍOS AND BLOODY CHRISTMAS POLICE BEATINGS

1　This chapter was presented to the Los Angeles History Group at The Huntington Library, San Marino, Calif., on Dec. 7, 2002 and published as Kenneth C. Burt, "Tony Ríos and Bloody Christmas: A Turning Point Between the Los Angeles Police Department and Latino Community," in the *Western Legal History: The Journal of the Ninth Judicial Circuit Historical Society* 14:2 (Summer/Fall 2001). See also Edward J. Escobar, "Bloody Christmas and the Irony of Police Professionalism: The Los Angeles Police Department, Mexican Americans, and Police Reform in the 1950s," *PHR* 72:2 (May 2003): 171-199.

2　Manuel and Aurora Hernández interview, Jan. 16, 2003; Jack Wilson interview, Jan. 16, 2003. The two victims said it was their first interview in fifty years and that they were not consulted in the making of the movie, *L.A. Confidential*, which includes a scene of their being beaten. The literature has inaccurately stated that the seven men (or alternatively six or five) were Latino.

3　"Cop-Beating Victim Tells 'Horror' Night," *LAM*, Aug. 8, 1952, p. 6.

4　Manuel and Aurora Hernández interview; Ralph H. Nutter interview, Mar. 6, 2002; Henry Nava interview; Edward Roybal interview; Tony Ríos interview; Konstantin Sparkuhl interview; Henrietta Villaescusa interview; "2 Policemen Beaten in Bar Brawl," *DN*, Dec. 25, 1951, p. 2; Clippings, b. 1, f. 5 & 6, CRCLA, SCLSSR; Letter, Ríos to Roger N. Baldwin, ACLU, n.d., b. 5, f. 1, Ross Papers; Fred Ross, unpublished ms., "Tony Ríos-Bloody Xmas," pp. 31-43, b. 21, f. 18, Ross Papers; Minutes, CSO Executive Committee, January 15, 1951, b. 5, f. 6, Ross Papers.

5　"Cop-Beating Victim Tells 'Horror' Night," *LAT*, Aug. 8, 1952, p. 6.

6   Manuel and Aurora Hernández interview; Konstantin Sparkuhl interview.
7   "Celebrate Christmas Eve By Beating Up Two Cops," *DN*, Dec. 25, 1951, in
    Clippings, CRCLA, SCLSSR. The *DN* on microfilm at the L.A. Main Library,
    upon which many of the citations are based, ran the same photo and a similar
    story: "2 Policemen Beaten in Bar Brawl," *DN*, Dec. 25, 1951, p. 2.
8   "Police Brutality in Spotlight," *DN*, Feb. 8, 1952, p. 5; "League Analyzes
    Councilmanic Races," *L.A. Fire & Police Protective League News*, Mar. 26,
    1951, Newspaper Clippings, Roybal Papers, CSULA.
9   Escobar, *Race, Police, and the Making of Political Identity*.
10 Don Parsons, "Injustice for Salcido: The Left Response to Police Brutality in
    Cold War Los Angeles," *SCQ* 87:2 (Summer 2004): 145-168.
11 Tony Ríos interview; Fred Ross, "Tony Ríos-Bloody Xmas, p. 25; "Urge
    Community-Police Cooperation: Closer Ties Stressed to Avert Crime," *ESJ*, July
    6, 1949, p. 1, Newspaper Clippings, Roybal Papers, CSULA. See also Martin
    Schiesl, "Behind the Shield: Social Discontent and the Los Angeles Police since
    1950," in Schiesl and Dodge, eds., *City of Promise*, pp. 139-140.
12 Tony Ríos Interview; Konstantin Sparkuhl interview; "Two Cops Named in Jury
    Probe of Bloody Christmas Beatings," *LAM*, Mar. 25, 1952, p. 4.
13 Tony Ríos interview; Edward Roybal interview; Minutes, General Meeting
    of CSO, Jan. 16, 1952, b. 5, f. 7, Ross Papers; Letter, Tony Ríos to Roger N.
    Baldwin, ACLU, op. cited; Fred Ross, "Tony Ríos-Bloody Xmas," pp. 31-49;
    Gómez-Quiñteros, *Chicano Politics*, p. 55.
14 Jack Wilson interview.
15 Fred Ross, "Tony Ríos-Bloody Xmas," p. 49.
16 Fred Ross, "Tony Ríos-Bloody Xmas," pp. 16, 48.
17 Margarita Durán Méndez interview.
18 Ralph Nutter interview; Margarita Durán Méndez interview; Tony Ríos inter-
    view; Edward Roybal Interview; Fred Ross, "Tony Ríos-Bloody Xmas," pp. 51-
    57; Letter, Tony Ríos to Roger N. Baldwin, ACLU, n.d., b. 5, f. 1, Ross Papers.
19 Letter, Tony Ríos to Roger N. Baldwin, ACLU, op. cited.
20 Tony Ríos interview.
21 Tony Ríos interview; Edward Roybal interview; Fred Ross, "Tony Ríos-Bloody
    Xmas," pp. 51-57; Letter, Tony Ríos to Roger N. Baldwin, ACLU, op. cited..
22 Alice Soto interview, Mar. 22, 2002. See also Joe Domanick, *To Protect and to
    Serve: The LAPD's Century of War in the City of Dreams* (New York: Pocket
    Books, 1994), p. 103; Daryl F. Gates, *Chief: My Life in the LAPD* (New York:
    Bantam Books, 1992), pp. 27-29.
23 Henry Nava interview.
24 William Barry interview.
25 Larry Margolis interview, Feb. 10, 1996, Mar. 24, 1996.
26 Tony Ríos interview; Ross, "Tony Ríos-Bloody Xmas," p. 48.
27 Tony Ríos interview.
28 Ralph Nutter interview.
29 Tony Ríos interview; Ross, "Tony Ríos-Bloody Xmas," pp. 31, 58.
30 "Police Brutality in Spotlight," *DN*, Feb. 8, 1952, p. 5.
31 Tony Ríos interview; "Café Owner Tells Threat By Policeman," *DN*, Mar. 6,
    1952, p. 3.
32 Tony Ríos interview.

33 Ibid.

34 Ralph Nutter interview.

35 Tony Ríos interview; Edward Roybal interview; "Brutality Claims Put Heat On Cops–Story on Page 2," p. 1, and "Air L.A. Police Brutality Charges: 50 Complaints Reported by Councilman Roybal," *DN*, Feb. 26, 1952, p. 2; "Chief Shrugs at Claim of Cop Brutality (story, page 4), *LAM*, Feb. 27, 1952, p. 1, "Police Brutality Gets Brush-off by Chief Parker," *LAM*, February 27, 1952, p. 4; Fred Ross, "Tony Ríos-Bloody Xmas," p. 60; Clippings, Anti-Defamation League Los Angeles; Clippings, CRCLA, SCLSSR.

36 Zane Meckler interview; Fred Ross, "Tony Ríos-Bloody Xmas," p. 65; "Chief Shuns Cop Brutality Charges: Inquiries Into Specific Cases Given Brush-Off," *DN*, Feb. 27, 1952, p. 2.

37 Hope and Harvey Schechter interview; Zane Meckler interview; Minutes, CSO General Meeting, July 16, 1952, b. 5, f. 7, Ross Papers; "Huge Cal. Tax Setup Explained," *DN*, Feb. 26, 1952, p. 5.

38 Acuña, *A Community Under Siege*, p. 36-37.

39 "Cop Chief Steps Away From Heat–Story on Page 2," *DN*, Feb. 28, 1952, p. 1 and "Chief Ducks Out of Brutality Quiz: Parker Passes Buck to Board," *DN*, Feb. 28, 1952, p. 2.

40 Hope Mendoza Schechter interview.

41 Harvey Schechter interview.

42 Ralph Nutter interview.

43 "Ríos-Ulloa Trial Opens," *CSO Reporter*, Feb. 28, 1952, p. 1, Clippings, CRCLA, SCLSSR.

44 "Jury Picked In Ríos Case," *CSO Reporter*, Feb. 28, 1952, p. 1, Clippings, CRCLA, SCLSSR.

45 Ralph Poblano interview.

46 "Near-Riot Charged To Police Critics: Officers Accursed of Brutality Party Tried to Incite Crowd to Prevent Arrest," *LAT*, Mar. 4, 1952, p. 2.

47 "'Police Brutality' Case Expects Jury Choice Today," *LAM*, Feb. 29, 1952, p. 12.

48 "Drunken Cops Beat Them, Say 2 Men on Trail Here," *DN*, Feb. 27, 1952, in Clippings, CRCLA, SCLSSR.

49 Tony Ríos interview; Ralph Nutter interview; "Says Najera Drunk When Arrest Made," *DN*, Feb. 29, 1952, p. 2; "Cops in Ríos Case Admits Taking Drink, *DN*, Mar. 3, 1952, p. 2; "Ríos Story Unshaken in Cross-Examination," *DN*, Mar. 5, 1952, p. 2; Ross, "Tony Ríos-Bloody Xmas," p. 60.

50 Clippings, CRCLA, SCLSSR.

51 Tony Ríos interview; Fred Ross, "Tony Ríos-Bloody Xmas," pp. 66, 71-72.

52 Ibid.; "Huge Cal. Tax Setup Explained," *DN*, Feb. 26, 1952, p. 5.

53 Tony Ríos interview; Fred Ross, "Tony Ríos-Bloody Xmas," pp. 71-72.

54 "Police Board Sets Brutality Quiz: Charges to Be Aired at Hearing," *DN*, Mar. 6, 1952, p. 3; Fred Ross, "Tony Ríos-Bloody Xmas," pp. 71-72.

55 "Ríos and Ulloa 'Not Guilty'," n.d., b. 23, f. 7, ACLU Papers, Special Collections, UCLA.

56 Tony Ríos interview; Fred Ross, "Tony Ríos-Bloody Xmas," p. 75.

57 "Salcido Case Victory in Court," *PW*, May 19, 1948, p. 3.

58 Manuel Hernández interview; Jack Wilson interview.

59 "Judge Urges Inquiry on Brutality," *LAT*, Mar. 13, 1952, p. 1.
60 Ibid.; "Police Methods Under FBI Scrutiny: Brutality Complaints Studied," *DN*, Mar. 13, 1952, p. 2.
61 Clippings, b. 23, f. 7, ACLU Papers, UCLA; Clippings, Anti-Defamation League Los Angeles; Clippings, CRCLA, SCLSSR.
62 "Board Will Not Tolerate Cruelty, Booth Declares," *DN*, Mar. 17, 1952, p. 2.
63 Tony Ríos interview; "Solons Eye L.A. Cop Brutality, *DN*, Mar. 17, 1952, p. 5; "Move for Attorney General to Enter L.A. Police Probe," *DN*, Mar. 21, 1952, p. 2; "Funds for Police Terror Probe Seen," *PW*, Apr. 5, 1950, p. 3.
64 Lou Cannon, *Official Negligence: How Rodney King and the Riots Changes Los Angeles and the LAPD* (Boulder, Colo.: Westview Press, 1999), p. 65.
65 "Grand Jury Vindicates Youths," *CSO Reporter*, Apr. 30, 1952, p. 4, in Clippings, CRCLA, SCLSSR.
66 Katherine Underwood, "Pioneering Minority Representation: Edward Roybal and the Los Angeles City Council, 1949-1062," *PHR* 66:3 (Aug. 1997): 401.
67 Escobar, "Bloody Christmas and the Irony of Police Professionalism," pp. 189-190.
68 "Hits at Reds Horning in on Cop Brutality," *DN*, April 4, 1952, in Clippings, CRCLA, SCLSSR. In an interview, Tony Ríos also claimed that the group used his name to raise money that it failed to turn over to his defense effort.
69 Kenneth C. Burt, "The Battle for Standard Coil: The United Electrical Workers, the Community Services Organization, and The Catholic Church in East Los Angeles," in Cherny, et al., eds., *American Labor and the Cold War*, pp. 118-140.
70 Manuel and Aurora Hernández interview; Tony Ríos interview; Acuña, *A Community Under Siege*, p. 43; Grebler, et al., *The Mexican American People*, pp. 533-534.
71 Escobar, "Bloody Christmas and the Irony of Police Professionalism," pp. 197-198.
72 Tony Ríos interview; "Julio Gonzales, 86; Helped Reach Out to Latinos," *LAT*, Dec. 14, 2003, p. B10; J. Gregory Payne and Scott Ratzan, *Tom Bradley: The Impossible Dream* (New York: PaperJacks, 1987), p. 52.
73 Camarillo, *Chicanos in California*, p. 82.
74 "New Chapter Formed in East Los Angeles," *The Open Forum,* Dec. 1956, Clippings, Roybal Papers, CSULA.
75 Katherine Underwood, "Pioneering Minority Representation," pp. 414-415.
76 "Farewell Party for Fred Ross Great Success," *CSO Reporter*, March 27, 1952, Newspaper Clippings, 1952, Roybal Papers, CSULA; Ernesto Galarza, "Program for Action," *CG* 9:4 (Summer 1949): 33-34.
77 "New from CSO," *Civil Liberties Newsletter* No. 6, p. 1, b.13, f.1, Galarza Papers.

CHAPTER 7
STATEWIDE CANDIDATES AND STATEWIDE NETWORKS

1 Hill, *Dancing Bear*, pp. 91-107.
2 Deverell and Sitton, eds., *California Progressivism Revisited*; Delmatier, et al., pp. 33-337; Rolle, *California*, pp. 575-579; Schuparra, *Triumph of the Right*, pp. 126.
3 García, *Mexican Americans*, pp. 212-213; Gutiérrez, *Walls and Mirrors,* pp. 161-170; Michael J. Ybarra, *Washington Gone Crazy: Senator Pat McCarran and the Great American Communist Hunt* (Hanover, N.H.: Steerfort Press, 2004).

4   Hope Mendoza and Harvey Schechter interview.

5   CSO, *Democracy is Not a Fake: The CSO Story, CSO Program . . . It's Future*
    [1965], p. 6, b. 13, f. 8, Galarza Papers; Gutiérrez, *Walls and Mirrors,* acknowl-
    edged that the bill "liberalized some parts of the nation's general immigration
    statutes" but like most historians emphasized the negative aspects of the bill (p.
    161). He credits CSO for reaching out to "potential citizens," to use Roybal's
    phrase, (pp. 171-172), but does not credit CSO for its role in changing the law.

6   Josephine Whitney Duveneck, *Life on Two Levels: An Autobiography* (Los
    Altos, Calif.: William Kaufmann, 1978), pp. 250-257. For more on CSO and
    San Jose, see Matthews, *Silicon Valley, Women, and the California Dream*; Pitti,
    The Devil in Silicon Valley, pp. 148-158.

7   Author's interview with George C. Higgins, July 20, 1995; Jeffrey M. Burns,
    "The Mexican Community in California," in Dolan and Hinojosa, eds., *Mexican
    Americans and the Catholic Church*, pp. 204-217.

8   Levy, *Cesar Chavez*, pp. 97-98. Feriss and Sandoval, *The Fight in the Fields*, pp.
    37-42; Ross, *Conquering Goliath*, p. 3. For an early account the CSO experience,
    see Cesar Chavez, "The Organizer's Tale," reprinted in Dennis Hale and Jonathan
    Eisen, eds., *The California Dream* (New York: Collier, 1968), pp. 106-115.

9   Jacques Levy, *Cesar Chavez*, p. 99.

10 Duveneck, *Life on Two Levels*, p. 255; Feriss and Sandoval, *The Fight in the
    Fields*, pp. 43, 45.

11 Duveneck, *Life on Two Levels*, p. 255; Levy, *Cesar Chavez*, pp. 104-105;
    Guzman, *The Political Socialization*, p. 141; Feriss and Sandoval, *The Fight in
    the Fields*, p. 48.

12 Levy, *Cesar Chavez*, pp. 105-108; Feriss and Sandoval, *The Fight in the Fields*,
    p. 49.

13 Levy, *Cesar Chavez*, pp. 107-108.

14 Ibid., pp. 115-118.

15 Gutiérrez, *Walls and Mirrors*, p. 171.

16 Margaret Rose, "Gender and Civic Action in Mexican American Barrios in
    California: The Community Services Organization, 1947-1962," in Meyerowitz,
    ed., *Not June Cleaver*, p. 194.

17 Tony Ríos interview; California State Department of Social Welfare, Digest of
    Social Welfare Legislation, 1953, p. 9, CSA.

18 Edward Roybal interview; Parson, *Making a Better World*, p. 114.

19 William Barry interview; Margarita Durán Méndez interview; Edward Roybal
    interview; Hope Mendoza Schechter interview; Email, Bruce Phillips to author,
    Feb. 6, 2003.

20 Margarita Durán Méndez interview.

21 Ibid.; Henry Nava interview; Hope Mendoza Schechter interview; quote from
    Charlotte Negrette White, "Women in the Political Process: The Community
    Service Organization of East Los Angeles," paper at Claremont College,
    December 5, 1994; Rose, "Gender and Civic Action in Mexican American
    Barrios in California," p. 193.

22 Tony Ríos interview; Henrietta Villaescusa interview; Ford, *Thirty Explosive
    Years in Los Angeles County*, p. 137; Catholic Institute Papers, Center for the
    Study of Los Angeles, Loyola Marymount University.

23 "Appoint Mexican Judge, Knight Asked," *PW*, Feb. 8, 1954, p. 3.

24 Tony Ríos interview.
25 Héctor Abeytia interview, Dec. 1981 and May 1982; Bert Corona interview, Dec. 17, 20, 1981, May 4, 1995; Henry López interview, Jan. 4, 1982; Edward Roybal interview; Joseph Sánchez, Sr. interview, Dec. 18, 1981; Henrietta Villaescusa interview; Jan G. Bernstein, "Realignment and Political Party-Building in California, 1952-1963," Ph.D. diss., Cornell University, 1986; Carney, *The Rise of the Democratic Clubs in California*; Fowle, *Cranston*, pp. 93-102; Mellow Carlotta Herman, "The Rise and Fall of Grass Roots Politics: The California Democratic Council, 1953-1966," Ph.D diss., Claremont, 1972; R. Fred Kugler, *Volunteers in Politics: The Twenty-seven Year History of the California Democratic Council, 1953-1980* (Los Angeles: CDC, 1981); Levy, *Cesar Chavez*, pp. 111-112; Frederick B. Tuttle, Jr., "The California Democrats: 1953-1966," Ph.D. diss, UCLA, 1975; Wilson, *The Amateur Democrat*.
26 Tuttle, Jr., "The California Democrats," p. 57.
27 Henrietta Villaescusa interview.
28 Bert Corona interview. CDC required all club members to be registered Democrats and allowed clubs to only endorse Democrats, but refused to enact anti-Communist loyalty disclaimers, Bernstein, "Realignment and Political Party-Building in California," p. 71; Tuttle, Jr., "The California Democrats," pp. 58-59. The FBI monitored CSO for years and maintained files on Corona, Ríos and Chávez, despite a 1954 report that there were few Communists in CSO. FBI files obtained under the FOIA. Cited document on CSO dated Dec. 27, 1954, and attached to FBI memo of May 3, 1955.
29 During the popular front period A. Philip Randolph served as the president of the National Negro Congress, the equivalent of El Congreso within the African American community. And like Quevedo, he left the post after the Hitler-Stalin pact. Little recognized was the role of the anti-Stalinist left in leading and staffing this critical civil rights committee. Becker staffed the labor desk for the 1948 Norman Thomas Socialist Party presidential campaign; the Jewish Labor Committee paid his salary at Cal Committee while he worked out of the AFL office in San Francisco. The second Cal Committee staff person was Max Mont, a Trotskyist (Schachtmanite) before becoming a Social Democrat. He ran the Cal Committee out of the Los Angeles offices of the Jewish Labor Committee, for whom he worked.
30 Bill Becker interview, Sept. 8, 1993 and Apr. 12, 1996; Herman Gallegos interview; Tony Ríos interview; Kenneth C. Burt, "Fighting for Fair Employment: Celebrating the 40th Anniversary of the FEPC," Program, JLC Annual Recognition Awards Brunch, June 6, 1999, Beverly Hills.
31 Carney, *The Rise of the Democratic Clubs in California*, pp. 3, 11.
32 Newspaper Clippings, Roybal Papers, CSULA; Herman, "The Rise and Fall of Grass Roots Politics," pp. 58-65; Hill, *Dancing Bear*, pp. 151-152; Tuttle, Jr., "The California Democrats," pp. 55-69; Katherine Underwood, "Pioneering Minority Representation: Edward Roybal and the Los Angeles City Council, 1949-1962," *PHR* 66:3 (Aug. 1997): 418.
33 Roger Johnson interview.
34 Letter, Ross to Roybal, February 16, 1954, b. 9, f. CSO-2, Roybal Papers, UCLA.
35 Ibid.; Finks, *The Radical Vision of Saul Alinsky*, pp. 62-64.
36 Ibid.
37 Roger Johnson interview.

38 Hill, *Dancing Bear*, pp. 142-143; Taft, *Labor Politics American Style*, p. 213.

39 "Friendship Day Camp Brings Together Kids of All Races, Creeds at Griffith Park," *ESS*, July 15, 1954; Tony Ríos interview; Ezra Weintraub interview, Sept. 3, 1997.

40 Armando Rodríguez interview.

41 Roger Johnson interview.

42 George Sotelo interview.

43 Richard Chávez interview, Apr. 16, 2005.

44 White, "Women in the Political Process."

45 "Women's Leader Appointed for Roybal Campaign," *ESJ*, Oct. 20, 1954.

46 "GOP Knight, Dem Roybal Strong Men," *LAM*, Nov. 4, 1954; Statement of Vote, CSA.

47 Assembly Interim Committee on Elections and Reapportionment, Transcript of Hearing, Dec. 15 and 16, 1960, in Los Angeles, p. 240.

48 Hope Mendoza Schechter interview; Tony Ríos interview; "Mexican-Americans Found a New Group," *PW*, June 8, 1951, p. 3; *Civil Liberties Newsletters*, b. 13, f. 1, Galarza Papers; b. 84, f. American Council of Spanish Speaking, Jackson Papers, FDR Library; Alan Axelrod, *Minority Rights in America* (Washington, D.C.: CQ Press, 2002), p. 22; García, *Mexican Americans*, pp. 221, 253.

49 Héctor García interview; George Sotelo interview; Robert A. Caro, *The Years of Lyndon Johnson: Master of the Senate* (New York: Knopf, 2002), pp. 740-755; Ramos, *The American GI Forum*, pp. 9-17.

50 Letter, Murray M. Chotiner to Vice President Richard Nixon, Nov. 8, 1954, PPS 300.353, RMN Library.

51 Bishops' Committee for the Spanish Speaking, *Newsletter*, No. 29 (Aug. 1954), p. 3, b. 13, f. 4, Galarza Papers; Guzman, *The Political Socialization*, pp. 162-169.

52 John O'Grady, "New Life Comes From the Bottom," *Catholic Charities Review,* Dec. 1955, b. 13, f. 7, Galarza Papers.

53 Minutes, National CSO Executive Board Meeting, July 16-17, 1955, Fresno, b. 3, f. CSO-2, Roybal Papers, UCLA.

54 Tony Ríos interview; CSO, "Highlights of the Past 20 Years," author's files.

55 White, "Women in the Political Process."

56 Charlie Erickson interview, Mar. 2, 2003; George Sotelo interview; Dionicio Morales interview; Grebler, et al., *The Mexican-American People*, p. 534.

57 "Council Downs FEP: One Vote Kills Roybal Proposal," *Free Press*, June 17, 1955, and "L.A. County Conference on Human Relations Celebrates 10th Birthday," *Herald Dispatch*, Dec. 13, 1956, Newspaper Clippings, Roybal Papers, CSULA.

58 "The Mexicans Among Us," *Readers Digest*, Mar. 1956, pp. 177-186.

59 "County FEPC Vote Slated For Tuesday," *CE*, June 21, 1956. Honorary Co-chairs included Roybal and CSO President J.J. Rodríquez. The secretary (and staff person) was Max Mont of the Jewish Labor Committee. B. 1, f. 16, Mont Papers.

60 "Friendship Festival Celebrated by 25,000," *LAE*, May 23, 1955, and "Ninth Annual Friendship Festival Reaches Climax with Record Crowd," *ESJ*, n.d., Newspaper Clippings, Roybal Papers, CSULA.

61 Amendments to Constitution, Propositions and Proposed Laws, General

Election, Nov. 6, 1956, p. 18, CSA.

62 "Stevenson Delegate Slate Filed in State: Names of 136 Democrats Hailed by Brown as Best Balanced in History," *LAT*, Mar. 8, 1956, p. 8; Charles A.H. Thomson and Frances M. Shattuck, *The 1956 Campaign* (Washington, DC: The Brookings Institution, 1960), pp. 56-61; Statement of the Vote, 1938-1956, CSA.

63 "Democratic Roundup: Roybal Says Campaign Is Missing Minorities," *Free Press*, Oct. 11, 1956, Newspaper Clippings, Roybal Papers, CSULA.

64 CSO estimated that a quarter million Latinos were not registered. Leaflet, "CSO's Target For 1956, b. 3, f. CSO-2, Roybal Papers, UCLA; Statement of the Vote, Nov. 6, 1956, p. 2, CSA.

65 Minutes, National CSO Executive Board Meeting, July 16-17, 1955, Fresno, p. 27, b. 3, f. CSO-2, Roybal Papers, UCLA; Memo, Sept. 24, 1956, Tony Ríos' FBI File, obtained by the author under the FOIA.

66 Letter, Eisenhower to the Thomas Kuchel, Sept. 15, 1954, with attachments, in Collection: Eisenhower: Records as President (extra files), 1953-61, Official File; Box: 881; File: OF 204 Mexico (2); and Letter, Eisenhower to Armando Torres, Aug.25, 1954, with attachments, in Collection: President's Personal File; Box 806; File: Confederation of Mexican Chamber of U.S; DDE Library.

67 Ad, "Reelija al Senador Kuchel," *LO*, Nov. 4, 1956, p. 8; Ad, "Keep America Strong, Re-elect President Eisenhower-Vice President Nixon," *LO*, Nov. 4, 1956, p. 3; Letter, Sherman Adams to Manuel Mesa, Nov. 3, 1956, and attachments, including letter, Manuel Mesa to Eisenhower, Nov. 7, 1956, with report from the Latin American Division of Eisenhower-Nixon. Eisenhower: Records as President (White House Central Files), 1953-61, General Files; b. 864, f. GF122-G 1956, DDE Library.

68 Ad, "Senator Kuchel Rally," *LO*, Oct. 14, 1956, p. 8.

69 *La Opinión*, Nov. 3-5, 1956.

70 Richard Santillan and Federico A. Subervi-Velez, "Latino Participation in Republican Party Politics in California," in Jackson and Preston, eds., *Racial and Ethnic Politics in California*, pp. 288-289; Thomson and. Shattuck, *The 1956 Campaign*, pp. 321, 433.

71 Augustine Flores interview, Dec. 16, 1982; Edward Ramírez interview, Aug. 31, 1996; Leopoldo Sánchez interview, Jan 4, 1982; George Sotelo interview.

72 Edward Ramírez interview.

73 Petition to Goodwin Knight, 1957, 56.30, Garcia Papers.

74 Edward Ramírez interview.

75 Cruz Reynoso interview, Mar. 25, 1982, Sept. 7, 2002.

76 Leopoldo Sánchez interview; George Sotelo interview; "Carlos M. Teran," *Martindale-Hubbell Law Directory*, 1957, p. 164; Ford, *Thirty Explosive Years in Los Angeles County*, p. 137.

77 Tony Ríos interview.

78 Chapter Reports, CSO, Fourth annual Convention, Fresno, Mar. 23-24, 1957, b. 3, f. CSO-3, Roybal Papers, UCLA.

79 One of the best networked Latinos in the U.S., Galarza had met with Truman's Labor Secretary, Maurice Tobin, on behalf of striking Latinos in Imperial County, accompanied by Monsignor George Higgins. Galarza, *Farm Workers and Agribusiness in California*; Majka and Majka, *Farm Workers, Agribusiness, and the State*, pp. 146-161; H.L. Mitchell, *Mean Things Happening in This Land: The Life and Times of H.L. Mitchell, Cofounder of the Southern Tenant Farmers Union*

(Montclair, N.J.: Allanheld, Osmun, 1979), pp. 245-278.

80 B. 13, f. 7, Galarza Papers; Allsup, *The American G.I Forum*, pp. 112-125; Majka and Majka, *Farm Workers, Agribusiness, and the State*, pp. 158-159. See also Galarza, *Merchants of Labor: The Mexican Bracero Story*; Anderson, *The Bracero Program in California.*

81 John O'Grady, "New Life Comes From the Bottom."

82 Richard Chávez interview.

83 Rose, "Gender and Civic Action in Mexican American Barrios in California," pp. 189-190.

84 Hope Mendoza Schechter interview.

85 Henrietta Villaescusa interview.

86 Hill, *Dancing Bear*, pp. 119-120

CHAPTER 8
HENRY LÓPEZ AND THE MEXICAN-AMERICAN POLITICAL ASSOCIATION

1   "State AFL Launches Fight Against 'Right-to-Work' campaign," *LAC,* Jan. 17, 1958, p. 5; Totton James Anderson, "The 1958 Election in California," *WPQ* XII (Mar. 1959); Taft, *Labor Politics American Style*, quote on p. 241.

2   Hill, *Dancing Bear*, pp. 139-159; Gayle B. Montgomery and James W. Johnson, *One Step From the White House: The Rise and Fall of Senator William Knowland* (Berkeley: University of California Press, 1998), pp. 228-254; Rarick, *California Rising*, pp. 87-110.

3   "NAACP Aid Says State Lacks Minority Rights," *Fresno Bee*, March 24, 1957, and other items in Newspaper Clippings, Roybal Papers, CSULA.

4   Edward Roybal interview.

5   Ford, *Thirty Explosive Years in Los Angeles County*, p. 137.

6   "Ford Names Roybal As Choice For His Job," *Roybal Newsletter*, [Spring 1958, p. 1,] b. 132, f. 18, Roybal Papers, CSULA.

7   *Roybal Newsletter*, [Spring 1958,] op. cit.

8   Henry López interview; Edward Roybal interview; John Anson Ford, OHI, 1961,1967 by L. Craig Cunningham and Elizabeth I. Dixon in, p. 137, OHP, UCLA; "For Secretary of State, Hank López, Officially Endorsed Democrat," [1958], b. 4, f. 5, Mellon Papers, Special Collections, UCLA; Mellon Carlotta Herman, "The Rise and Fall of Grass Roots Politics: The California Democratic Council, 1953-1966," Ph.D diss., Claremont, 1972, p. 89.

9   Henry López interview; Edward Roybal interview; John Anson Ford Oral History, p. 137; Daniel M. Luevano Oral History, p. 66; "Democrats Back Lopez Over Ford: Secretary of State Endorsement Won by L.A. Attorney," *LAT*, Jan. 13, 1958, p. 1; Carney, *The Rise of the Democratic Clubs in California*, pp. 13, 32; Dr. R. Fred Kugler, *Volunteers in Politics: The Twenty-seven Year History of the California Democratic Council, 1953-1980* (Los Angeles: CDC, 1981).

10 Fowle, *Cranston: The Senator From California*, p. 111.

11 "Voter League Endorsements," *LAC*, May 30, 1958, p. 1.

12 "At Council Luncheon for President's Committee," *LAC*, Mar. 7, 1958, p. 1; "Vice-President Nixon Praises American Unions," *LAC*, p. 8; "Hits Job Discrimination: Mitchell Says Minority Group Ban Is Wasting Manpower," *LAC*, Feb. 21, 1958, p. 1.

13 Brown's CSO visit was arranged by Héctor Abeytia, apparently without the group's prior approval. Héctor Abeytia interview, Sanger, Dec. 6, 1981; Fred Ross, Activity Report, Jan. 11, 1958, b. 2, f. 27, Ross, Sr. Papers.

14 Schedules, Mar. 15, 1958, and Letter, Dan Curtin to Fredrick Dutton, May 9, 1958, in b. 56, f. Schedules, and b. 56, f. Minority Group Data, "Pat" Brown Papers; "Brown Asks Start On Feather River: Democratic Governor Candidate Favors Action On Project Without Amendment," *SDU*, Apr. 4, 1958, p. A-15.

15 Parson, *Making a Better World*, pp. 173-181.

16 Greenstone, *Labor in American Politic*, p. 160; Statement of the Vote, June 3, 1958, CSA.

17 Roger Johnson interview; Hope Mendoza Schechter interview; Tony Ríos interview; J. David Greenstone, *Labor in American Politics*, pp. 254-255.

18 Anderson, "The 1958 Election in California," p. 299; Taft, *Labor Politics American Style*, p. 241.

19 "Serious Business at Labor Day Fete," *LAC*, Sept. 5, 1958, p. 1; William Issel, "'A Stern Struggle': Catholic Activism and San Francisco Labor, 1934-1958," Cherny, et al., eds., *American Labor and the Cold War*, p. 168.

20 "Speakers Set For Human Rights Meet," *LAC*, Sept. 12, 1958, p. 1; "Praises Labor As Champion Civil Rights, *LAC*, Oct. 17, 1958, p. 1.

21 "Eastside Rally Against 18 Saturday," *LAC*, Oct. 17, 1958, p. 1; "Eastside Leaders Told Evils of Proposition 18," *LAC*, Oct. 24, 1958, p. 1.

22 "No Permita que las Fuerzas Anti-Derechos Cívicos Engañen," *LO*, Oct. 19, 1958, p. 8; "An Open Letter to Our Fellow Citizens," *LO*, Oct. 31, 1958, p. 7.

23 Brown, Statement on Civil Rights, 1958, b. 56, f. Minority Group Data, Pat Brown Papers, Berkeley.

24 Letter, Edward Rodriguez, to "Hello," Sept. 3, 1958, b. 3, f. Governor Brown, Roybal Papers, UCLA; Hill, *Dancing Bear*, pp. 150-151; George J. Sánchez, "'What's Good for Boyle Heights Is Good for the Jews': Creating Multiracialism on the Eastside During the 1950s," *AQ* 56:3 (Sept. 2004), p. 644.

25 Louis Flores interview, Oct. 26, 2003; Photo caption, "Prometen Llevar A Brown La Victoria," *LO*, Oct. 17, 1958, p. 7.

26 Louis Flores interview; Henry López interview; George Sotelo interview; Mailing Directory, CSO, [1958], b. 13, f. 8, Galarza Papers; Photo caption, "Henry López Con Harry Truman," *LO*, October 19, 1958, Sec. Two, p. 1; "Voter League Endorsements," *LAC*, Oct. 24, 1958, p. 4; Jan G. Bernstein, "Realignment and Political Party-Building in California, 1952-1963," Ph.D. diss., Cornell University, 1986, p. 154.

27 Ferriss and Sandoval, *The Fight in the Fields*, p. 52-60.

28 Ross, *Conquering Goliath*, pp. 18-26; "CSO Opens Drive To Get Out Vote," *OPC*, Nov. 1, 1958, p. 8; "Vujovich, Catlin Elected; Ramirez Likely on Board," *OPC*, Nov. 5, 1958, p. 1.

29 Brochure, "Roybal for Supervisor," Box 9, Roybal Papers, UCLA.

30 Totton James Anderson, "The 1958 Election in California," pp. 292-294.

31 Flyer, "Grand Open-Air Rally," b. 64, f. 48, Healey Papers.

32 Katherine Underwood, "Pioneering Minority Representation: Edward Roybal and the Los Angeles City Council, 1949-1962," *PHR* 66:3 (Aug. 1997), p. 420.

33 Tony Ríos interview; Greenstone, *Labor in American Politics*, p. 160; Anderson, "The 1958 Election in California," pp. 291, 300.

34 "La elección de Roybal y López, sigue indecisa," *LO*, Nov. 5, 1958, p. 1.

35 "Complete L.A. Vote Returns: 10,000-Vote Error; Roybal Upsets Debs," *LAEH&E*, Nov. 6, 1958, p. 1; "Debs Trailing Roybal But Still Thinks He Will Win, " *LAM*, Nov. 6, 1958, p. 1.

36   "Debs Vence A Roybal, En Un Nuevo Recuento," *LO*, Nov. 7, 1958, p. 1.

37   "Roybal Forces 'Storm' as Debs Again Leads: May Demand New Election," *HE,* Nov. 7, 1958, p. 1.

38   Roger Johnson interview; Hope Mendoza Schechter interview; Bill Boyarsky interview, 2002-2004.

39   "Hubo ayer un nuevo recuento: Aumentó Debs su delantera — López sigue avanzando," *LO*, Nov. 9, 1958, p. 1; Acuña, *Anything But Mexican*, p. 46.

40   "Democrats Take Nearly 2-1 Majority in State House: Greatest Victory Since 1883," *LAT,* Nov. 6, 1958, p. 1; Bernstein, "Realignment and Political Party-Building in California," pp. 182-184; Fowle, *Cranston*, p. 98; Hill, *Dancing Bear*, pp. 150-162; Herman, "The Rise and Fall of Grass Roots Politics," pp. 97-100; Montgomery and Johnson, *One Step From the White House*, pp. 228-254; Frederick B. Tuttle, Jr., "The California Democrats: 1953-1966," Ph.D. diss, UCLA, 1975, pp. 134-135; Statement of Vote, Nov. 1958, CSA.

41   Henry López interview.

42   Anderson, "The 1958 Election in California," p. 285.

43   Herman Sillas interview, Aug. 22, 2003.

44   Stephen I. Zetterberg, OHI, 1990 and 1993, p. 40, OHP, CGS, for CSAOHP.

45   Hill, *Dancing Bear*, p. 219.

46   *CSO Reporter*, [1958,] b. 26, f. 9, UFW-Office of the President, ALUA, WSU.

47   Martin Schiesl, "The Struggle for Equality: Racial Reform and Party Politics in California, 1950-1966," in Schiesl, ed., *Responsible Liberalism*, p. 105. For more on the larger Brown agenda see "Summary of Governor Brown's 1959 Legislative Record," b. 4, f. Governor Brown, Roybal Papers, UCLA.

48   Bill Becker interview; Schiesl, "The Struggle for Equality," pp. 103, 105.

49   Ibid.; Hope Mendoza Schechter interview; Ford, *Thirty Explosive Years in Los Angeles County*, p. 139.

50   Alan Cranston interview; Henry López interview; Hope Mendoza Schechter interview; George Sotelo interview; b. 3, f. Governor Brown, Roybal Papers, UCLA.

51   Press release, "Pensions for Non Citizens Bill," b. 13, f. 8, Galarza Papers. Bill Becker interview; Dolores Huerta interview, 1997-2004; Tony Ríos interview.

52   Dolores Huerta interview.

53   Committee for Extension of Old Age Assistance to Non-Citizens Fact Sheet, b. 26, f. Aid to Non Citizens, Roybal Papers, UCLA.

54   Letter, Munnell to Roybal, May 19, 1959, b. 26, f. Aid to Non Citizens, Roybal Papers, UCLA.

55   Letter, Bane to Roybal, May 21, 1959, b. 26, f. Aid to Non Citizens, Roybal Papers, UCLA.

56   Press release, "Pensions for Non Citizens Bill," b. 13, f. 8, Galarza Papers.

57   Ibid.

58   Ross, *Conquering Goliath*, pp. 55-57.

59   Héctor Abeytia interview; Dolores Huerta interview; Minutes, Industrial Welfare Commission, Jan. 8, 1960, and Orders 13-61 and 14-61, IWC, San Francisco; Jeffrey M. Burns, "The Mexican Community in California," in Dolan and Hinojosa, eds., *Mexican Americans and the Catholic Church*, pp. 119-220.

60   Wilson Carey McWilliams observed in a 1960 essay that: "The minority delegates, almost all middle-class, aspire to the leadership of their respective groups. They speak, eloquently, for the excluded, and with utmost sincerity, but for them

politics is a drive for status and professional advance. These, in fact, are the would-be new professionals, the new Irish, for whom politics is still a matter of clear and definite goals, of local grievances and general solutions." McWilliams, "The C.D.C.: The Yearning for Community," reprinted in *The California Dream* (New York: Collier Books, 1968), p. 74.

61 Edward Roybal interview. See also Guzman, *The Political Socialization*, pp. 143-144; Harvey, *The Dynamics of California Government*, p. 281.

62 Edward Roybal interview; Héctor Abeytia interview; Bert Corona interview; Julius Castelan interview, Nov. 13, 1981, Feb. 26, 1982; Henry López interview; George Sotelo interview.

63 Juan Acevedo interview, Nov. 3, 1981; Resume, Juan Acevedo [1959], b. 4, f. Pat Brown, Roybal Papers, UCLA.

64 "Governor Appoints Judge Teran to Superior Court; Begins Duties," *BC*, Jan. 7, 1960; "Governor Brown Speaks at Judge Teran Testimonial Tonight," *BC*, Feb. 25, 1960.

65 Letter, Edward Roybal to Dear Friend, Feb. 26, 1960, quoted in Kenneth C. Burt, "The History of the Mexican American Political Association and Chicano Politics in California," Honors Thesis, UC, Berkeley, 1982, p. 26.

66 Letter, Roybal to Nick Martinez, March 22, 1960, cited in Burt thesis, p. 273.

67 Fred W. Ross, "Mexican-Americans on the March," *Catholic Charities Review*, June 1960, reprint, b. 13, f. 7, Galarza Papers.

68 Alex M. Saragoza, *Fresno's Hispanic Heritage* (San Diego Federal Savings and Loan Association, 1980), pp. 55-61.

69 "The following were present," Apr. 23, 24, 1960, b. 23, f. MAPA, Roybal Papers, UCLA.

70 "Mexican-American Political Association, First Annual Conference, Tentative Program, Apr. 23 and 24, b. 23, f. MAPA, Roybal Papers, UCLA. See also "American, Mexican Political Group Formed," *SFC*, Apr. 27, 1960, p. 6.

71 Henry López interview.

72 Burt, *The History of the Mexican-American Political*, p. 5.

73 George Sotelo interview.

74 David Broder, *Changing of the Guard: Power and Leadership in America*, with a new Introduction (New York: Penguin, 1981), p. 285.

75 Wilson, *The Amateur Democrat*, pp. 286-287.

76 List, "California Delegation," in Collection: White House Conference on Children and Youth, Box: 48, File: California—Delegate Information, DDE Library.

77 Ford, *Thirty Explosive Years in Los Angeles County*, p. 137.

78 Wilson, *The Amateur Democrat*, p. 362.

79 Camarillo, *Chicanos In California*, p. 87. See note 73.

CHAPTER 9
VIVA KENNEDY AND THE STRUGGLE FOR REPRESENTATION

1 "The minimum qualification for the Latino vote to make a difference is the gap between winning and losing candidate must be no larger than the gap in the partisan split of the Latino vote," according to DeSipio, *Counting on the Latino Vote*, p. 71.

2 Carlos McCormick interview, Apr. 3, 1984, July 1984; Birth Certificate, James Carlos McCormick, Sept. 7, 1934, Santa Barbara County; "J. Carlos McCormick, Supreme President," *Alianza* 57:2 (May 1962), 59.54, Garcia

Papers; "Frontiersmen (j.g.): Do They All Want to Be President?" *Newsweek*, Mar. 19, 1962, pp. 34-35.

3   Carlos McCormick interview; "Sen. Kennedy Sends Warm Message To GI Forum in Los Angeles," *FNB*, Sept. 1959, and "Sen. Kennedy Joins GI Forum," *FNB*, June 1960, Garcia Papers.

4   Clark Clifford interview, Apr. 24, 1984.

5   Carlos McCormick interview.

6   Héctor García interview, July 1984.

7   César Chávez, OHI, pp. 3-4, JFK Library; Carlos McCormick interview.

8   Speech, JFK, "The New Frontier," July 15, 1960, on the JFK Library website.

9   Carlos McCormick interview.

10 Ibid. McCormick reported to Bill Henry, who oversaw the specialized campaigns, who reported to John Seigenthaller, who reported to Robert Kennedy. Because of his tenure on the Senator's staff, McCormick enjoyed a personal relationship with Seigenthaler and Kennedy, to whom he had direct access, a reality confirmed by Seigenthaler in author interview, Apr. 23, 1996.

11 Allsup, *The American G.I Forum*, p. 132; García, *Viva Kennedy*, p. 54.

12 Lorenzo Tapia interview, July 1984.

13 Carlos McCormick interview.

14 Frank Zaragoza interview, Apr. 1, 2000.

15 E.J. Salcines interview, July 9, 2002.

16 CSO brochure, [1962], b. 2, f. 1, UFW-Office of the President, ALUA, WSU; Allsup, *American G.I. Forum*, p. 132; Bok and Dunlap, *Labor*, p. 422; Statement of Vote, Nov. 8, 1960, p. 2, CSA.

17 Dolores Huerta interview; "Democrats: Little Brother is Watching," *Time*, Oct. 10, 1960; Schlesinger, *Robert Kennedy*, p. 852.

18 Herman Gallegos, OHI, 1989, ROHO, UCB, pp. 19-20.

19 "Viva Kennedy Clubs of California, Official Directory," undated, *CVKWB*, Oct. 3, 1960, *CVKWB*, Oct. 17, 1960, RFK Pre-Administration Files, Box 40, JFK Library.

20 Henry López interview.

21 *CVKWB*, Oct. 17, 1960, pp. 15-16, op. cited.

22 Richard Santillan and Federico A. Subervi-Velez, "Latino Participation in Republican Party Politics in California," in Jackson and Preston, eds., *Racial and Ethnic Politics*, p. 290.

23 César Chávez, OHI, p. 16, JFK Library.

24 Carlos McCormick interview.

25 Sidney Kraus, *The Great Debates* (Bloomington: Indiana Press, 1962), p. 348.

26 Henry López interview; Carlos McCormick interview; "Civil Rights Bulletin," Oct. 31, 1960, 143.16, Garcia Papers; García, *Viva Kennedy*, pp. 56-57; Ramos, *American GI Forum*, p. 36.

27 "Jackie Talks to Latins," *Riverside Press*, Oct. 13, 1960, in Scrapbook, 4.2, Garcia Papers.

28 Carlos McCormick interview; TV Commercial, Audio Archives, JFK Library.

29 Armando Rodríguez interview.

30 Misc. articles, 4.4, Garcia Papers.

31 "Sen. Kennedy Here Today for Talk, Rallies," *LAT*, Nov. 1, 1960, p. 1; "200,000 Welcome Kennedy in Downtown L.A. Motorcade," *LAT*, Nov. 2, 1960, p. 1.

32 Joseph R. Cerrell interview, Sept. 29, 1998; Carlos McCormick interview; Theodore H. White, *The Making of the President 1960* (New York: Book-of-the-Month Club, 1988), p. 363; Pre-Presidential Papers, Senate Files, Speech Files, East Los Angeles College Stadium, California, 11-1-60, Box 914, JFK Library.

33 Joseph Sánchez, Sr. interview, Dec. 18, 1981.

34 Leopoldo Sánchez interview; Edward Ramírez interview; George Sotelo interview; Memo to Files, Jan. 12, 1960, Re: L.A. Municipal Court, b. 70, f. AD 51-Munnell, Pat Brown Papers; "Forumeer Defeats A Gov. Brown Picked Candidate: See November Victory As Sanchez's Candidacy Assures Big Turnout," *FNB*, June 1960, 1, Garcia Papers.

35 Henry López interview; Carlos McCormick interview; "Crowds Greets Ted Kennedy," *Santa Barbara News-Press*, October 27, 1960; "Viva Kennedy Clubs Urge Big Voter Turnout," *Fresno Bee*, November 7, 1960, Scrapbook 4.2, Garcia Papers.

36 Statement of Vote, 1948-1960, CSA.

37 Frank Cullen, Sr. interview, 2001-2002.

38 Carlos McCormick interview; Allsup, *American G.I Forum*, p. 132; Levy and. Kramer, *The Ethnic Factor*, pp. 77, 256-257; Telegram, Kennedy to Garcia, Nov. 10, 1960, n.n., and "On Hand for Aztec Eagle Award," *Forumer*, Mar.-Apr. 1960, p. 11, Garcia Papers.

39 J. R. Feagin and C. B. Feagin, *Racial and Ethnic Relations*, 7th ed. (Upper Saddle River, N.J.: Prentice Hall, 2003), p. 315; Levy and Kramer, *The Ethnic Factor*, pp. 256-259; Polenberg, *One Nation Divisible*, p. 168.

40 Carlos McCormick interview.

41 Ibid.; b. 35, Roybal Papers, UCLA.

42 Letter, Garcia to Kennedy, Jan. 11, 1961, n.n., and Letter, Héctor [García] to Manuel Avila, Jr., Feb. 25, 1961, 46.27, and Letter, Garcia to Lawrence F. O'Brien, Feb. 25, 1961, 51.49, Garcia Papers.

43 Carlos McCormick interview; *The New Frontiersmen: Profiles of the Men Around Kennedy* (Washington, D.C.: Public Affairs Press, 1961), p. 30.

44 Carlos McCormick interview.

45 Henry López interview; Carlos McCormick interview.

46 Carlos McCormick interview.

47 Tom Rees interview, July 9, 1997.

48 Carlos McCormick interview.

49 "L.A. Judge May Get Envoy Post," *LAE*, Feb. 8, 1961, p. 1; "Judge Carlos Teran Mentioned as Envoy," *LAM*, 53.26, Garcia Papers.

50 Letter, Manuel Avila, Jr. to Dr. Hector P. Garcia, Feb. 4, 1961, 53.2, Garcia Papers.

51 Letter, Manuel Avila, Jr. to Dr. Hector P. Garcia, Feb. 15, 1961, 53.26, Garcia Papers.

52 Henry López interview; Carlos McCormick interview; Brochure, Democratic National Committee, "Our Goal Is Progress," 62.48, Garcia Papers.

53 Joseph Breckenridge interview, Sept. 4, 2002; Brochure, Democratic National Committee, "Our Goal Is Progress," 62.48, Garcia Papers.

54 Ralph Guzmán interview, Mar. 2, 1982; Henrietta Villaescusa interview.

55 Minutes, California Committee for Fair Housing Practices, Nov. 30, 1960, b. 1, f. 2, Mont Papers.

56 Ibid.

57 Bill Becker interview; Dolores Huerta interview; Tony Ríos interview; Fred Ross, Jr. interview, 1996-2001; Jacobs, *A Rage for Justice*, p. 78; Gov. Brown, July 12, 1961, AB 5, Chapter 1970, Gov. Files, CSA.

58 Dolores Huerta interview. See John Jacobs, *A Rage for Justice*, p. 79.

59 Bill Becker interview; Tony Ríos interview.

60 Address by Brown, LULAC Convention, May 6, 1961, b. 78, f. Mexican American Speeches, and b. 508, f. Social Welfare-June-Dec. [1961], Pat Brown Papers.

61 "Welfare Bills Approved by Committee," Associated Press, May 25, 1961, b. 508, f. Old Age Pension, Pat Brown Papers.

62 Dolores Huerta interview.

63 Brown, July 12, 1961, AB 5, Chapter 1970, Gov. Files, CSA; CSO, "Que Dia Tan Maravilloso!," and Dolores Huerta, CSO Legislative Report-1961, b. 26, f. 29, UFW-Office of the Pres., and CSO brochure, [1962], 2/1, UFW Papers; Gutiérrez, *Walls and Mirrors,* p. 172.

64 CSO, "The CSO Story: American Democracy is Not A Fake," b. 13, f. 8, Galarza Papers.

65 Bill Becker interview; Dolores Huerta interview; Tony Ríos interview.

66 Dolores Huerta, CSO Legislative Report-1961, b. 26, f. 29, UFW Papers.

67 Address by Brown, LULAC Convention, May 6, 1961, b. 78, f. Mexican American Speeches, Pat Brown Papers.

68 "Recognition, Appointments Urged By Judge," *ELAG*, Oct. 8, 1961, 51.50, Garcia Papers; Address by Governor Edmund G. Brown, Oct. 4, 1961," b. 78, f. Mexican American Speeches, Pat Brown Papers.

69 Benjamin J. B. Allen, *Amigos Sam?: Mayor Sam Yorty and the Latino Community of Los Angeles*, Thesis, Department of History, Harvard University, Mar. 23, 2000, p. 26; Banfield, *Big City Politics*, pp. 85-86; Greenstone, *Labor in American Politics*, pp. 147-149; Sonenshein, *Politics in Black and White*, pp. 38-39.

70 George Sotelo interview; Edward Ramírez interview; Leopoldo Sánchez interview; Richard Tafoya interview, May 31, 1997; Letter, Raul Morin to Dear Friend, May 19, 1961, that includes list of pro-Yorty Latinos, in b. 2, f. 8, Quevedo Papers; Parson, *Making a Better World*, pp. 183-185.

71 "Group Voting in the 1961 Los Angeles Mayoral Election," *BGR Observer* (Bureau of Governmental Research, UCLA), Nov. 1961.

72 Norris Poulson, OHI, 1966, OHP, UCLA, p. 441.

73 "Los Angeles: Upset," *Newsweek*, June 12, 1961, p. 38.

74 George Sotelo interview; Edward Ramírez interview; Richard Tafoya interview. See also Benjamin John Bridgeman Allen, *Amigos Sam?* p. 48.

75 Assembly Interim Committee on Elections and Reapportionment, Transcript of Hearing, Dec. 15, 16, 1960, in Los Angeles, pp. 237-238.

76 Roger Johnson interview; Newspaper Clippings, Roybal Papers, CSULA.

77 Carlos McCormick interview.

78 Letter, Carlos McCormick to Garcia, Apr. 16, 1962, 59.54, Garcia Papers.

79 Henry Lacayo interview, Jan. 4, 1997, 2000-2006; Keith M. Seegmiller interview, Jan. 15, 1997; Greenstone, *Labor in American Politics*, pp. 224-225, 238-239, 301; "Gov. Olson Gives Nod to Roybal," *Westlake Post* and *Wilshire Post*, Mar. 22, 1962, Roybal Papers, CSULA; Statement of the Vote, June 5, 1962, p. 20, CSA.

80 Bert Corona interview; "Mexican Group Elects Castelan," *SFC*, June 17, 1962, p. 17.

81 Arthur L. Alarcon, OHI, 1988, OHP, UCLA, for the CSAOHP, p. 56.
82 Ibid, pp 59, 71-73, 245, 252-265.
83 Bert Corona interview.
84 "Brown voted Support of U.S. Mexican Group," *LAT*, Aug. 12, 1962.
85 Democratic National Committee, "Our Goal Is Progress," [1st version] 62.48, Garcia Papers, and "Our Is Progress," [2nd. version] Newspaper Clippings, Roybal Papers, CSULA.
86 Roger Johnson interview; Henry Lacayo interview; Hope Mendoza Schechter interview; Keith Seegmiller interview; Newspaper Clippings, Roybal Papers, CSULA.
87 "Presidential Tour Slated for District," *30ᵗʰ CD Demo*, and campaign mailer of White House letter, October 23, 1962, Newspaper Clippings, Roybal Papers, CSULA.
88 Jackson Putman, "Jesse and Pat: A Creative Conflict in California Political History, 1955-1966," in Schiesl, *Responsible Liberalism*, pp. 155-156; Rapoport, *California Dreaming*, p. 75.
89 Statement of the Vote, Nov. 6, 1962, CSA.
90 "LA Congressmen-Elect Is Speaker at CSO Banquet," *The Hanford Sentinel*, Nov. 10, 1962, Newspaper Clippings, Roybal Papers, CSULA.
91 Philip Soto interview, Mar. 9, 1982; quote from Philip L. Soto, OHI, 1988, OHP, UCLA, for the CSAOHP; "Pioneering Eastside Assemblyman John Moreno Dies at 72," *LAT*, Aug. 29, 1999; Statement of the Vote, June 5, 1962, and Nov. 6, 1962, CSA.
92 Philip Soto interview; Henrietta Villaescusa interview.
93 "Roybal Speaks, Interview Council Candidates at Mass Meeting," n.p, n.d., Clippings, Roybal Papers, CSULA.
94 Ibid.
95 Newspaper Clippings, Roybal Papers, CSULA; Sorenshein, *Politics in Black and White*, pp. 40-46.
96 Richard Tafoya interview.
97 Ibid., George Sotelo interview.
98 Carlos McCormick interview; "Will Opposed Bracero Program Use Next Year, Brown Says: Reluctantly Supported Present Extension, Governor Tells Mexican-American Parley," *LAT*, Nov. 10, 1963, p. 21.
99 "Kennedy Lauds Roybal Plan for JFK Play Area at Hazard," *ESS*, July 23, [1964,] and "For 'Kennedy Playground': Bobby to Attend Park Board Meeting," *Citizen News*, July 19, [1964,] Newspaper Clippings, Roybal Papers, CSULA.

CHAPTER 10
VIVA JOHNSON, GOVERNOR BROWN, & THE BIRTH OF THE UNITED FARM WORKERS

1 "Johnson Warns Reds on Vietnam War: U.S., Mexico Chiefs Meet in L.A., Tighten Bonds of Friendship," *LAT*, Feb. 22, 1964, p. 1; "Brown Urges Closer Ties with Mexico," *SFC*, Feb. 18, 1964, p. 8; Pierre Salinger, *With Kennedy* (Garden City, N.Y.: Doubleday, 1966), p. 343.
2 "Gift at Fiesta Surprises Lady Bird," *LAT*, Feb. 23, 1964, p. 2; "Johnson, Lopez Mateos Vow to Continue Work for Peace: Presidents End 2-Day Meeting, Cheered by Sports Arena Crowd," *LAT*, Feb. 23, 1964, p. 1.
3 Dionicio Morales interview.
4 "Lyndon in Town: Seeing 'Everybody'," *LAEH&E*, Aug. 9, 1963, Photo cap-

tion, Vice President Arrives," *LAT*, Aug. 10, 1963, p. 2; "Mexican-American Groups: Host Vice President Today, Rep. Roybal, Brown Attend," *BC*, Aug. 8, 1963, Newspaper Clippings, Roybal Papers, CSULA; Morales, *Dionicio Morales,* pp. 170-177.

5   Leopoldo Sánchez interview; Edward Ramírez interview; "Johnson Urges Latin Citizens to Report Bias," *LAT*, Aug. 10, 1963, p. 1; Letter, Raul Morin to Robert Hernandez, Aug. 6, 1963, Semi-Process Area, Garcia Papers.

6   "LA Convention: Governor, Congressman to Address MAPA Members," *ESS*, Nov. 7, 1963; "Will Oppose Bracero Program Use Next Year, Brown Says: Reluctantly Supported Present Extension, Governor Tells Mexican-American Parley," *LAT*, Nov. 10, 1963, p. 21; Report on the proceeding of the MAPA convention, in the FBI's file on Bert Corona, obtained by author under the FOIA.

7   George Sotelo interview; Edward Ramírez interview; Letter, Raul Morin to Bob Sanchez, November 30, 1963, 51.5, Garcia Papers; Pycior, *LBJ & Mexican Americans*, p. 131; Memo, George E. Reedy from Hobart Taylor, Jan. 11, 1964, Re: The Los Angeles Conference, with attachment, Container 23, Mexican, Aides Files: George Reedy, LBJ Library.

8   Daniel Luevano interview; "Luevano Named Assistant to Army Secretary," *San Francisco Chronicle*, March 1, 1964, p. 20; Lou Cannon, *Ronnie and Jessie* (Garden City, N.Y.: Doubleday, 1969), p. 117.

9   Raúl Yzaguirre interview.

10   Brochure, All Americans Council/Viva Johnson Clubs, "Continuemos Adelante Viva Johnson Y Humphrey," [1964], and Brochure, Spanish-Speaking Californians for President Lyndon B. Johnson, "Let Us Continue," [1964,] Newspaper Clippings, Roybal Papers, CSULA.

11   *Official Proceedings, Democratic Party National Convention, Atlantic City, New Jersey, August 24-27, 1964* (Washington, D.C.: DNC, 1968), pp. 138-145.

12   Statement of Vote, June 2, 1964, p. 5, CSA.

13   Armando Rodríguez interview.

14   Carlos McCormick interview; Vicente Ximenes interview, June 1984; Allsup, *American G.I. Forum*, pp. 59-60.

15   Email, Amador to author, Aug. 9, 2005.

16   Vicente Ximenes interview; Edward Ramírez interview; "Three Named for North State Drive," *SFC*, Sept. 3, 1964, p. 8; Newspaper Clippings, 1964, Roybal Papers, CSULA; Viva Johnson Club," [undated], DNC Research, Container 166, LBJ Library.

17   Bert Corona interview; "Call For Unity Is Issued At Political Parley," *FB*, June 14, 1964; "Mexican-American Assn. Backs Negro 'Coalition'," *LAT*, June 15, 1964; "Latin-Negro Unity Move Launched: Politicians Hope to Obtain 'Balance of Election Power'," *LAT*, July 5, 1964.

18   "Tight Security Set for Johnson Visit: Heaviest Force in City History to Guard Motorcade Route Today," *LAT*, Oct. 28, 1964, p. 1; "H. Humphrey: Viva Johnson-Humphrey Fiesta at East LA Stadium Sunday," *BC*.

19   Levy and. Kramer, *The Ethnic Factor*, pp. 78, 256-256.

20   Héctor Abeytia interview; Bill Becker interview; Bert Corona interview; Alfonso Gonzáles interview, Nov. 24, 1981, May 10, 1982; Governor's Meeting With Mexican American Community, Roster, Dec. 28,1964; Memorandum, to Governor Brown from Helen Amick, Subject: Mexican American Lunch Today, Jan. 14, 1965, b. 92, f. Mexican Americans, "Pat" Brown Papers.

21 "Will Opposed Bracero Program Use Next Year, Brown Says: Reluctantly Supported Present Extension, Governor Tells Mexican-American Parley," *LAT*, Nov. 10, 1963, p. 21.

22 Héctor Abeytia interview; Bert Corona interview; Press release, Mexican American Organizations, Jan. 5, 1965, b. 15, f. 12, Mont Papers.

23 Minutes, MAPA Board of Directors Meeting, Aug. 24, 1963, pp. 4-5, as cited in Kenneth C. Burt, "The History of the Mexican American Political Association and Chicano Politics in California," Honors Thesis, UC, Berkeley, 1982, p. 58.

24 Héctor Abeytia interview.

25 Bert Corona interview; Dallek, *The Right Moment,* p. 46.

26 Héctor Abeytia interview; Bill Becker interview; Bert Corona interview; Albert Tieburg interview.

27 Héctor Abeytia interview.

28 Meister and Loftis, *A Long Time Coming*, pp. 89-90.

29 Héctor Abeytia; Press release, Mexican-American Unity Council, [May 9, 1965], b. 15, f. 14, Mont Papers.

30 "Area Domestic Farm Worker Recruitment Called Success," *SJM*, Sept. 26, 1965, and "War on Poverty Program Officers Opportunity," *SMJ*, Sept. 19, 1965, in Luis Juarez, *Mexican-American Notes, 1965-1976*, California Room, King Library, San Jose State University.

31 Héctor Abeytia interview; Bill Becker interview; Bert Corona interview; Albert Tieburg interview; Chronology of events, 5-9-65 to 6-4-65, prepared by Albert Pinon, MAUC, b. 15, f. 14, Mont Papers; *CF*, Jan.-June 1965.

32 "Mexican-American Groups Demand Separate Services," *CF*," June 5, 1965, p. 8.

33 "Mexican Group Will Open Parley Tonight, " *FB*, July 23, 1965; "Convention Gets Praise and Pickets," *FB*, July 25, 1965; "MAPA Asks Voice in Poverty War," *FB*, July 26, 1965.

34 Héctor Abeytia interview; Bert Corona interview; Paul Schrade interview.

35 Héctor Abeytia interview; Bert Corona interview; Anthony Ramos interview, July 30, 1998.

36 George G. Higgins, *Organized labor and the Church: Reflections of a 'Labor Priest'* (New York: Paulist Press, 1993), p. 87.

37 Héctor Abeytia interview; Bert Corona interview.

38 Bert Corona interview.

39 Hoffman, *Ministry of the Dispossessed*, p. 27. The Emergency Committee to Aid Farm Workers was staffed by the Jewish Labor Committee. See Mont Papers.

40 Ferris and Sandoval, *The Fight in the Fields*, pp. 102-103.

41 Henry Lacayo interview; Paul Schrade interview. Lacayo was a Social Democrat.

42 Ralph Arriola interview.

43 Henry Lacayo interview.

44 Paul Schrade interview; Ferriss and Sandoval, *The Fight in the Fields*, pp. 114-115. For coverage, see "Grapes of Wrath," *Newsweek*, Dec. 27, 1965, pp. 57-58.

45 Flyer, "Viva La Huelga," b. 13, f. 4, Mont Papers.

46 Leopoldo Sánchez interview; George Sotelo interview; Address by Governor Edmund G. Brown, Testimonial dinner for Judge Leopoldo Sanchez, Feb. 13, 1966, b. 78, f. Mexican American Speeches, Pat Brown Papers.

47 Paul Schrade interview; Peter B. Edelman, OHI 1969, no. 1, pp. 125-126, JFK Library.

48   Bert Corona interview; Pycior, *LBJ & Mexican Americans*, p. 165.

49   "Amending Migratory Labor Laws," Hearings on S. 1864 et al., U.S. Senate Committee on Labor and Public Welfare, Subcommittee on Migratory Labor, 89th Congress, 1st, 2nd session (Washington, DC: GPO, 1966).

50   Peter B. Edelman, OHI, no. 1, pp. 126-129, JFK Library.

51   César E. Chávez, OHI, 1969, pp. 5-8, JFK Library.

52   Henry Santiestevan interview.

53   Dunne, *Delano*, pp. 121-135; Hammerback and Jensen, *The Rhetorical Career of César Chávez*, p. 87.

54   Minutes, Board of Directors, CLRA, May 14, 1966, author's files.

55   "For Spanish Speaking: Abeytia Heads State Job-Training Project," *FB*, Feb. 24, 1966.

56   B. 78, f. Mexican American Speeches, Pat Brown Papers.

57   Ainsworth, *Maverick Mayor,* p. 231; Joseph Lewis, *What Makes Reagan Run?* (New York: McGraw-Hill, 1968), p. 151.

58   Robert E. Gonzales interview.

59   Levy, *Cesar Chavez*, p. 231; Dunne, *Delano*, p. 147, Majka and Majka, *Farm Workers,* p. 181.

60   Héctor Abeytia interview; Bert Corona interview; "Brown, Reagan Court Mexican Americans," *LAT*, June 26, 1966.

61   Address by Governor Edmund G. Brown, MAPA Luncheon, June 25, 1966, b. 78, f. Mexican American Speeches, Pat Brown Papers.

62   Héctor Abeytia interview; Bert Corona interview; Dunne, *Delano,* p. 147; Levy, *Cesar Chavez*, p. 231; Taylor, *Chavez And The Farm Workers*, pp. 193-195.

63   Héctor Abeytia interview; Bill Becker interview; Bert Corona interview; "Governor Pledges Probe of DiGiorgio Vote Dispute," *FB*, June 28, 1966; Levy, *Cesar Chavez*, p. 231.

64   Meister and Loftis, *A Long Time Coming*, pp. 149-150; Taylor, *Chavez and the Farm Workers*, pp. 194-202.

65   Henry Santiestevan interview; *IUE Agenda*, July 1966.

66   "Latins Form Committee to Back Brown," *LAT*, Aug. 12, 1966; Newspaper Clippings, Roybal Papers, CSULA.

67   "Ted Kennedy Keeps Busy Pace in Southland Tour for Party," *LAT*, Oct. 2, 1966, p. B; "Crowds Cheer Ted, Brown," *LAEH&E*, Oct. 2, 1966, p. A-3; "Politics at the Palladium: Behind the Other Conference," *PW*, Oct. 8, 1966, p. 2.

68   "Reagan Matches Forces With Brown on East L.A. Tour," *LAT*, Oct. 2, 1966, p. B.

69   *Lewis, What Makes Reagan Run?* pp. 149-150; Schuparra, *Triumph of the Right*, pp. 140-141; Richard Santillan and Federico A. Subervi-Velez, "Latino Participation in Republican Party Politics in California," in Jackson and Preston, *Racial and Ethnic Politics in California*, pp. 293-294.

70   Carton 67, Pat Brown Papers, Berkeley.

71   Margaret Cruz interview, Nov. 12, 1981, Apr. 10, 1982; "USF Appearance: Bobby's Talk Is Tomorrow," *SFC*, Oct. 22, 1966, p. 6.

72   "East LA College: Sen. Kennedy to Appear at Democratic Rally," *BC*, Oct. 20, 1966, Clippings, Roybal Papers, CSULA; "Reagan's Racism Flares Up as Campaign Heads for Polls," *PW*, Oct. 29, 1966, p. 12; "RFK Calls California World Inspiration," *FB*, Oct. 23, 1868, p. 1.

73 Bert Corona interview; Henry Lacayo interview; Paul Schrade interview; Remarks by Governor Edmund G. Brown, MAPA Salute to Mexican American Labor Leaders, Nov. 3, 1966, b. 78, f. Mexican Americans, Pat Brown Papers.

74 Cannon, *Governor Reagan,* p. 160.

75 Hill, *Dancing Bear,* p. 254; Lewis, *What Makes Reagan Run?* p. 152; Rarick, *California Rising,* pp. 341-366; Santillan and Subervi-Velez, "Latino Participation in Republican Party Politics in California," p. 294. Alberto Juárez, "The Emergence of El Partido de la Raza Unida," *Aztlan* 3:2 (1973): 197, Bravo claimed Reagan appointed 54 Latinos to "non-civil service jobs" in his first term.

76 Luis Juarez, "Governor Reagan's Choices Lauded," *SJM*, Apr. 23, 1967.

77 "Julio Gonzales, 86; Helped Reach Out to Latinos," *LAT*, Dec. 14, 2003, p. B10; Torso del Junco, OHI, 1982, ROHO, UCB, p. 8.

78 Guzman, *The Political Socialization,* p. 173.

79 Cannon, *Governor Reagan*; Dallek, *The Right Moment,* pp. 211-239; Matt Dallek, "Up From Liberalism: Pat Brown, Ronald Reagan, and the 1966 Gubernatorial Election," in Schiesl, *Responsible Liberalism,* pp. 193-216; Rarick, *California Rising,* pp. 255-366.

80 See note 76.

81 "Assemblyman Thought to be Finished Politically," *The Eagles,* Jan. 25, 1964, p. 1, Hispanic Link News Service files.

82 Dionicio Morales interview; Philip Soto interview. This examination of the defeat of Soto and Moreno reevaluates the literature. According to Chávez, *¡Mi Raza Primero,* p. 37, "these [electoral] achievements became short-lived, when the districts were almost immediately reapportioned, leading to the defeat of Moreno and Soto." Moreno lost prior to the 1966 reapportionment and Soto lost largely to the Reagan landslide.

83 Newspaper Clippings, Roybal Papers, CSULA; Statement of Vote, Primary Election, June 7, 1966, CSA.

84 Henry Lacayo interview; Leo Grebler, Joan W. Moore, Guzman, *The Mexican American People,* pp. 561; Acuña, *Anything But Mexican,* p. 49.

85 Charlie Erickson interview, Mar. 2, 2003; Nava, *Julian Nava,* p. 71.

86 *MAPA News,* May 24, 1967, p. 8, Chicano, Sub. File, SCLSSR; Nava, *Julian Nava,* pp. 71-73.

87 Nava, *Julian Nava,* pp. 70-81.

Chapter 11
President Johnson, Vietnam, and the Politics of Race

1 Edward Ramírez interview; Daniel Luevano interview.

2 "Proposition 14 Opponents Schedule Rally Here Sunday," *BC*, Oct. 15, 1964, and "Roybal, Soto Head Latin 'No' on 14 Group," n.p., n.d., and mailer, MAPA, "Discrimination & Segregation Is Aimed At Us," in Newspaper Clippings, Roybal Papers, CSULA; "State Gathering: Mexican Group Hails Church for Prop. 14 Fight," *SFC*, Oct. 4, 1964, p. 1A; Martin Schiesl, "The Struggle for Equality," in Schiesl, ed., *Responsible Liberalism,* pp. 113-117.

3 Héctor Abeytia interview; Bert Corona interview; "Condemn Racial Violence: Congressmen Urge Action in Alabama," *BC*, Mar. 16, 1965, and "5000 March Here In Selma Protest," *LAEH&E*, Mar. 13, 1965, Newspaper Clippings, Roybal Papers, CSULA.

4   Héctor Abeytia interview; Bert Corona interview; Minutes, MAPA Executive
    Board Meeting, Downey, Apr. 24, 1965, cited in Kenneth C. Burt, "The
    History of the Mexican American Political Association and Chicano Politics in
    California," Honors Thesis, UC, Berkeley, 1982, p. 78.

5   B. 177, f. Mexican-American White House Conference, Roybal Papers, CSULA.

6   B. 177, f. Recommendations-Mexican-Americans, 1963-1969, Roybal Papers,
    CSULA; Pycior, *LBJ & Mexican Americans*, pp. 154-155.

7   "CSO '65: Reflections by Rosie Vasquez," [1996], author's files; Rosie Vásquez
    interview, 2000-2004.

8   Armando Rodríguez interview.

9   Ibid.

10 News Release, Albuquerque, Mar. 28, 1966, 105.14, Garcia Papers; News re-
    lease, National Mexican-American Ad Hoc Committee on Equal Employment
    Opportunity, b. 7, f. 16, UFWOC Papers, ALUA, WSU; Memo, Franklin D.
    Roosevelt, Jr. to The President, [April 7, 1966], ExHu2-1/MC, LBJ Library.

11 Hope Mendoza Schechter interview; "L.A. Community Service Organization
    Honors Members Appointed to FEPC and State Industrial Welfare
    Commission," *ESS*, July 15, 1965, Newspaper Clippings, Roybal Papers,
    CSULA.

12 "Democratic National Committee Called 'Lax': Spanish Voters Ignored, Solon
    Says," *Albuquerque Journal*, April 3, 1966, 105.14, Garcia Papers; García,
    Memories of Chicano History, pp. 224-225.

13 *Public Papers of the Presidents of the United States: Lyndon B. Johnson: 1966*,
    Vol.1 (Washington, DC: GPO, 1967), pp. 388-389.

14 Bert Corona interview; Joseph A. Califano, Jr., *The Triumph & Tragedy of
    Lyndon Johnson: The White House Years* (New York: Simon & Schuster, 1991),
    pp. 135-137; Pycior, *LBJ & Mexican Americans*, pp. 169-170.

15 Memo, Harry McPherson to Joe Califano, February 17 [1967], "Mexican
    Americans," Office Files of Harry McPherson, Container 11, LBJ Library.

16 B. 177, f. Mexican-American White House Conference, Roybal Papers, CSULA
    Papers; Memo, Irv Sprague to Joe Califano, Mar. 1, 1967, "Mexican American
    Conference (2)," Office Files of Irvine Sprague, Container 7, LBJ Library.

17 "Ambitious Program for Spanish Speaking Meet," *PW*, Mar. 11, 1966, p. 2;
    "Mexican Americans Form Militant Alliance," *PW*, Mar. 25, 1967, p. 1.

18 Bert Corona interview; "Minorities Speak Out: Civil Rights Commission Is Put
    on Trial in West," *Washington Post*, May 4, 1967; Memorandum, 5/5/67, with
    attached flyer, MAPA FBI File obtained by author.

19 Bert Corona interview; MAPA Roster of Officers, May 1, 1967, b. 67, f. 3, UFW
    Papers.

20 "Johnson Creates Group to Aid Latin-Americans," *LAT*, June 10, 1967.

21 Vicente Ximenes interview.

22 Raúl Yzaguirre interview.

23 Telegram, Corona to The President, June 12, 1967, EX FG 655/A, Container
    382, LBJ Library.

24 Memo, John W. Macy, Jr. to The President, June 16, 1967, EX FG 655/A,
    Container 382, LBJ Library.

25 Minutes, Informal Meeting, Riverside, July 15, 1967 and Minutes, Pre-White
    House Conference, Los Angeles, July 22, 1967, b. 177, f. Mexican American
    White House Conference, Roybal Papers, CSULA.

26 "¡Bien Hecho, Senior Presidente!" DNC, 1968 Campaign, Candidates: LBJ, Printed Materials, 1968(2), 150.F.13.8(F), MHS.

27 Vicente Ximenes interview; Press Release, "Press Conference of Vicente Ximenes," Sept. 12, 1967, IACMAA, Wirtz, NA.

28 Letter, Acevedo to Roybal, Sept. 14, 1967, with attached list; Letter, Acevedo to Ximenes, Sept. 27, 1967, b. 177, f. Mexican American White House Conference, Roybal Papers, CSULA.

29 Letter, Acevedo to Roybal, Sept. 25, 1967, 177/Mexican American White House Conference, Roybal Papers, CSULA.

30 Memo, To Ed Moreno, et al., from Conference Steering Committee, Juan Acevedo, Coordinator, California Pre-White House Conference, Sept. 22, 1967, b. 65 f. 11, UFW Papers.

31 Letter, Chavez to Ximenes, Sept. 27, 1967, b. 65, f. 11, UFW Papers.

32 Letter, Roybal to David Santiago, Oct. 11, 1967, and letter, Ximenes to Roybal, Oct. 18, 1967, in b. 177, f. Mexican-American White House Conference, Roybal Papers, CSULA.

33 "Latin Position Papers Readied for White House Conference," *BC*, Oct. 12, 1967, Newspaper Clippings, Roybal Papers, CSULA.

34 "State's Latin Citizens Demand Action to End Poverty Status," *LAT*, Oct. 9, 1967.

35 Bert Corona FBI File obtained by the author.

36 "30 Congressmen Ask LBJ to Halt Bombing," *LAEH&E*, Oct. 13, 1967.

37 "Mexican-American Unit to Boycott Conference," *LAT*, Oct. 17, 1967.

38 Louis Flores interview.

39 Bert Corona interview; Louis Flores interview; Robert E. Gonzales interview.

40 *Testimony Presented at the Cabinet Committee Hearings on Mexican American Affairs, El Paso, Texas, October 26-28, 1967* ([Washington, DC:] U.S. Inter-Agency Committee on Mexican-American Affairs, [1967]).

41 Armando Rodríguez interview.

42 "La Voz De Mexico, En El Capitolio: Díaz Ordaz Habla en Congreso; Luego, un Comunicado Conjunto," *LO*, Oct. 28, 1967, p.1; "HHH, Ante Los Mexicanamericanos: Les Señala Derroteros en El Paso," *LO*, Oct. 28, 1967, p. 1.

43 Remarks of Vice President Hubert H. Humphrey, Hearing on Mexican American Affairs, El Paso, Texas, Oct. 27, 1997, Groups: Ethnics: Mexican Americans, Jan-June 1968, 150.F.14.8(F), MHS.

44 *Transcript of Proceedings on Labor Affairs, Cabinet Committee Hearings on Mexican American Affairs,* ([Washington, DC:] U.S. Inter-Agency Committee on Mexican American Affairs, [1967]); Letter, Vicente T. Ximenes to W. Willard Wirtz, October 25, 1967 and "Participants Program," Cabinet Committee Hearings on Mexican American Affairs, IACMAA, Wirtz, NA.

45 Philip Newman interview; "El Chamizal Es Ya Suelo de Mexico: 300,000 Aclaman den Juarez a los 2 Presidentes: Johns y Díaz Ordaz Selan con un Abrazo el Historico Acuerdo," *LO*, Oct. 29, 1967, p. 1; Bill Henry, "Friendship Cemented," *LAT*, Nov. 1, 1967.

46 Ramos, *The American GI Forum*, p. 105. See also "Victory Claimed At El Paso Meet: ELA Leaders Hail US Cabinet Level Talks On Problems," *ELAT*, Nov. 2, 1967, IACMAA, Wirtz, NA.

47 Dionicio Morales interview.

48 "LBJ Aide Ximenes To Be Here Saturday," *ELAT*, Nov. 23, 1967, and Letter, Roybal and Brown to Ximenes, Dec. 1, 1967, with attached, "A Voice in

Washington: Mexican American Affairs Championed," *LAEH&E*, Nov. 28, 1967, Newspaper Clippings, Roybal Papers, CSULA.

49 "ELA Leaders Say Survey is Result of El Paso Meet," ELAT, Nov. 9, 1967, Newspaper Clippings, Roybal Papers, CSULA.

50 Bert Corona interview; Robert E. Gonzales interview; Henry Santiestevan interview; Carl Alsup, *American G.I Forum*, pp. 140-141; Castro, *Chicano Power*, pp. 137-138; García, *Memories of Chicano History*, pp. 225-227.

51 Samora, ed., *La Raza*, p. 202.

52 Henry Santiestevan interview; Camarillo, *Chicanos in California*, pp. 88, 95; National Council of La Raza Papers, Special Collections, Stanford University.

53 Nava, *Julian Nava*, p. 75.

54 Daniel M. Luevano, OHI, 1988 OHP, UCLA for the CSAOHP, pp. 406-407.

55 Armando Rodríguez interview.

56 Eymann and Wollenberg, eds., *What's Going On?*

57 Raúl Yzaguirre interview.

CHAPTER 12
ROBERT KENNEDY, HUMPHREY AND THE 1968 PRESIDENTIAL ELECTION

1 "Lies About Rural Legal Assistance Defeat: Reagan Backs Away From Showdown With Shriver," *LAC*, Jan. 26, 1968, p. 1; "They Refused to Sit with Unionists: Panel on Braceros Set Up Despite State, Growers," *LAC*, Mar. 22, 1968, p. 1.

2 Vicente Ximenes interview; Raúl Yzaguirre interview; "Statement by the President Summarizing Actions on the Recommendations of the Inter-Agency committee on Mexican-Americans Affairs," in *Public Papers of the Presidents of the United States: Lyndon B. Johnson, 1968-69* (Washington, D.C.: GPO, 1970), pp. 266-268. See also HHH Papers, Political Affairs: Political Parties: Minority Group, 150.F.13.6(F), and Groups: Ethnic: Mexican American, Jan-June 1968, 150.F.14.8(F), MHS.

3 Henry Lacayo interview; "Pro-Johnson Delegation Picked for Convention," *Wilshire Press*, Mar. 21, 1968, Newspaper Clippings, Roybal Papers, CSULA.

4 Rodolfo Acuña interview, Nov. 7, 1997; List of delegates, in Statement of Vote, June 4, 1968, p. 6, CSA; RFK, 1968 Pres. Camp., Black Books, Calif.-Delegate Info., JFK Library.

5 Jack Ortega interview, Dec. 21, 1981; Bert Corona interview.

6 Majka and Majka, *Farm Workers*, pp. 162-163.

7 "Roybal Supports Objectives of Student Protest," *ES*, Mar. 14, 1968.

8 Muñuz, *Youth, Power, Identity*, 64.

9 Henry González interview, Dec. 29, 1998; Henry J. Gutiérrez, "Racial Politics in Los Angeles: Black and Mexican American Challenges to Unequal Education in the 1960s," *SCQ* 78:1 (Spring 1996): 67-69; Muñoz, *Youth, Power, Identity*, p. 203.

10 Dolores Huerta interview.

11 Cesar Chavez, JFKOHP, JFKL, pp. 20-21.

12 Schlesinger, *Robert Kennedy*, p. 904; Theodore H. White, *The Making of the President, 1968* (New York: Atheneum, 1969), pp. 3-30; Jules Witcover, *1968: The Year The Dream Died* (New York: Warner, 1997), pp. 94-101.

13 RFK 1968 Pres. Camp., Media, TV & Radio Ads: Planning Notebook, JFK Library.

14 RFK 1968 Pres Cam, National HQs Pres Div.: Subject File: CA: Spanish Press,

JFK Library.

15 Memo, Dave Hackett, March 21, 1968, RFK, 1968 Pres. Camp., Black Books, Calif., Background & Intelligence, JFK Library.

16 Chávez, *Eastside Landmark*, pp. 26-45.

17 Henry Santiestevan interview.

18 Hope Mendoza Schechter interview; Paul Schrade interview; Personal Papers of RFK, 1968 Pres. Camp. Black Books, Calif., Newsclips, JFK Library.

19 Paul Schrade interview.

20 Dolores Huerta interview.

21 Personal Papers of RFK, 1968 Pres. Camp. Black Books, Calif., Newsclips and Speeches Issues, JFK Library.

22 "Chavez Slates Appearance At Voter Drive," *SB*, Mar. 23, 1968.

23 Flyer, "You Can Vote, But Are Your Registered?" UFWOC, b. 7, f. 6, ALUA, WSU.

24 Rosie Vásquez interview, 2000-2002.

25 Richard D. Mahoney, *Sons & Brothers* (New York: Arcade, 1999), p. 370.

26 Memo, Nolan to Barron, Re: Viva Kennedy Rally in California, Apr. 29, 1968, Personal Papers of RFK, 1968 Pres. Camp., Black Books, Calif.-Background & Intelligence, JFK Library.

27 Herbert S. Parmet, *The Democrats: The Years After FDR* (New York: Macmillan, 1976), p. 273; Personal Papers of RFK, 1968 Pres. Camp., Black Books, Calif., Background & Intelligence and Newsclips, JFK Library.

28 Bert Corona interview; Jack Ortega interview; Paul Schrade interview; Personal Papers of RFK, 1968 Pres. Camp., Black Books, Indiana, Background & Intelligence, JFK Library.

29 Personal Papers of RFK, 1968 Pres. Camp. Black Books, Indiana, Background & Intelligence, JFK Library.

30 Bert Corona interview; Jack Ortega interview; RFK 1968 Pres. Camp., National HQ Press Division; Newsclips: State File: Indiana, JFK Library; Note, Henry Santiestevan to Cesar [Chávez] with attached letter, and *Latin Times*, May 3, 1968, UFWOC, b. 7, f. 6, ALUA, WSU.

31 RFK 1968 Pres. Camp., National HQ Press Division; Newsclips: State File: Indiana, JFK Library.

32 Herman Gallegos interview; Armando Rodríguez interview; Henry and Stina Santiestevan interview; Schlesinger, *Robert Kennedy*, p. 975; Personal Papers of RFK, 1968 Camp. Black Books, Calif.-Background & Intelligence, JFK Library.

33 Memo, Bacca to David Becket, May 16, 1968, p. 4, Personal Papers of RFK, 1968 Camp. Black Books, Calif.-Background & Intelligence, JFK Library.

34 Esteban Torres interview, Apr. 14, 1968; Henry Santiestevan interview; Paul Schrade interview; Newspaper Clippings, Roybal Papers, CSULA; Personal Papers of RFK, 1968 Camp. Black Books, Calif.-Background & Intelligence, JFK Library.

35 Jayne Ruiz interview, Mar. 13, 1982.

36 Louis Flores interview.

37 Letter, Vincent Godina to author, Oct. 12, 1998; Personal Papers of RFK, 1968 Pres. Camp. Black Books, Calif., Correspondence, JFK Library.

38 Cesar Chavez, OHI, pp. 24-26, JFK Library.

39 Leaflet #1, RFK, 1968 Pres. Camp., Black Books, Calif., Background & Intelligence, JFK Library.

40 Tabloid, *Viva Kennedy*, UFWOC, b. 7, f. 7, ALUA, WSU.

41 Henry G. González interview.

42 Dolores Huerta interview; Henry G. González interview; Hope M. Schechter interview; Esteban E. Torres interview; César Chávez, OHI, JFK Library; Personal Papers of RFK, 1968 Camp. Black Books, Calif.-Corr., 4-16-68-5-27-68; RFK 1968 Pres. Camp., Media, TV and Radio Ads, Transcripts #515-562; RFK 1968 Pres. Camp., National HQ's Press Division: Sub. File, Presidential Camp.: General Information, JFK Library.

43 César Chávez, OHI, p. 26, JFK Library.

44 Ralph Arriola interview, Sylmar, Jan. 24, 1998.

45 Alice Soto interview; Adam Walinsky, JFKOHP, JFKL, 1969-1979, p. 744; Witcover, *85 Days*, pp. 235-236.

46 "ABC News, Issues & Answers, Special Report," copy at JFKL; Mills, *Robert Kennedy*, pp. 442-443; Schlesinger, *Robert Kennedy*, pp. 978-979; Lewis Chester, Godfrey Hodgson, Bruce Page, *An American Melodrama: The Presidential Campaign of 1968* (New York: Viking Press, 1969), pp. 338-349.

47 "Roundup of Political Activity," *SFC*, May 28, 1968, p. 15; Schlesinger, *Robert Kennedy*, p. 975.

48 "Chavez Charges Reagan Plot to Wreck Farm Union," *LAC*, May 31, 1968, p. 1.

49 Margaret Cruz interview, Nov. 12, 1981, Apr. 10, 1982, Feb. 24, 2001.

50 Frank and Lucy Casado interview, Nov. 3, 1981.

51 Phillip C. Castruita interview, May 28, 1998; Raúl Henderson interview, May 28, 1998.

52 Castro, *Chicano Power*, p. 4; Pycior, *LBJ & Mexican Americans*, pp. 224-225. Statewide precinct results based on records at CSA.

53 Dolores Huerta interview.

54 "U.S. Mexican Leaders Vow To Hold RFK Ideals," *FB*, June 8, 1968.

55 Levy, *Cesar Chavez*, p. 291.

56 Louis Flores interview.

57 Pycior, *LBJ & Mexican Americans*, p. 225.

58 Henry Lacayo interview; Statement of the Vote, June 4, 1968, CSA. The United Mexican American Students supported unionist James Cruz, according to Alberto Juárez, "The Emergence of El Partido de la Raza Unida," *Aztlan* 3:2 (1973), p. 196.

59 Bert Corona interview; Robert E. González interview; George Sotelo interview; Oropeza, *¡Raza Si! ¡Guerra No,* pp. 66-67.

60 FBI Informant's Report, June 29, 1968, MAPA FBI Files.

61 Robert E. González interview.

62 Louis Flores interview.

63 Release, Statement by Vice President Hubert Humphrey, June 27, 1968, Groups: Ethnic: Mexican American, Jan.-June 1968, 150.F.14.8(F), MHS.

64 Hubert H. Humphrey, *Beyond Civil Rights,* p. 140.

65 Address by Vice President Hubert Humphrey, GI Forum Convention, "Battle in the Cause of Human Rights," Aug. 9, 1968, HHH Papers, Groups: Ethnic: Mexican American, July 1968, 150.F.14.8(F); and HHH Papers, Groups: Ethnic: Mexican American, Newspaper clippings, 1968, 150.F.14.8(8), MHS.

66 Ibid.

67 Ibid.

68 Candidates: Person: HHH Misc. 1968 (1), 150.F.13.8(F), MHS.

69 Henry Lacayo interview; Hope Mendoza Schechter interview; John Morton Blum, *Years of Discord: American Politics and Society, 1961-1974* (New York: Norton, 1991), pp. 305-310; Chester, et al., *An American Melodrama*, pp. 503-604; White, *The Making of the President, 1968*, pp. 257-313; Todd Gitlin, *The Sixties: Years of Hope, Days of Rage* (New York: Bantam Books, 1993), pp. 319-340.

70 Richard Santillan and Fedrico A. Subervi-Velez, "Latino Participation in Republican Party Politics in California," in Jackson and Preston, eds., *Racial and Ethnic Politics*, pp. 294-295.

71 California Broadcast, "Nixon Answers," July 16, 1968, PPS 208 (1968). 49, RMN Library.

72 Hon. James G. O'Hara, "Nixon's Deception on Grape Boycott: Candidate Nixon and the California Farmworkers," *Cong. Rec.*, Oct. 2, 1968.

73 Dolores Huerta interview.

74 "Cranston States His Principles to MAPA," *FB*, Sept. 8, 1968.

75 "Latins Balk at Presidential Endorsement," *LAT*, Sept. 9, 1968; "MAPA Shuns Presidential Candidates," *FB*, Sept. 9, 1968; *State (MAPA) Newsletter*, Oct. 1968, pp. 1, 7, author's files; Pycior, *LBJ & Mexican Americans*, p. 231.

76 Robert E. Gonzales interview.

77 Lewis Chester, *An American Melodrama*, p. 741.

78 Todd Gitlin, *Letters To A Young Activist* (New York: Basic Books, 2003), pp. 78-82.

79 "Humphrey Stays Firm Against Bombing Halt Now," *WP*, Sept. 26, 1968; Campaign Memo, Sept. 26, 1968, 1968 Campaign Files: Citizens for Humphrey: Regional: Region 4: California, 150.F.15.8(F), MHS.

80 Quote in "Humphrey Stays Firm Against Bombing Halt Now," *WP*, Sept. 26, 1968; Chester, *An American Melodrama*, pp. 607-650; White, *The Making of the President, 1968*, pp. 352-356.

81 "A First For S.F.: A Mexican American Named to School Board," *SFC*, Sept. 11, 1968, p. 3; "The New S.F. Supervisor," *SFC*, Nov. 8, 1968, p. 1; Hartman, *The Transformation of San Francisco*, pp. 29-30.

82 Press Release, "Nationalities Organization Backs Humphrey-Muskie," CHM, HHH Papers, Groups: Ethnic: Mexican American, Oct-Nov 1968, 150.F.14.8(8); "1968 Guide to Nationality Observances," DNC, HHH Papers, 1968 Campaign, Candidates: LBJ, Printed Materials, 1968(2), 150.F.13.8(F), MHS.

83 Henry and Stina Santiestevan interview; "Activists Are Hostile to Montoya as Leader," *Albuquerque Journal*, Sept. 29, 1968, Groups: Ethnic: Mexican Americans: Newspaper Clippings, 1968, 150.F.14.8(F), MHS.

84 Bert Corona interview; Frank Zaragoza interview; Release, "Humphrey to Talk with Peña, Other Democratic Leaders Friday," Oct. 10 [1968], HHH Papers, Groups: Ethnic: Mexican American, Oct-Nov 1968, 150.F.14.8(8), MHS.

85 Memo, Aldrete to Senator Montoya, et al., Oct. 11, 1968, HHH Papers, Groups: Ethnic: Mexican American, Oct-Nov 1968, 150.F.14.8(8), MHS.

86 Memos, Oct. 9, 1968, 1968 Campaign Files: Citizens for Humphrey: Regional: Region 4: California, 150.F.15.8(F), MHS.

87 Dolores Huerta interview.

88 Memos, Oct. 9, 1968, 1968 Campaign Files: Citizens for Humphrey: Regional: Region 4: California, 150.F.15.8(F), MHS.

89 Bert Corona interview; Press release, Peña, et al, n.d., b. 65, f. 11, UFW Papers.

90 Burt, *The History of the Mexican American Political Association*, p. 15.

91 Ray Solis interview, Hayward, May 25, 1982; Minutes, State Executive Board Meeting, November 30, 1968, cited in Kenneth C. Burt, "The History of the Mexican American Political Association and Chicano Politics in California," Honors Thesis, UC, Berkeley, 1982, p. 115.

92 Bert Corona interview.

93 Release, "'Viva Humphrey-Muskie' Nationwide Organization Announced by Democratic National Chairman O'Brien," DNC, Oct. 17, 1968, HHH Papers, Groups: Ethnic: Mexican American, Oct-Nov 1968, 150.F.14.8(8), MHS.

94 HHH Papers, Groups: Ethnic: Mexican American, Oct-Nov 1968, 150.F.14.8(8), MHS.

95 Henry Santiestevan interview; HHH Papers, Groups: Ethnic: Mexican American, Oct-Nov 1968, 150.F.14.8(8), MHS.

96 Ibid.

97 Remarks of Humphrey, Viva Humphrey Rally, East Los Angeles, October 23, 1968, HHH Papers, Groups: Ethnic: Mexican American, Oct-Nov 1968, 150. F.14.8(8), MHS.

98 "Thousands Hail Humphrey in Downtown L.A.: Vice President Answers cheers with Cry, 'We're Going to Sock It to 'em'," *LAT*, Nov. 5, 1968, p. 1

99 Pycior, *LBJ & Mexican Americans*, p. 232; Eymann and Wollenberg, eds., *What's Going On?*

100 Tony Castro, *Chicano Power*, pp. 198-214.

101 Email, Rodolfo Acuña to author, Apr. 7, 2002.

102 Chet Holifield, "Election of Roybal—Democracy at Work," *Cong. Rec.*, Aug. 9, 1949.

CHAPTER 13
REPUBLICANS, CHICANOS AND LATINO POLITICAL MACHINES

1 de la Isla, *The Rise of Hispanic Political Power*, pp. 22-56; Kaplowitz, *LULAC*, pp. 134-140; Castro, *Chicano Power*, pp. 198-214.

2 Richard A. Santillan, "El Partido La Raza Unida: Chicanos in Politics," *The Black Politician*, July 1971, pp. 45-52, and reprinted in F. Chris Garcia, ed., *Chicano Politics: Readings* (New York: MSS Information Corp., 1973).

3 Muñoz, *Youth, Identity, Power*, p. 49; García, *Chicanismo*; Juan Manuel Herra, "A View from Within: 'Years of Shout' Seem Over in Chicano Politics," *CJ*, May 1973, pp. 155-158; Parson, *Making a Better World*, p. 199; Pulido, *Black, Brown, Yellow, & Left*. See Ernesto Galarza's 1971 autobiography, *Barrio Boy* (Notre Dame: University of Notre Dame Press, 1971), p. 2.

4 See Arroyo, *Prophets Denied Honor.*

5 Ibid.; Dolan and Deck, eds., *Hispanic Catholic Culture in the U.S.*; Richard E. Martínez, *PADRES: The National Chicano Priest Movement* (Austin: University of Texas Press, 2005); Lara Medina: *Las Hermanas: Chicana/Latina Religious-Political Activism in the U.S. Catholic Church* (Philadelphia: Temple University Press, 2004).

6 Albert Hernández interview, Dec. 30, 1998; *LCLAA at 20: An Officers Report to the Membership*, with Addendum (Washington, D.C.: LCLAA, 1992).

7 Roger Cardenás interviews, 1980-2005; "Tour Helps Image: MCO Impresses Top Reagan Aide," *SFC*, July 19, 1970, p. 3; "21 Named to The Mission Study Panel," *SFC*, Oct. 17, 1970, p. 6; "Coalition Split: Mission Group's Internal Strife," *SFC*, Oct. 12, 1973, p. 49; "Coalition Leader Hails Rules Change," *SFC*, Oct. 19, 1970, p. 3.

8 Henry Nava interview; Tony Ríos interview; Mariscal, ed., *Aztlan and Viet Nam*, pp. 193-194; Oropeza, *¡Raza Si! ¡Guerra No!*, pp. 152-153; Martin Schiesl, "Behind the Shield," in Schiesl and Dodge, *City of Promise*, p. 151. For more on Salazar, see García, ed., *Ruben Salazar*.

9 "Chicanos Cheer Third Party Idea, Hear Candidates Ask For Endorsement," *SB*, Apr. 19, 1970; "MAPA Spurs Big-Name Candidates," *SFC*, Apr. 19, 1970; "MAPA Backs Romo for Governor Spot," *FB*, Apr. 20, 1970.

10 "Mexican-American Group Snubs Unruh Bid, Backs Chicano," *LAT*, Aug. 3, 1970; Navarro, *La Raza Unida*, p. 110.

11 "Political Campaign Goals Never Attained by Group," *SJM*, Jan. 17, 1971.

12 Richard Alatorre interview, 1980; "Richard Alatorre: Political Innocent to Powerful Assembly Post," *HE*, Feb. 2, 1982; Castro, *Chicano Power*, pp. 171-172; Navarro, *La Raza Unida*, pp. 141-144; José de la Isla, *The Rise of Hispanic Power*, p. 25; Santillan, *Chicano Politics*, p. 86; T. Anthony Quinn, *Carving Up California: A History of Redistricting, 1951-1984* (Claremont McKenna College, Rose Institute of State and Local Government, n.d.), pp. 17-19. See also Bert Corona, "Why Labor and La Raza Should Break with the Republican and Democratic Parties," *The Militant*, Apr. 7, 1972, pp. 12-13. For more on CASA, see Pulido, *Black, Brown, Yellow & Red*, pp. 124-133.

13 Alberto Juárez, "The Emergence of El Partido de la Raza Unida," *Aztlan* 3:2 (1973): 197.

14 Levy, *Cesar Chavez*, pp. 447-448.

15 Vincent S. Ancona, "When the Elephants March Out of San Diego: The 1972 Convention Fiasco," JSDH 30:4 (Fall 1992): 237.

16 Hope Mendoza Schechter interview.

17 Theo Lippman, Jr., *Senator Ted Kennedy: The Career Behind the Image* (New York: Norton, 1997), p. 98.

18 John C. Bollens and G. Robert Williams, *Jerry Brown: In a Plain Brown Wrapper* (Pacific Palisades, Calif.: Palisades Publishers, 1978), pp. 69-73.

19 Castro, *Chicano Power*, pp. 198-214; de la Isla, *Rise of Hispanic Power*, pp. 22-56.

20 Ibid.

21 Ibid.

22 Luis Juarez, "Chicano GOP 'Too Quiet," *SJM*, Aug. 8, 1975.

23 Castro, *Chicano Power*, p. 214.

24 Héctor Abeytia interview; Marc Grossman interview; "In 25the Dist. Demo Primary: Abeytia Gets MAPA Nod," *SJM*, Jan. 30, 1970.

25 Statement of the Vote, CSA; Biographies in *Legislative Handbook* (Sacramento: California Legislature, 1970-1975).

26 Mary Ellen Leary, *Phantom Politics: Campaigning in California* (Washington, DC: Public Affairs Press, 1977); J.D. Lorenz, *Jerry Brown: The Man on the White Horse* (Boston: Houghton Mifflin, 1978), p. 76.

27 Republican Flournoy was nominated by a member of the La Raza Unida Party. "Fresno Convention: MAPA Eyes Political Choices," *FB*, Aug. 11, 1974; "MAPA Backs Brown, Bagley," *FB*, Aug. 12, 1974. Also see, "Why Chicanos Don't Vote," *CJ*, July 1975, pp. 245-246.

28 Margaret Cruz interview; Robert E. Gonzáles interview; Armando O. Rodríquez interview; Convention Program, MAPA 13th Annual Convention, San Bernardino, July 20-22, 1973, cited in K. C. Burt, "The History of the Mexican American Political Association and Chicano Politics in California," Honors Thesis, UC, Berkeley, 1982, pp. 179-180; "Chicano Leader Denies Takeover

Role at Rally: Tapia Concedes S.F. War Protest Program Disintegrated After He Went to Platform," *LAT*, Apr. 27, 1971; "Rodriquez: A Moderate Looks At MAPA," *FB*, Aug. 3, 1971; "Quit, Says MAPA of Nixon," *FB*, July 23, 1973.

29 Frank C. Lemus, *National Roster, California Section, Spanish-Surnamed Elected Officials* (Los Angeles: Urban Affairs Institute, 1973).

30 Frank Casado interview; "L.A.'s El Adobe: California's Political Restaurant," *CJ*, Dec. 1981, pp. 421-422; Burt, *The History of MAPA*; Bollens and Williams, *Jerry Brown*; Lorenz, *Jerry Brown;* Culver and Syer, *Power and Politics in California*, pp. 188-193; Skerry, *Mexican Americans*.

31 "Opponents Rebuked: Brown: Anti-Reynoso Move 'Orchestrated, Almost Racist,'" *SB*, Jan. 22, 1982.

32 "Debunking the Myth of Chicano Conservatism," *CJ*, June 1979, pp. 218-219. Brown recognized that Latinos were "his most loyal constituency," in "Missing: The Chicano Candidate," *CJ*, May 1978, pp. 143-145. See "The Myth of the Chicano 'Sleeping Giant,'" *CJ*, Feb. 1979, pp. 46-47; Bernard L. Hyink, Seyom Brown, and Ernest W. Thacker, *Politics and Government in California*, 10th ed. (New York: Harper & Row, 1979), pp. 247-248.

33 "Brown's Farm Labor Coup: Agreement Became Possible Once the Rhetoric Stopped," *CJ*, June 1975, pp. 190-192; Journdane, *El Cortito*.

34 "Carter Endorsed by Chicano Group," *LAT*, Oct. 3, 1976.

35 Henry Lacayo interview.

36 Ibid.

37 Ibid.; Chávez, *Eastside Landmark*, pp. 139-143, 172-180.

38 Margaret Cruz interview.

39 Fox, *Hispanic Nation*, pp. 160-163; Donald E. Miller, Roger Gustafson, and Timothy Sato, *Power, Justice, Faith: Conversations with the IAF* (Los Angeles: USC, Center for Religion and Civic Culture, 2000); M. R. Warren, *Dry Bones Rattling: Community Building to Revitalize American Democracy* (Princeton: Princeton University Press, 2001).

40 Fox, *Hispanic Nation*, p. 158.

41 Hammerback, et al., *A War of Words*, p. 106.

42 DeSipio, *Counting on the Latino Vote*, p. 40.

43 Herman Gallegos interview; Henry Santiestevan interview; Raúl Yzaguirre interview.

44 de la Isla, *The Rise of Hispanic Politics*, pp. 161, 167; Gutiérrez, *Walls and Mirrors*, pp. 200-202.

45 Ad, "We Have Doubts About You, President Carter," *LAT*, May 5, 1979.

46 "Mexico Wealth Aids US: Nava: Ambassador to Mexico Cites Increased Trade," *FB*, Oct. 5, 1980. See Nava, *Julian Nava*, pp. 136-165.

47 Chávez, *Eastside Landmark*, pp. 184-186.

48 Marc Grossman interview. See M. J. Ross, *California: Its Government and Politics*, 3rd ed. (Pacific Grove, Calif.: Brooks/Cole, 1988), pp. 149-150.

49 Gottlieb, et al., *The Next Los Angeles*, pp. 143-144.

50 Ray Solis interview.

51 Marc Grossman interview; Statement of the Vote, 1980, CSA.

52 State of California, Fair Political Practices Commission, "Campaign Contribution and Spending Report, Nov. 4, 1980 General Election," p. C-2, and Campaign disclosures, National Farm Workers Union (NFWU), 1980, CSA. Late filings placed the union among top ten donors.

53 Dolores Huerta interview; Marc Grossman interview; "Chavez Attacks Switch on Speaker: Calls for Appeals to Democrats Who Now Support Brown," *LAT*, Nov. 29, 1980; Frank del Olmo, "For Chicanos, a Political Bloodletting: Feud Over Assembly Speakership is Wide and Deep," *LAT*, Dec. 11, 1980.

54 *LAT* columnist Al Martínez foresaw such a development. "Willie [Brown] has one clear agenda." " He's propping Leo [McCarthy] up for now only because he needs him. But when Leo's dead, Willie will carry the casket." Quoted in Culver and Syer, *Power and Politics in California*, pp. 165-166.

55 Hispanic Americans in Congress web page sponsored by Library of Congress.

56 Richard A. Clacus, *Willie Brown and the California Assembly* (Berkeley: Institute of Governmental Studies Press, UC, 1995); Fernando J. Guerra, "The Career Paths of Minority Elected Politicians," in Jackson and Preston, eds., *Racial and Ethnic Politics*, pp. 117-131; James Richardson, *Willie Brown* (Berkeley: University of California Press, 1996), p. 225; Skerry, *Mexican Americans*.

57 "Hispanics Decide to Further Study Senate Remapping," *Sacramento Union*, Sept. 17, 1981.

58 de la Isla, *The Rise of Hispanic Political Power,* pp. 148-209.

59 "Chicano Power," *New West*, Sept. 11, 1978, pp. 35-40, examines Latino politics in the late 1970s, noting MAPA's Sandoval had "applied the techniques of Saul Alinsky and Fred Ross in dealing with the problems of the Mission District."

60 "Effort By Republicans To Woo Hispanics Welcomed At MAPA State Convention," *SB*, July 19, 1981; Burt, *The History of the MAPA*, pp. 22-26. Calderón discusses his party switches and frustrations in "Politics—The Art of Making the Irrational Rational," *La Prensa San Diego*, Feb. 22, 2002.

61 Raphael J. Sonenshein, "Coalition Building in Los Angeles," in Lawrence B. de Graaf, Kevin Mulroy, & Quintard Taylor, *Seeking El Dorado: African Americans in California* (Los Angeles: Autry Museum of Western Heritage, 2001), p. 454.

62 Frank del Olmo, "Who Will Take Obledo Seriously if He Runs?" *LAT*, Oct. 8, 1981; Culver and Syer, *Power and Politics in California*, p. 85.

63 "Reynoso Wins Confirmation: Will Become First Latino on High Court," *LAT*, Jan. 21, 1982.

64 J. Gregory Payne and Scott Ratzan, *Tom Bradley: The Impossible Dream* (New York: Paperjacks Ltd.), p. 254.

65 Kenneth C. Burt, "Competing with the Democrats for the Growing Hispanic Vote," *CJ*, May 1983, pp. 192.

66 For background on the death penalty, which first became a political problem for Governor Pat Brown, see Bernard L. Hyink, *Politics and Government in California*, pp. 260-262.

67 Frank del Olmo, "Let Governor Prove Himself by Naming Another Latino," *LAT*, Nov. 13, 1986, p. 5; "Deukmejian's Supreme Court Nominees: John A. Arguelles, A Latino and Democrat, He's Conservative Who Tries to Conform to Legal Precedents," *LAT*, Feb. 19, 1987, p. 22.

68 Marc Grossman interview.

69 Ibid. On Deukmejian, see Culver and Syer, *Power and Politics in California*, pp. 194-198.

70 Marc Grossman interview; Campaign disclosures, NFWU, 1982, CSA.

71 Culver and Syer, *Power and Politics in California*, p. 85.

72 State of California, Fair Political Practices Commission, "1982 Legislative Winners," p. II, and Campaign disclosures, NFWU, 1982, CSA.

73 James Richardson, "The Members' Speaker: How Willie Brown Held Center Stage in California, 1980-1995," in Preston, et al., *Racial and Ethnic Politics in California*, Vol. 2, pp. 137-158.

74 Ross, *California: Its Government and Politics*, pp. 64-65, 83.

75 Latinos served as the mayor in a number of smaller cities, including Colton, Cypress, El Centro, Lompoc, Los Gatos, Mountain View, Pittsburg, San Gabriel, and Southgate. Two were Latinas, Connie Cisneros of Colton and Patricia Figueroa of Mountain View. One was a labor leader. UAW staffer Henry C. González served as mayor of Southgate. Arthur D. Martinez, *Who's Who: Chicano Officeholders, 1983-84* (Silver City, N.M.: self-published), p. 51.

76 Biography of Joe Serna, CSUS, 2000; Kenneth Burt, "'Citizenship for Service' Has a Long History," *Hispanic Link Weekly Report*, May 5, 2003.

77 Biography of Mayor Ronald Gonzalez, City of San Jose, 2005; Matthews, *Silicon Valley*, pp. 171-172.

78 Browning, et al., *Protest Is Not Enough* discusses the importance of coalitions in electing Latinos. Culver and Syer, *Power and Politics in California*, p. 76, applied the model to state politics.

79 Cain, *The Reapportionment Puzzle*, pp. 166-178; DeSipio, *Counting on the Latino Vote*, p. 78. "Court Overturns Federal Rule for Voter Redistricting Plans," *SB*, May 13, 1977, p. A6; "High Court Again Bars Race-Based Redistricting," *LAT*, June 30, 1997, p. A12.

80 Clacus, *Willie Brown and the California Assembly*, p. 122; Richardson, *Willie Brown*, p. 329; Skerry, *Mexican Americans*, p. 332; Sonenshien, "Coalition Building in Los Angeles," pp. 454-455; Dan Walters, *The New California*, p. 33.

81 The legal breakthrough came in a Watsonville case. See Joaquin G. Avila, *Latino Political Empowerment: A Perspective* (self published, [1990?]), p. 21.

82 "The Quiet Fire of Joaquin Avila," [SJM] *WEST*, Jan. 5, 1992.

83 Culver and Syer, *Power and Politics in California*, p. 85, noted that "This contest pitted two Latinos against each other, both backed by different coalitions."

84 Chávez, *Eastside Landmark*, pp. 242-246; Skerry, *Mexican Americans*, pp. 333-335, with "stole" quote on p. 334; Jaime Regalado, "Conflicts Over Redistricting in Los Angeles: Who Wins? Who Loses," in Jackson and Preston, eds., *Racial and Ethnic Politics*, pp. 373-394; Walters, *The New California*, p. 24.

85 Statement of the Vote, 1990-1992, CSA; DeSipio, *Counting on the Latino Vote*, p. 78; Raymond A. Rocco, "Latino Los Angeles," in Allan J. Scott and Edward W. Soja, eds., *The City: Los Angeles and Urban Theory at the End of the Twentieth Century* (Berkeley: University of California Press, 1996), pp. 365-389.

86 DeSipio, *Counting on the Latino Vote*, p. 41.

87 "A Tradition Reborn with New Glory: The 2005 Charter Banquet Gala," *California Monthly*, Mar./Apr. 2005, p. 41.

88 Chávez, *Eastside Landmark*, p. 253.

89 CET website.

90 Biography, Senator Liz Figueroa, 2004.

91 César Chávez address to Commonwealth Club, November 9, 1984. Reprinted as "UFW Made Change a Possibility, Then a Reality," *SB*, Sept. 4, 2006, p. B5.

92 Fernando Guerra, "Latino Politics in California," in Preston, et al., *Racial and Ethnic Politics in California*, pp. 446-447.

93 Walters, *The New California*, p. 19; Richard Santillan and Federico A. Subevi-Velez, "Latino Participation in Republican Party Politics in California," in Preston, et al., *Racial and Ethnic Politics in California*, pp. 285-319.

94 "Schwarzenegger Courting Latinos," *SB*, Sept. 3, 2006, p. A3.

CHAPTER 14
PROPOSITION 187 AND THE REBIRTH OF LABOR-BASED COALITIONS

1 Gutiérrez, *Walls and Mirrors*, pp. 179-205; Bernard L. Hyink, et al., *Politics and Government in California*, 10th ed. (New York: Harper & Row, 1979), p. 249.

2 George Skelton, "Straddling the Line on Illegal Immigration," *LAT*, Aug. 26, 1983, p. A3.

3 "State's Diversity Doesn't Reach Voting Booth," *LAT*, Nov. 10, 1994, p. A1; "Prop. 187 May Show Clergy's Political Role is Dwindling," *LAT*, Nov. 20, 1994, p. A3; "Despite Gains, Latino Voters Still Lack Clout," *LAT*, Dec. 4, 1994, p. A1; H. Eric Schockman, "California's Ethnic Experiment and the Unsolvable Immigration Issue: Proposition 187 and Beyond," and "Nativism, Partisanship, and Immigration: An Analysis of Prop. 198," both in Preston, et al., *Racial and Ethnic Politics*, pp. 233-304.

4 See above notes. For Torres first quote, see "Despite Gains, Latino Voters Still Lack Clout," *LAT*, Dec. 4, 1994, p. A1; for his second quote see "Angelides Seen as a Drag on the Party: Democratic leaders, saying he has failed to redefine a campaign that thus far has gone badly, fear repeating the '94 ticket-wide collapse," *LAT*, Oct. 9, 2006, p. B1. For Pedro Villarroya's quote, see "State's Diversity Doesn't Reach Voting Booth," *LAT*, Nov. 10, 1994, p. A1.

5 "House GOP Charts California Agenda," *LAT*, Nov. 13, 1994, p. A1.

6 Schockman, "California's Ethnic Experiment and the Unsolvable Immigration Issue," op. cit., p. 261.

7 Art Torres biography, California Democratic Party.

8 See Michael B. Preston and James S. Lai, "The Symbolic Politics of Affirmative Action," Preston, et al., *Racial and Ethnic Politics*, pp. 161-198.

9 Bruce E. Cain and Karin MacDonald, "Race and Party Politics in the 1996 U.S. Presidential Election," in Preston, et al., *Racial and Ethnic Politics*, p. 200.

10 Harry P. Pachon, "Latino Politics in the Golden State: Ready for the 21st Century?" in Preston, et al., *Racial and Ethnic Politics*, p. 420.

11 John B. Judis and Roy Teixeira, *The Emerging Democratic Majority* (New York: Scribner, 2002), p. 29.

12 Fox, *Hispanic Nation*, p. 165.

13 Hayes-Bautista, *La Nueva California*, pp. 136-138.

14 Gottlieb, et al., *The Next Los Angeles*, p. 166. Thanks to *SB* reporter Aurelio Rojas for pointing out how key individuals used organized labor and immigrant rights groups as a bridge between MEChA and CASA, and electoral politics. See also, Ruth Milkman and Kim Voss, eds., *Rebuilding Labor: Organizing and Organizers in the New Union Movement* (Ithaca, N.Y.: IRL Press, Cornell University Press, 2004), particularly Marshal Ganz, et al., "Against the Tide: Projects and Pathways of the New Generation of Union Leaders, 1984-2001."

15 Wood was a protégé of Max Mont who built the labor-based civil rights coalitions, and was a social democrat. The Social Democrats USA were the "more conservative" of the two factions affiliated with the Socialist International. The Democratic Socialists of America (DSA) were the "more liberal."

16 Biography based on numerous sources, including interviews with Miguel Contreras (1977-1984), Atara Mont (1977-1980), and Roger Cardenás. For the state of immigrant labor organizing when Contreras assumed control of the Los Angeles County Federation of Labor, see Ruth Milkman, ed., *Organizing Immigrants: The Challenge for Unions in Contemporary California* (Ithaca, N.Y.: ILR Press, Cornell University Press, 2000).

17 Biography, Art Pulaski, California Labor Federation.

18 "The Making of a Catholic Labor Leader: The Story of John F. Sweeney," *America*, Aug. 28-Sept. 4, 2006, pp. 16-18.

19 Biography, Linda Chávez-Thompson, AFL-CIO website.

20 For the new labor movement, see Milkman and Voss, *Rebuilding Labor*.

21 John Pérez, born in New York to Puerto Rican parents, traveled as UTLA president to El Salvador to better understand the district's new students.

22 Miguel Contreras interview, Mar. 28, 1977.

23 Biography, Antonio Villaraigosa, City of Los Angeles; Robert Gottlieb, et al., *The Next Los Angeles*, p. 166.

24 "Volunteers Hit Streets to Register New Voters," *DN*, Nov. 6, 1996.

25 Bill Boyarsky, "Latino Middle Class Emerges as a Force," *LAT*, Apr. 10, 1997, p. 1.

26 "Southland Elections: Record Percentage of Latinos Turn Out to Vote, Exit Polls Find; Analysis: School Bond Measure Appeals to have Drawn the Larger than Usual Response," *LAT*, Apr. 9, 1997, p. 17; Election '97: Predictable Results and Big Surprises; Amid the yawns, flashes of electoral energy and interest," *LAT*, Apr. 10, 1997, p. 8; "Latino Turnout a Breakthrough; Group's Heavy Balloting Could Signal a Historic Pivot Point for Political Relations in Los Angeles," *LAT*, Apr. 9, 1997, p. 1.

27 Fernando Guerra, "Latino Politics in California: The Necessary Conditions for Success," in Preston, et al., *Racial and Ethnic Politics*, p. 450.

28 Larry Frank and Kent Wong, "Dynamic Political Mobilization: The Los Angeles County Federation of Labor," *WUSA* 8:2 (Dec. 2004): 154-181.

29 Valle and Torres, *Latino Metropolis*.

30 María Elena Durazo, talk, "Living a Commitment to the Worker," Fifth John F. Henning Conference, "Partners in a Sacred Trust: The Church and the Worker in the Modern World," Saint Mary's College of California, Oct. 30, 2004.

31 Dennis King interview, Oct. 19, 2004. See also Barbara Byrd and Nari Rhee, "Building Power in the New Economy: The South Gay Labor Council," *WUSA* 8:2 (Dec. 2004), pp. 131-153.

32 "A significant question, especially for political incorporation theorists, is whether the incorporation of communities of color will be more difficult to achieve, and sustain, under term limits.... It seems likely that, since mass-based electoral and community coalitions have historically been difficult to maintain over time, it would be difficult to consistently create/or maintain electoral coalitions to replace 'termed' council members." Jaime Regalado, in "Minority Political Incorporation in Los Angeles: A Broader Consideration," Preston, et al., *Racial and Ethnic Politics*, p. 393.

33 Contreras interviews; Gottlieb, et al., *The Next Los Angeles*, pp. 158-171.

34 T. Anthony Quinn interview, Sept. 20, 2006; Biographies, Abel Maldonado, Robert "Bob" Pacheco, Rod Pacheco, and Charlene Zettle, California legislature; Statement of the Vote, 1996-2004, CSA.

35 "Governor Trips Himself Up on Illegal Immigrants, *SB*, May 6. 2004. p. B7.

36 Carlos Moreno interview, 2003; "Determined to Deliver on a Dream: Profile: Carlos Moreno worked and studied hard to advance from a modest L.A. background to his Nomination to the State Supreme Court," *LAT*, Sept. 30, 2001.

37 "Out With the Ho-Hum: L.A. Times Endorsement: Villaraigosa for Mayor," *LAT*, May 8, 2005.

38 "The 2005 Mayoral Election Compared to 2001," *LAT*, May 19, 2005, p. A19.

39 "Leader Who Restored Labor's Clout in L.A. Dies," *LAT*, May 7, 2005.

40 Luis Ricardo Fraga and Richard Ramírez, "Latino Political Incorporation in California, 1990-2000," in López and Jimenez, eds., *Latinos and Public Policy in California*, p. 309.

41 Ibid. pp. 309-310.

42 "A Rising Voice: Univision's 'Voz y Voto' takes on the state's top politicos—and not just about Latino issues," *SB*, Aug. 22, 2006, p. E1.

43 DeSipio, *Counting on the Latino Vote*, pp. 167-183. He postulates that to most fully incorporate Latino voters, candidates must compete for their votes as part of a larger coalition, reduce barriers to participation, and the address issues of concern to new voters, which "would challenge the party to return to its New Deal and Great Society roots" (p. 173).

44 "Governor gains among Latinos," *SB*, Nov. 21, 2006, p.3. Thanks to T. Anthony Quinn for the historical analogy to the earlier Republican governors.

SELECTED BIBLIOGRAPHY

Acuña, Rodolfo F. *A Community Under Siege: A Chronicle of Chicanos East of the Los Angeles River, 1945-1975*. Los Angeles: Chicano Studies Research Center Publications, UCLA, 1984.

_____. *Occupied America: A History of Chicanos*, 4th ed. New York: Longman, 2000.

_____. *Anything but Mexican: Chicanos in Contemporary Los Angeles*. New York: Verso, 1996.

Ainsworth, Ed. *Maverick Mayor: A Biography of Sam Yorty of Los Angeles*. Garden City, N.Y.: Doubleday, 1966.

Allsup, Carl. *The American G.I Forum: Origins and Evolution*. Austin: Center for Mexican American Studies, University of Texas at Austin, 1982.

Anderson, Henry. *The Bracero Program in California*. New York: Arno Press, 1976.

Arroyo, Antonio M. Stevens. *Prophets Denied Honor: An Anthology of the Hispanic Church in the United States*. Maryknoll, N.Y.: Orbis, 1980.

Baldassare, Mark. *California in the New Millennium: The Changing Social and Political Landscape*. Berkeley: University of California Press, 2000.

Banfield, Edward C. *Big City Politics: A Comparative Guide to the Political Systems of Atlanta, Boston, Detroit, El Paso, Los Angeles, Miami, Philadelphia, St. Louis, Seattle*. New York: Random House, 1965.

Bok, Derek C., and John T. Dunlap, *Labor and the American Community*. New York: Simon & Schuster, 1970.

Browning, Rufus P., Dale Rogers Marshall, and David H. Tabb, *Protest Is Not Enough: The Struggle of Blacks and Hispanics for Equity in Urban Politics*. Berkeley University of California Press, 1984.

Burke, Robert E. *Olson's New Deal for California*. Berkeley: University of California, 1953.

Burt, Kenneth C. *The History of the Mexican-American Political Association and Chicano Politics in California*. Sacramento: MAPA, 1982.

Bynum, Lindley, and Idwal Jones. *Biscailuz: Sheriff of the New West*. New York: William Morrow, 1950.

Cain, Bruce E. *The Reapportionment Puzzle*. Berkeley: University of California Press, 1984.

Califano, Joseph A. *The Triumph & Tragedy of Lyndon Johnson: The White House Years*. New York: Simon & Schuster, 1991.

Camarillo, Albert. *Chicanos In California: A History of Mexican Americans in California*. San Francisco: Boyd & Fraser, 1984.

Cannon, Lou. *Ronnie and Jessie: A Political Odyssey*. Garden City, N.Y.: Doubleday, 1969.

_____. *Governor Reagan: His Rise to Power.* New York: Public Affairs, 2003.

Carney, Frances. *The Rise of the Democratic Clubs in California.* Eagleton Institute at Rutgers/McGraw-Hill, 1960.

Carrillo, Leo. *The California I Love.* Englewood Cliffs, N.J.: Prentice-Hall, 1961.

Castro, Tony. *Chicano Power: The Emergence of Mexican American America.* New York: Saturday Review Press/E.P. Dutton, 1974.

Chávez, Ernesto. *¡My People First! ¡Mi Raza Primero!: Nationalism, Identity, and Insurgency in the Chicano Movement in Los Angeles.* Berkeley: University of California Press, 2002.

Chávez, John R. *Eastside Landmark: A History of the Los Angeles Community Union, 1968-1993.* Stanford: Stanford University Press, 1998.

Chávez, Lydia. *The Color Bind: California's Battle To End Affirmative Action.* Berkeley: University of California Press, 1998.

Cherny, Robert W, William Issel, and Kieran Walsh Taylor. *American Labor and the Cold War: Grassroots Politics and Postwar Political Culture.* New Brunswick, N.J.: Rutgers University Press, 2004.

Clacus, Richard A. *Willie Brown and the California Assembly.* Berkeley: Institute of Governmental Studies Press, UC, 1995.

Culver, John C. and John Hyde. *American Dreamer: A Life of Henry A. Wallace.* New York: Norton, 2000.

Culver, John H. and John C. Syer, *Power and Politics in California,* 3rd ed. New York: Macmillan, 1988.

Dallek, Mathew. *The Right Moment: Ronald Reagan's First Victory and the Decisive Turning Point in American Politics.* New York: Free Press, 2000.

de Graaf, Lawrence B., Kevin Mulroy, and Quintard Taylor, eds. *Seeking El Dorado: African Americans in California.* Los Angeles: Autry Museum of Western Heritage, in association with University of Washington Press, 2001.

de la Garza, Rodolfo O., Martha Menchaca, and Louis DeSipio, *Barrio Ballots: Latino Politics in the 1990 Elections.* Boulder, Colo.: Westview Press, 1994.

de la Isla, José. *The Rise of Hispanic Political Power.* Los Angeles: Archer Books, 2003.

Delmatier, Royce D. Clarence F. McIntosh, and Earl G. Waters, *The Rumble of California Politics, 1948-1970.* New York: John Wiley, 1970.

DeSipio, Louis. *Counting on the Latino Vote: Latinos as a New Electorate.* Charlottesville: University Press of Virginia, 1996.

Denning, Michael. *The Cultural Front: The Laboring of American Culture in the Twentieth Century.* New York: Verso, 1997.

Deverell, William and Tom Sitton, eds. *California Progressivism Revisited.* Berkeley: University of California Press, 1994.

Dolan, Jay P. and Allan Figueroa Deck, eds. *Hispanic Catholic Culture in the U.S.: Issues and Concerns.* Notre Dame: University of Notre Dame Press, 1994.

Dolan, Jay P. and Gilberto M. Hinojosa. *Mexican Americans and the Catholic Church, 1900-1965.* Notre Dame: University of Notre Dame Press, 1994.

Dunne, John Gregory. *Delano: The Story of the California Grape Strike*. New York: Farrar, Straus & Giuroux, 1966.

Eymann, Marcia A. and Charles Wollenberg, eds. *What's Going On? California and the Vietnam Era*. Berkeley: Oakland Museum of California and University of California Press, 2004.

Escobar, Edward J. *Race, Police, and the Making of a Political Identity: Mexican Americans and the Los Angeles Police Department, 1900-1945*. Berkeley: University of California Press, 1999.

Feriss, Susan, and Richard Sandoval. *The Fight in the Fields: Cesar Chavez and the Farmworkers Movement*. San Diego: Harcourt Brace, 1997.

Finks, P. David. *The Radical Vision of Saul Alinsky*. New York: Paulist Press, 1984.

Ford, John Anson. *Thirty Explosive Years in Los Angeles County*. San Marino, Calif.: The Huntington Library, 1961.

Fowle, Eleanor. *Cranston: The Senator from California*. San Rafael, Calif.: Presidio Press, 1980.

Fox, Geoffrey. *Hispanic Nation: Culture, Politics, and the Construction of Identity*. Tucson: University of Arizona Press, 1996.

Galarza, Ernesto. *Merchants of Labor: The Mexican Bracero Story*. Santa Barbara: McNally & Loftin, 1964.

_____. *Farm Workers and Agri-business in California, 1947-1960*. Notre Dame: University of Notre Dame Press, 1977.

———, Herman Gallegos, and Julian Samora, *Mexican-Americans in the Southwest*. Santa Barbara: McNally & Loftin, 1969.

García, Ignacio M. *Chicanismo: The Forging of a Militant Ethos Among Mexican Americans*. Tucson: University of Arizona Press, 1998.

_____. *Viva Kennedy: Mexican Americans in Search of Camelot*. College Station: Texas A&M University Press, 2000.

García, Mario T. *The Making of Mexican American Mayor: Raymond L. Telles of El Paso*. El Paso: Texas Western Press, University of Texas at El Paso, 1998.

———. *Mexican Americans: Leadership, Ideology, & Identity, 1930-1960*. New Haven: Yale University Press, 1989.

_____. *Memories of Chicano History: The Life and Narrative of Bert Corona*. Berkeley: University of California Press, 1984.

_____. *Ruben Salazar: Border Correspondent*. Berkeley: University of California Press, 1995.

Garcia, Matt. *A World of Its Own: Race, Labor, and Citrus in the Making of Greater Los Angeles, 1900-1970*. Chapel Hill: University of North Carolina Press, 2001.

Gillon, Steven M. *Politics and Vision: The ADA and American Liberalism, 1947-1985*. New York: Oxford University, 1987.

Gluck, Sherna Berger. *Rosie The Riveter Revisited: Women, the War and Social Change*. New York: Meridian, 1987.

Gómez-Quiñones, Juan. *Chicano Politics: Reality & Promise, 1940-1990*. Albuquerque: University of New Mexico Press, 1990.

_____. *Roots of Chicano Politics, 1600-1940*. Albuquerque: University of New Mexico Press, 1994.

_____. *Mexican American Labor, 1790-1990*. Albuquerque: University of New Mexico Press, 1994.

Gonzalez, Gilbert G. *Chicano Education in the Era of Segregation*. Philadelphia: The Balch Institute Press, 1990.

Gottlieb, Robert, Mark Vallianatos, Regina Freer, and Peter Dreier, *The Next Los Angeles: The Struggle for a Livable City*. Berkeley: University of California Press, 2005.

Grebler, Leo, Joan W. Moore, Ralph C. Guzman, *The Mexican American People: The Nation's Second Largest Minority*. New York: The Free Press, 1970.

Greenstone, J. David. *Labor in American Politics*. New York: Alfred A. Knopf, 1969.

Gutiérrez, David G. *Walls Mirrors: Mexican Americans, Mexican Immigrants, and the Politics of Ethnicity*. Berkeley: University of California Press, 1995.

Guzman, Ralph C. *The Political Socialization of the Mexican American People*. New York: Arno Press, 1976.

———. *The Mexican American People: The Nation's Second Largest Minority*. New York: The Free Press, 1970.

Hammerback John C. and Richard J. Jensen, *The Rhetorical Career of César Chávez*. College Station: Texas A&M University Press, 1998.

Hartman, Chester. *The Transformation of San Francisco*. Totowa, N.J.: Roman & Allanfeld, 1984.

Harvey, Richard B. *The Dynamics of California Government and Politics*. Belmont, Calif.: Wadsworth,1970.

———. *Earl Warren, Governor of California: A Political Profile of California's Most Prominent Statesmen and One of America's Leading Figures*. New York: Exposition Press, 1969.

Hayes-Bautista, David E. *La Nueva California: Latinos in the Golden State*. Berkeley: University of California Press, 2004.

Healey, Dorothy Ray and Maurice Isserman. *California Red: A Life in the American Communist Party*. Urbana: University of Chicago, 1993.

Heineman, Kenneth. *A Catholic New Deal: Religion and Reform in Depression Pittsburg*. University Park: The Pennsylvania State University Press, 1999.

Higgins, George G. *Organized Labor and the Church: Reflections of a 'Labor Priest'*. New York: Paulist Press, 1993.

Hill, Gladwin. *Dancing Bear: An Inside Look at California Politics*. Cleveland: World Publishing, 1968.

Hoffman, Pat. *Ministry of the Dispossessed: Learning from the Farm Worker Movement*. Los Angeles: Wallace Press, 1987.

Horwitt, Sanford D. *Let Them Call Me Rebel: Saul Alinsky, His Life and Legacy*. New York: Alfred A. Knopf, 1989.

Hovas, Himilce. *The Hispanic 100: A Ranking of the Latino Men and Women Who Have Most Influenced American Thought and Culture*. New York: Citadel Press, 1995.

Humphrey, Hubert H. *Beyond Civil Rights: A New Day of Equality*. New York: Random House, 1968.

Jackson, Byran O. and Michael B. Preston, ed. *Racial and Ethnic Politics in California*. Berkeley: Institute of Governmental Studies Press, University of California, 1991.

Jacobs, John. *A Rage for Justice: The Passion and Politics of Philip Burton*. Berkeley: University of California Press, 1995.

Journdane, Maurice "Mo". *El Cortito: The Struggle for the Health and Legal Protection of Farm Workers*. Houston: Arte Público, 2004.

Kaplowitz, Craig A. *LULAC: Mexican Americans and National Policy*. College Station: Texas A&M University Press, 2005.

Kennedy, David M. *Freedom From Fear: The American People in Depression and War, 1929-1945*. New York: Oxford University Press, 1999.

Kennedy, John F. *A Nation of Immigrants*, rev. & enlarged ed. New York: Harper Torchbooks, 1964.

Kennedy, Robert. *To Seek a Newer World*. Garden City, N.Y.: Doubleday, 1967.

Klehr, Harvey. *The Heyday of American Communism: The Depression Decade*. New York: Basic Books, 1984.

Leary, Mary Ellen. *Phantom Politics: Campaigning in California*. Washington, DC: Public Affairs Press, 1977.

Leuchtenburg, William E. *Franklin D. Roosevelt and the New Deal, 1932-1940*. New York: Harper & Row, 1963.

_____. *A Troubled Feast: American Society Since 1945*, revised edition. Boston: Little, Brown, 1979.

Levy, Jacques. *Cesar Chavez: Autobiography of La Causa*. New York: Norton, 1975.

Levy, Mark R., and Michael S. Kramer. *The Ethnic Factor: How Minorities Decide Elections*. New York: Simon & Schuster, 1973.

Lewis, Joseph. *What Makes Reagan Run?* New York: McGraw-Hill, 1968.

López, David, and Andres Jimenez, eds. *Latinos and Public Policy in California: An Agenda For Opportunity*. Berkeley: Institute of Governmental Studies, UC, 2003.

Lorenz, J.D. *Jerry Brown: The Man on the White Horse*. Boston: Houghton Mifflin, 1978.

Lubell, Samuel. *The Future of American Politics*, 2nd ed. Garden City, N.Y.: Doubleday, 1956.

McWilliams, Carey. *California: The Great Exception*. Reprint. Berkeley: University of California Press, 1999.

_____. *The Education of Carey McWilliams*. New York: Simon & Schuster, 1978.

Majka, Linda C. and Theo J. Majka. *Farm Workers, Agribusiness, and the State*. Philadelphia: Temple University Press, 1982.

Mariscal, George, ed. *Aztlan and Viet Nam: Chicano and Chicana Experiences of the War*. Berkeley: University of California Press, 1999.

Márquez, Benjamin. *LULAC: The Evolution of a Mexican American Political Organization*. Austin: University of Texas Press, 1993.

Matthews, Glenna. *Silicon Valley, Women, and the California Dream: Gender, Class, and Opportunity in the Twentieth Century*. Stanford: Stanford University Press, 2003.

Meister, Dick, and Anne Loftis. *A Long Time Coming: The Struggle to Unionize America's Farm Workers*. New York: MacMillan, 1977.

Meyerowitz, Joanne, ed. *Not June Cleaver: Women and Gender in Postwar America, 1945-1960*. Philadelphia: Temple University Press, 1994.

Mitchell, H.L. *Mean Things Happening in This Land: The Life and Times of H. L. Mitchell, Cofounder of the Southern Tenant Farmers Union*. Montclair, N.J.: Allanheld, Osmun, 1979.

Mills, James R. *A Disorderly House: The Brown-Unruh Years in Sacramento*. Berkeley: Heyday Books, 1987.

Mills, Judie. *Robert Kennedy*. Brookfield, Conn.: The Millbrook Press, 1998.

Morales, Dionicio. *Dionicio Morales: A Life in Two Cultures*. Houston: Arte Público Press /Piñata Books, 1997.

Moore, Deborah Dash. *To the Golden Cities: Pursuing the American Jewish Dream in Miami and L.A.* New York: The Free Press, 1994.

Moore, Joan W., with Harry Pachon, *Mexican Americans*, 2nd ed. Englewood Cliffs, New Jersey: Prentice-Hall, 1976.

Morin, Raul. *Among The Valiant: Mexican Americans in WWII and Korea*. Alhambra, CA: Borden, 1963.

Muñoz, Jr., Carlos. *Youth, Identity, Power: The Chicano Movement*. New York: Verso, 1989.

Nava, Julian. *Julian Nava: My Mexican-American Journey*. Houston: Arte Público Press, 2002.

Navarro, Armando. *La Raza Unida: A Chicano Challenge to the U.S. Two-Party Dictatorship*. Philadelphia: Temple University Press, 2000.

Ochoa, Enrique C., Gilda L. Ochoa. *Latino Los Angeles: Transformations, Communities, and Activism*. Tucson: University of Arizona Press, 2005.

Oropeza, Lorena. *¡Raza Si! ¡Guerra No!: Chicano Protest and Patriotism During the Viet Nam War Era*. Berkeley: University of California Press, 2005.

Pachon, Harry, and Louis DeSipio, *New Americans By Choice: Political Perspectives of Latino Immigrant*. Boulder, Colo.: Westview Press, 1994.

Pagáa, Eduardo Obregon. *Murder at the Sleepy Lagoon: Zoot Suits, Race, and Riot in Wartime L.A.* Chapel Hill: University of North Carolina Press, 2003.

Parson, Don. *Making a Better World: Public Housing, the Red Scare, and the Direction of Modern Los Angeles*. Minneapolis: University of Minnesota Press, 2005.

Pitti, Stephen J. *The Devil in Silicon Valley: Northern California, Race, and Mexican Americans*. Princeton: Princeton University Press, 2003.

Polenberg, Richard. *One Nation Divisible: Class, Race, and Ethnicity in the United States Since 1938*. New York: Penguin Books, 1980.

Privett, Stephen A. *The U.S. Catholic Church and Its Hispanic Members: The Pastoral*

Vision of Archbishop Robert E. Lucy. San Antonio: Trinity University Press, 1988.

Preston, Michael B., Bruce Cain, and Sandra Bass, eds. *Racial and Ethnic Politics in California*, Vol. 2. Berkeley: Institute of Governmental Studies Press, UC, 1998.

Pulido, Laura. *Black, Brown, Yellow, & Left: Radical Activism in Los Angeles*. Berkeley: University of California Press, 2006.

Pycior, Julie Leininger. *LBJ & Mexican Americans: The Paradox of Power*. Austin: University of Texas Press, 1997.

Ramos, Henry A. J. *The American GI Forum: In Pursuit of the Dream, 1948-1983*. Houston: Arte Público Press, 1998.

Rapoport, Roger. *California Dreaming: The Political Odyssey Pat and Jerry Brown*. Berkeley: Nolo Press, 1982.

Rarick, Ethan. *California Rising: The Life and Times of Pat Brown*. Berkeley: University of California Press, 2005.

Richardson, James. *Willie Brown: A Biography*. Berkeley: University of California Press, 1996.

Rolle, Andrew. *California: A History*, 6th ed. Wheeling, Ill.: Harlan Davidson, 2003.

Ross, Fred. *Conquering Goliath: Cesar Chavez at the Beginning*. Keene, CA: El Taller Grafico Press, 1989.

Ruiz, Vicki L. *Cannery Women, Cannery Lives: Mexican Women, Unionization, and the California Food Processing Industry, 1930-1950*. Albuquerque: University of New Mexico Press, 1987.

———. *From Out Of The Shadows: Mexican Women in Twentieth Century America*. New York: Oxford University Press, 1988.

Samora, Julian, ed. *La Raza: Forgotten Americans*. Norte Dame: University of Notre Dame Press, 1966.

Samora, Julian, and Patricia Vandel Simon. *A History of the Mexican-American People*. Notre Dame: University of Notre Dame Press, 1977.

Sánchez, George J. *Becoming Mexican American: Ethnicity, Culture and Identity in Chicano Los Angeles, 1900-1945*. New York: Oxford University Press, 1993.

Schiesl, Martin, ed. *Responsible Liberalism: Edmund G. "Pat" Brown and Reform Government in California, 1958-1967*. Los Angeles: California State University, Los Angeles, Edmund G. "Pat" Brown Institute of Public Affairs, 2003.

———, and Mark M. Dodge, eds. *City of Promise: Race and Historical Change in Los Angeles*, Claremont, Calif.: Regina Books, 2006.

Schlesinger, Arthur M., Jr. *Robert Kennedy and His Times*. New York: Random House, 1978.

Schuparra, Kurt. *Triumph of the Right: The Rise of the California Conservative Movement, 1945-1966*. Amonk, N.Y.: M.E. Sharp, 1998.

Skerry, Peter. *Mexican Americans: The Ambivalent Minority*. New York: The Free Press, 1994.

Sonenshein, Raphael J. *Politics in Black and White: Race and Power in Los Angeles*. Princeton, N.J.: Princeton University Press, 1993.

Starr, Kevin. *Endangered Dreams: The Great Depression in California.* New York: Oxford University Press, 1996.

_____. *Embattled Dreams: California in War and Peace, 1940-1950.* New York: Oxford University Press, 2002.

————. *Inventing the Dream: California Through the Progressive Era.* New York: Oxford University Press, 1985.

Stevenson, Janet. *The Undiminished Man: A Political Biography of Robert Walker Kenny.* Novato, Calif.: Chandler & Sharp, 1980.

Stromquist, Shelton, ed. *Labor's Cold War: Local Politics in a Global Context.* Urbana: University of Illinois, 2007.

Taft, Philip. *Labor Politics American Style: The California Federation of Labor.* Cambridge: Harvard University Press, 1968.

Taylor, Ronald B. *Chavez and the Farm Workers.* Boston: Beacon Press, 1975.

Valle, Victor M., and Rodolfo D. Torres. *Latino Metropolis.* Minneapolis: University of Minnesota Press, 2000.

Vargas, Zaragosa. *Labor Rights Are Civil Rights: Mexican American Workers in Twentieth-Century America.* Berkeley: University of California Press, 2005.

Walters, Dan. *The New California: Facing the 21st Century,* second edition. Sacramento: California Journal Press, 1992.

Weber, Devra. *Dark Sweat, White Gold: California Farm Workers, Cotton, and the New Deal.* Berkeley: University of California Press, 1994.

Wilson, James Q. *The Amateur Democrat: Clubs in Three Cities.* Chicago: University of Chicago Press, 1962.

Zieger, Robert H. *The CIO: 1935-1955.* Chapel Hill: University of North Carolina Press, 1995.

INDEX